T0305745

Innovation under the Radar

Investigating the nature, drivers and sources of innovation in Africa, this book examines the channels for effective diffusion of innovation in and to Africa under institutional, resource and affordability constraints. Xiaolan Fu draws on almost a decade of research on innovation in Africa to explore these issues and unpack the process, combining a rigorous statistical analysis of a purposely designed multi-wave, multi-country survey with in-depth studies of representative cases. Building on this research, Fu argues that African firms are innovative but unsupported. Those 'under-the-radar' innovations that widely exist in Africa as a result of the constraints are not sufficient to enable Africa to leapfrog the innovation gap in the era of the Fourth Industrial Revolution. This is the first comprehensive analysis of the creation and diffusion of innovation in low-income countries. It also provides the first survey-based analysis of innovation in the informal economy.

Xiaolan Fu is the Founding Director of the Technology and Management Centre for Development and Professor of Technology and International Development at the University of Oxford. She led the UK Foreign, Commonwealth and Development Office (FCDO) and Economic and Social Research Council (ESRC) funded research on 'Diffusion of Innovation in Low-income Countries' and is appointed by the Secretary-General of the United Nations to the Council of the Technology Bank for the Least Developed Countries and the 10-Member High-Level Advisory Group of the Technology Facilitation Mechanism for sustainable development.

Innovation under the Radar

The Nature and Sources of Innovation in Africa

Xiaolan Fu

University of Oxford

CAMBRIDGE
UNIVERSITY PRESS

CAMBRIDGE
UNIVERSITY PRESS

University Printing House, Cambridge CB2 8BS, United Kingdom

One Liberty Plaza, 20th Floor, New York, NY 10006, USA

477 Williamstown Road, Port Melbourne, VIC 3207, Australia

314–321, 3rd Floor, Plot 3, Splendor Forum, Jasola District Centre, New Delhi – 110025, India

79 Anson Road, #06–04/06, Singapore 079906

Cambridge University Press is part of the University of Cambridge.

It furthers the University's mission by disseminating knowledge in the pursuit of education, learning, and research at the highest international levels of excellence.

www.cambridge.org
Information on this title: www.cambridge.org/9781107183100
DOI: 10.1017/9781316869482

First published 2020

A catalogue record for this publication is available from the British Library.

Library of Congress Cataloging-in-Publication Data
Names: Fu, Xiaolan, 1967– author.
Title: Innovation under the radar : the nature and sources of innovation in Africa / Xiaolan Fu.
Description: 1 Edition. | New York : Cambridge University Press, 2020. | Includes bibliographical references and index.
Identifiers: LCCN 2020024233 | ISBN 9781107183100 (hardback) | ISBN 9781316869482 (ebook)
Subjects: LCSH: Technological innovations – Africa. | Information technology – Economic aspects – Africa.
Classification: LCC HC800.Z9 F8 2020 | DDC 338/.064096–dc23
LC record available at https://lccn.loc.gov/2020024233

ISBN 978-1-107-18310-0 Hardback

To my beloved dad Baisong, mum Hualin, for the love that enlightened my life; husband Shaohui and son Yujie, for your love and support over the years.

Contents

Figures

Tables

Foreword

This book, bringing together Xiaolan Fu's research on the nature and sources of innovation in Africa over the last seven years, represents a rather unique piece of academic research. Based on careful, empirical, in-depth research on two countries – Ghana in West Africa and Tanzania in East Africa (as well as a case study in Kenya) – the author brings to the forefront the various and diverse ways in which innovation in Africa takes place. This is not based on R&D as is the case in industrialized countries, nor purely 'frugal' or 'inclusive' in nature as assumed in many Asian low-income countries, but innovative in a creative African way – low-cost innovations, based on individual creativity, practice, organizational learning and adaptation. What the author calls 'innovation under the radar'. Most of these activities are incremental in nature, strongly demand-led and implemented across the board: in significantly improved, sometimes even new, products or processes, in non-technological areas such as management and marketing, in design. Innovation within a context of constraints to firms on all sides. In short: innovation to survive. No traditional innovation indicator will capture such activities.

The mirror picture of such invisible innovation is reflected in the lack of input from science and engineering in this African innovation process and the lack of the diffusion of foreign technology, including managerial knowledge. As the book highlights (containing also some contributions written with a couple of African colleagues of Xiaolan Fu), within the context of the global digital Fourth Industrial Revolution, this will be one of Africa's major challenges in the years to come. Xiaolan Fu's emphasis on the policy need to build up digital competencies in the African continent, both with respect to infrastructure and human skills, for Africa to 'leapfrog innovation' as illustrated in cases such as M-PESA, is well made. Coming from a world-class Chinese scholar who acknowledges in the conclusions that her interpretation of some of the results obtained might have been constrained by her lack of 'knowledge of the rich history, culture and economic and social diversity' of the African continent, one rather welcomes this detailed analysis of the nature and sources of innovation in Africa, often undetected by scholars more know-ledgeable about the history and industrial development of the contin-ent. I strongly recommend this book.

LUC SOETE

Acknowledgements

The book arises from my research on innovation in low-income countries since 2012. It is a serious academic book based on seven years of research and reflection. It aims to present a systematic, comprehensive and coherent study of the nature, origin and diffusion of innovation in Africa and the challenges and opportunities faced in the era of the Fourth Industrial Revolution. Although most of the chapters are fairly self-contained, the hope is that the whole will add up to more than the sum of its parts and enable us to develop a comprehensive understanding of this under-researched area of innovation, which is itself an outcome of system engineering.

Many acknowledgements and thanks are due. Among the numerous colleagues and friends I wish to thank for helpful and constructive comments and discussions are Pierre Mohnen, George Essegbey, Anne Miroux, Yong Li, Luc Soete, Bengt-Åke Lundvall, Christopher Adam, Marc Ventresca, Bitrina Diyamett, Anne Kingiri, Martin Bell, Raphie Kaplinsky, Adrian Wood, Valpy FitzGerald, Mammo Muchie, David Kaplan, Maria Sanova, Tomasso Ciarli, Shamika Sirimanne, Dong Wu, Dirk Willem te Velde, Augusto Luis Alcorta, Wunsch-Vincent, Sacha, Razzaque, Mohammad, Heide Hackmann, William Colglazier, David O'Connor, Oliver Schwank, Richard Roehrl, Wei Liu, Pervez Ghauri, Juha Vaatanen, Godfred Frempong, Shyama Ramani, Suraksha Gupta, Sonia Kabir, Douglas Gollin, Diego Sanchez-Ancochea, Calestous Juma, Jorge Katz and Jizhen Li; editors of Cambridge University Press, Valerie Appleby and Laura Parish; as well as five anonymous reviewers of the book proposal.

Chapter 6 is co-authored with Giacomo Zanello, Chapter 8 with Mammo Muchie and Abiodun Egbetokun, Chapter 9 with George Essegbey and Bitrina Diyamett, Chapter 14 with Jun Hou and Chapter 15 with Anne Kigiri. Luc Soete has kindly written a foreword for the book.

In particular, I would like to extend my thanks to Carmen Contreras for her valuable assistance in the analysis of the new innovation survey data from Ghana and Tanzania; to Giacomo Zanello and Jun Hou for their excellent work in the first stage of the DILIC project; to Shaomeng Li, Mavis Akuffobea and Lanta Daniel for their assistance in background data collection for Chapter 3; to Pu Yan for assistance to a background paper for the United Nations Conference on Trade and Development (UNCTAD) which partly contributed to Chapter 13; and to Geraldine Adiku, Elvis Avenyo and Patricia Dudman for their careful assistance in the editing and proofreading of the whole book manuscript at different stages of its development. The support of Valerie Appleby and Laura Parish of Cambridge University Press was essential for the publication of the book.

Much of the research was sponsored by the Economic and Social Research Council (ESRC), the Foreign, Commonwealth and Development Office (FCDO), formerly the Department for International Development (DFID), and the European Commission FP7, and was carried out in collaboration with my partners in Africa, the United Kingdom and other European countries, and beyond. The fieldwork and data collection have benefited from the support of the Science and Technology Policy Research Institute (STEPRI) of the Council for Scientific and Industrial Research (CSIR) of Ghana and the Science, Technology and Innovation Policy Research Organisation (STIPRO) of Tanzania. I would also like to thank UNCTAD, UNIDO, UN DESA and Luc Soete of UNU-MERIT for their support and helpful comments throughout the research process. The visits to Oxford University by Anne Kingiri and Abiodun Egbetokun were supported by an Africa-Oxford Travel Grant. I am grateful to the DFID-ESRC Growth Research Program (DEGRP) and the European Commission FP7 for their support on the dissemination, outreach and impact of some of the research, especially those related to the studies on 'Diffusion of innovation in low-income countries' and the 'MNEs and sustainable development'.

I am also grateful to the copyright holders of the following journals and the United Nations for permitting me, with acknowledgement, to present full or part of the papers that have appeared in their journals or reports in a suitably revised form: Giacomo Zanello, Xiaolan Fu, Pierre Mohnen and Marc Ventresca, 'Innovation in low income countries: a literature review', *Journal of Economic Survey* (30) 2016 (part of Chapter 2); Xiaolan Fu, Pierre Mohnen and Giacomo Zanello, 'Innovation and productivity in formal and informal firms in Ghana', *Technological Forecasting & Social Change* (131) 2017 (part of Chapter 6); Xiaolan Fu and Hao Xu, 'Knowledge transfer in MNEs in Africa: A comparison of Chinese and European MNEs in Ghana', chapter 5 in *Multinationals, Local Capabilities, and Development*, 2019 (part of Chapter 12); and 'Building digital competencies to benefit from frontier technologies', by UNCTAD, © (2019) United Nations (part of Chapter 13). I would like to thank my co-authors for allowing the results of our joint research to be included in this book.

I would also like to thank my colleagues at the 10-Member Group of United Nations (UN) Technology Facilitation Mechanism (TFM), the Council of the Technology Bank for the Least Developed Countries of the United Nations and the Leadership Council of the Sustainable Development Solutions Network (SDSN). The constant interactions with them and the intensive discussions at the meetings helped me to reflect and sharpen my thinking on technology and innovation for sustainable development in the developing countries, especially in low-income countries.

Prototypes of various chapters have been presented, in past years, at various conferences and seminars in many universities, which cannot all be acknowledged here in detail. A few examples of these conferences include the 'UNU-WIDER Development Conference 2013' in Helsinki, 'Expert Meeting on Innovation of the General Assembly of the United Nations 2014', 'Development Cooperation Forum 2015', 'Academy of Innovation and Entrepreneurship 2013 Annual Conference' in Oxford, 'Development Studies Association Annual Conference', '1st African Innovation Summit', 'DILIC Innovation Conference' in Ghana, 'DILIC End of Project Conference' in London, '2017 ILO Future of Work Forum', 'United Nations STI Forum in New York 2016 and 2017', 'UNCTAD Multi-Year Expert Group Meeting', 'UNIDO 50 Years Anniversary Conference', 'UK-China Innovation Round Table Meeting', 'UK-China Innovation and Development Forum', and other conferences or workshops organized by UNCTAD Committee of Sciences and Technology for Development, UN DESA, UNCTAD, UNIDO and the International Council for Sciences. I am grateful to the organizers and participants for providing me with these opportunities to obtain helpful feedback on the research from experts and practitioners, and to share findings from the research with the wider community on technology, innovation and development.

The research has attracted attention and gained strong support from international organizations: UNCTAD, UNIDO, UN DESA, WIPO and ITU. It has been a great privilege to realize that the findings from this body of research will be able to contribute to the international debate and policymaking concerning the role of innovation in the global effort to achieve the sustainable development goals (SDGs), and in international efforts to strengthen the innovation and technological capabilities and technology facilitation in developing countries.

I thank the Department of International Development of Oxford University for hosting the research. I also thank colleagues, associate fellows and students of the Technology and Management Centre for Development, Oxford University, for stimulating discussions and help. The collegiality of the Fellowship of Green Templeton College, Oxford, has also been an inspirational support.

Finally, I would like to express my enormous gratitude to my family, especially my husband, Shaohui, and my son, Yujie, for their great love, patience and support. Without their support, the research would not have been as successful as it is today, and the book would not have come to fruition.

1 Introduction

1.1 Motivation and Objectives of the Research

Innovation is a major driver of long-term economic growth (Aghion and Howitt, 2009; Lundvall, 2016; Romer, 1990) and sustainable development (UN, 2015). As extensively documented in Fagerberg et al. (2010), two factors have been identified as critical factors in the endogenous economic growth models: adoption of technologies developed elsewhere and indigenous innovative capacity. While science, technology and innovation have received increasing attention in academic research and policymaking, most of the research in this area has been carried out in the context of the developed countries. Our understanding about the determinants and the impact of innovations is therefore obtained in the context of the developed countries.

The nature, the source and the role of innovations in developing countries, especially in low (including both low and lower-middle) income countries, which have similar development levels and economic structure, such as countries in sub-Saharan Africa, are largely overlooked. The levels of economic, technical and institutional development in these countries are significantly lower than those in developed countries. Therefore, our knowledge about innovation in developed countries may not be appropriate for innovation, if any, in low-income countries. Reasons underlining this overlook are not only the lack of data and attention but also doubts which question whether firms and societies in these economies are innovative, and whether innovation is a rich-countries-only business and is therefore not relevant for low-income countries.

Is innovation relevant for low-income countries (LICs)? For some researchers, the answer is a clear 'yes', but other people may argue that there are other more important issues in LICs, such as food security, water, health and conflict, among others. This history supports the claim that the development process in LICs can be accelerated by tapping existing knowledge and know-how from foreign countries or by facilitating the exchange of both external and local knowledge within a country. Where the technological gap between developed and developing countries is significantly wide, better implementation of basic technologies can have a greater impact in recipient countries than the adoption of new technologies (Prahalad, 2012). The transfer, adoption and adaptation of knowledge to LICs hence constitute an important issue to understand and promote economic growth and global development. Moreover, only innovation and technical progress can provide fundamental solutions to challenges of LICs, such as poverty reduction, environment and resource constraints, and sustainable development. Therefore, innovation should be regarded not as an outcome of development but as a means to achieving it.

Are African economies innovative? Is there any innovation in sub-Saharan Africa? If so, what kinds of innovations are prospering there? Are innovations important to Africa and LICs? Until a decade ago, innovation in LICs was the focus of only a handful of studies every year (Zanello et al., 2013). Until then, innovation was often associated with patents or groundbreaking discoveries. Those are the results of costly, risky and lengthy processes which require intense knowledge and capital investment to create something 'new'. The *Oslo Manual* has been a standard reference for surveys of innovation in advanced economies and, from its third edition, in developing countries. Its definition of innovation as '[. . .] the implementation of a new or significantly improved product (good or service), or process, a new marketing method, or a new organisational method in business practices, workplace organisation or external relations' (OECD, 2005: p. 46) highlights two important features. First, innovation can take a multitude of forms (product innovations, process innovations, marketing innovations, and managerial and organizational innovations). Second, innovation can be developed by an original idea but could also emerge from diffusion, absorption or imitation of the new methods that are observed. Because of that, it could simply be new to the firm and have an impact on productivity and employment.

The recognized growing role of innovation in developing countries has opened new sub-fields of research at the intersection of innovation and management studies and development studies. The collection of work by Lundvall et al. (2011) explored the development of innovation systems in developing countries. Kraemer-Mbula and Wunsch-Vincent (2016) made an insightful investigation of the informal economy as a hidden engine of innovation in developing countries, based on case studies. In the context of Africa, Juma (2015) is a seminal research study on agricultural innovation in Africa. The effort of African Science, Technology and Innovation Indicators Initiative (ASTII) led by the New Partnership for Africa's Development (NEPAD) made valuable progress on the measurement and the relevant discussions of science, technology and innovation (STI) policies in Africa. The African Innovation Outlook published in 2014 reported that while R&D intensity in most of African countries is still far below the level of 1 per cent, innovation is pervasive (NPCA, 2014).

In recent years, there have been more studies on innovation for the poor. The stream of literature on inclusive innovation focuses on the impact of innovation on the people living in the lowest income groups (Chataway et al., 2014). In particular, it refers to the production or delivery of new products and services for and/or by those people that so far were largely excluded by markets. At the same time, the constrained ingenuity and resilience of the people living on the poverty line have been recognized as an incubator for local innovation. This focus on 'frugal innovation' (Bhatti and Ventresca, 2012) introduces further considerations to understand the sources and impact of innovation in LICs. In order to effectively access new markets, companies may need to re-think the production and delivery of goods, often re-engineering products in order to reduce the complexity and cost of production. The innovation process could involve reverse diffusion (Govindarajan and Ramamurti, 2011), when an innovation is adopted first in LICs before spreading to advanced industrial economies; *jugaad* innovation (Gulati, 2010), in the case when the innovation involves arrangement or workaround and is born out of lack of resources; or design thinking processes, in which consumers are involved in the design of a product or services. Alongside these developments, in a study of innovation in the emerging Asian economies, China and India in particular, Kaplinsky (2011) and Kaplinsky et al. (2009) suggested that 'innovation for the poor and innovation appropriate for production in low-wage and poor-infrastructure environments has increasingly become an arena for profitable production'. According to them, such 'appropriate technologies below the radar' observed in China and India are likely to become the dominant sources of innovation for the poor.

While all these studies made valuable progress in advancing our knowledge of innovation for the poor and have great relevance for Africa, most of these findings are discovered in the context of emerging Asia, especially in India and China. While the evidence published by NEPAD of innovation in Africa is valuable and encouraging, most countries, except South Africa and Uganda, did not use a stratified random sample or project the sample results to the population of firms for the surveys of innovation in 2008–2010 (NPCA, 2014). Although the NEPAD surveys also adopt the *Oslo Manual* definition of innovation, which is a step forward from only relying on R&D and patents, these surveys have not moved further in localizing the sources of innovation in the Africa context.[1] Moreover, the diffusion mechanisms of innovation to and within African countries were not its focus and hence received limited attention. What is more important, the informal economy is not covered in the NEPAD survey. Innovation in the informal economy remains under-researched, especially that based on large survey data. Finally, our understanding of the origin and diffusion of non-technological management innovation in Africa remains limited. These are important gaps in the literature that await investigation.

In a continent that rarely has formal R&D labs and has invested less than 1 per cent of the world's total R&D expenditure, what is the nature of the innovations created there? What are the major domestic and foreign sources of these innovations? What are the important mechanisms for the diffusion of these innovations? How do African firms manage to innovate given the resources, skills and institutional constraints? Are the innovations purely created through the frugal process? To what extent does the informal sector innovate? How do informal firms innovate? What are the scale, the nature, the sources and the constraints of the innovation in the informal sector? Moreover, what are the sources of non-technological, management and marketing innovations in the African firms, especially the informal firms? What is the role of innovation in the informal sector? Finally, what is the role of government policy? Which policies have effectively benefited the African firms? Where are the problems? Our understanding of innovation in the African continent is limited. Broadly speaking, as a published review on the origins and evolution of the field of science policy and innovation studies points out, innovation studies are a consolidated research field in the developed world, while innovation studies in developing countries have not received much attention so far (Fagerberg and Verspagen, 2009; Martin, 2012).

Defining innovation as a new product or process, or new management, organizational or marketing practices (where 'new' means new to the world or new to the country or the firm), using evidence from firm-level

---

[1] For example, the pattern of innovation expenditure is categorized following the European Community Innovation Survey, into intramural (in-house) R&D, extramural (outsourced) R&D, acquisition of machinery and acquisition of external knowledge.

surveys in Ghana and Tanzania, plus in-depth case studies in Ghana and Kenya, this book aims to fill this knowledge gap by exploring the nature of innovation in Africa, the determinants and transmission channels for effective innovation creation, diffusion and adoption in these countries under institutional, resource and affordability constraints, and opportunities and challenges of the Fourth Industrial Revolution for innovations in Africa. In particular, it aims to

• understand the nature and type of innovations in Africa, in both the formal and informal sectors;
• examine the sources and strategies of innovation creation and diffusion in Africa, comparing the formal and informal sectors;
• analyse the channels of external knowledge diffusion to Africa and their effectiveness;
• explore the sources and diffusion mechanisms of management innovation in Africa;
• investigate the opportunities and challenges of the Fourth Industrial Revolution for innovations in African economies; and
• discuss the space for innovation policy in LICs.

In order to achieve these objectives, the book carries out a systematic, comprehensive yet pioneering analysis of the nature and type of innovations in Africa, the internal and external sources of innovation in these countries, using economic, management, development and evolutionary theories, institutional analysis and political economy. It provides unique survey-based evidence on innovation in the informal sector, which is very important for the African economies while being seriously under-researched. It is one of the first systematic and in-depth academic studies of innovation in Africa that covers both the formal and the informal sectors. In particular, it presents the first large survey-data-based evidence of innovation in the informal economy in the LICs; it also delivers some pioneering analysis of the origin and diffusion of innovative management practices in Africa, using evidence at both organizational and individual levels.

Findings from this research have wide and important policy and practical implications for innovation in other LICs.

Innovation can be developed from an original idea but also emerges from diffusion, absorption or imitation of the new methods that are observed. Admittedly, fundamental innovation is costly, risky and path-dependent, and to date, important innovative work is highly concentrated in a few wealthy countries, with specific forms of research capacity, and amongst a few companies. Therefore, external sources of technology account for a large component of productivity growth in most developing countries. If foreign technologies are easy to diffuse and adopt, a country with meagre technological capacity can follow a catch-up strategy to acquire and more rapidly deploy the most advanced technologies (Bell and Pavitt, 1993). In the current times, this is one emerging insight from the broad diffusion and impacts of mobile technologies and affiliated value-adding financial and health services (Aker and Mbiti, 2010). This view is also supported by evidence from the European industrialization process in the nineteenth century and the Japanese economic reconstruction after the Second World War. Soete (1985) showed how during the first Industrial Revolution, the United States and other European countries successfully reduced the technological gap with the United Kingdom, the main innovator at that time, thanks to a successful imitation and catching-up process. Again, after the Second World War, the reconstruction and growth of the Japanese economy was absorptive in nature and based on integrating foreign technologies (Blumenthal, 1976). Similar paths to imitate the Japanese growth and structural changes were attempted in the past decades by other Asian countries as well, with South Korea and Taiwan being success stories (Biggart and Guillen, 1999).

However, technology diffusion to and adoption by LICs is costly and conditional on factors that support the process (Keller, 2004). It relies on substantial and well-directed technological efforts (Lall, 1992) as well as sufficient human and financial resources and absorptive capacity in firms and industries (Cohen and Levinthal, 1989; Keller, 1996). It also requires appropriate institutions and policies to guide incentives and facilitate the process, in addition to strong local capabilities to identify the right technology and appropriate transfer mechanism, and to absorb and make adaptations according to local economic, social, technical and environmental conditions (Fu and Gong, 2011).

Therefore, unlike most other innovation studies which focus on the inputs and outcomes of innovation activities, this book puts special emphasis on the transmission mechanisms of knowledge diffusion and detailed processes and provides unique and important analysis and evidence in this important regard. Moreover, different from most other research which is based on case studies of a particular industry, the studies reported in this book cover a wide range of industries that are important in Africa and in other LICs.

The results of this study challenge the opinion that innovation may not be relevant in Africa, and a much more diverse picture emerges. Firms in Africa are innovative and there are wide ranges of creative activities taking place. These include significantly improved products and production practices as well as novel marketing and management practices. The innovations in Africa are clearly not R&D-based, as are those that are often observed in industrialized countries. They are also not purely frugal. Nor are they all the so-called inclusive innovations that serve the base of the pyramid. However, they share some common characteristics, which suggest innovations in Africa are mostly innovations 'under-the-radar'. Most of these activities are incremental in nature and based on organizational or individual learning and adaptation, practice or individual creativity in the countries under study. They are often demand-led, learning and non-R&D based, low-cost innovations as a result of the constraints that the African firms face and the responses that they made to survive and grow. They are visible in new or significantly improved products or processes, but more than that, they are just everywhere in non-technological areas such as management and marketing practices used by the African firms. They do exist in Africa and other LICs, but they are not detectable by the traditional innovation indicators such as R&D investment and patent application/grant numbers. They do allow the African firms to survive and grow. But the clear limitation of the lack of inputs from modern science and engineering makes it difficult for the African firms to catch up with the firms in the industrialized countries which are supported by rapid progress in science and technology.

This concept of 'under-the-radar innovation' based on research in Africa has its roots in what Kaplinsky (2011) identified as 'innovation below the radar' in the Asian Drivers. It argues that much of the previously dominant innovation value chains are either ignorant of the needs of consumers at the bottom of the pyramid or lack the technologies and organizational structures to meet these needs effectively. It also argues that innovation for the poor and innovation appropriate for production in low-wage and poor-infrastructure environments has increasingly become an arena for profitable production. It goes further to fully elaborate the meaning of 'under-the-radar innovation' in the low-income or lower-middle-income context and how this is created and diffused in such an eco-social and physi-technical context.

The study reported in the book also finds that the diffusion of foreign technological and managerial knowledge to these counties is limited, especially at inter-organizational level. The limited collaboration between businesses was also stifling creativity. The new information and communication technologies have facilitated the innovation diffusion but could have played a more significant role. The opportunities for Africa in the Fourth Industrial Revolution will only be genuine and substantial when policies and international co-operations are in place to build up the digital competencies in the African continent; not only skills but also infrastructure and an enabling environment. Otherwise, they will miss the opportunities and face significant challenges. The role of policymakers should therefore be aimed at implementing policies that build national and international business networks, create incentives for innovators and provide funding to overcome common financial restraints.

1.2   Research Design

The book uses the rigorous statistical analysis of purposely designed surveys as well as in-depth case studies of representative cases. But a systematic approach is adopted: an analytical framework of an open national innovation system approach is introduced to organize the analysis that coherently spans a wide array of perspectives. Economic and management theory of innovation, development and evolutionary theory, institutional analysis and political economy are used to explain the nature, motivation, sources, obstacles and policy measures of innovation in the context of LICs, and the roles played by the domestic and international actors, the market and non-market institutions.

To capture the diversity of innovation in LICs, this book uses a broad definition of the term 'innovation' as previously stated. This includes not only the adoption of new product or process but also new management and marketing practices (where 'new' means new to the world or new to the country or the firm). On the one hand, this accounts for the different innovation activities and isolates their impact on the business of the firms. On the other hand, this book discusses innovation that could simply be new to the firm and have an impact because it is so. Importantly, this allows the research to distinguish groundbreaking novel innovation from imitative and incremental innovations.

1.2.1   Choice of Country for the Study

With regard to the country choice for the case study, Ghana is regarded as one of the most promising cases of industrial development in West Africa (AfDB et al., 2014). The country recently moved up from a low-income country to a lower-middle-income country. The development level and stability of its institutions and education system provide a potentially fertile soil for innovation in an LIC setting. Innovation has also been at the core of Ghana's long-term strategic political vision of being at the frontline of African development. In 2010, the Government of Ghana established an Industrial Policy, which was accomplished through a comprehensive and inclusive process based on analysis and wide consultation with stakeholders (Government of Ghana, 2010). In 2013, Ghana's industrial sector contributed 29 per cent of the total GDP. In the same year, agriculture accounted for 22 per cent of GDP and the remaining 49 per cent was the contribution of the services sector. Apparel and food processing are major manufacturing industries in its industrial sector. The contribution of the construction industry also increased from 5.7 to 8.6 per cent between 2006 and 2010. All these make Ghana a good case for the study of innovation in Africa (and also innovation in LICs).

Tanzania, being an East African country and a low-income country, is a good case to complement Ghana. Tanzania is among the countries in sub-Saharan Africa that have shown a sustained high growth rate in recent years (between 2009 and 2017), with an average growth at between 6 per cent and 7 per cent.[2] In terms of economic structure, the country is not very different from Ghana. Just like Ghana, it has service sectors as a major contributor to the GDP, contributing 47.6 per cent, with agriculture contributing 23.4 per cent and industry (mining, construction and manufacturing) contributing 28.6 per cent.[3] However, in terms of the industrialization process, that is the contribution of the manufacturing sector to GDP, the country is not doing very well – the contribution has never exceeded 10 per cent in the long history of attempts to industrialize since independence; it was as low as 5.6 per cent in 2016. The country has however, renewed its industrialization vigour and it is the country's top development agenda. Currently, the country has a development vision that envisions the country to be semi-industrialized by 2025, that is, the manufacturing contribution reaching 23 per cent of GDP, up from 5.6 per cent; the President himself is spearheading the industrialization agenda. Moreover, Tanzania is one of the very first African countries to realize the role of science and technology in the industrialization process; its first science and technology policy came into effect in 1986. The policy has been reviewed twice since then. Currently, the Global Innovation index 2018 report shows Tanzania to be the top-ranked low-income country, holding the 92nd position globally, having moved up four positions from the previous report. Notably, the report showed Tanzania to have achieved high innovation output scores relative to its input scores.[4] A lot is happening in the country, and this makes Tanzania an interesting case representing emerging low-income resource-rich countries and the economies in East Africa.

---

[2] Index Mundi, 2018 – www.indexmundi.com/tanzania/economy_profile.html retrieved on 2 January 2019.
[3] Ibid.
[4] www.sipotra.it/wp-content/uploads/2018/09/GLOBAL-INNOVATION-INDEX-2018 .pdf retrieved on 2 January 2019.

1.2.2 Methods

This book attempts to fill a gap in the literature and the market by providing the first systematic and comprehensive analysis of the creation and diffusion of innovation in Africa through an in-depth study of innovation in Ghana and Tanzania. It also provides a valuable, large survey-based analysis and evidence of innovation in the informal economy, which is also rarely researched. Therefore, it uses a mixed methods approach, which combines both qualitative case studies and statistical analysis of data from large firm-level surveys, to understand the overall innovation performance in Ghanaian and Tanzanian firms and the process of creation and diffusion of innovation in these firms. The quantitative and qualitative approaches are used to triangulate the results and provide a more complete picture of the current innovation activities in Ghana and Tanzania.

Such a research design using survey evidence from two representative countries in East and West Africa over time, instead of a single-country cross-section survey, allows us to identify the major characteristics and key sources as well as linkages for innovation in sub-Saharan Africa which are common to different countries and robust over time. This is then supplemented by a case study in a third country, Kenya, and some general analysis in the context of LICs. In this study, we emphasize the shared characteristics and factors that are common in a wider African context, instead of comparing the differences. The institutional and economic factors that underline the differences between these countries are not the main focus of this study due to the space limit of this book. This leaves space for future studies, which I will discuss in the concluding chapter.

The advantage of such a research design is that it offers us an opportunity to discover the general patterns of innovation, the sources and diffusion mechanisms in sub-Saharan Africa through in-depth and systematic studies without the heavy cost of demanding firm-level surveys in each of the African countries. It also offers the advantage of in-depth and systematic analysis of each major case-study country and avoids the limitation of having to narrow the analysis of innovation in each country into one or two chapters. I have to admit, at the same time, that the study may have not covered all the major types of innovations in Africa. Hence caution should be exercised when drawing strong arguments about innovation in the African continent.

In analysing the creation and diffusion of innovation in Ghana and Tanzania, it is important to recognize the structural peculiarities of most of the developing countries, where a dual economy system coexists, and besides formal registered firms, an informal sector is active (La Porta and Shleifer, 2014). The nature of the informal sector prevents an assessment of its magnitude; however, it has been estimated that the weighted average size of the shadow economy (as a percentage of GDP in the period 1999–2007) in sub-Saharan Africa is around 40 per cent (Schneider et al., 2011) and up to 80 per cent of non-agricultural employment (Chen et al., 1999). The different firms' capabilities in the formal and informal sectors are likely to shape the innovation adoption and diffusion. For example, formal establishments may have the human and capital resources to collaborate in innovation activities with other firms, research and development institutions, or, in the case of larger firms, with foreign institutions (Oyelaran-Oyeyinka et al., 1996). In contrast, informal firms are unlikely to have strong capabilities and therefore may be more likely to innovate from entrepreneurs' initiatives and in response to specific constraints of the context in which they operate (Robson et al., 2009). Therefore, the research and the survey have placed a special emphasis on innovation in the informal sector.

The book draws on evidence from the 'Diffusion of innovation in the low-income countries' (DILIC) project in 2012–2015 funded by ESRC-FCDO and the follow-up research in Ghana and Tanzania supported by the ESRC and the European Commission Framework Program 7, commissioned by the United Nations, as well as other related research by the author in collaboration with researchers in Africa and Europe to explore these issues and unpack the process. The DILIC Project was designed to shed some light on this issue investigating the role of innovation in LICs, by exploring the nature of innovation in the private sector and the determinant factors and transmission channels for effective innovation creation, diffusion and adoption in LICs under institutional, resource and affordability constraints. The project was led by the Principal Investigator, Professor Xiaolan Fu from the University of Oxford (UK). The research group includes Professor Pierre Mohnen of UNU-MERIT (Maastricht), Dr Giacomo Zanello and Dr Jun Hou of the University of Oxford, Dr George Essegbey of the Science and Technology Policy Research Institute (STEPRI) of the Council for Scientific and Industrial Research (CSIR) of Ghana.

The DILIC project designed and administrated a representative survey of the firms' population in Ghana and collected detailed information on the innovation activities of more than 500 formal and informal firms. This survey is the first survey in LICs dedicated to the origin and diffusion of innovation within and to these countries. The unique design of the survey provided unprecedented insights on the transmission mechanisms of innovation, expanding our understanding and going beyond the traditional input and output indicators. Such a survey is not only unique for LICs but also for middle- and high-income countries, where transmission mechanisms have not been receiving the attention they deserve. This carefully designed pioneering survey offers distinctive evidence on the form and nature of innovations in the LICs' context, the origins and the effective channels for the diffusion of innovation within the country and from foreign sources to these countries, the barriers to innovation creation and diffusion and the space for innovation policy in these economies. Details of the case studies and the design of the survey are reported in Appendices 1 and 2 at the end of the book.

After the completion of the DILIC project, the research on innovation in LICs was extended to include both Ghana and Tanzania (and also Uganda by the World Intellectual Property Organization). Follow-up surveys were carried out in Ghana and Tanzania between end of 2015 and early 2016. In order to minimize the influence of cultural differences and the differences in the definitions of innovation in the two countries, the surveys were carried out in person by trained survey assistants, who were trained for a week and had to pass a test before going out into the field. Moreover, the survey team in Tanzania was trained by staff of the Ghanaian survey team to further ensure the consistency and comparability of the surveys.

The firm-level survey is then supplemented by (1) an in-depth case study of thirty-two firms in Ghana, (2) a case study of the mobile payment technology development in Kenya, and (3) a general study of the impact of the Fourth Industrial Revolution on developing countries. The decision to include the case study of M-Pesa not only enriches the study by adding the insights of the success of Africa in digital financial innovations, but also describes the innovation experience in another major economy in Africa. The GDP of Kenya in PPP terms was $163.7 billion in 2017, ranking the country 74th in the world. The development in digital finance in Kenya is commendable, setting an example for the hope of developing a digital economy in other African countries. Therefore, in-depth studies of some successful innovation in Kenya, especially in the application of information and communication technologies, provide valuable insights into the success factors for innovation in Africa.

1.3   The Structure of the Book

In light of the technology and innovation theories on the nature, sources and diffusion of innovation, the book is organized into three parts focusing on the nature and domestic sources of innovation in Africa, the diffusion of foreign innovation into Africa, and emerging technologies and innovation in Africa, in addition to the Introduction and concluding chapters. Before embarking on these analyses, a systematic literature review and an overview of Ghana's and Tanzania's industrial sectors are presented in Chapters 2 and 3.

Part I on the nature and domestic sources of innovation in Africa includes five chapters. Chapter 4 examines the nature of innovation in Africa using a mixed methods approach combining both qualitative case studies and statistical analysis of unique firm-level survey data. It finds innovations in a multitude of sectors, both in formal and informal firms. Innovation strategies tend to primarily address the resources, skills and institutional constraints and meet the affordability and accessibility of local consumers. Successful innovations are therefore user-led, learning-based, and economically and technically appropriate. Firms also tend to adopt low-cost, non-technological hidden innovations in management and marketing. Chapter 5 analyses how African firms overcome the resources, skills and institutional constraints of innovation and the high risks of innovation through opening up to collaboration and external information searching. Special focus is placed on the role of universities, clusters, and regional and global value chains and their impact on technology upgrading and diversification in African industries. Chapter 6 assesses the impact of innovation on the growth of African firms based on evidence from a firm-level survey and in-depth cases studies in Ghana and Tanzania, and studies of innovation and upgrading in African countries. It finds that firms survive because they innovate. Innovation also has had a significant positive impact on the labour productivity of firms; learning-based innovation is a significant factor in firm growth in these countries. The effect is significantly greater for informal establishments. Evidence from this chapter suggests that innovation is a factor that may push developing informal firms to the formal economy. Evidence based on secondary country-level panel data also suggests that innovation contributes positively to export upgrading in LICs, including Africa. Chapter 7 discusses the role played by women entrepreneurs and the challenges to innovation encountered by women entrepreneurs in Africa. Our findings suggest that women entrepreneurs in our study countries score lesser in product, process and management innovations than their male counterparts. The results show, however, that women entrepreneurs perform better than male entrepreneurs in market innovations. Chapter 8 analyses the role of the state in innovation in Africa, questioning whether the state has been a driver or barrier to innovation in the continent. Our findings show that while sampled firms acknowledged the importance of the state through policy interventions, they lamented about the implementation of policies. The sampled firms noted that most of the policies, such as the

S&T policies, are poorly implemented and hence ineffective. However, firms in Ghana and Tanzania seem to have benefited from available government subsidy and training programmes.

Part II on the diffusion of foreign innovation into Africa includes two chapters. Chapter 9 examines the channels for the diffusion of foreign innovation to Africa, in particular, trade, foreign direct investment (FDI) and diasporas. The results from the empirical analyses suggest that some innovations in Ghana and Tanzania are imported from abroad and/or result from spillovers emanating from multinational companies. Firms are identified to acquire external knowledge, specifically from abroad, through networks, labour mobility, and imports and exports. The importation and exportation of products (goods and services) are important conduits through which local firms engage and potentially adopt innovations. In addition, formal firms engage in the global value chain via the downstream manufacturing sectors, which is a very effective way to obtain innovation from abroad. Chapter 10 studies the transfer of innovative managerial knowledge within MNE subsidiaries, with a special focus on the role of social and business networks. The findings suggest that clusters provide greater support to firms through the exchange of relevant production and technology information and a greater collaboration on pricing. Our results also suggest that regional value chains that enable firms to be part of a vertical production network are a more realistic and feasible step for African firms to gradually upgrade and integrate into the global production network.

Part III on the emerging technologies and innovation in Africa includes three chapters. Chapter 11 examines the role of information technology in knowledge diffusion and innovation in Ghana. The chapter finds that the use of ICT in firms' production processes offers unique and integrated opportunities for interacting with innovation activities through the facilitation of in-house innovation. The 'internet' was found as the most important knowledge source that has helped firms to utilize the effect of in-house innovation activities and eventually yield high innovation sales which are new to the market. Chapter 12 presents a case study of catch-up in the digital economy based on the story of M-Pesa in Kenya. The chapter shows the importance of public–private partnership. The findings show that a private sector company, Safaricom, played a crucial role in developing a vertical production chain of services and user community. These innovations led to additional product and process innovations. In addition, the chapter emphasized the significant role the Kenyan mobile policy evolution provides to the public–private partnership. A facilitative but firm regulatory role of the state was found to be critical for effective legitimization of M-Pesa. The Central Bank of Kenya was identified to have played multiple but very critical policy-oriented roles, but it also remained an honest broker throughout the formative phase and beyond. Chapter 13 investigates the implications of the Fourth Industrial Revolution on innovations in Africa, assessing both the opportunities and challenges. The chapter recognizes that the Fourth Industrial Revolution (4IR) offers key opportunities and challenges to African economies. The chapter argues that the 4IR holds great prospects in enhancing connectivity and efficiency of African businesses as well as empowering people in Africa through the bridging of the digital divide. The 4IR will speed up access to knowledge, information and services at much faster speed and convenience at much lower costs. These lower costs would be expected to generate greater variety of products that would benefit consumers in the continent.

Finally, Chapter 14 summarizes the main findings of the book and discusses whether Africa can leapfrog the innovation gap in the context of these findings. It also discusses the policy implications for the African and other developing countries and identifies issues for future research.

2 Innovation in Low-Income Countries
Received Wisdom

2.1 Introduction

Innovation is regularly recognized as a critical component of industrialization and catch-up in developing countries. Literature on the diffusion of innovations in developing countries is growing and taking different directions (Altenburg, 2009). It is critical to identify what we have learnt so far, what evidence is inconclusive and what we still do not know enough about. The main purpose of this chapter is to review the state of the research in this area, shed some light on the dynamics that drive the diffusion of innovation in low-income countries (LICs) based on existing literature and identify the gaps for future research. Specifically, this chapter focuses on the diffusion of innovation among firms in the private sector of LICs, a sector in developing countries which has a greater space for improvement, since they are often working far from the technological frontier. From past studies, this chapter aims to collect study cases and empirical evidence that will contribute to answer three questions: (1) what are the barriers to innovation creation and diffusion *in* LICs? (2) what are the channels of innovation diffusion *within* LICs? (3) what are the channels of diffusion of external innovation *to* LICs?

This chapter adopts a systematic review protocol – a rigorous and transparent form of literature review. As DFID (2012) stated, 'systematic reviews are a well-established and rigorous method to map the evidence base in an unbiased way as possible, assess the quality of the evidence and synthesize it'.

This chapter is extracted from Zanello et al. (2016). I am grateful to Giacomo Zanello, Pierre Mohnen and Marc Ventresca as well as to the publisher for kindly allowing the extracted part to be reprinted in this chapter.

2.2   The Nature of Innovation in LICs

A fundamental question for the literature review is how to reliably measure sources, forms and impact of innovation. From the *Oslo Manual*'s definition, two dimensions of innovation emerge. First, innovation can be a new or significantly improved product (good or service), process, marketing or organizational activity or process. It is relevant, in order to account for the different innovation modes, to isolate their diffusion patterns and their impact on firm performance. For example, recent evidence suggests that in the Organisation for Economic Cooperation and Development (OECD) countries, product innovations have a significant impact on revenue productivity, while the impact of process innovation is less clear (Hall, 2011). Second, innovation does not necessarily have to be new to the market or to the world as a whole but could simply be new to the firm and have an impact on productivity and growth because of that. In addition, that impact could be competence-enhancing or competence-destroying for the individual firm or even for an industry (Tushman and Anderson, 1986). This suggests that innovation can be either a groundbreaking novel innovation or an imitative innovation; both forms of innovation can add considerable value, albeit through different implementation processes and on different timescales (Kaplinsky, 2018). According to Lundvall (2016), groundbreaking or radical innovations often form the basis for incremental, imitative innovations. Given the characteristics of the developing countries, technological capabilities in the context of LICs are not only research and development (R&D) but also incremental (Lundvall et al., 2009).

Creation, diffusion and adoption of innovation form a complete chain of process. It is important to clarify the distinction between adoption and diffusion. Adoption is the individual process that an agent (individual, firm) experiences from first learning about a technology, product or idea to finally implementing it. The diffusion process, instead, analyses the dynamics that influence how an innovation spreads among adopters. Overall, the diffusion process essentially encompasses the adoption process of several individuals over time. Because of the risk, cost and accumulative nature of innovation, groundbreaking novel innovation is less likely to occur in LICs, while imitative and incremental innovation may play an important role. In the review, we therefore focus on the diffusion of innovation in LICs, although often we refer to adoption as well.

The social organization of economic activities varies substantially across countries, in both industrialized and developing economies, and is critical to the understanding of the diffusion of innovation

(Hamilton and Biggart, 1988). These institutional differences between the developed and developing countries are under-recognized in many treatments of LICs and, correspondingly, in many studies (Biggart and Guillen, 1999). In addition to the institutional arrangements, the nature of diffusion itself may be under-specified. Strang and colleagues (Strang and Meyer, 1993; Strang and Soule, 1998) in their work on 'institutional conditions for diffusion' critique the standard methods' toolkit for diffusion and review useful improvements in the study of diffusion. They argue that the network-dominant accounts of diffusion (Rogers, 2003) neglect (1) the texture of the terrain in which diffusion occurs, (2) the ways that the diffused innovation or technology is transformed over time and (3) temporal variables that affect diffusion. In a thoughtful discussion about 'theorization', they argue that the work of abstraction and the provision of standard 'accounts' allow some elements to diffuse more rapidly and widely, relative to elements that stay moored in a 'local' context. Their insights are particularly relevant to the understanding of some differences in innovation in LICs, relative to industrialized economies regarding the role of intermediaries: the overall apparatus of 'theorization' whether through legal infrastructure, experts, industry standard bodies or trade associations is overall less well developed in most LICs. This means that even 'good ideas' may have more difficulty spreading in these contexts, where both potential adoptions and potential adopters are more routinely grounded in the 'local' rather than in the broader cosmopolitan (e.g. expert, profession-alized) activity, values and practices.

As noted in Chapter 1, the so-called inclusive innovation literature focuses on the impact of innovation on people at the bottom of the pyramid (Chataway et al., 2013). On the other hand, the constrained ingenuity and resilience of the people living on the poverty line have been recognized as an incubator for local innovation. Often this process is called 'frugal innovation', in which non-essential features are removed from a product or service to contain costs and be marketed for lower-income customers. The innovation process could involve (1) reverse diffusion (Govindarajan and Ramamurti, 2011); (2) reverse engineering; (3) *jugaad* (Gulati, 2010; Radjou et al., 2012), when the innovation involves a low-cost solution to any problem in an intelligent way and is born out of lack of resources; or (4) design thinking processes, in which consumers are involved in the design of a product or service. Frugal innovation can be thought to be a subset of inclusive innovation, although in the literature the two definitions and concepts have sometimes been used interchangeably. Nevertheless, both processes recognize the role of innovation within the LICs' socio-economic and political contexts and aim to create value for underserved markets.

2.3 Barriers to Innovation Creation and Diffusion in LICs

The findings from the systematic review are presented in three sections. The first investigates the nature of innovation in LICs and includes two subsections, respectively covering external and internal barriers to innovation. The second section presents evidence of the innovation diffusion within LICs, while the last section reports on the drivers of innovation diffusion to LICs.

2.3.1 External Factors: Political, Economic and Institutional Constraints

Factors outside the firms may prevent or promote mechanisms of innovation creation and diffusion which, in turn, determine the speed and pattern of diffusion among firms within a country (Cohen and Levinthal, 1989; Keller, 2004). The existing literature suggests that these barriers include political factors, such as a weak political system and widespread corruption across society; economic characteristics, such as openness of an economy and level of economic development; inadequate infrastructure; institutional factors, such as intellectual property rights and the interaction between private (firms) and public sectors (research institutes and universities); and cultural and linguistic distances. Each of these is a critical barrier to the diffusion of innovation in LICs.

A large number of studies have reviewed the impact of political and economic barriers on innovation. In a cross-sectional study of 107 countries, Allard et al. (2012) found evidence that national systems of innovation were most likely to flourish in developed, politically stable countries and less likely to prosper in historically unstable countries. Innovation capabilities require education and technical skills which can only be developed with long-term investments and are unlikely to exist in unstable countries. A further consequence of unstable political powers is the lack of trust between private sector and policymakers which inhibits innovation activities (Meagher, 2007). Srholec (2011) argued that the way a political system is organized has powerful indirect effects on development through innovativeness of firms. From an analysis of more than 14,000 firms in thirty-two developing countries surveyed in the Productivity and Investment Climate Survey (PICS) by the World Bank, he found that democratic governments are likely to provide better incentives to the innovation systems. The level of corruption in a country is also an important barrier to innovation. De Waldemar (2012), analysing 1,600 Indian firms from the World Bank Enterprise Survey, found that corruption, in the form of bribes, levied a de facto tax that diminished the probability of new products being introduced. To mitigate the possible endogeneity effect of corruption and innovation, he used an instrumental variable approach and estimated that an increase of one standard deviation in the bribery 'tax' decreased the probability of innovation by 5 per cent. Analysing data from nineteen countries in sub-Saharan Africa, Amendolagine et al. (2013) found that efficient institutions and a reliable legal system are preconditions for boosting the linkages between foreign firms and local firms. Property rights also affect the diffusion of innovation. A study of small-scale furniture makers in the city of Mwanza (Tanzania) revealed the lack of property rights manifested in the lack of control that business owners have over assets and that this created disincentives to invest in site improvements or fixed capital (Murphy, 2007).

Literature further suggests that the level of economic development of a country is not as decisive as the openness of the economy and trade policies for the creation and diffusion of innovation (Tybout, 2000). Trade is the main access to foreign goods and technology for countries (Coe et al., 1997; Eaton and Kortum, 2002). Lucke (1993) tested the hypothesis that industrial process innovations in the textile and steel industries had diffused more slowly in developing countries than in industrialized countries. He concluded that overall, the level of economic development had only a modest impact on the adoption of innovations. Instead, multiple studies stress the importance of economic openness as a determinant for diffusion of innovation. Using firm-level data across forty-three developing countries, Almeida and Fernandes (2008) found a strong positive correlation between openness and technology adoption. After controlling for firm characteristics and country and industry fixed effects, minority for-eign-owned firms, importing firms and exporting firms were, respect-ively, 4.5, 6.4 and 3.1 per cent significantly more likely to engage in technological innovations than firms without these characteristics. More recently, Fu and Gong (2011) explored the different impacts of foreign and domestic investment on R&D. From a panel data set of more than 50,000 Chinese firms, they found that the major drivers of technology upgrading of indigenous firms were internal R&D activities, whereas foreign investment appeared to contribute to static industry capabilities. This suggests that indigenous capacity is likely to result in innovation, whereas foreign direct investment (FDI) tends to reinforce existing industrial capacity. Openness of an economy can be supported by specific policies, but infrastructure to physically move people and goods is often necessary to realize the full benefits/impacts of openness. This more precise specification reinforces our observations about absorptive capacity and local infrastructure that converts abstract potential (e.g. R&D expenditures) into realized benefits. Kinda (2010) uses firm-level data from seventy-seven LICs and shows how the lack of physical infrastructure discourages FDIs.

A large literature regarding developed economies points to the role of national innovation 'systems' that link key institutions in a value-creating cycle (Lundvall, 2016; Lundvall et al., 2002; Nelson, 1992). In the context of LICs, obsolete national innovation systems in relation to the economic development of a country and lack of market competition are both barriers to innovation. In developing countries which are less successful in technological catching-up, to be effective, the national innovation systems must be linked to the economic structural development level. Using Thailand as a case study, Intarakumnerd et al. (2002) found that while the country moved from agricultural to an increasingly industrial economy, its national innovation system remained weak and fragmented. That undermined the innovation capabilities. A functional national innovation system seems to be critical for the acquisition, adaptation and development of more advanced technologies. Fu and Zhang (2011) analysed the solar photovoltaic industry in China and India and found that in both countries, the national innovation systems successfully developed and supported the capacity for the industry to mix and sequence different technology transfers and indigenous innovation mechanisms. Similarly, innovation capabilities can also be nurtured by market competition. From a sample of 291 Indian manufacturing firms, Kumar and Saqib (1996) showed that in the case where the entry of new firms in a market is restricted by government policy, the absence of competitive pressure reduces the likelihood of firms to undertake R&D. However, they found that the competitive pressure did not influence the intensity of R&D expenditures of firms once they have decided to invest in R&D.

Diffusion and creation of innovation are also restricted by weak interaction between private and public sectors. A number of the issues associated with the lack of innovation activity in North-West Frontier Province Pakistani industries could be linked to the fact that Pakistan has not had an established tradition of interaction between the public and the private sectors in technology policymaking (Bashir et al., 2010). Meagher (2007) remarks that industrial development is better facilitated if the mechanisms driving it are embedded in the social institutions, capabilities and competences found in a region. In this way, spillovers between different sectors are facilitated. Katrak (1997b) looked at the poor performances of the partnership between the Indian national chemical laboratories and the local firms. It was found that the lack of complementary capabilities in the private firms and the inadequate technology developed in the labs were the main factors that weakened the relationship.

A further barrier to innovation creation and diffusion is the lack of connections between universities and the private sector (Kruss et al., 2012). From a study of fifty firms in Nigeria, Oyelaran-Oyeyinka et al. (1996) found that research and development institutions (RDIs) interacted more with firms that did not undertake any R&D but relied on RDIs for solutions to bottlenecks rather than developing new products and processes. More recently, Srholec (2011) used a multilevel model of innovation to find a lack of evidence on the extent of public research infrastructure and the propensity of firms in developing countries to innovate.

Entrepreneurship policies are also determinant factors that can promote or prevent innovation in LICs. Hall et al. (2012) examined the participation of people at the Base of Pyramid (BoP) as entrepreneurs and not as consumers. They argue that weak institutions encourage undesirable outcomes, especially if entrepreneurship policies are based solely on economic indicators. They added that policies addressing both economic and social perspectives may foster more productive entrepreneurial outcomes, albeit at a more constrained economic pace. Allard et al. (2012) found that pro-business market reforms consistently showed a strong effect that counterbalanced the negative impact of political instability, especially in those developing country environments where science and technology were lagging behind.

Cultural and linguistic distances also have an impact on the diffusion of innovation, particularly regarding FDI spillovers. Analysing patents' data to measure international diffusion of technological knowledge, MacGarvie (2005) found that diffusion is enhanced by sharing a common language, together with physical and technological proximity. Instead, Rodriguez-Clare (1996) built a theoretical model in which the difference of languages between host and source countries can actually foster the diffusion of innovation. The rationale is that when the costs of communication between headquarters and production site are higher, there is a stronger incentive to buy specialized inputs in loco. Similarly, a different cultural background between host and source countries can increase domestic firms' opportunity to learn through exposure to different systems of technologies, management practices and cultural values. These are the findings from a panel study of Chinese firms (Zhang et al., 2010). Ethnicity is an important bounding factor in economic transactions, and Huang et al. (2013) explored the impact of FDI on ethnic Chinese firms. Their results seem not to support the vision of ethnic ties as factors that can close the information gap and contribute to contract enforcement in environments where legal institutions are underdeveloped, but rather as factors that privilege insiders at the expense of outsiders with a consequential reduction in economic efficiency.

Finally, Weinhold and Nair-Reichert (2009) highlighted two additional barriers to innovation: inequality (measured as proportion of middle class) and intellectual property rights (IPRs). They used data on patents granted to residents and non-residents from 1994 to 2000 across a sample of fifty-three countries, including several LICs, to capture the innovation level. Taking into account the likely endogenous nature of innovation, their findings indicate that the size of the middle class, and to some extent IPRs, explains resident, but not non-resident, patterns of patenting. They argue that the middle-class impact on creation of innovation is likely to operate through increased market participation, which directly increases domestic, but not necessarily non-resident, innovation. Kumar and Saqib (1996), Javorcik (2004), Shi and Pray (2012), Yang and Maskus (2009), and Yongmin and Puttitanun (2005) found similar evidence of the negative impact of weak IPRs on innovation. Zhao (2006) showed how multinational enterprises (MNEs) undertaking R&D in LICs take advantage of the arbitrage opportunities presented by the institutional gap across countries. Using data for over a thousand US firms, she found that technologies developed in countries with weak IPR protection are used more internally and as a consequence they show stronger internal linkages. The results suggest that firms may use internal organizations to substitute for inadequate external institutions. However, it is important to contextualize those results to the nature of innovation in LICs. For many of these, innovation is often imitation and adaptation of imported technologies, and this is not reflected in the patents' data.

2.3.2 *Internal Factors: Capabilities and Resources Constraints*

We also find in the literature frequent references to factors internal to the firm that can stand in the way of innovation and affect the competitive strategy of a firm. The predominant factors are the lack of human capital (education and managerial skills), resources (financial capital and information) and networking capabilities.

Bell and Albu (1999) argued that the diffusion of innovation in LICs should be assisted with systems of knowledge accumulation, rather than just production systems. They developed a conceptual framework of clusters' active capabilities for generating and diffusing knowledge and highlight the critical role of external sources of knowledge. Numerous studies have empirically tested the role of knowledge. Using data from 100 manufacturing firms in Nigeria, Abereijo et al. (2007) found a strong positive correlation among the few firms that showed some level of innovation abilities and the level of education of the managers, which included higher academic degrees and education in science or engineering. Similar findings are reported in studies of firms in a multi-country setting (Wang and Wong, 2012), in Ghana (McDade and Malecki, 1997; Robson et al., 2009), Tanzania (Hall et al., 2012), Uganda (Oyelaran-Oyeyinka and Lal, 2006) and Nigeria (Egbetokun et al., 2012; Ilori et al., 2000). Fu (2008) provided evidence showing that in regions of China with more highly educated and skilled workers, FDI spillovers are greater. As Huang et al. (2003) point out, intellectual capabilities are also critical in the process of learning from failure. In many of the previous references, education is regarded as a necessary, although not a sufficient, condition to innovation. From a survey of 201 small business owners involved in a microcredit programme in Kenya, Bradley et al. (2012) advocate that capital is not a 'silver bullet' and education and human capital are the major constraints of innovation. Robson et al. (2009) stress how the lack of access to educational opportunities in many developing countries further disadvantages female entrepreneurs in the pursuit of an entrepreneurial career. The lack of resources in the education systems in many LICs, mainly in rural areas, make non-formal training the main source for learning, together with 'learning-by-doing' (Oyelaran-Oyeyinka and Lal, 2006). In addition to education, managerial skills have received increased attention as a factor explaining differences in firms' performance in LICs (Bruhn et al., 2010). Mano et al. (2012) ran a randomized experiment in Ghana where 167 metalworkers received a three-week training programme. Compared to the control group, the treatment group showed improved business practices (keeping business records and visiting customers) and better performance.

Technical innovations can be expensive, and firms cannot afford to implement them. For example, in the specific case of paper-manufacturing firms in Northern Vietnam, the financial constraint was a more critical obstacle to overcome than the lack of skill to adopt and use a new technology (Kimura, 2011). Kugler (2006) draws similar conclusions from a sample of Colombian manufacturing firms. Subsidies and grants become a concrete support for innovation in LICs. Vishwasrao and Bosshardt (2001), analysing data from Indian firms, concluded that not only should machinery and assets be subsidized but skills, capabilities and linkages should be as well. Egbetokun et al. (2012) argue that tax reduction for firms could achieve the same result.

Back in 1992, Bagachwa (1992) studied the performance of small- and large-scale grain milling techniques in Tanzania to explain why some firms select inappropriate techniques and products. Besides the lack of financial capital, he found that an important factor was the lack of information about the appropriate technology. In fact, about 80 per cent of the mill owners did not have sufficient prior knowledge about costs of alternative milling equipment and their operating characteristics. The lack of information and knowledge was also responsible for an initial failure of the electronic banking system of a commercial bank in Nigeria (Huang et al., 2003). A first implementation of internet banking did not work, and given the lack of technological capability within the bank, it was not possible to simply generate a solution based on the organization's existing knowledge. They then argue that technology is not necessarily a panacea for innovation, and learning from experience can be equally relevant. McDade and Malecki (1997) showed how the lack of comprehensive information and experience in larger-scale manufacturing seemed to be the largest impediment to improving Ghana's industrial capacity. Kumar and Saqib (1996) pointed out how the lack of the right technology was also a barrier for the manufacturing sector in India. A different approach is taken by Van Dijk and Szirmai (2006). Based on a comprehensive sample of Indonesian paper manufactures from 1923 to 2000, they built an index of machinery efficiency that captured the technological distance of each firm to the world technological frontier. They found evidence of quick catch-up by the industry, although some firms (which had the finance and capabilities to adopt large-scale modern machinery) installed state-of-the-art machinery, while others installed older vintages. Some studies also considered the firm size as a barrier to innovation (Chen et al., 2011; Robson et al., 2009). However, arguably, the size of a firm and its resources are likely to be correlated.

Additional internal factors that facilitate the diffusion of knowledge and innovation are the openness and networking capabilities of the firm. According to Lundvall (2016), innovations diffuse mainly through user–producer interactions where producers communicate the 'use-value characteristics' of innovative products to 'potential users'. In an empirical study, Murphy (2002) collected data from forty-one manufacturing firms in Tanzania and found not only that a firm's capacity for innovation was related to the quality of the social structures available to it (i.e. the institutions) but that innovation was also driven by the social capabilities or competences of the managers within the firm. He also emphasized how trust between actors, which often is not captured in empirical estimations, may be associated with different forms of innovation. In fact, trust has an important function as a binding and bridging mechanism in social relations that ultimately may facilitate information exchange and collective knowledge creation. Similar conclusions come from Meagher (2007), who found trust to be a determinant factor in the success of clusters in Nigeria. Finally, the lack of communication technologies could also be a barrier for knowledge diffusion. In a study at the dawn of the diffusion of mobile phones in developing countries, Overå (2006) found that prompt communication between economic agents in Ghanaian firms had a significant effect on the diffusion of market knowledge.

2.4   Innovation Creation and Diffusion in LICs

The literature review highlights three main vectors of innovation diffusion in LICs. Simple forms of clusters allow firms and entrepreneurs to share capabilities in the existing value chain. Case studies on the link between public (universities) and private sectors underline how public funding can support the knowledge diffusion and innovation. Finally, a new and growing branch of research looks at the innovation diffusion within the BoPs that innovate on the value chain itself. The focus is two-fold: to rethink the value chain of products and to provide affordable services and products.

The evidence suggests that clusters in LICs do not seem to directly involve the creation of new products or processes; however, they go farther than merely exploiting economies of scale. McDade and Malecki (1997) investigated the type of inter-firm interactions that take place among entrepreneurs of small-scale enterprises in the industrial district of Odawna (Ghana). Most of the interactions are associated with sharing tools or pieces of equipment, in addition to the role of word-of-mouth advertising. Although many examples are reported of ingenious innovations in the adaptation of material resources, much of the energy seems to be consumed in finding ways to accommodate the scarcity of basic economic and material resources. Murphy (2007), instead, found that in the industrial clusters in Mwanza (Tanzania), there was no high-end innovation or high-quality production, but rather situations exploited for market access and the collective efficiencies associated with tool sharing, labour pooling and ready access to inputs. Both examples seem to fall within the category of 'survival clusters' where micro- and small-scale enterprises produce low-quality consumer goods for local markets, mainly in activities where barriers to entry are low (Altenburg and Meyer-Stamer, 1999). This example emphasizes the importance of geographical location for the diffusion of innovation. Robson et al. (2009) found that more innovative Ghanaian firms were located in large towns, where the opportunities for personal interactions and exchange of information increased the likelihood that the entrepreneurs would be exposed to new ideas. A more recent study, instead, found stronger evidence for the role of clusters in enhancing innovation diffusion among their members. Gebreeyesus and Mohnen (2013) studied the learning process of informal shoemaking firms in a cluster in Ethiopia. In an environment where innovation is mainly imitative in nature, they found that firms with more ties in local business networks tend to perform better in terms of innovation. Their findings suggest connectedness as the main factor of knowledge transfer, while co-location is not a sufficient determinant for diffusion of innovation.

The importance of the interaction between university and industry is recognized in the innovation literature (Lundvall, 2016). Several empirical studies highlight the importance of connections between the public (universities and public research institutes) and the private sector in various technological fields, such as vaccine production in Vietnam (Ca, 2007), chemical and mineral extraction in Pakistan (Bashir et al., 2010), and cable and wire manufacturing industry in Nigeria (Egbetokun et al., 2012). Each study emphasizes how the web of connection is crucially a win-win solution for both actors: the involvement of the private sector is essential for industrial competitiveness, which in turn is crucial to formulate and implement innovation policies. Nonetheless, Kruss et al. (2012) remark that there is a high degree of heterogeneity among LICs. For example, the nature of university–firm interaction in South Africa is more direct, formal and knowledge intensive than in Uganda and Nigeria. In turn, policy advances and university-level interventions in Uganda have stimulated the emergence, albeit on a small scale, of more knowledge-intensive firms than in Nigeria. Eun et al. (2006) provided a good example of how the interactions between universities and the private sector could assume different forms. Since the market-oriented reform, Chinese universities have a strong propensity to pursue economic gains and strong internal resources to launch start-ups and thus establish their own firms (the so-called University-run Enterprises). The main reasons provided to explain this evolution – low absorptive capacity of industrial firms and underdeveloped intermediary institutions – could be informative for LICs.

In the past decade, the recognition of the people living at the BoPs as innovators and new potential consumers has opened up a new sub-field of innovation studies. Prahalad and Mashelkar (2010) created the definition of 'Gandhian innovation' to describe the process in India of designing inexpensive products and manufacturing them with limited capital, and on a scale so vast that their prices are affordable for customers who cannot afford products marketed by Western companies. Affordability and sustainability, not premium pricing and abundance, become the new goals of effective innovation. To address the needs of this new market segment, firms must learn how to enhance new product adoption despite the barriers of poverty. An efficient approach is to work backward from the constraints and circumstances, to ensure that the innovation is well received (Nakata and Weidner, 2012). At the same time, Prahalad (2012) claims that in such environments, innovation can come from focusing on awareness, access, affordability and availability (4As). He retraces the commercialization of a biomass stove for the rural poor in India to show how from a product-centric approach the focus is on business model innovation, of which the product is just a subset. The BoP is clearly a huge market, but in some countries, it can be too small for multinationals and this opens opportunities for local companies. Analysing the e-commerce sector in Nepal, Kshetri (2007) advocates that one of the reasons why the local web portal Thamel.com succeeded is because the Nepalese e-commerce market was too small to be attractive for multinationals like Google or Yahoo.

Hall et al. (2012) focused on the participation of the poor as entrepreneurs and not as consumers. Drawing on data collected from Brazilian tourism destinations, they found that tourism entrepreneurship provided the BoP with opportunities to improve social welfare but at the same time it was the cause of wider social problems. This, therefore, suggests that policies should address both economic and social perspectives, although at the expense of a more constrained pace of economic development. Again, a different perspective is given by Ramachandran et al. (2012) who investigated a BoP producer, a member of the BoP population who creates value by producing goods and services for sale in non-local markets. Using as a case study Fabindia, an Indian handloom retailer, they coined the concept of 'bridging enterprise', a business enterprise that originated at the intersection of specific BoP communities and the corresponding non-local markets. In return, BoP producers would obtain access to market, access to organization and access to ecosystem with potential impact on poverty alleviation. Ramani et al. (2012), instead, used an ethnographic analysis to identify and analyse the actual field practices of sanitation entrepreneurs in India, specifically in the delivery of pro-poor innovations. They found that sanitation entrepreneurs followed their target beneficiaries through three phases (pre-construction, construction and post-construction activities), the last one being the most crucial for the success of sanitation diffusion, and therein lies the most valuable lessons. This example shows how the innovation process goes beyond a standard linear model of assessing need and appropriateness of technology. Innovation for and within BoP is often demand driven. In the rural areas of Bangladesh, in most cases the innovations are based on the farmers' perception of their needs and the available indigenous capability of the artisans (Uddin, 2006). The innovation process is kindled by the knowledge of producers gained through 'learning-by-doing' and the experience of farmers through 'learning-by-using'.

2.5   Innovation Diffusion to LICs

The applied literature on innovation and developing economies has mostly focused on four channels of technology transfer across country borders: trade, FDI, migration and licensing (Fagerberg et al., 2010). However, most of the empirical studies have mainly given attention to the first two, since data for migration and licensing are scarce in LICs. Due to the challenges related to assessing innovation in LICs, the studies reviewed have predominantly looked at the direct impact of knowledge diffusion on productivity. Literature suggests that openness is a pre-requisite for diffusion of external knowledge; however, the magnitude of FDI and trade depends on host-country policies. This highlights again the importance of local governance to nurture innovation in local firms, attracting foreign knowledge and technologies (Dollar et al., 2005; Franco et al., 2011).

The trade and the degree of openness of an economy are critical factors for knowledge diffusion. Coe et al. (1997) are the first to have shown that productivity capacity in developing countries is significantly related to the R&D activities in the country's trade partners, providing evidence of spillover effects between developed and developing countries. A 1 per cent increase in the R&D capital stock in the industrial countries on average raises output in the developing countries by 0.06 per cent. Analysing a mix of ninety-three developed and developing countries, Edwards (1998) investigated the robustness of the relationship between openness and total factor productivity growth. He used nine alternative openness indicators, and in the vast majority of cases he found a positive and significant correlation with total factor productivity. Similar findings relate to the positive correlation between imports and local R&D (Kumar and Saqib, 1996), the attraction of foreign R&D activities in LICs (Bashir et al., 2010; Ca, 2007; Robson et al., 2009), increased international trade (Shi and Pray, 2012) and firms' decisions to export (Abor et al., 2008). Both imports and exports can give access to foreign goods and technologies. Furthermore, favourable foreign investment can potentially bring positive spillovers to local firms. Almeida and Fernandes (2008) use data from forty-three developing countries to investigate whether exporting and importing activities are important channels for technology transfer to LICs. They adopted a broad definition of innovation that included the creation of new production processes and also the adoption and adaptation of existing technologies to local conditions. They found a strong positive correlation between openness and technology adoption, importing firms being up to 6.4 per cent more likely to engage in technological innovations than autarky firms. Although they ran several robustness checks, they did not fully address the potential endogeneity nature of innovation in their model. More recently, Seker (2012) draws similar conclusions. Again, the cross-sectional nature of the data used makes it difficult to interpret the relationship between trade and innovation as causal. Two studies overcome this limitation by using panel data. Thanks to a detailed panel of Indonesian manufacturing firms, Blalock and Veloso (2007) showed that firms in industries supplying import-intensive sectors had higher productivity growth than other firms. Moreover, they found that early exposure to downstream imports gave the greatest opportunities for learning.

A rather large literature provides evidence of a link between a firm's efficiency and becoming an exporter (Aw and Hwang, 1995; Chen and Tang, 1987). However, only recently scholars have focused on determining the direction of causality. Analysing firm-level data from Colombia, Mexico and Morocco, Clerides et al. (1998) could not identify the causal relationship and concluded that the relationship between exporting and efficiency is mainly explained by self-selection of the more efficient firms into the export market. Hallward-Driemeier et al. (2002) argued that it is not self-selection, but the fact that firms that aim for export markets make different decisions regarding investment, training, technology and inputs, which all together raise firms' productivity. Their conclusions are based on analysing the years before entering a foreign market of 2,700 manufacturing establishments in five

Southeast Asian countries (Indonesia, Korea, Malaysia, the Philippines and Thailand).

The openness of an economy can also positively attract FDI. Wang and Wong (2012) used panel data of seventy-seven countries and a stochastic frontier analysis to study the effect of foreign R&D transferred through imports and FDI on domestic technical efficiency. They found that foreign R&D transferred through both inward FDI and imports on average accounted for almost 10 per cent of the world technical efficiency over the period 1986–2007, with the largest contribution in OECD countries at 12 per cent and the smallest contribution in sub-Saharan Africa at 7 per cent. The authors argued that the lack of human capital in local firms is a critical factor in the missing link between FDI and innovation. This confirms the theoretical work of Keller (1996) that underlines the distinction between technological information and human capital. Both are needed for a sustainable growth, although human capital is costly to accumulate and needs largely to be home-provided even in an outward-oriented regime.

In economic theory, we find three channels through which FDI can generate productivity growth for host-country producers: spillovers, linkage externalities and competition.[1] Kugler (2006) analysed data from Colombian firms to assess the impact of each of these factors. He found limited *intra*-industry externalities but widespread *inter*-industry spillovers from FDIs. The findings also revealed outsourcing relationships of MNCs with local upstream suppliers. Young and Lan (1997) pointed out that policies of host countries are critical factors in exploiting the potential of FDI as an instrument of technological development. Using a mix of quantitative and qualitative methodology, they concluded that in China the impact of FDI is greater than theory would suggest, and given the size and growth of the market, substantial opportunities exist for increased technology transfer with appropriate policy changes. In particular, they advocated that Chinese policies have encouraged the quantity rather than the quality of FDI. In this respect, Glass and Saggi (1998) built a theoretical model in which they linked the quality of technology transferred through FDI to the technology gap between the developed and developing countries, as determined by the rate of imitation relative to innovation. The capacity of imitation of LICs allows FDI to transfer more advanced technologies, while the innovation rate of developed countries limits the transfer of more advanced technologies. However,

---

[1] Spillovers in emerging economies from multinational firms have received much attention in the literature. For a review of evidence, see Blomström and Kokko (1998) and Görg and Strobl (2001).

the transfer of technology associated with FDI may have a different effect in local firms. Analysing data from Indonesian chemical and pharmaceutical firms, Suyanto et al. (2009) found that FDI spillovers have a significant impact in enhancing the local technological level, although it does not seem to significantly change technical and scale efficiency. Remarkably, a study of Indonesian manufacturing firms found that knowledge spillovers seem to be significant only in FDI of foreign firms that perform R&D (Todo and Miyamoto, 2006).

The positive effects of FDI on technology transfer strongly depend on the host country's characteristics and policies (Blomström and Kokko, 2001). Besides fiscal incentives and performance and technology transfer requirements, they argued that the efficacy of FDI can be increased by policies in support of local technological capability and policies that ensure that the foreign affiliates operate in a competitive environment. Spillovers to local agents need fertile environments and also time to allow local absorption. Amendolagine et al. (2013) investigated the type of FDI that maximizes the likelihood of creating local linkages between MNEs and domestic suppliers in sub-Saharan Africa. Using data from nineteen different countries, they find that time since entry of foreign firms is associated with higher local linkages. The FDI's impact can also depend on the host's economic structure. Thompson (2002) analysed data of Hong Kong garment firms with manufacturing investments in Mainland China to empirically test whether FDI within geographical industry clusters transfers technology more that FDI that is geographically dispersed. He found that clustered FDI is significantly better than dispersed FDI at transferring technology, implying that industry clusters and FDI policies should be designed in tandem rather than separately.

Several studies looked at the different channels – vertical and horizontal – through which knowledge is transmitted along the production chain. Using a panel dataset of Indonesian manufacturing firms, Blalock and Gertler (2008) tested the hypothesis that not just the foreign-owned firm but all firms downstream of that supply market were able to obtain lower prices. They found strong evidence of productivity gains, greater competition and lower prices among local firms in markets that supplied foreign entrants. This finding suggests that linkages through vertical supply relationships are the channel through which import-driven technology transfer occurs. Similar conclusions that foreign-owned firms are more likely to benefit from trade than domestic firms are found in the research of Vishwasrao and Bosshardt (2001) and Blalock and Veloso (2007). Bwalya (2006) investigates the nature of productivity spillovers from foreign to local firms using firm-level data on manufacturing firms in Zambia. The main findings bring weak evidence in support of productivity spillovers from foreign firms to local firms through horizontal channels, whereas there are significant knowledge spillovers occurring through backward linkages, from foreign firms in upstream sectors to local firms in downstream sectors. Goedhuys (2007) instead found horizontal linkage among local manufacturing firms in Tanzania. Foreign firms were more likely to innovate through connections with foreign firms, hiring better-skilled personnel and investing heavily in machinery and equipment. Instead, she found that local firms mainly innovated in collaboration with other local firms.

Finally, we find limited evidence on two additional channels of potential knowledge transmission to LICs, international cooperation and remittances. Sawada et al. (2012) built a panel dataset with eighty-five countries to investigate the role of international technical cooperation from developed to developing countries. They found that technical cooperation mainly complements the lack of human capital in hosting countries and its impact on technology transfer is only second to openness of the economy. Ca (2007) investigated the production of vaccines on the basis of research and technology transfer in Vietnam. He found that international cooperation on R&D was a critical factor in the success of turning Vietnamese research institutes into business operations. In this case, the lack of capabilities of the local firms was supported by international cooperation efforts. Thanh and Bodman (2011) investigated whether skilled workers from LICs, living and working overseas, can effectively channel technological knowledge back to their home country. They found that remittances have a positive and significant impact on the growth rate of donor countries, which suggests that openness to international migration can contribute to the economic development. This is the only study in our sample that looks at the impact of migration on innovation; however, the endogeneity issues in the models are not fully considered.

2.6   The Diffusion of Innovations in LICs within the General Theoretical Framework of Innovation Diffusion

Hall's review on diffusion of innovation (2004) claims that most of the studies that have looked at the diffusion of innovations in developed countries used some variations of the theoretical framework provided in Rogers' seminal book *Diffusion of Innovations*. Rogers (2003) conceptualized the factors that influence the diffusion of innovations and described the attributes that affect the decision of potential adopters of innovations. According to Rogers, 'diffusion is the process by which an innovation is communicated through different channels in a certain period of time among the members of a social system' (Rogers, 2003: p. 5). Two factors are involved in the diffusion: the innovation must have a nature suitable for the context in which it is spreading, and the vectors of communication diffusion must be in place in order to transmit information. Rogers based his work on studying and observing the diffusion of innovations in developed countries. How do the local socio-economic, cultural and political environments of developing countries shape and characterize the ways in which innovations are spread? The review allows us to integrate and contextualize the evidence collected in the existing theoretical framework.

Innovation in LICs, as everywhere, is context-dependent. The nature of innovation in these countries is strongly shaped by the composition of the industrial sector, institutional capacity and economic performance overall. Altenburg (2009) highlights five main structural differences between LICs and industrialized countries: (1) LIC economies have a less diversified sectoral composition than advanced economies, primarily comprising agriculture and extractive industries; (2) At the same time, the levels of specialization and interaction among the firms in an industry are low; (3) Informal arrangements are widespread across many aspects of economic transactions; (4) The majority of businesses are organized informally: they do not work within a framework of rules and regulations, the payment of wages and salaries is irregular, and they do not tend to have social security obligations; (5) Finally, the share of FDI in the total fixed capital formation tends to be high. These five differences must be taken into account in how we conceptualize 'innovation' in LICs and the way they are embedded in the current diffusion of innovation theoretical framework.

The nature of the innovation strongly influences the spread and the speed of diffusion. Some low-tech innovations do not rely much on channels of transmission and do not require demanding pre-conditional capacity (in term of skills and capital), and therefore the diffusion amongst potential adopters in LICs may be faster. On the contrary, more advanced innovations, such as high-technology equipment, may not find locally the absorptive capacity that would enable the diffusion in the host country. For those reasons, innovations developed in LICs are likely to be more easily spread within a country, since the within-country context is likely not to be very different as between developing and developed countries, as is the case for imported innovation. The nature of innovation also includes the objective and use of the innovation itself. A further constraint in the diffusion of imported innovations in developing countries is given by the fact that those may not be designed by people with similar needs, and therefore may not address local needs. Adaptability, that is, the skills and tools needed to perform the modification, is an important component enabling innovation, which allows imported innovation to meet local specifications and needs.

Communication channels are essential vectors of innovations' diffusion: potential adopters will embrace an innovation only if they come across it or hear of it. The channels may involve transmission of information (e.g. ICTs), but also transport infrastructures (e.g. roads, harbours and airports) for moving goods from outside and within a country. The latter was tacit in Rogers' work, although it is a relevant factor in LICs. Lundvall (2016) also recognized the importance of user-producer communication in both the innovation process and the diffusion of innovations. The efficiency of communication depends on the level of development of infrastructures and on the geographical and cultural distances between the actors involved in the communication. Developed countries have efficient transport systems that facilitate the diffusion of knowledge and goods. In many LICs, the quality and efficiency of infrastructures limit the transport of goods both from other countries and internally thereby hampering the spread of innovation. Moreover, in many cases developing countries set high import duties on imported products which limit the choice of technology, or compromise on the quality of imported technologies. Geographical distance affects not only the transport of goods but also the communication. In the case of imported innovation, communication from the owner of the innovation and the potential adopters in the developing country is likely to be heterophilous, that is, the actors may not share common meanings, languages or personal and social characteristics. Misunderstandings and cultural differences on the way to carrying out the negotiations can affect the diffusion. This is less common amongst developed countries, where the differences in local absorptive capacity and social capabilities across countries are less extreme compared to such differences between some developed and developing countries.

A large part of diffusion of innovation within countries takes place by means of communication between firms and through intermediaries (trade associations, government policies, movement of personnel). In high-income countries, we observe a larger concentration of firms, which can allow greater interactions among them and exchange of skilled personnel. This is particularly important for innovations that involve the communication of tacit knowledge. Instead, LICs have usually less diversified sectors, fewer larger firms, and limited intra-firm workers' mobility, which reduce the capacity of collaborations and spillovers. In this respect, the formation of clusters supports the diffusion of innovation. Moreover, the typical composition of the economic sectors in developing countries may affect the internal spread of innovations. While the private sector of high-income countries is based on formal firms, most of the markets in LICs – as we have seen – are formed by the activities of informal firms. This may create two levels of innovation diffusion: diffusion amongst firms with similar characteristics (formal and informal) and also between the two groups. For example, the spread of innovation between formal and informal firms could move the latter to become formal.

The review collected strong evidence on how incomplete, outdated or under-developed institutional arrangements, which include socio-political environments, are the telling obstacles to innovation diffusion in LICs relative to developed countries, where these capacities are often taken for granted and 'standard'. Developed countries can rely on reasonable conventional and stable economic and political environments, while this is often not the case in developing countries. For example, political instability and weak law enforcement discourage foreign investments and the opportunity of diffusion of innovation from outside countries. Developing countries also lag behind developed countries on the agility and relevance of national innovation system features and on the level of interaction and partnership between private and public sectors. Outdated or resource constrained national innovation systems do not meet the original objectives for which they were designed. Diffusion and creation of innovation in LICs are also restricted by weak interactions and cooperation between private and public sectors. Those obstacles are typical of developing countries and occur less obviously or less routinely among more developed economies.

Diffusion and adoption of innovation are closely related (Metcalfe, 1988) in a way that the diffusion process covers the adoption process of a population of individuals over time. Rogers (2003) also formalized six factors that influence the adoption of innovation (ACCORD framework): (1) whether the new technology provides a relative advantage to the user; (2) its compatibility with previous technologies already adopted by the user; (3) the difficulty to use; (4) and understand; (5) whether the innovation can be tested and trialled prior to purchase; and (6) the extent to which an innovation is visible to others in such a way it communicates its presence to its peers. The six factors are all determined by adaptors' and innovation characteristics.

Internal factors of the firms, such as limited financial resources and lack of advanced and specific skills, are factors that hamper both diffusion and adoption of innovation in developed as well as developing countries. However, those constraints have a stronger impact in LICs, where the financial and knowledge gap is greater. Limited financial resources of people living in developing countries narrow down the affordability of innovation, and the lack of technical knowledge may prevent some adoption of innovations that are too complicated or require technical adaptation. At the same time, a constraint for innovation adoption, such as the lack of financial means, has been a leverage for innovation itself, pushing producers to manufacture cheaper products and services affordable to the poorest categories.

Figure 2.1 summarizes the factors affecting the diffusion of innovation and the interaction with the adoption. Most of the obstacles to innovation diffusion in LICs seem to be connected to structural issues that are related to the current conditions and are a consequence of aspects related to history and geography. This arguably provides an additional argument for the reinforcing role of innovation diffusion and adoption and economic growth of a country. A similar conclusion is supported by Fagerberg and Srholec (2008), when they analyse the causes behind the weakness of innovation systems in developing countries. However, some of the lack of diffusion of innovation may not derive from weak or missing transmission channels. Sometimes, innovations in developing countries do not spread simply because they do not fit the local needs: something that solves a problem in developed countries may not be useful in a different context. For each innovation that is not spread, it is essential to assess whether this is due to a design fault, missing channels or lack of local capacities.

Despite the technological conquests witnessed in the past century and the technologies that made possible and ease the transmission of information and movement of goods worldwide, innovation adoption and creation in developing countries are still greatly influenced by the acumen and skills of entrepreneurs to an extent that we do not find in developed countries. In less structured establishments, innovation is driven by people with characteristics that allow them to overcome the constraints distinctive of LICs. Entrepreneurial skills and attitude, including marked curiosity and inclination to pursue personal relationships, are important factors in the diffusion and adoption of innovations.

In modelling the diffusion of innovation in LICs, Rogers' framework provides critical intuitions but is heavily centred on developed countries, with specific and fairly homogenous environments and economic structures. Once the economic, political and cultural differences of LICs are introduced, on the one hand, the framework does not consider the role of infrastructure and capacity; on the other hand, it fails to address the diffusion among heterogeneous agents. As we have seen, both elements have a great role in facilitating or impeding: (1) how innovations reach a country; (2) how innovations diffuse within a bounded firm; and (3) the role of intermediaries at several levels in the process. The critique of Strang and colleagues (Strang and Meyer, 1993; Strang and Soule, 1998) on Rogers' framework seems to address many shortcomings of its application in LICs.

Regardless of the multiple obstacles that LICs face, the benefits from the spread of innovations are likely to be greater than in more advanced economies. Most of the firms in developing countries work far from the potential technological production frontiers; therefore, small changes in their activities may have greater impact in the production and wealth distribution. Given the current state of local capacity, incremental and low-tech innovations are more likely to be adopted and have greater chances of success. Moreover, in the past decades we witness a massive and rapid spread of ICTs (internet and mobile phones) in most LICs that has reduced the state of 'informational isolation' of many countries. Entrepreneurs can rely on information found on the internet, and the use of mobile phones allows more reliable and quicker communication within a country. This could also support a greater integration of national institutions, for example better connecting and coordinating universities and research institutes.

2.7   Conclusions

This chapter reviewed the state-of-the-art research on the diffusion of innovation in the private sectors in LICs to identify the gaps for future research. A robust protocol of the systematic review and a rigorous procedure selected eighty-one studies which contributed to the identification of the barriers to innovation creation and diffusion in LICs, and the factors of knowledge diffusion *in* and *to* LICs. Most of the studies reviewed have been published in the past five years. This is an evidence of both the early and partial nature of the findings, and also of the importance and energy for this research sub-field. This research attention coincides with the fact that in the last decade several developing countries moved out of the poverty trap, spurring an agenda among governments and international donors for knowledge about how to strengthen a private sector in agrarian transitional economies.

Literature shows that value-creating innovation in LICs is about creation or adoption of new ideas and technologies; but various studies point to the on-going importance of diverse capacity for innovation embedded in and constituted by dynamics between geographical, socio-economic, political and legal subsystems. Several factors appear as predominant barriers to innovation across different settings and geographical areas. Weak education systems (from basic education to training and universities), unstable political powers, fragile legal systems (unsecure property rights, weak intellectual property rights, and lack of law enforcement), limited financial resources, poor infrastructure (from transportation to market facilities), and cultural and linguistic distances are all factors that hamper the diffusion of innovations. The diffusion of knowledge within LICs is facilitated by the institution of clusters, the link between public (universities) and private sector, and the empowerment of the poor. Instead, knowledge diffusion to developing countries is conditioned by the degree of openness of an economy and host-country policies and characteristics that can favour FDI and international trade. It also emerged that innovation in LICs is a phenomenon that involves institutional and environmental factors as well as personal and entrepreneurial characteristics. Firm owners' entrepreneurial acumen is as critical as firms' characteristics for innovation adoption. The review highlighted scattered evidence on this, De Mel et al. (2009) being the only study we found that takes into account both entrepreneurs' and firms' characteristics in the adoption of innovations.

The evidence collected seems to show a heterogeneous picture of obstacles and channels of innovation diffusion, in which countries face different challenges that are related to socio-political and geographical factors. At the same time, it becomes evident that those factors are all connected on structural issues related to the current economic conditions. It is beyond the scope of this study to find a 'one-size-fits-all' recipe for innovation diffusion in LICs. However, some patterns have emerged. Successful cases seem to arise from strengthening innovation diffusion within countries and supporting local innovation. This could further support the facilitation of diffusion of innovation developed in similar contexts, with a potential role of South-South collaborations.

The findings also suggest that data on innovation should give priority to capturing incremental innovation, much of which will document the diffusions of competence-extending innovation, rather than more disruptive innovation. In particular, it is critical to collect data that go beyond aggregate measures of innovation capacity such as R&D expenditures and patents. These are important indicators, but they tend to over-attend to aggregate potential and to under-specify the critical need for more fine-grained, pervasive absorptive capacity, such that individual firms can benefit from the general diffusion of innovations. This emphasis on imitative and incremental innovation is consistent with the evidence that matters for innovation impact for LICs. Given the current capacity of LICs, policies should therefore focus more on incremental innovations of existing technologies that are nevertheless new to firms and therefore have an impact because of that.

The review also highlighted four relevant research areas that have not received much attention so far: the determinants of innovation diffusion in the informal sector; the potential role of open innovation networks in LICs; the knowledge transmission through South-South trade and investment; and case studies focusing on learning from policy failures.

Innovation diffusion in LICs can take different shapes and the picture seems to be more heterogeneous compared to studies of innovation in developed countries. Innovation is not just a driver for economic growth but also a tool for poverty reduction. Most of the studies reviewed take into account the first perspective and recognize the BoP as an unexplored vast market segment that has pushed international but also local firms to build affordable and sustainable products. Possibly more interesting – but also more unexplored – is the consideration of BoP as a user group of innovators. The ingenuity and constraints on which the BoP population lives are rich soil for innovation. The lack of research in this area originates from the fact that most of the studies focus on the formal sector. However, given the typical economic environment of LICs, this is a limitation that provides only a partial evidence of the diffusion of innovation in LICs. Possibly, the transmission of knowledge and the dynamics in which the informal sectors adopt and create innovation are different. Again, the success of informal businesses may be determined by not only the skills but also the acumen of entrepreneurs. Pro-active attitude, curiosity and perseverance are all factors that may influence the diffusion and creation of innovation among those groups. Moreover, the diffusion of mobile phones and the internet in developing countries allows users to access relevant contacts and content previously unavailable. Informal entrepreneurs may use these tools to overcome local constraints. The magnitude of the informal sectors in many LICs urges researchers to explore and better understand these phenomena. Researchers could also investigate how informal firms work or cooperate with formal firms. In particular, are formal and informal firms, competitors or partners? How does innovation spread from one to the others? Again, what role can intermediaries play to support the innovation activities of informal firms?

In the last decade, there has been an increasing interest around open innovation networks in advanced economies.[2] However, in the review process we could not find studies or evidence that report examples of open innovation networks in LICs. Investigating whether and where

---

[2] Open innovation is defined as the process that occurs when an organization engages customers, suppliers, employees and other key stakeholders in the collaborative development of a product, service, experience, process, or idea that creates real value for them.

those occur, and with what impact, would be relevant since they may be a tool for contrasting under-developed innovation institutions, in the formal as well as the informal sectors. For example, firms with low innovation capabilities could benefit from inter-firm networks or university–industry linkages. Again, in survival clusters, such as Suame in Ghana or Mwanza in Tanzania, there may be situations where entrepreneurs and workers share capabilities to add value to their activities along the value chain of the products.

Recently, the potential benefit of South-South trade and FDI for diffusion of innovation in developing countries has gained attention (Fu and Gong, 2011). The rationale is that the knowledge transferred to LICs is likely to be more appropriate since it comes from countries with similar factor endowment and at a similar development stage. Absorptive capacity of a LIC recipient may also be more effective in receiving similar levels of technologies (Glass and Saggi, 1998). Nevertheless, in this review, it was difficult to find empirical studies that focus on South-South flows or separate the impact of North-South with South-South FDI. Arguably, in this regard the lack of data is a major obstacle that needs to be addressed.

Lastly, implementation of policies to favour innovation in LICs may not have worked as policymakers expected. The case studies reviewed tend to focus on successful examples and seldom analyse learning from failures. The cases of incomplete or failed initiatives, along with documentation of unintended consequences, would provide an empirical base for understanding the interplay of context, institutional capacity and form/intensity of innovation. This would be a useful addition to the current body of literature, together with a comparative analysis.

Appendices

Appendix 2.1

Table 2.1 *Geographical coverage*

Geographical coverage			
China (9)	Nigeria (5)	Brazil (1)	Multi-Countries (28)
India (7)	Ghana (4)	Colombia (1)	Multi-Countries in Africa (4)
Indonesia (4)	Tanzania (4)		Multi-Countries in Latin America (1)

Table 2.1 *(cont.)*

Geographical coverage			
Taiwan (2)	Ethiopia (1)		Multi-Countries in Asia (1)
Vietnam (2)	Kenya (1)		
Bangladesh (1)	Zambia (1)		
Nepal (1)			
Pakistan (1)			
Thailand (1)			
Sri Lanka (1)			
Asia: 29 (36%)	Africa: 16 (20%)	Latin America: 2 (2%)	Multi-Country: 34 (42%)

Note: Number of studies in parentheses.

Table 2.2 *Sectoral coverage (number of studies in parentheses)*

Sectoral coverage		
Manufacturing (32)	Universities (2)	Multi-sector (43)
Biotechnologies (1)	Finance (1)	
Sanitation (1)	Tourism (1)	
Industry: 34 (42%)	Services: 4 (5%)	Multi-sector: 43 (53%)

Appendix 2.2

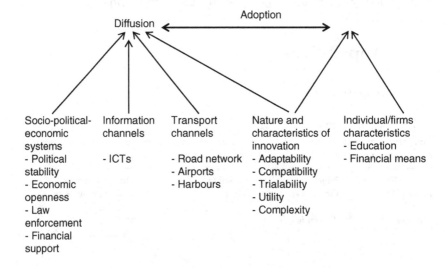

Figure 2.1 Framework of diffusion of innovation in LICs

3 The Economy of Ghana and Tanzania
An Overview

3.1 Introduction

This chapter introduces and partly discusses the structural realities of Ghana and Tanzania using current data. The chapter emphasizes the current economic structure, trade patterns and the informal sector in both countries. The chapter also describes the industrial sector and its structure from a historical perspective in both countries.

Ghana and Tanzania are both sub-Saharan African economies located in different parts of the continent. Despite the geographical distance and other differences between the two countries, both countries are also similar, particularly in terms of economic, institutional and socio-historical structures. This is due, in part, to the fact that both countries were former colonies of the United Kingdom, and as a result have similar socio-political structures and institutions. Other socio-economic factors – the economic recovery and structural adjustment programmes (ERP and SAP), poverty, religion, and corruption, among others – have also fundamentally, independently and/or jointly, shaped the economic activities, institutions and socio-political characteristics of these countries as well as the very way economic activities are organized, undertaken and exchanged. For instance, in both countries, the economic recovery programme (ERP) and the structural adjustment programme (SAP) were implemented in the mid-1980s and the 1990s, respectively. These policies oversaw the massive devaluation of both countries' currencies by a stroke of the pen, increases in taxes, trade liberalization, reduction in government expenditure particularly in the provision of important social services, increased unemployment due to the massive retrenchment of workers as a result of the privatization of state-owned enterprises, reduction in the real income of workers and growth in corruption, among others.

While several authors and policymakers have indicated that the ERP and the SAP, in part, reversed the worsening economic decline experienced in both countries in the 1970s and early 1980s, these policies also opened up the newly established and non-competitive industries to competition from industrialized countries, led to the concentration on the production and export of agricultural products and the excessive import-ation of manufactured goods with consequent balance of payment prob-lems. These policies arguably cemented Ghana's and Tanzania's economies as primary/traditional goods producers and net importers of industrial products. On the other hand, the ERP and the SAP also contributed to the development and expansion of alternative and dual economic sectors – 'traditional and modern' – and institutions, leading to the emergence of the hybrid system found in both countries today. The majority of the labour force, in both countries, that were adversely affected by these programmes resorted to the 'traditional' sector for buffer and livelihood. There was also the rural-urban exodus in search for better economic means leading to the rapid expansion of cities with limited housing, sanitation and health facilities. Arguably, these socio-economic and historical factors partly shaped the current socio-economic structures in both Ghana and Tanzania, and the remainder of this chapter looks at the nature of these structures.

Section 3.2 presents an overview of Ghana's and Tanzania's economies by comparing and contrasting the contributions of each sector in both countries. Sections 3.3, 3.4, 3.5 and 3.6 examine the patterns of trade, foreign direct investment inflows, human capital development, and digi-tal technology development in both countries respectively. Historical analyses of the structure and performance of the industrial sectors in both countries are presented in Section 3.7. Section 3.8 examines the informal sector in Ghana and Tanzania, whereas Section 3.9 summarizes the chapter.

3.2   The Economy and Industry

Ghana, the first country in sub-Saharan Africa to attain independence from British colonial rule in 1957, is a resource-rich and agriculture-based economy located in West Africa. After independence, the Ghanaian economy was booming until the mid-1960s, when there was a downward spiral because of political and social turmoil. With the introduction of the IMF/World Bank-sponsored ERP in 1983, Ghana undertook a relatively successful transition from a government-controlled system of economic management to a market-oriented economy. The economy is increasingly becoming diversified, with the service sector playing a more central role. The service sector contributes the most in terms of value added to the economy, followed by the agriculture and industry sectors. Table 3.1 Panel A shows their percentage contribution to the economy as follows: 50 per cent, 30 per cent and 20 per cent, respectively. Ghana's industry sector has achieved considerable development over the past fifteen years. The value added by the industry sector grew from $4.3 billion in 2006 to $13.7 billion in 2013 and recorded slightly lower growth rates in the subsequent years before reaching $12.0 billion in 2016.

Tanzania, on the other hand, gained its independence in 1961 and is one of the major economies in East Africa. Similar to Ghana, it is also a resource-rich and an agriculture-based economy. Since dismantling the socialist *ujamaa* economic controls in the mid-1980s, the Tanzanian economy has been performing well over the years, growing steadily from $4.1 billion in 2006 to $12.9 billion in 2016. Table 3.1 Panel A shows that like Ghana, the service sector contributes most to the economy, followed by the agriculture and then the industry sectors. While there is an increasing trend in Tanzania's agricultural sector, the agricultural value added in Ghana has decreased to $8.4 billion in recent years from its highest peak of $11.1 billion in 2013. Overall, the size of the two economies in terms of GDP are more or less similar to each other, from around US $20 billion in 2006 in both countries to US $42 and 47 billion in Ghana and Tanzania, respectively. In the ten years from 2006 to 2016, Tanzania has experienced a strong and stable economic growth. Ghana, however, has experienced an unstable economic performance over the same period.

With regards to employment, as Table 3.1 Panel B indicates, Tanzania has a larger labour force than Ghana. The total number of employees in Tanzania was 23,143 thousand in comparison to 12,465 thousand in Ghana in 2016. This is a 20 per cent increase in Tanzania since 2006, and a 43 per cent increase in Ghana over the same period. Combining Panels A and B of Table 3.1, we can infer that Ghana has a higher labour productivity than that of Tanzania. It is noteworthy that the overall labour productivity of Tanzania has improved significantly. The 20 per cent increase in employment accounted for 150 per cent growth in GDP from 2006 to 2016. In contrast, Ghana was weaker in this respect in comparison to Tanzania. In terms of the sectoral distribution of employment, the agriculture sector has been the most visible source of job vacancies in both economies. In Ghana, around 50 per cent of the labour force engaged in agricultural activities, while in Tanzania this proportion was 20 per cent higher. In both countries, over the 2006 to 2016 period, this ratio was decreasing over the years, which suggests a shift in

Table 3.1 *GDP and employment, Ghana and Tanzania (2006–2016)*

Panel A: Distribution of value added across broad sectors, billion USD

Year	Agriculture				Industry				Services				GDP	
	Ghana		Tanzania		Ghana		Tanzania		Ghana		Tanzania		Ghana	Tanzania
	$	%	$	%	$	%	$	%	$	%	$	%	$	$
2006	6.4	31.1	5.8	31.0	4.3	21.3	4.1	22.1	9.7	47.6	8.7	46.9	20.4	18.6
2007	7.4	29.7	6.2	28.8	5.3	21.2	4.7	21.7	12.1	49.0	10.7	49.5	24.8	21.5
2008	9.1	31.7	8.4	30.8	6.0	20.9	6.0	21.9	13.5	47.3	12.9	47.3	28.5	27.4
2009	8.5	32.9	9.2	32.4	5.1	19.7	5.7	19.9	12.3	47.4	13.6	47.7	26.0	28.6
2010	9.9	30.8	10.0	32.0	6.4	19.8	6.8	21.7	15.9	49.4	14.6	46.3	32.2	31.4
2011	10.3	26.0	10.6	31.3	10.4	26.2	8.2	24.3	18.9	47.7	15.0	44.4	39.6	33.9
2012	9.9	23.6	13.0	33.2	12.1	28.9	9.1	23.3	19.9	47.5	17.0	43.6	41.9	39.1
2013	11.1	23.2	14.8	33.3	13.7	28.7	10.7	24.2	23.0	48.1	18.8	42.5	47.8	44.3
2014	8.6	22.4	14.9	31.0	10.7	27.7	12.0	25.0	19.3	49.9	21.2	44.0	38.6	48.2
2015	7.9	21.0	14.2	31.1	10.4	27.6	11.9	26.1	19.3	51.4	19.6	42.9	37.5	45.6
2016	8.4	19.6	14.7	31.1	12.0	28.2	12.9	27.2	22.3	52.2	19.8	41.8	42.7	47.4

Panel B: Distribution of employment across broad sectors, thousand people

Year	Agriculture				Industry				Services				GDP	
	Ghana		Tanzania		Ghana		Tanzania		Ghana		Tanzania		Ghana	Tanzania
	#	%	#	%	#	%	#	%	#	%	#	%	#	#
2006	4982	57.3	14334	74.6	1184	13.6	959	5.0	2534	29.1	3915	20.4	8700	19208
2007	4908	57.3	14808	74.8	1116	13.0	987	5.0	2546	29.7	3991	20.2	8570	19786
2008	5269	56.3	14783	73.6	1212	12.9	1072	5.3	2885	30.8	4220	21.0	9366	20075
2009	5255	55.2	14871	72.9	1214	12.8	1073	5.3	3043	32.0	4465	21.9	9512	20409
2010	5553	53.4	14904	72.2	1368	13.1	1126	5.5	3483	33.5	4606	22.3	10404	20636
2011	5319	48.9	14827	71.4	1537	14.1	1214	5.8	4022	37.0	4735	22.8	10878	20776
2012	5326	47.1	14608	69.5	1623	14.3	1270	6.0	4364	38.6	5133	24.4	11313	21011
2013	5196	44.7	14353	68.4	1674	14.4	1320	6.3	4754	40.9	5318	25.3	11624	20991
2014	5244	44.0	14863	68.1	1724	14.5	1366	6.3	4955	41.6	5612	25.7	11923	21841
2015	5288	43.4	15217	67.7	1753	14.4	1412	6.3	5151	42.2	5838	26.0	12192	22467
2016	5345	42.9	15575	67.3	1770	14.2	1461	6.3	5350	42.9	6105	26.4	12465	23141

Source: World Bank national accounts data, OECD National Accounts data files and International Labour Organization

employment to the industry and services sectors. Although most of the labour force was employed in the agriculture sector, labour productivity was lower compared to those in the service and industry sectors.

Ghana's industry sector experienced an upward trend, accounting for a 10 per cent increase in GDP contribution between 2010 and 2012. The change in economic structure towards growth in this sector is quite similar in Tanzania, where there were some fluctuations producing about 5 per cent increase between 2009 and 2011. Ghana experienced a significant decrease in GDP contribution by the agriculture sector between 2009 and 2016, while undergoing a considerable increase in the service sector. By contrast, Tanzania experienced a steady growth in the agriculture sector but a 6 per cent reduction in GDP contribution in the service sector. Overall, the two countries experienced an upward trend in economic growth between 2006 and 2013, but Ghana experienced a decline from 2014 onwards.

Over the nine years, mining, manufacturing and utilities have been important for Ghana, but the share of GDP in these sectors has been decreasing. There was a considerable growth in the sector in 2011, as seen in value added to the mining, manufacturing and utilities sectors as a proportion of the GDP. In 2009 and 2014, Ghana fell into recession which resulted in 5–25 per cent economic shrinkage in the above sectors. The recession of the Ghanaian economy was the result of an energy crisis and was not financial in nature (of course, it had financial implications). Lack of electricity meant that factories and companies could not work to full capacity. In other years, there were different extents of growth in GDP. Although Tanzania faced financial crisis in 2009, the performance of the economy was different from that of Ghana. Agriculture, industry and construction, and mining sectors were all seriously affected. But the country managed a quicker recovery. In 2014, Tanzania's economy stood strong as compared to Ghana's economy. The overall economic performance of Tanzania appeared to be better, although there was a slight reduction in GDP after 2013.

3.3   Trade

Both Ghana and Tanzania have actively participated in international trade. As Table 3.2 indicates, the import of merchandise into Ghana has been increasing since 2006. From as low as $6.8 billion in 2006, imports increased considerably, reaching $17.8 billion at their peak in 2012 and reducing to $13.4 billion in 2016. Import of merchandise into Tanzania has also been increasing from 2006, reaching $12.1 billion in 2013 before declining to $9.5 billion in 2016. Ghana's merchandise

Table 3.2 *Total merchandise trade (2006–2016)*

(Billions of US$)	2006	2007	2008	2009	2010	2011	2012	2013	2014	2015	2016
Merchandise Import											
Ghana	6.8	8.1	10.3	8.0	10.9	15.8	17.8	17.6	14.6	13.5	13.4
Tanzania	4.2	5.3	7.7	6.4	7.9	10.8	11.3	12.1	12.0	10.8	9.5
Merchandise Export											
Ghana	3.7	4.2	5.3	5.8	8.0	12.8	13.6	13.8	13.2	10.3	11.3
Tanzania	1.9	2.2	3.1	3.0	4.1	4.7	5.5	4.6	4.6	4.9	5.2
Merchandise Balance											
Ghana	−3.0	−3.9	−5.0	−2.2	−3.0	−3.1	−4.2	−3.8	−1.4	−3.1	−2.1
Tanzania	−2.3	−3.1	−4.6	−3.4	−3.8	−6.1	−5.8	−7.5	−7.4	−5.9	−4.3

Source: UNCTADstat

exports showed the same trend in volume. Tanzania is the 77th largest export economy in the world. In 2006 and 2016, Tanzania exported $1.9 billion and $5.2 billion, and imported $4.2 billion and $9.5 billion, resulting in a negative trade balance of $2.3 billion and $4.3 billion, respectively. Ghana on the other hand ranked the 71st largest export economy, exported $3.7 billion and $11.3 billion, and imported $6.8 billion and $13.4 billion in 2006 and 2016, respectively, resulting in a negative trade balance of $3.0 billion and $2.1 billion, respectively. This reveals that the trade deficit in Tanzania is bigger than that in Ghana.

The growth and changes in the direction of Ghana's trade over time, as reported in Table 3.2, indicate a better integration of the country into the world's trade. Since the early 1980s when Ghana signed onto the SAP and increasingly opened up its economy to international trade, growth remained positive as compared to the earlier period. Food items remain the leading foreign exchange earner in gross terms since 2006 for both countries (Table 3.3). Evidently, this is slightly different in Tanzania, where besides food items, the share of minerals in total merchandise exports also led the foreign exchange earnings. This has been increasing since 2006, reaching its peak in 2011 and declining thereafter. However, its contribution in net terms might not be very significant. This is because of the generous incentives given to mining firms, especially with regards to the retention of part of the sales from mineral products in foreign accounts.

Ghana, like other sub-Saharan African countries, engages more in extra-regional trade than intra-regional trade as Figures 3.1, 3.2 and 3.3 highlight. Nigeria was Ghana's major trade partner (import) in the

Table 3.3 *Import and export structure by product group, Ghana and Tanzania (2006–2016)*

(millions of US$)	2006	2007	2008	2009	2010	2011	2012	2013	2014	2015	2016
Import structure by product group: Ghana											
All food items	928	1,053	1,461	1,211	1,600	2,473	2,507	2,897	2,232	2,076	2,160
Ores and metals	92	109	112	91	142	185	167	165	146	132	131
Fuels	1,373	1,129	1,794	749	911	1,798	1,805	1,750	1,504	1,061	938
Manufactured goods	4,171	4,799	6,654	5,639	7,977	11,009	12,863	12,392	10,500	10,003	9,934
Other	190	189	247	356	292	372	421	396	217	193	188
Tanzania											
All food items	561	703	686	635	864	1,148	1,168	1,057	1,142	722	790
Ores and metals	83	78	124	73	88	112	172	199	178	92	98
Fuels	741	1,152	1,859	1,204	1,747	2,848	2,878	4,156	3,360	4,274	2,129
Manufactured goods	3,041	3,862	5,283	4,482	5,181	6,905	7,152	6,901	7,807	5,541	6,455
Other	100	125	137	136	133	171	346	211	205	160	139
Export structure by product group: Ghana											
All food items	1,963	2,246	2,737	2,830	3,810	3,929	3,464	2,903	3,046	2,557	3,234
Ores and metals	295	340	686	362	498	486	418	423	402	289	477
Fuels	155	133	197	103	153	4,531	3,677	3,584	3,463	1,569	1,492
Manufactured goods	471	414	419	539	550	843	765	1,141	705	513	626
Other	731	1,061	1,230	2,005	2,949	2,996	5,228	4,593	4,536	4,561	4,545
Tanzania											
All food items	677	840	1,048	956	1,192	1,299	1,523	1,303	1,909	1,887	2,004
Ores and metals	237	278	358	410	841	976	722	508	586	494	440
Fuels	41	39	94	72	113	68	68	144	79	76	78
Manufactured goods	241	321	621	449	657	661	735	583	557	860	717
Other	669	661	1,000	1,095	1,247	1,730	2,498	1,875	1,496	1,612	1,501

Source: UNCTADstat

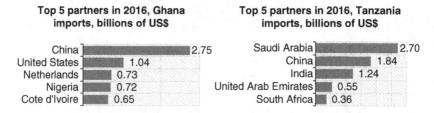

Figure 3.1 Top five partners of import, Ghana and Tanzania
Source: UNdata

Figure 3.2 Top five partners of export, Ghana and Tanzania
Source: UNdata

ECOWAS sub-region, accounting for over $1 billion trade, while the EU also remained important to Ghana's international trading activities. Over the years, China and the EU have been Ghana's largest trading partners in terms of import and export, respectively. Since 2008, China has displaced Nigeria as the leading import origin for Ghana. In 2011, China contributed $2.95 billion to Ghana's total imports. In the EU, the Netherlands and the United Kingdom were Ghana's major export destinations in 2006, contributing $0.43 billion and $0.28 billion, respectively. In most recent years, Switzerland, India and China took over as Ghana's major recipients of exports. In 2016, for instance, $1.80 billion of Ghana's total exports went to Switzerland, followed by India, $1.44 billion, and China, $0.94 billion, thereby displacing the United Kingdom and the Netherlands as the major destinations of Ghana's exports.

Tanzania showed a similar pattern. However, the most important trade partners remain China and India. Tanzania shows a similar trade pattern and also engages more in extra-regional trade than intra-regional trade, as the figures below indicate. South Africa was Tanzania's major trade partner (import) in Africa, accounting for $0.36 billion trade, while Saudi Arabia has remained important to Tanzania's international trading activities in terms of imports. Over the years, India has been Tanzania's

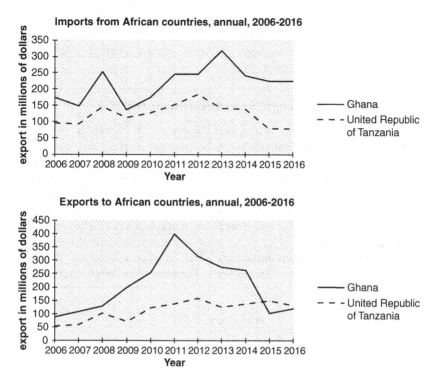

Figure 3.3 Intra-Africa trade, Ghana and Tanzania, 2006–2016
Source: UNCTADstat

largest trading partner in terms of exports. Exports to India reached
$0.74 billion in 2016. In Europe, Switzerland was Tanzania's major
export destination in 2016, contributing $0.62 billion to the economy.
In most recent years, China has increasingly become an important trade
partner for Tanzania in terms of imports and exports. In 2016, for
instance, $1.84 billion of Tanzania's total imports came from China
and total exports to China stood at $0.35 billion.

Figure 3.3 shows the intra-Africa trade patterns of Ghana and Tanzania
in the period 2006–2016. The figure indicates that both countries experienced decline in trade activity with the rest of Africa over the period. The
figure suggests that Ghana engages more in intra-Africa trade – both in
terms of exports and imports – than Tanzania. Tanzania's exports to the
rest of the African continent surpassed that of Ghana in 2015.

The foregoing indicates that there have been radical changes in the
patterns of trade in both Ghana and Tanzania. In the last decade,

China has emerged as a key trading partner to both Ghana and Tanzania, displacing the traditional trade partners. Ghana and Tanzania's trade patterns with the rest of the African continent have also dimmed in recent years.

3.4   Inflows of Foreign Direct Investment (FDI)

FDI has had direct and multiplier effects on the level of employment, its quality and the skills of the labour force. But in some sectors, it has not contributed to promoting labour-intensive activities. In mining, for example, capital intensive production has created relatively few low-skilled jobs, but has led to productivity improvements and skills upgrading. FDI is also important for the development of exports, and there are clear linkages between FDI and trade patterns. Most of the goods and services with the highest export growth have been linked to FDI. In Figure 3.4, we observe that inflow of FDI into Ghana and Tanzania has been increasing

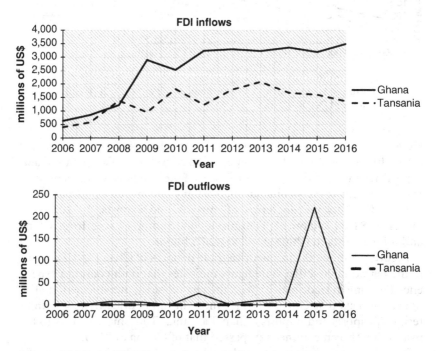

Figure 3.4 FDI flows, Ghana and Tanzania, 2006–2016
Source: UNCTAD FDI/TNC database.

since 2006. Despite the rising flow of FDI inflows into both countries over the years and its expected positive impact on economic growth, the amount is significantly different. Total FDI inflows to Ghana in 2006, valued at about $600 million, is close to that of Tanzania in 2006. It further grew to $3,500 million in 2016, twice more than for Tanzania. In addition, we found that both countries rarely invest in other counties.

3.5   Human Capital

Human capital is a key determinant of innovation and economic growth. Education is a major source of human capital development. Table 3.4 shows that the Ghanaian government has spent a slightly higher proportion of GDP on education than Tanzania. Education expenditure in total government spending is also higher in Ghana than in Tanzania. The significant difference comes from the school enrolment. Although the difference in primary school enrolment is small, the difference in secondary and tertiary education between the two countries is significant. In the year 2017, the secondary school enrolment ratio in Ghana was 69.95 per cent, while that in Tanzania was only 25.84 per cent. For tertiary education enrolment, the ratio for Ghana was 15.84 per cent, while that in Tanzania was only 3.92 per cent. This is a huge difference reflecting the governments' emphasis and support for education. This also reflects the difference between the two countries in economic and human development.

3.6   Digital Technology Development

The past fifteen years have witnessed a rapid diffusion of mobile phone technology in Africa (Asongu and Nwachukwu, 2016). This is also, arguably, the only area of technological progress where Africa has kept pace with the rest of the world in terms of growth rate, despite the gap in absolute level of adoption. By the year 2012, Ghana had already achieved 100 mobile cellular subscriptions per 100 people. Tanzania did less well than Ghana, but it still had achieved 50 mobile cellular subscriptions per 100 people by 2011. This rate has been around 70 per 100 people since 2015 (Figure 3.5). This is to some extent attributable to the lower cost of the infrastructure and hence the subscription fees, as well as the significant reduction in the price of the mobile phones, which is about a quarter or even less of the original price of the big brands. This greatly facilitates the diffusion of information and knowledge in Africa and in particular in the poor communities of Africa.

Table 3.4 *Educational expenditure and school enrolment in Ghana and Tanzania*

Educational expenditure and school enrolment.

		2008	2009	2010	2011	2012	2013	2014	2015	2016	2017
Government expenditure on education											
As % of GDP	Ghana	5.76	5.32	5.54	8.14	7.92	6.1	6.16	5.94	5.77	4.51
	Tanzania	4.25	4.04	4.62	...	...	...	3.48	...	...	...
As % of Total Government Expenditure	Ghana	24.04	22.5	20.7	30.63	37.52	21.22	20.99	23.81	22.09	20.17
	Tanzania	18.78	17.41	19.65	...	...	...	17.3	...	...	...
Gross enrolment ratio (%)											
Primary Education	Ghana	102.67	101.74	...	104.28	108.04	107.25	105.37	108.64	106.47	104.78
	Tanzania	...	101.17	97.4	92.02	89.27	85.54	82.62	80.74	81.51	85.26
Secondary Education	Ghana	48.33	49.62	...	56.08	56.96	68.44	64.75	68.71	69.81	69.95
	Tanzania	...	...	30.64	...	...	31.67	...	...	...	25.84
Tertiary Education	Ghana	8.63	9.01	...	12.09	12.23	14.03	15.57	15.84	15.67	16.16
	Tanzania	...	...	2.12	...	3.9	3.61	...	3.92	...	...

Source: UNESCO Institute of Statistics

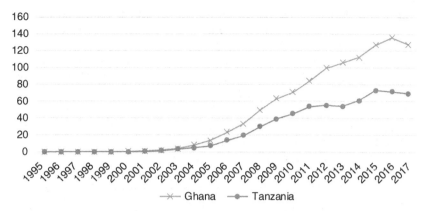

Figure 3.5 Mobile phone subscription in Ghana and Tanzania (per 100 people)
Data source: Word Development Indicator.

3.7   The Industrial Sector in Ghana and Tanzania

3.7.1   Ghana

The industrial sector of Ghana comprises the following industries: (1) Mining and Quarrying (Bauxite, Gold, Manganese and Diamond); (2) Manufacturing (e.g. Iron and Steel, Food and Beverages, Cement, Metal, Pharmaceuticals, Sawmill and Wood Products); (3) Electricity, Water and Sewage Plants; (4) Construction; and (5) Petroleum.

The mining industry has been a huge contributor to the growth of the industrial sector in Ghana, though it has been beset with a number of challenges in recent times, resulting in staff retrenchment to reduce operational costs. In 2012, the sector performed appreciably well, with gold leading the industry at a growth rate of nearly 24 per cent. According to the Gold Fields Mineral Survey, Ghana was the 8th leading producer of gold in the world, and its output increased by 6 per cent – a rise in position in 2011 from 9th. Overall, the industrial sector is the second largest sector in Ghana. The sector grew by only 0.8 per cent in 2014, a far cry from its growth rate of 6.6 per cent in 2013 (ISSER, 2015). Performance over the years in the sector has been underpinned primarily by growth in the mining and quarrying industries, with petroleum being the main contributor. The exception to this is the manufacturing and the water/sewage plant industry, which recorded marginally higher growth rates on their 2013 figures; all other sectors grew more slowly than this industry in 2014 (ISSER, 2013, 2014, 2015).

However, Ghana's performance in terms of global industrial innovation has improved over the years. The World Economic Forum Global Competitiveness Index Report in 2018 indicates that out of the 137 countries that were studied, Ghana was ranked 111th, an improvement over the ranking in 2015/2016, which was 119th. In some key areas of innovation, according to the Global Competitiveness Index, Ghana is ranked as follows:
• Capacity for innovation – 63th (a decline from 56th in 2015/2016)
• Quality of scientific research institutions – 74th
• Availability of scientists and engineers – 81st
• University–Industry collaboration in R&D – 65th

The statistics suggest that globally, Ghana's capacity for innovation and scientific capability (in terms of human resources and institutions) is respectable. However, the low score for university–industry collaboration suggests there is a need for an improvement. This further implies that should Ghana create an effective bridge between the R&D system and industry, Ghana's global competitiveness could be enhanced. Therefore, the industrial sector of Ghana could have an improved outlook if it is augmented with effective R&D support systems and collaboration.

With regard to industrial policy[1] in Ghana, the main document supporting the industrial sector of Ghana is the Industrial Policy developed by the Ministry of Trade and Industry. In 2010, the Government of Ghana established an Industrial Policy which was accomplished through a comprehensive and inclusive process based on analysis and wide consultation with stakeholders (Government of Ghana, 2010). The key development objectives of the Industrial Policy are to expand productive employment in the manufacturing sector; expand technological capacity in the manufacturing sector; promote agro-based industrial development; and promote spatial distribution of industries in order to achieve reduction in poverty and income inequalities.

Innovation is at the core of Ghana's long-term strategic political vision of being in the frontline of African development. In such a context, science, innovation and technology (STI) are at the core of the process. The Ghana Shared Growth and Development Agenda (GSGDA II – 2014–2017) envisioned the structural transformation of Ghana's economy, with STI driving the national development. Most recently, the Coordinated Programme of Economic and Social Development Policies (2017–2024) was introduced, which, in general, underscores the same

[1] Accessed from www.moti.gov.gh/home/index.php?option=com_docman&task=doc_vie w&gid=24&tmpl=component&format=raw&Itemid=128 on 3 June 2016.

structural transformation through STI in the context of the latest development in the technological arena.

However, the Industrial Policy underscores the fact that Ghana's manufacturing sector has not responded well to the various economic and trade policy reforms pursued over time. Manufacturing firms have faced considerable challenges in the form of increased competition in the domestic and export markets and high production and distribution costs arising from high interest rates, obsolete equipment, inefficient infrastructural services and low productivity. As part of the policy, the government intends to initiate and implement programmes to develop requisite skills, ensure adequate and cost-competitive production inputs and services, and also provide financing for industrial development.

The overdependence of Ghana's industrial sector on exports, resulting in higher pricing of raw materials, was acknowledged by the Industrial Policy. To overcome this constraint, the Industrial Policy set a policy goal 'to ensure availability of competitively priced imported raw materials for manufacturing'. The policy measures introduced include the following: encouraging the private sector to set up consignment stocking of critical imported raw materials in a customs bonded warehouse; supporting industry groups to negotiate favourable port charges and shipping costs; improving handling facilities and turnaround times at the ports; and exploring opportunities with private sector partners for regional and sub-regional joint sourcing arrangements.

Even though all these plans have been targeted by the government to boost the industrial sector, much of it has not materialized as the country continues to experience serious setbacks of power cuts every now and then. The power crisis has been largely curtailed; however, the need for a solid and sustainable energy supply-demand system remains. In line with the sustainability goal, the national energy policy aims at 10 per cent renewable content in the national energy mix by 2030. The majority of the policy directions for a 'cost effective and adequate supply of electricity and water' have not been met, and these plans are still being debated. If the industrial sector is to see a significant boost and a greater contribution to the country's growth, adequate infrastructure systems are critical.

3.7.2   Tanzania

Tanzania is the second largest economy in East Africa. Since the 1940s, Tanzania's industrialization has been characterized by the shift in the roles between the central government and the private sector. Up to the mid-1960s, Tanzania was in a private sector-driven industrialization, followed by a mixed economy, especially due to its gaining independence in 1961. The mixed economy was a result of inheritance of the already existing colonial economic structure, with the existence of foreign private-owned industries along with some government involvement. In 1967, the famous Arusha declaration engineered by Mwalimu Julius Kambarage Nyerere, Tanzania's first president, came into effect. This declaration shifted the industrialization strategy into a state-led import substitution up until mid-1970, when productivity in many of the parastatal industries started to drop mainly because of chronic underutilization of their capacity and lack of indigenous technological capabilities. Such decline led to the adoption of the SAP that was prescribed by the IMF and WB in the late 1980s.[2] The SAP policies brought back the private sector as a major engine of growth and therefore led to the industrialization process.

Tanzania's pre-independence production structure was mainly dominated by raw materials for export purposes. Among the very early industries that Tanzania had were those of ginning – separating cotton from its seeds – which dated back to the 1920s.[3] By the 1950s and 1960s, Tanzania had already built some appreciable capabilities in agro and textile industries; by 1970, Tanzania was doing very well in the fabrics industries. Other kinds of firms that existed in the 1960s also included ironsmiths, pottery, weaving and woodworking, which were inherited after independence and continued to do well up until the early 1980s, when things started to fall apart.

Currently, Tanzania's industrial sector contributes around 25 per cent of the country's GDP.[4] The industrial sector includes manufacturing – mainly agro processing due to the country's dependence on agriculture. Others are textile manufacturing industries, furniture, rubber and plastic manufacturing industries. The manufacturing sector contributes 13.25 per cent to the country's GDP.[5]

Despite the important part that manufacturing has to play in industrialization, its performance remains unimpressive. The sector still relies heavily on the low-value-added manufacturing and mining sectors. In addition, manufacturing value added is highly concentrated in a few low-tech sectors, which, in turn, has a negative effect on the ability to learn and innovate.[6]

Mining is known to be at the centre of the Tanzania Industrial Sector. The mining industry consists of extraction of minerals including gold,

---

[2] Wangwe et al. (2014).   [3] Baffes (2002).
[4] www.tanzaniainvest.com/industry retrieved on 24 December 2018
[5] www2.deloitte.com/content/dam/Deloitte/tz/Documents/tax/tz-budget-economic-outook-2017.pdf retrieved on 24 December 2018
[6] www.unido.org/sites/default/files/2013-08/TanzaniaIndustrialCompetitivenessRepor t2012-ebook_0.pdf retrieved on 20December 2018

diamonds, tanzanite (which is found only in Tanzania), iron, silver, copper, nickel, uranium and manganese. Others are cement, graphite, limestone and coal. In 2016, mining accounted for 2.8 per cent of GDP.[7]

In terms of global competitiveness, Tanzania has improved and managed to move up three positions according to the World Economic Forum's (WEF) Global Competitiveness Index (GCI) ranking. In 2017–2018, Tanzania was ranked in the 113th position, out of the 137 countries, as opposed to the 116th position in the previous report. The country has shown improvement, as just three years earlier, in 2014, the report ranked the country in the 125th position.

In terms of industrial policy, Tanzania's current path towards industrialization is guided by several documents. These include the Sustainable Industrial Development Policy (SIDP2020) initiated in 1996, whose major purpose was to slowly phase out the government's direct investment in production activities and allow the private sector to take the leading role. The policy was broken down into three phases: the first phase was aimed at rehabilitating and consolidating the existing industrial capacities; the second phase aimed at generating new capacities in areas with potential for creating competitive advantage through the use of efficient technology and learning processes; and the last phase aimed at achieving major investments in basic capital goods industries supporting industrial structures developed in the first two phases.

The Development Vision 2025 of 1999 is yet another document with an emphasis on the role of the industrial sector for development so as to ultimately make the nation semi-industrialized by 2025. It emphasizes nurturing industrialization for economic transformation and human capital development.[8] The Export Processing Zones (EPZs) Act that was passed in April 2002 with the aim of creating international competitiveness for export-led economic growth is also one of the documents that shapes Tanzania's industrial path. Other documents include the SME Development Policy (SMEDP), with the objective to stimulate development and growth of SME activities through improved infrastructure, enhanced service provision and creation of a conducive legal and institutional framework so as to achieve competitiveness.[9] Integrated Industrial Development Strategy (IIDS) is yet another document guiding the path towards Tanzania's industrialization agenda.[10]

[7] www.economiesafricaines.com/en/countries/tanzania/economic-sectors/the-industrial-sector retrieved on 24 December 2018

[8] www.mof.go.tz/mofdocs/overarch/Vision2025.pdf retrieved on 27 December 2018

[9] URT (2002). Small and Medium Enterprises Development Policy

[10] URT (2011). Integrated Industrial Development Strategy 2025 also found at www.tzdpg.or.tz/fileadmin/_migrated/content_uploads/IIDS_Main_Report.pdf

To date, despite the political will and commitment as indicated in the promulgation of various policies and strategies for developing the industrial sector as indicated above, Tanzania still very much lags behind in terms of a robust industrial sector. However, there is some light at the end of the tunnel, as Tanzania has put the development of the manufacturing sector as its top development priority, and the President himself is spearheading this.

3.8   The Informal Sector in Ghana and Tanzania

The informal economy remains a key feature of labour markets in both developed and developing countries, and Ghana and Tanzania are no exceptions. With varying economic significance across regions and countries, the informal economy serves as a source of livelihood to many, employing more than 60 per cent of workers globally (ILO, 2018). In Africa, where informality is highest, about 85.8 per cent of employment is estimated to be in the informal economy (ILO, 2018). The informal economy is therefore significant.

The informal sector and informal sector activities in Africa are dominant, contributing mainly to employment (about 76 per cent) through micro-, small- and medium-scale economic activities (ILO, 2018). While there is a significant variation in the share of the informal sector in Ghana and Tanzania, informal economic units remain key contributors to economic activity in both economies. In Ghana, employment and economic units are mainly informal. The informal sector in Ghana, for instance, employs about 86.1 per cent of the labour force (Ghana Statistical Service, 2012). The informal sector and informal sector activities in Tanzania also continue to grow, contributing immensely to both socio-economic and political development of Tanzania (Muhanga, 2017). The informal sector has been found to be a dynamic job creator (Aikaeli and Mkenda, 2014), a major source of consumer demand (Muhanga, 2017), and also serves as an avenue for breeding of new entrepreneurs and skills.

Figure 3.6 shows the size and development of the informal economy in Ghana and Tanzania from 1991 to 2015. The figure suggests that the contribution of the informal economy declined from 46.07 per cent and 60.32 per cent, respectively, in 1991 to about 39 per cent in both countries. Despite the decline in the contribution of the informal economy in Ghana and Tanzania, the informal economy shows a high level of persistence, suggesting that it is a 'permanent' feature of both economies.

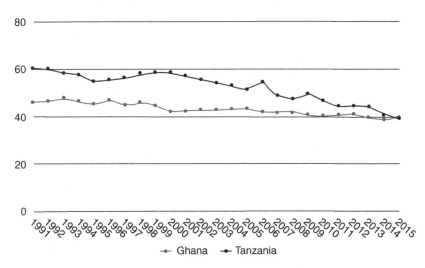

Figure 3.6 Size and development of the informal economy in Ghana and Tanzania
Data source: Medina and Schneider (2018).

3.9   Summaries

The economic outlook for both countries is improving gradually. Even though agriculture remains an important sector for both economies, other sectors like industry and services are also increasingly making significant contributions to the economy. Both countries, at various points in the past ten years, have experienced various levels of economic fluctuations and instability leading to periods of recession, especially in Ghana. However, by 2016, both countries were experiencing a resurgence in their economic outlook. In terms of trade, even though intra-regional trade is perceptible for both countries, extra-regional trade is a significant part of the economy. Both countries import more than they export, leading to trade deficits. While imports of advanced machineries may bring in superior technology, this trade imbalance has led to some worries of 'over'-liberalization of the economy, which has opened the floodgates for all manner of imports, which may affect the growth of local industry. FDI into Ghana and Tanzania has been increasing since 2006; however by 2016, FDI into Ghana was twice that into Tanzania. The informal sector and informal sector activities remain an integral characteristic of both economies, serving as the main source of livelihood to the majority of the labour force in Ghana and Tanzania.

Part I

The Nature and Domestic Sources
of Innovation in Africa

4 Innovation under the Radar as a Response to Constraints
The Nature of Innovation in Africa

Xiaolan Fu and Giacomo Zanello

4.1 Introduction

According to Schumpeter, innovation is creative destruction. It is 'industrial mutation that revolutionizes the economic structure from within, destroying the old one, creating a new one'. Innovation means that 'new products and new methods compete with the old methods not in equal terms, but at a decisive advantage that may mean the death of the latter' (Schumpeter, 1934). Looking at the history of human civilization, the examples of creative constructions include, for example, the history of the iron and steel industry from charcoal furnaces to current technology; the history of transportation from mail-coach to the airplane; and the history of organization from craft-shops to multinational enterprises (MNEs).

Despite the classical definition of innovation by Schumpeter, innovation has for a long time been measured by a country's or an organization's investment in research and development (R&D), number of patents applied for or granted, or number of scientific publications, although it is widely accepted that these are only partial indicators of innovation. In order to capture wider innovation, the Oslo Manual has broadened the definition of innovation. The Oslo Manual has been a standard reference for surveys of innovation in advanced economies and, from its third edition, in developing countries. Its definition of innovation as '[. . .] the implementation of a new or significantly improved product (good or service) or process, a new marketing method, or a new organizational method in business practices, workplace organization, or external relations' (OECD, 2005: p. 46) highlights several important features of innovation.

As Africa accounted for only less than 1 per cent of the world's total R&D investment and less than 1 per cent of the world's total patents granted, some assume that Africa is not innovative. Not just a small number of African policymakers, the general public also thought that innovation is somebody else's business. While the survey carried out by NEPAD and the '2014 African Innovation Outlook' published by NPCA reported an encouraging picture of innovation in the African continent, questions still remain about the scale, the nature and the sources of innovation in the informal economy in Africa – the most important sector in most low-income countries – and how they compare with the situation in the formal sector, as described in the NEPAD survey.

Moreover, much of the existing literature on innovation focuses on developed countries (Martin, 2012). Innovation, in the traditional literature, often originates from research and development in dedicated laboratories. This study recognizes that given the current technological capabilities in the context of low-income countries, innovation is more than research and development (R&D) (Lundvall et al., 2011). It may also come from technological learning, which is found to be important, especially in developing countries (Bell, 1984; Morrison et al., 2008). What are the major sources of innovation in Africa? As a systematic literature report in Chapter 2 suggests, although there is valuable research on the role of technological learning (Lundvall et al., 2011), the role of MNEs (Fu, 2015; Javorcik, 2008; Lall, 1996) and the role of clusters (Bell and Albu, 1999), a systematic and comprehensive study of the sources of innovation in Africa, especially based on multi-country large firm-level surveys, is rare.

Although innovative capacity in LICs is critical for the successful transfer and adaptation of knowledge, it is inevitable for firms in developing countries to encounter obstacles during the process of knowledge adoption and innovation. An innovation obstacle is perceived as a factor that potentially prevents an innovation decision or increases the difficulties, timeframe and cost of the process. Limited by their inadequate resources and experiences, firms in LICs are likely to face substantial barriers to innovation compared to firms in advanced economies. Given all these obstacles, how do the firms in Africa manage to innovate? What are the major domestic sources of innovation in such an environment?

At a structural level, most low-income countries are characterized by a dual-economic system in which there is an active informal sector alongside formal registered firms. Ghana and Tanzania are no exception. The differences in the capabilities of firms in the two sectors are likely to shape the innovation adoption and diffusion. Formal establishments usually have the human and capital resources to undertake innovation processes with other research and development institutions, or, for larger firms, with foreign institutions. Instead, informal firms are unlikely to have

strong capabilities and therefore are more likely to innovate from entrepreneurs' initiatives and in response to specific constraints in the context
in which they operate.

This chapter aims to address these important questions, in particular:
(1) What is the scale and nature of innovation in Africa? (2) How do
innovations in the informal sector differ from those in the formal sector?
(3) What are the domestic sources of innovation in Africa? (4) How do
firms in Africa develop their ways to innovation given the skills, resources
and institutional constraints in these countries?

The chapter addresses these questions using a mixed method
approach, which combines both qualitative case studies and statistical
analysis of unique firm-level survey data in Ghana and Tanzania, to
understand the nature and sources of innovation in Africa. It is based
on evidence from case studies of 32 firms and a statistical analysis of three
dedicated firm-level innovation surveys of 500 formal and informal firms
in 2013 and 498 firms in 2015 in Ghana as well as 278 formal and
informal firms in Tanzania in 2015. As discussed in the Introduction
chapter, the use of a combination of these three surveys allows us to
identify the major characteristics of innovations that are common and
robust over time in Ghana and Tanzania. The analysis adopts the *Oslo
Manual's* definition of innovation, which suggests that, first, innovation
can take a multitude of forms (product innovations, process innovations,
marketing innovations, and managerial and organizational innovations).
Second, innovation can be developed from an original idea but also
emerges from diffusion, absorption or imitation of new methods that
are observed. Because of that, it could simply be new to the firm and
have an impact on productivity and employment.

The rest of this chapter is organised as follows. In the next section (4.2),
we present the methodology employed in the chapter. Sections 4.3–4.7
discuss the nature, the novelty, innovation barriers, innovations under
constraints and sources of external knowledge in Ghana and Tanzania.
Section 4.8 synthesises the discussions in the previous sections with field-
qualitative data, and the last section (4.9) concludes the chapter.

4.2   Methodology

4.2.1   Data

This chapter uses a mixed method approach which combines both qualitative case studies and descriptive statistical analysis of large firm-level
survey data to understand the process of the creation and diffusion of
innovation in Ghanaian and Tanzanian firms. The quantitative and

qualitative approaches are used to triangulate the results and provide a more complete picture of the current innovation activities in these economies.

The study initially approached the research questions through a qualitative approach. This phase aimed to better understand how the concept of innovation may have had different meanings for different actors and how the adoption is influenced by various factors that could be embedded in the social and cultural environments of the respondents. The data were collected through in-depth interviews in Ghana in early 2013 and covered four main dimensions: innovation activities, the process of knowledge sourcing for innovation, which includes knowledge and sources' identification, acquisition, adoption and adaptation, barriers to innovation transmission and space for innovation policies.

The analysis focuses on three sectors of the industry relevant for the Ghanaian economy: (i) food processing, where Ghana may hold a potential competitive advantage in addition to the relevance of being strictly linked with the agricultural sector; (ii) textile and garments, which is populated by micro and small entrepreneurs and engages a large share of the population; (iii) firms supplying construction businesses, which have had a remarkable growth in the past years and where local firms collaborate with and supply foreign firms. To capture how the characteristics and constraints typical of informal settlements can shape the nature of innovation and the way innovation is adopted or created, half of the firms sampled in the food and textile sectors were from the informal sector.

The firms were selected using a purposive sampling technique to identify and approach only innovative firms. We randomly selected textile, food processing and firms in the construction business from the Association of Ghana Industries' database that in the previous innovation survey in Ghana identified themselves as innovators. Such methodology allowed us to capture richer information and insights on innovation activities in Ghanaian firms. However, it does not uncover factors and, in particular, barriers that prevent firms from innovating.

We selected a total of ten firms in which we carried out thirty-two in-depth interviews that included a range of actors: senior managers, departmental managers (production, marketing and human resources), R&D staff, technicians and workers. Interviewees were seen individually to avoid biases in the responses, and the choice of interviewees depended on the access to the respondents and the nature of the firms. The data were analysed in different dimensions, within-case and cross-case

(Eisenhardt, 1989). The former were meant to gather information within a firm and sector, while the latter aimed to find within-group (industry and sector) similarities and intergroup differences. This allowed us to discern patters and relationships and to compare relevant findings with previous literature. Table 4.1 summarizes the main characteristics of the firms interviewed.

Following the in-depth interviews in Ghana, a national firm-level survey was carried out in Ghana in 2013 using a questionnaire based on findings from the qualitative interviews, and in 2015, two follow-up surveys were carried out in Ghana and Tanzania using the same questionnaire and sampling framework as described in the Introduction chapter. The analysis in this chapter is therefore based on a combination of statistical analysis of these large-scale firm-level surveys and evidence from the in-depth interviews.

4.2.2   Characteristics and Environment of Sampled Firms

Table 4.2 reports some key characteristics of Ghanaian firms from the surveys of 2013 and 2015, and compares the differences between formal and informal firms. The group of formal and informal firms present statistically different averages in all variables, identifying two different realities in the economy of Ghana. On average, the surveyed firms have been active for 16 years, with formal firms relatively older than informal firms (21 vs. 14). Informal firms employed, on average, just over five employees with no change between surveys. Turnover too has increased for both types of firms between surveys. Almost all of the informal and formal firms predominantly trade in local and regional markets.

The percentage of employees with a university degree, which is an important indicator of human capital for innovation and also of absorptive capacity, is significantly different in formal and informal firms. Formal firms have three times more employees with a university degree than informal firms. There are also significant differences between the formal and informal firms in terms of access to foreign investors, public grid and the internet. Twelve per cent of formal firms have foreign investors while less than 1 per cent of informal firms engage with foreign investors. There were consistently 40 per cent of formal firms that had access to the internet in 2013 and 2015, while the proportion of informal firms with internet access remained significantly lower than that in the formal sector, seeing limited improvement over the two survey periods, from 5 per cent in 2013 to 7 per cent in 2015. A significant improvement was a large increase in the proportion of firms with access to the public grid over

Table 4.1 *Description of firms*

Firm	Nature	Sector	Core business	No. of employees	Markets	Turnover in 2010 ('000 GHc)	Interviewees
A	Formal	FP	Processing cocoa beans	270	Global	89,000	MM, HRM, DMD, R&D, PM
B	Formal	FP	Soups, jam, drinks	40	Ghana, ECOWAS, Europe	720	MD, AO, PM, QA, WK
C	Informal	FP	Pepper sauces and peanut products	10	Ghana	250	MD, MO, PS, WK
D	Informal	FP	Mushroom grower and processor	2	Ghana	15	MD
E	Formal	TX	Garments in large scale	450	Ghana, USA, Europe, Asia	2,000	MD, OD
F	Formal	TX	Uniforms	15	Ghana, West Africa	60	MD, 2 WK
G	Informal	TX	Men's and ladies' wear, uniforms	10	Ghana	35	MD, DMD, 2 WK
H	Informal	TX	Fashion designer	10	Ghana, US, Europe	50	MD, 2 WK
I	Formal	CS	PVC pipes	750	Ghana, ECOWAS	35,000	MM, EM, PM, PS
J	Formal	CS	Concrete products	400	Ghana, ECOWAS	10,000	PM

Legend: Sector: food processing (FP), textile (TX), construction business (CS). Interviewees: accounts officer (AO), deputy managing director (DMD), human resource manager (HRM), export manager (EM), managing director (MD), marketing manager (MM), marketing officer (MO), operations director (OD), production manager (PM), production supervisor (PS), quality assurance officer (QA), research and development manager (R&D), generic worker (WK).

Table 4.2 *Key firm characteristics (by nature of firm) in Ghana (2015)*

		2015		
	All	Informal (1)	Formal (2)	Difference (1)-(2)
Age of the firm (years)	16.3	13.5	20.5	-***
Active mainly in the local market (%)	89.4	95.6	80.3	+***
Number of employees	39.8	5.4	90.0	-***
Turnover ('000 GH₵)	1,083.1	33.3	2,608.1	-***
Turnover ('000 USD)	339.0	10.4	816.3	
Employees with a university degree (%)	6.4	3.6	10.6	-***
Foreign investor (%)	5.4	0.7	12.3	-***
Access to public grid (%)	84.7	76.3	97.0	-***
Access to internet (%)	20.9	7.5	40.4	-***

Note: One, two and three asterisks respectively indicate significance at the 10 per cent, 5 per cent and 1 per cent levels. Exchange rate of Ghanaian cedi to USD on Dec 30, 2014 USD/GHS = 3.1950, source: www.xe.com/currencycharts/?from=USD&to=TZS&view=5Y

the 2013–2015 period. The proportion of informal firms with access to the public grid increased from 9 per cent in 2013 to 76 per cent in 2015, and this proportion increased from 43 per cent to 97 per cent amongst the formal firms over the same period. While there is still a considerable difference between the formal and informal sectors, this is a commendable achievement in the Ghanaian economy.

Table 4.3 shows the features of surveyed firms in Tanzania in 2015 based on available variables in the Tanzanian dataset. It can be observed that Tanzanian firms are younger than those in Ghana, with an average age of 11 years. Informal firms are younger with 7 years of existence, while formal firms are double this age. Both groups of firms largely sell in the local market, a higher proportion than for Ghanaian firms. The share of firms with foreign investors is larger than in Ghana, for both informal and formal firms in the sample. This suggests that the Tanzanian sample may have over-sampled the foreign invested firms, as overall Ghana has attracted more FDI than Tanzania as shown in Chapter 3. The data also shows that Tanzanian firms tend to have higher access to infrastructure than Ghanaian firms. For instance, access to public electricity grids is available for almost all formal and informal firms in Tanzania at higher rates than in Ghana. A higher proportion of firms in Tanzania has access to the internet, with 35 per cent of informal firms and 89 per cent of formal firms having access to the internet.

Table 4.3 *Key firm characteristics (by nature of firm) in Tanzania (2015)*

	All	Informal (1)	Formal (2)	Difference (1)-(2)
Age of the firm (years)	11.3	6.9	14.5	-***
Active mainly in the local market (%)	75.8	85.5	68.3	+***
Number of employees	251.0	7.45	393.43	-***
Turnover ('000 shilling)	299,000	75,000	445,000	-***
Turnover ('000 USD)	172.8	43.4	257.2	-***
Employees with a university degree (%)	37.5	22.5	46.2	-***
Foreign investor (%)	15.5	4.3	23.6	-***
Access to public grid (%)	98.6	97.4	99.4	-*
Access to internet (%)	66.5	35.0	89.4	-***

Note: One, two and three asterisks respectively indicate significance at the 10 per cent, 5 per cent and 1 per cent levels. Exchange rate of Tanzania shilling to USD on Dec 30, 2014 USD/TZS = 1730, source: www.xe.com/currencycharts/?from=USD&to=TZS&view=5Y

4.3   The Nature of Innovation Activities

As explained earlier, to capture the diversity of innovation in Ghana and Tanzania, we used a broad definition of the term 'innovation'. This includes the adoption of a new product or process, or new organizational and marketing practices (where 'new' means new to the world or new to the country or the firm). This also allows us to distinguish between ground-breaking, genuinely novel innovation and imitative and incremental innovation. This emphasis on imitative and incremental innovation is more compatible with the type of evidence that is more likely to be relevant and available for Ghana and Tanzania, and LICs in general. According to Kaplinsky (2018), these imitative and incremental innovations are key steps in building capabilities of firms for catch-up.

Evidence from the surveys shows that incremental innovation is a widespread phenomenon in the private sector in both Ghana and Tanzania (Figures 4.1 and 4.2). From the sample, most of the Ghanaian firms (78 per cent in 2013 and 84 per cent in 2015) are active in some innovation activity. Formal firms seem to perform better than informal firms. The proportions of formal firms reporting to have introduced innovation were 90 per cent in both surveys. Amongst the informal firms, almost three out of four have engaged in innovation activities in the period 2011–2013. This increased to 80 per cent in 2015, suggesting some advancement in innovation in the informal sector in Ghana.

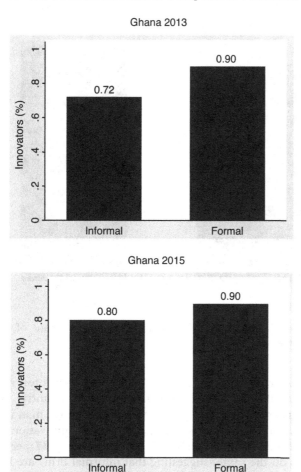

Figure 4.1 Proportion of innovative firms (by nature of firm) in Ghana

In Tanzania, 94 per cent of surveyed firms reported that they had engaged in innovation in the 2013–2015 period (Figure 4.2). This is an even larger proportion in comparison to that in Ghana. As was the case in Ghana, formal firms innovated more (96 per cent) than informal firms (89 per cent). The difference between the proportion of formal and informal firms that innovated is similar for both countries.

Firms may have different patterns of innovation. Figures 4.3 and 4.4 show the different types of innovations reported by our sampled firms in

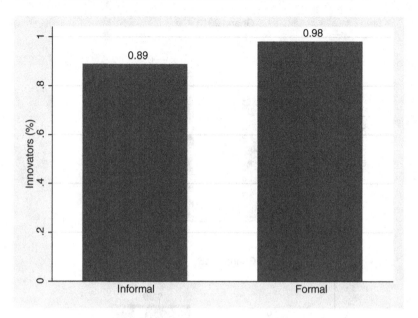

Figure 4.2 Proportion of innovative firms (by nature of firm) in Tanzania

Ghana and Tanzania, respectively. The pattern of innovation activities for formal and informal firms is similar within each country. Overall, formal firms are more active in technological innovations than informal firms. The major difference is found in process innovation. While 59 per cent of formal firms innovate in processes, only 37 per cent of informal firms do the same, suggesting that informal firms are less efficient as compared with their formal counterparts. However, the difference between formal and informal firms is less pronounced in management and marketing innovations. In Tanzania, the informal firms even appear to be more active in marketing innovation than the formal firms, bringing to fore the dominance of informal firms in the retail sector.

Looking at the proportion of firms engaged in product, process, management and marketing innovations, both Ghanaian and Tanzanian firms have demonstrated strong resilience in innovation across the board. In both countries, more than half of firms reported to have introduced product or marketing innovation. However, the difference between the two countries in each category becomes more evident, with Tanzania showing a high proportion of innovations in all

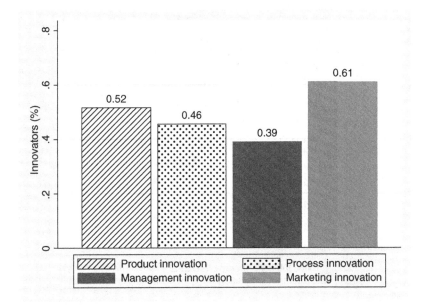

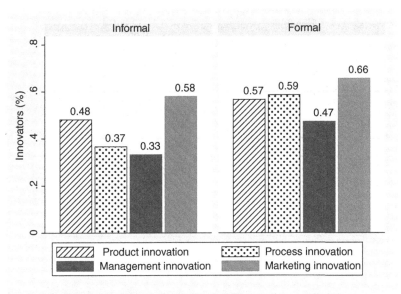

Figure 4.3 Proportion of firms active in innovations: (left) by nature of innovation and (right) by nature of innovation and firm in Ghana (2015)

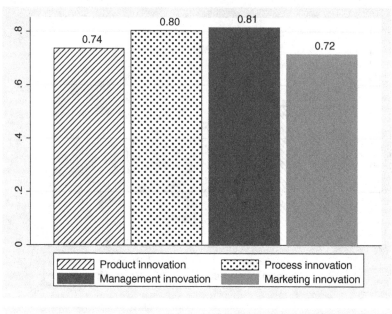

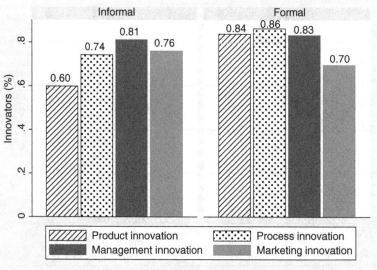

Figure 4.4 Proportion of firms active in innovations: (left) by nature of innovation and (right) by nature of innovation and firm in Tanzania (2015)

categories. Marketing innovation is the area which sees the smallest difference between the two countries. Sixty-one per cent of Ghanaian firms were involved in marketing innovation in 2015 (Figure 4.3) in comparison to 72 per cent in Tanzania. About half of Ghanaian firms introduced new or significantly improved goods or services between 2012 and 2014, while in Tanzania the proportion of product innovators was 74 per cent.

Comparing innovation in the formal and informal firms in Tanzania, a higher proportion of formal firms innovate in each category, and there are several differences between formal and informal firms. Within informal firms, the higher rate of innovation is found in management (81 per cent) followed by marketing and process innovation (76 and 74 per cent respectively); while products or services innovation registered the lowest rate of innovation (60 per cent). For formal firms, the highest rates of innovations are found in process, product and management innovations (86, 84 and 83 per cent respectively), while the lowest proportion of firms (70 per cent) engage in marketing innovations. These patterns of innovation in Tanzanian firms make evident that informal firms innovate more in non-technological types of innovation, while formal firms innovate more in technological processes.

The biggest differences between Ghana and Tanzania are in process innovation and management innovation. While 47 per cent of the Ghanaian firms innovate in their processes, around 80 per cent of Tanzanian firms have introduced process innovation over the 2012–2014 period. While only 39 per cent of Ghanaian firms developed management innovation – introduced new or made significant changes or improvements in management practices over the sample period – this ratio is as high as 81 per cent among Tanzanian firms, more than double that in Ghana. These suggest that Tanzanian firms are more efficient and are better managed than Ghanaian firms.

Such significant differences in the proportions of innovative firms between these two countries are interesting. The NEPAD survey for the 2008–2010 period reported the percentage of innovation active firm in completed returns was 72.5 per cent for Ghana (for a sample of 500 firms with 10 or more employees) and 61.3 per cent for Tanzania (for a sample of 200 firms with 5 or more employees). Although the result may be caused by the cultural differences and differences in definitions in the two countries, this has been minimized to a considerable extent as the survey was carried out in person by our survey assistants, who are trained for a week before going into the field. The survey team in Tanzania was trained by staff of the Ghanaian survey team to ensure the consistency and comparability of the surveys. A possible explanation of such differences may be that the DILIC survey reported here includes 250 informal and 250 formal firms. The inclusion of the informal sector, which is less innovative than the formal firms, may bring down the overall ratio of innovative firms in Ghana. Secondly, the Tanzania survey seems to have over-sampled foreign invested firms, which are more innovative than the local firms.[1] This may boost the overall ratio of innovative firms in Tanzania. A factor which may explain such a consistently high proportion of innovations in Tanzanian firms in all categories is that many of the Tanzanian firms carry out different innovations simultaneously. This will be discussed in detail in Section 4.4.

4.4   The Novelty of Innovation

Not all innovations are equal. In order to capture the different nature of innovations, the study follows the *Oslo Manual* and Kaplinsky (2018) to capture the degree of ingenuity of innovations, that is, whether an innovation was new to the firm, new to the country, or new to the world. The vast majority of innovations recorded are new to the firm, with some evidence of new to the country product and process innovations. This supports the wider spread of incremental innovations, rather than innovations that leap-frog or redefine value-creation processes.

This is captured in Figures 4.5 and 4.6 where the proportion of firms engaging in product or process innovations that are new to the firm or new to the world are presented. In Ghana and Tanzania, most firms conduct product and process innovations that are only new to the firm, evidencing that firms in LICs mostly adapt innovations from other markets.

In Ghana, only 1.8 per cent of firms innovate in products or services new to the world, while processes new to the world are generated by almost no firms (0.2 per cent). Just one in one hundred informal firms innovate in a product or service new to the world, while this is almost three in one hundred for formal firms.

The qualitative research from fieldwork sheds some light on the nature of innovations. For example, a food processing firm introduced a new product (canned groundnut soup base) which is the first in Ghana and West Africa. The product was developed in collaboration with a foreign university in order to fill a production gap when the main ingredient for the main core product of the firm was not in season. Again, another food processing firm introduced a modified version of a local sauce made of mushrooms instead of pepper. The idea for such a product was a result of

---

[1] The proportion of firms with a foreign investor was 15 per cent in the Tanzania sample. See Table 4.3.

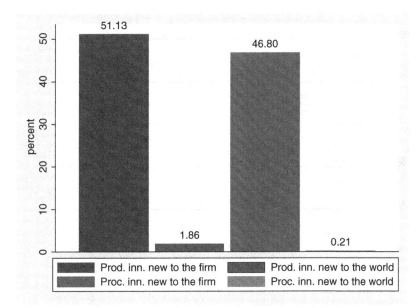

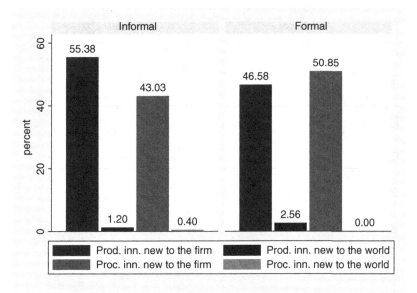

Figure 4.5 Proportion of firms' engagement in new-to-the-firm and new-to-the-world product/process innovations in 2015: (left) by nature of innovation and (right) by sector of firm in Ghana

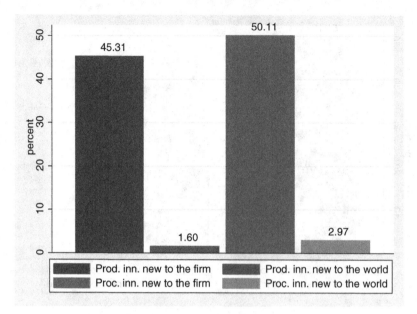

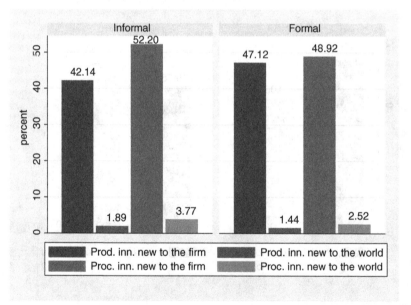

Figure 4.6 Proportion of firms' engagement in new-to-the-firm and new-to-the-world product/process innovations in 2015: (left) by nature of innovation and (right) by sector of firm in Tanzania

an oversupply of mushrooms, the core business of the firm. The idea and the launch of the new product both allowed the firm to introduce a new line of products and reduce production waste. At the time of the survey, no such product was available in the national market. We also found some evidence of product and process innovations thought to be new to the world, although the diffusion is very small. A firm in the construction business introduced a modified version of plastic as a supporting structure used in the construction of drainage gullies beside roads. The original device is made of wood, which makes it prone to rotting and limits the number of times it can be re-used. The different material allows builders to re-use the structure with significant savings in costs and time. To the best of the company's knowledge, it is the only firm in the world to produce such a device.

For Tanzania, there are more firms innovating in processes new to the world than in the Ghanaian case, but still the number of firms producing technological innovations new to the world is extremely low. Almost 3 per cent of firms generated process innovations new to the world, while only 1.6 per cent of firms innovated in products or services new to the world. Informal firms reported higher rates of innovations new to the world compared to formal firms. This finding may be due to the limited information that informal firms have about products globally. The survey questions are designed as firms' self-assessment, so it might be a case that an informal firm thought that it developed a new-to-the-world production process, which may not be true because of their limited knowledge of the external world. This finding, therefore, needs further investigation.

The private benefits of new products and services produced are captured by the percentage of the total turnover from the new products introduced (Tables 4.4 and 4.5). For Ghanaian firms, product

Table 4.4 *Percentage of total turnover of goods or service innovations introduced in Ghana (2014)*

	2014			
	Total	Informal	Formal	Difference
Goods and service innovations new to your market	22.64	23.54	21.54	1.99
Goods and service innovations were only new to the firm	49.79	58.29	39.49	18.80***

Note: Only for firms that introduced product innovations (n = 261). One, two and three asterisks respectively indicate significance at the 10 per cent, 5 per cent and 1 per cent levels.

Table 4.5 *Percentage of total turnover of goods or service innovations introduced in Tanzania (2014)*

	Total	Informal	Formal	Difference
Goods and service innovations new to your market	35.98	36.43	35.74	0.69
Goods and service innovations were only new to the firm	43.98	38.31	46.91	-8.60**

Note: Only for firms that introduced product innovations (n = 205). One, two and three asterisks respectively indicate significance at the 10 per cent, 5 per cent and 1 per cent levels.

innovations that were new to firms accounted only for around 50 per cent of the total turnover, while the contribution of product innovations new to the market provided around 23 per cent. Product innovations new to firms and new to the country were relatively more relevant for informal than for formal firms, although the difference is statistically significant only for the turnover from innovations new to the firm. Turnover from products new to the firm was about 44 per cent in Tanzania, while the share of turnover from products and services new to the market was 36 per cent. In Tanzania, formal firms seemed to benefit more from product innovations new to the firm (47 per cent of turnover) in comparison to informal firms (38 per cent).

The foregoing suggests that innovations new to the firm matter more for firms' turnover in both Ghana and Tanzania than higher degrees of product novelty. Also, informal enterprises in Tanzania lag behind their informal counterparts in Ghana in terms of turnover from innovations.

4.5   Innovation Barriers Faced by Firms in Ghana and Tanzania

Evidence from the surveys suggests that firms in Africa face several difficulties during the innovation process, and some obstacles can even deter firms from engaging in innovation activities. The survey conducted in Ghana and Tanzania in 2015 asked for eighteen factors that might impede innovation, which were grouped in five categories.

Figure 4.7 shows the average importance of the categories of obstacles hampering innovation in Ghanaian firms. Similar innovation constraints are observed for formal and informal firms. Results in 2015 are also similar to the ones observed in 2013. The main changes are a reduction of about 1 point in the importance of other

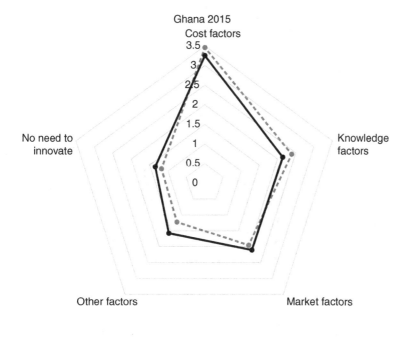

Figure 4.7 Importance of obstacles to innovation for formal (solid line) and informal (dotted line) Ghanaian firms in 2015 (1 = insignificant, 5 = crucial, average values)

factors impeding innovation and the perception of firms that they do not need to innovate. There are small differences between informal and formal firms. Informal firms consider knowledge factors more obstructive for innovation, while considering other factors as less relevant as obstacles for innovation. Overall, the most relevant factors impeding innovation in Ghanaian firms are the costs associated with the innovation processes (scores of 3.5 for informal firms and 3.3 for formal firms) and inadequate knowledge resources (scores of 2.4 for informal firms and 2.1 for formal firms).

Figure 4.8 exhibits the importance of innovation obstacles perceived by Tanzanian firms. In Tanzania, there are more differences in the perception of innovation obstacles between formal and informal firms. As in Ghana, the most relevant constraints impeding innovation are the costs and knowledge factors, which are perceived as much more restrictive for informal firms than formal firms. Informal firms consider the relevance of

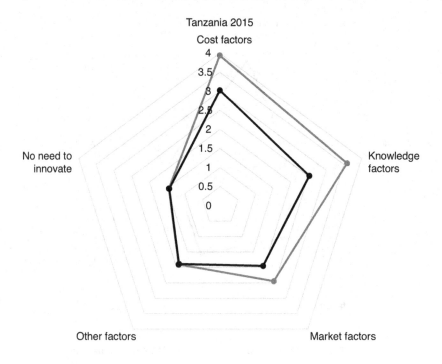

Tanzania 2015
Cost factors

━●━TANZANIA 2015 Informal firms   ━●━TANZANIA 2015 Formal Firms

Figure 4.8 Importance of obstacles to innovation for formal (grey) and
informal (black) Tanzanian firms in 2015 (1 = insignificant, 5 = crucial,
average values)

costs and knowledge factors with an average of 3.9 and 3.6 points,
respectively, while formal firms show an average of 3.0 and 2.5, respectively. Market factors are the third most relevant factor impeding innovation in informal Tanzanian firms (2.4 points on average), but for formal
firms this factor is less relevant (2.0 points). Other factors and the perception that innovation is not needed are the least relevant factors hin-
dering innovation, and their importance is the same for formal and
informal firms.

Tables 4.6 and 4.7 present the breakdown of the categories of factors
that hamper innovation in LICs. The average differences between formal
and informal firms were tested statistically to identify significant differences between formal and informal firms in both countries.

Table 4.6 *Importance of obstacles hampering innovation for formal and informal firms in Ghana (2013 and 2015)* (1 = insignificant, 5 = crucial, average values)

		2013				2015			
		All	Informal	Formal	Diff.	All	Informal	Formal	Diff.
Cost factors	Lack of funds within your enterprise or group	3.93	4.01	3.79	−0.22	4.48	4.61	4.30	0.31***
	Lack of finance from sources outside your enterprise	2.84	2.91	2.73	0.17	3.17	3.27	3.01	0.26*
	Innovation costs too high	3.12	3.07	3.20	−0.13	3.04	3.09	2.97	0.12
	Excessive perceived economic risks	2.65	2.62	2.71	−0.09	2.80	2.86	2.72	0.13
Knowledge factors	Lack of qualified personnel	2.14	2.12	2.18	−0.06	2.15	2.24	2.00	0.24*
	Lack of information on technology	2.17	2.16	2.19	−0.03	2.51	2.65	2.31	0.34**
	Lack of information on markets	2.20	2.19	2.22	−0.03	2.29	2.38	2.15	0.23*
	Difficulty in finding co-operation partners for innovation	2.29	2.40	2.09	0.31*	2.22	2.29	2.11	0.17
Market factors	Market dominated by established enterprises	2.17	2.18	2.17	0.01	2.36	2.34	2.38	−0.04
	Uncertain demand for innovative goods or services	1.97	1.97	1.96	0.01	2.01	2.02	1.99	0.03
	Innovation is easy to imitate	1.71	1.69	1.74	−0.05	2.21	2.00	2.51	−0.51***
	Little competition in the market and hence no need to innovate	1.47	1.46	1.50	−0.04	1.30	1.20	1.44	−0.23**
	Too much competition in the market and too low perceived return of innovation investment	1.94	1.83	2.13	−0.30*	2.21	2.20	2.21	−0.00
Other factors	Organizational rigidities within the enterprise	1.54	1.51	1.59	−0.08	1.19	1.01	1.45	−0.45***
	Workers do not have the incentive to innovate.	1.91	1.88	1.94	−0.06	1.50	1.41	1.64	−0.22
	Insufficient flexibility of regulations or standards	1.72	1.73	1.71	0.02	1.37	1.25	1.54	−0.28**
	Limitations of science and technology public policies	1.77	1.81	1.70	0.11	1.60	1.43	1.84	−0.41***
	Weak intellectual property rights protection	2.43	2.49	2.34	0.15	1.77	1.55	2.08	−0.53***
	Practices used by informal firms	1.77	1.82	1.68	0.14	1.68	1.45	2.01	−0.56***
No need to innovate	No need due to prior innovations	2.10	2.17	1.98	0.20	1.15	1.05	1.30	−0.25**
	No need because of no demand for innovations	1.51	1.48	1.58	−0.10	1.20	1.08	1.38	−0.30**
	Social or cultural factors	1.58	1.64	1.46	0.18	1.39	1.41	1.37	0.04

Note: More than one answer allowed. Significance at the 10 per cent, 5 per cent and 1 per cent levels are indicated by one, two and three asterisks respectively.

The evidence from Table 4.6 indicates that firms in Ghana perceived cost factors as the most important obstacle to innovation in both 2013 and 2015. The results further suggest that there is

Table 4.7 *Importance of obstacles hampering innovation for formal and informal firms in Tanzania (2015) (1 = insignificant, 5 = crucial, average values).*

		All	Informal	Formal	Diff.
Cost factors	Lack of funds within your enterprise or group	4.08	4.62	3.69	0.93***
	Lack of finance from sources outside your enterprise	3.79	4.19	3.50	0.69***
	Innovation costs too high	3.16	3.97	2.58	1.39***
	Excessive perceived economic risks	2.61	2.98	2.34	0.64***
Knowledge factors	Lack of qualified personnel	3.17	3.69	2.80	0.89***
	Lack of information on technology	3.08	3.76	2.60	1.16***
	Lack of information on markets	2.84	3.57	2.32	1.26***
	Difficulty in finding co-operation partners for innovation	2.79	3.35	2.38	0.97***
Market factors	Market dominated by established enterprises	3.12	3.87	2.58	1.29***
	Uncertain demand for innovative goods or services	2.46	3.00	2.08	0.93***
	Innovation is easy to imitate	1.84	1.63	1.99	−0.36**
	Little competition in the market and hence no need to innovate	1.32	1.25	1.36	−0.11
	Too much competition in the market and too low perceived return of innovation investment	2.06	2.48	1.76	0.72***
Other factors	Organizational rigidities within the enterprise	1.25	1.07	1.39	−0.32**
	Workers do not have the incentive to innovate.	1.50	1.50	1.50	−0.00
	Insufficient flexibility of regulations or standards	1.81	1.83	1.80	0.03
	Limitations of science and technology public policies	2.81	2.67	2.91	−0.24
	Weak intellectual property rights protection	2.91	2.88	2.93	−0.05
	Practices used by informal firms	2.16	2.50	1.91	0.59***
No need to innovate	No need due to prior innovations	1.17	1.13	1.19	−0.06
	No need because of no demand for innovations	1.16	1.06	1.23	−0.17*
	Social or cultural factors	1.99	2.15	1.88	0.27

Note: More than one answer allowed. Significance at the 10 per cent, 5 per cent and 1 per cent levels are indicated by one, two and three asterisks respectively.

a significant difference between informal and formal firms' access to internal and external funds for innovation within the enterprise or group. Informal enterprises on average tend to lack funds and are much inhibited by the lack of funds for innovation activities than their formal counterparts. These results evidence the absence of a developed financial system in LICs for financing innovation activities, and also the bias against informal firms in the credit market. Our findings in Tanzania, although similar to Ghana in general terms, present a situation where informal firms are more constrained. As shown in Table 4.7, informal firms in Tanzania consider almost all the barriers to innovation to be more restrictive than formal firms. The most relevant obstacles, for formal and informal firms, are all costs and knowledge factors, particularly the lack of funds in the company or economic group. Findings from our qualitative research and the wider literature corroborate this finding. The qualitative research found that financial constraints were a common barrier to innovation in most firms. Although funds would support firms to make investments in a range of areas, from expanding the factory to buying new machinery and increasing the productivity, the loan interest rate at the time (~20 per cent) was unaffordable for most firms. A formal firm expressed the inability to generate enough profit to repay the interest of a debt. This is common in other LIC settings; from North Vietnam (Kimura, 2011) to Colombia (Kugler, 2006).

Knowledge-related factors are the second-most relevant obstacles to innovation in 2013 and 2015. In particular, we found in Ghana that the lack of information on technologies is a highly relevant obstacle for informal firms in 2015, followed by lack of personnel and information on markets. Other internal constraints to innovate are 'Organizational rigidities within the enterprise' and 'Workers do not have the incentive to innovate', which are more relevant for formal firms (Table 4.6). These internal restrictions can be addressed by changes in managerial practices that represent a potential source of innovation that can be addressed by diffusion of organizational practices promoting innovation within the firm. Table 4.7 also shows knowledge factors as a key obstacle in Tanzania. Our qualitative research supports this finding, suggesting that lack of skills and human resource is a general challenge in LICs. This was how one respondent explained it to us:

"Efficiency on production depends on the technical ability for designing, but getting people with the right skills is sometimes a constraint, skills to even operate machines and establishing design patterns is difficult. In this regard Asia is ahead of Ghana because they have the right and qualified human resource base." (MD, Firm E)

A majority of empirical studies in the literature focused on the correlation between the level of innovation abilities and the level of education of the managers. This includes studies in a multi-country setting (Wang and Wong, 2012), in Ghana (McDade and Malecki, 1997; Robson et al., 2009), Tanzania (Hall et al., 2012), Uganda (Oyelaran-Oyeyinka and Lal, 2006), and Nigeria (Egbetokun et al., 2012; Ilori et al., 2000). The importance of the skills of workers has received less attention. Fu (2008) provided evidence of how in regions of China where there are more highly educated and skilled workers, the spillovers from FDI are greater. The same respondent added:

"This constraint is of utmost importance to us as a firm and so our commitment in providing on the job training." (MD, Firm E)

This highlights the importance of training of workers within firms to mitigate the lack of human resources in both countries. According to Kaplinsky (2018), this process of capability building is a long-term process and also sector specific as it varies from sector to sector.

Market and institutional factors can constrain innovations. In both Ghana and Tanzania, our analysis shows that the most relevant market factors that constrain innovations are the dominance of established firms in the market and the perception of high levels of competition. In 2015, the risk that innovations can be copied easily is significantly more relevant for formal firms. This fact, together with the high importance of the factors 'Weak intellectual property rights protection' and 'Practices used by informal firms' perceived by formal firms, presents a scenario where regulations regarding patents, copyrights and trademarks can produce a change in the innovation behaviour of firms, particularly in Ghana. Increasing competition in Ghanaian markets can push formal firms to innovate more. In Tanzania, the perception that innovations are easy to imitate deters innovation mainly in formal firms, although the practices used by informal firms affect mostly the innovations of other informal firms.

Expanding markets to nearby countries is also critical for the growth of local firms. However, even if firms' capability could accommodate larger production, the capabilities and institutions of host countries can hamper the ability to export. Firms A and E mentioned the difficulties of entering foreign markets, a concern shared by the construction firms as well. All of them highlighted the difficulties of finding permanent committed local representatives that are able to manage their business.

Finally, factors related to institutional constraints, such as the insufficient flexibility of regulations or standards, limitations of public policies relating to science and technology, weak intellectual property rights (IPR) protection, and practices used by informal firms, are not as relevant for formal firms. However, these factors present significant differences for formal and informal firms in 2015. In general, formal firms perceive the innovation policies, regulations and the existing regime as an obstacle more often than informal firms. This may be due to the reason that formal firms are directly affected by innovation policies and regulations, while informal firms operate in the shadow with little understanding and regard for innovation policies and regulations. In Tanzania, public policies, regulations and the weakness of property rights protection are also considered as relevant obstacles to innovation. There are no significant differences in these perceptions between formal or informal firms. This suggests that the protection of property rights and the development of public policies such as science and technology policies in line with local conditions are critical and should be a priority for the Tanzanian Government.

Generally, weak institutions such as intellectual property rights (IPR) protection have a negative impact on current innovation activities in LICs. In many LICs, overall institutional development still lags behind and so protection of IPR is still weak. This has clear implications for the diffusion of innovation. On the one hand, the lack of protection of IPR weakens incentives for inventors and for innovators, with a strong detrimental effect on innovation. On the other hand, too strict an IPR protection may inhibit the diffusion of innovation, especially in LICs where firms, people, and the government lack financial resources to pay royalties. Therefore, the solution probably has to be on a case-by-case and sector-by-sector basis. For some of the technologies and innovations and in some countries, there may be a need to encourage protection and incentivize the innovators. In some sectors, especially luxury goods and in areas not directly affecting people's welfare, governments can put in place strong IPR protection.

4.6 Innovation under the Constraints: Domestic Sources of Innovation

The literature suggests that innovations may originate from supply-side efforts such as R&D activities, technological learning or even from discovery by chance. They may also originate from demand-side efforts such as inspiration and co-creation. The different ways in which an innovation can materialise in Ghana and Tanzania are reported in Tables 4.8 and 4.9, respectively.

4.6.1   Customer Demand as a Major Inspiration of Innovation

Innovations are, argued Jacob Schmookler, to be shaped by the nature of demand; this can be traced to the work of Griliches and Schmookler (1963) and Schmookler (1966). Demand played a leading role in determining both the direction and magnitude of inventive activity (Scherer, 1982). Utterback (1974) finds that 'Market factors appear to be the primary influence on innovation. About 60 to 80 per cent of important innovations in a large number of fields have been in response to market demands and needs. The remainder have originated in response to new scientific or technological advances and opportunities.'

The patterns in the materialization of technological innovations in Ghana in 2015 are similar to the patterns observed in 2013. Consistent with the findings from the literature (e.g. Godin and Lane, 2013; OECD, 2011; Schmookler, 1966; Utterback, 1974), the customer is a major inspiration for innovation in Africa. Most of the technological innovations in Ghana (77 per cent) are modifications to the firms' products in response to customers' requirements. This is also observed for most informal (73 per cent) and formal (81 per cent) firms. This shows how the market is an inspiration for innovation and how a strong connection between firms and customers can be mutually beneficial. The picture in Tanzania is consistent with that in Ghana in this regard (Table 4.9). Innovations, as a response to customers' requirements, also drive the technological and management innovation processes. Seventy-four of the technological innovations in Tanzania made modifications to the firms' products in response to customers' requirements. This is also observed for most informal (87 per cent) and formal (65 per cent) firms.

Evidence from qualitative interviews also suggests that these are important channels for the diffusion of innovation both within and to the country. Visits to textile establishments confirmed that many product innovations are born from observing other products in the market. In the textile sector, where machinery can produce a multitude of garments and the design and material are important factors in tailoring a product, the visit to local markets can be an inspiration for new styles or products (Firms G and H[2]). Similarly, Firm H was used to take inspirations from fashion magazines. In the case of a firm supplying construction firms (Firm J), the production of a new product was initiated following a specific request from a large customer. Once the order was confirmed, the firm could invest in new machinery and transfer knowledge gained from producing similar products. The same product is still in the firm's portfolio and it was later successfully sold to other customers.

---

[2] Characteristics of the interviewed firms are given in Table 4.1.

4.6.2   In-house versus Extra-mural Innovation Sourcing

As evidenced from Tables 4.8 and 4.9, more than half of the technological innovations appear to be developed primarily within the firm. Sixty-three per cent and 55 per cent of the firms developed technological and management innovations within the firm, respectively. This is higher in the formal firms. Seventy-eight per cent of formal firms developed innovations in-house, with no external collaboration with other institutions. For informal firms, the proportion is significantly lower (50 per cent), though still relevant. Only 15 per cent of the firms reported that they create the innovation together with other enterprises or institutions.

In Tanzania, most of the firms developed technological and management innovations within the firm (87 and 80 per cent respectively). This is

Table 4.8 *Materialization of innovation in Ghana (2015, percentages of innovating firms)*

	Technological Innovations			
	Total	Informal	Formal	Diff.
The product or process was mainly developed within the enterprise	62.9	50.0	77.8	−27.8***
The firm developed the innovation in a research & development department	9.2	3.4	15.9	−12.5***
Technicians in the firm created the innovation as a solution to a problem that constrains the production or competitiveness of the company	18.0	7.5	30.2	−22.6***
Skilled workers in the firm find a better way for the production process after some experiments	38.6	27.4	51.6	−24.2***
The firm modified the product in response to customers' requirements	76.5	72.6	81.0	−8.4*
The firm adapted or modified goods or services originally developed by other enterprises or institutions	50.0	44.5	56.3	−11.8**
The firm created the innovation together with other enterprises or institutions	14.7	17.8	11.1	6.7*
The firm acquired technology originally developed by others by licensing and adapted or modified it	23.6	20.5	27.2	−6.7*
The firm acquired technology originally developed by others by licensing without any adaptation and modification	5.9	3.4	8.8	−5.4**
The firm observed or heard of the innovation by other companies and imitated it directly	47.2	47.3	47.2	0.1
The firm observed or heard of the innovation by other companies and imitated it with some modification	59.4	50.7	69.6	−18.9***

Table 4.9 *Materialization of innovation in Tanzania (2015, percentages of innovating firms)*

	Technological Innovations			
	Total	Informal	Formal	Diff.
The product or process was mainly developed within the enterprise	86.6	96.0	80.3	15.8***
The firm developed the innovation in a research & development department	25.3	1.0	41.4	−40.5***
Technicians in the firm created the innovation as a solution to a problem that constrains the production or competitiveness of the company	54.5	46.5	59.9	−13.3**
Skilled workers in the firm find a better way for the production process after some experiments	53.8	53.5	53.9	−0.5
The firm modified the product in response to customers' requirements	73.5	87.1	64.5	22.7***
The firm adapted or modified goods or services originally developed by other enterprises or institutions	43.1	53.5	36.2	17.3***
The firm created the innovation together with other enterprises or institutions	23.7	17.8	27.6	−9.8**
The firm acquired technology originally developed by others by licensing and adapted or modified it	19.4	9.9	25.7	−15.8***
The firm acquired technology originally developed by others by licensing without any adaptation and modification	20.9	4.0	32.2	−28.3***
The firm observed or heard of the innovation by other companies and imitated it directly	29.6	40.6	22.4	18.2***
The firm observed or heard of the innovation by other companies and imitated it with some modification	41.1	46.5	37.5	9.0*

considerably higher than those reported in Ghana. Similar to the case in Ghana, only 23 per cent of the firms developed technological and management innovations within the firm. All these suggest that African firms rely mainly on their own capacity for innovation. They are not very open to external sources in innovation.

4.6.3   Technological Learning versus Traditional R&D

Nearly half of the firms in Ghana and Tanzania report that they adapted or modified goods or services originally developed by other enterprises or institutions. The ratio is 50 per cent and 43 per cent of firms in Ghana and

Tanzania, respectively (Tables 4.8 and 4.9). The contribution of technicians and skilled workers in the technological innovation process is relevant mainly for formal firms (30 and 52 per cent for formal firms, while only 8 and 27 per cent for informal firms). About half of formal firms introduced processes of innovations that were produced by skilled workers who found better ways to produce after some experiments in a trial-and-error approach. These results evidence the importance of skilled workers in firms as a source for innovations in LICs.

This is the same in Tanzania, where formal and informal firms rely heavily on their skilled workers and technicians to develop technological and non-technological innovations. In fact, a significantly larger proportion of informal firms (47 per cent) developed management innovations through experimentation by skilled workers.

In comparison, only 9 per cent of firms (3 per cent informal firms and 16 per cent of formal firms) developed technological innovations with an internal department of R&D. In Tanzania, on average, 25 per cent of the firms developed technological innovations in an R&D department. This is mainly in the formal firms, where 41 per cent of them have technological innovation developed in formal R&D departments.

Overall, innovations in Africa mainly come from technological learning and skilled workers who carry out informal experiments or explorations instead of in formal R&D departments.

4.6.4   Technological Learning through Spillovers versus Formal Licensing

Imitation of innovations and minor adaptations of technologies or products are common practices in Ghana for formal and informal firms. In fact, 70 per cent of formal firms and 51 per cent of informal firms imitated other companies' innovations and did so with minor modifications.

In Tanzania, imitation and adaptation of innovations or products developed by other firms seem to play a less important role for Tanzanian firms than for those in Ghana. The difference lies mainly in the formal firms. About 38 per cent of formal firms and 47 per cent of informal firms imitated other companies' innovations and did so with minor modifications. This is consistent with the finding that more Tanzanian firms report to have R&D departments and 25 per cent of them reported to have innovations created in their R&D units.

In comparison, in both countries, the proportion of firms reporting to have acquired technology originally developed by others by licensing and adaptation or modification is much less. This figure was only 24 per cent in Ghana and 19 per cent in Tanzania. All these findings suggest that in Africa, knowledge spillover, imitation and adaptation are the main mechanisms of innovative knowledge transfer, rather than licensing. This may be partly explained by the constraints in finance faced by the African firms and the difficulties in the pricing of technology in a way that the buyer and the seller both convincingly agree with each other.

In addition to observing and learning along the value chains, for example, from customers and the suppliers in particular, social networks and competitors are also important sources of knowledge spillovers and technological learning. Social networks, which include not only family members but also being a member of associations, also appear to be important domestic sources of innovative ideas. Moreover, the importance of the market is not only seen by customers but also by competitors. Competitors are the fifth most important source of innovation in Ghana. This was confirmed by observing the portfolio of products of a construction business, which decided to include a specific product after a competitor started to sell an identical item (Firm I in Table 4.1).

4.6.5   Management and Technological Innovations

Most of the management innovations in both Ghana and Tanzania are a response to customers' requirements. As Table 4.10 shows, the ratio of firms that introduced management innovations, including new marketing practices, as a response to customers' requirements was 60 per cent for Ghanaian firms and 57 per cent for Tanzanian. In Tanzania, ideas from within the company are the most important knowledge source of management innovation, with 80 per cent of the firms reporting that this is the case, while knowledge spillovers played a less important role. Only 35 per cent of the Tanzanian firms reported that their management innovation originated from something they observed or heard from other companies and imitated it with some modifications. However, in Ghana the picture is different. Around half of the Ghanaian firms (55 per cent) reported that their new management practices were developed inside the company, while 67 per cent of them reported to have sourced their new management practices from knowledge spillovers. Despite these differences, these are the top 3 sources of knowledge for management innovation in these countries.

Interestingly, in Ghana, informal firms rely significantly more on knowledge developed within the firm; while in Tanzania, informal firms imitate others' innovations more often than formal firms in their introduction of management innovations.

Table 4.10 *Sources of management innovation in Ghana and Tanzania (2015, percentages of innovating firms)*

	Management Innovations – Ghana				Management Innovations – Tanzania			
	Total	Informal	Formal	Diff.	Total	Informal	Formal	Diff.
Mainly developed within the enterprise	54.5	67.7	45.1	22.6***	79.8	82.2	78.1	4.0
In response to customers' requirements	60.3	67.7	54.9	12.8*	56.7	63.4	52.3	11.0**
The firm observed or heard of the innovation by other companies and imitated it with some modification	67.3	62.1	71.1	−9.0	35.1	47.0	27.2	19.8***

4.7   Local Sources of External Knowledge and Information

Local information and knowledge are essential components for innovation. Figures 4.9 and 4.10 report the importance of different local sources of information for Ghana and Tanzania, respectively. The sources are grouped into four categories: internal to the firm, membership of networks (clusters or associations), market and institutional resources, and other sources, which include ICTs, conferences and publications. Results are presented for informal and formal firms, and for technological and management innovations.

Overall, as Figure 4.9 summarises, Ghanaian firms most frequently use internal sources such as colleagues in the firm as sources of knowledge. They have also made good use of networks to search external knowledge and innovation, especially for technological innovation in the informal firms. Market sources are important for all types of innovations in both formal and informal firms, scoring averages around 3 in a 0–5 range. Institutional and other sources such as the internet, associations and conferences have not been well used in knowledge searching. Internal and market sources of knowledge are most relevant for technological innovations in formal firms, while informal firms place more value on the knowledge acquired from internal and networks sources.

Knowledge sources for management innovations are almost equally relevant for formal firms, and knowledge from networks of firms is slightly

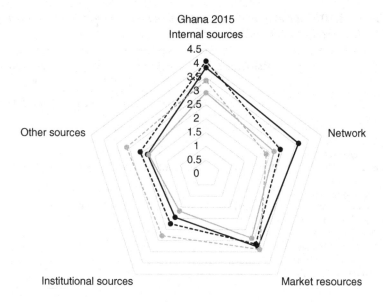

Figure 4.9 Importance of local sources of information for formal (dotted lines) and informal (solid lines) Ghanaian firms in 2015 (1 = insignificant, 5 = crucial, average values).

less relevant. For informal firms, internal, market and network sources of knowledge are equally relevant in management innovations. For management innovations, the informal firms appear to have gained limited benefits from external knowledge searching.

For Tanzanian firms, as shown in Figure 4.10, market sources such as customers, suppliers and competitors appear to be the most important source of information and knowledge. Internal sources such as colleagues rank as the second most important. Different from the case in Ghana, other sources such as the internet and journal articles appear to be an important knowledge source for the formal firms. However, the importance of networks such as being a member of clusters and associations is not valued highly by Tanzanian firms, only scoring between 2 and 3 on average for both technological and management innovations in both

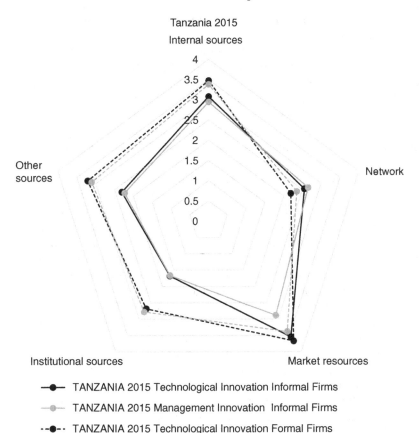

Figure 4.10 Importance of local sources of information for formal (dotted lines) and informal (solid lines) Tanzanian firms in 2015 (1 = insignificant, 5 = crucial, average values).

formal and informal sectors. Similar to the case in Ghana, the informal firms gain limited benefits from external knowledge searching for management innovation. Market sources and ideas internal to the firms are the most important knowledge sources for them.

There are differences between informal and formal firms. Informal firms value more the knowledge from their networks of firms than formal firms. Formal firms highly value market resources, internal sources, other sources and institutional sources of knowledge. Informal firms also highly value market resources for technological innovations, and for management innovations it is also considered relevant but less than for formal firms.

The detailed importance of the sources of knowledge is reported in Table 4.11 for Ghana and Table 4.12 for Tanzania. In Ghana, knowledge sources within the firm are the most important source of information for both formal and informal firms, and for both technological and managerial innovations. Also, clients and customers, competitors or other enterprises in the same sector and other firms within the group are an important source of information for technological and management innovations.

Firms also rely on information on innovations provided by other firms, members of a cluster or an association. Clusters and associations can generate knowledge spillovers, facilitating knowledge diffusion and innovation. The importance of networks is higher for informal firms suggesting that informal sector innovations are based on 'common' knowledge and team work. The relevance of clusters and associations is also higher in management innovations, where knowledge specific to the context, the sector and the markets is highly relevant.

Institutional sources of knowledge, such as universities and public research institutes, together with consultants and private R&D institutes, are more valued by formal firms. This is understandable, as only formal firms have access to these 'formal' institutions. This result holds for technological and management innovations, although for the latter, the relevance is larger. This can be attributed to the orientation of innovations in Ghana, where innovations of product and process are relatively lower than innovations in management and marketing.

Finally, it is important to highlight the role of other sources of information for innovation. Overall, formal firms place more value on these sources of knowledge and they are also more valued for management innovations. Among the sub-group of sources, it is possible to identify general sources (such as radio and internet) and technical sources (such as trade fairs, scientific journals and industry associations). The most relevant general source is the internet. However, formal firms use this source of knowledge significantly more, which can be attributable to the large differences in access to and the ability to use the internet between informal and formal firms. This is relevant, considering the potential which the internet holds to overcome the lack of information in low-income countries and allow users to find specific information at a low cost.

Firms in Tanzania also most value the internal sources of knowledge, particularly within the firm. Information from firms in an economic group is only relevant for formal firms. The second more important group of

Table 4.11 *Importance of local sources of information for formal and informal firms in Ghana (2015) (1 = insignificant, 5 = crucial, average values)*

		Technological Innovations				Management Innovations			
		Total	Informal	Formal	Diff.	Total	Informal	Formal	Diff.
Internal sources	Sources within the firm (colleagues)	4.37	4.18	4.54	−0.36**	4.19	4.54	3.99	0.55***
	Sources within the group (if you have subsidiary)	3.05	3.22	2.89	0.33	3.45	3.58	3.36	0.21
Network	Member of cluster	3.40	3.82	2.88	0.94***	3.63	4.20	3.05	1.15***
	Member of associations	3.30	3.58	3.04	0.54**	3.92	4.17	3.73	0.45*
Market resources	Suppliers of equipment, material, components, software	2.88	3.11	2.71	0.40*	2.63	2.26	2.86	−0.60**
	Clients or customers	3.98	4.02	3.95	0.08	3.77	3.81	3.74	0.07
	Competitors or other enterprises in your sector	2.94	2.97	2.91	0.07	2.87	2.39	3.17	−0.78***
	Consultants, commercial labs or private R&D institutes	2.24	2.02	2.46	−0.44**	2.52	2.21	2.84	−0.64**
Institutional sources	National universities or other higher education inst.	2.06	1.75	2.22	−0.47	2.59	1.94	2.97	−1.02**
Other sources	Government or public research institutes	2.08	1.88	2.30	−0.42*	2.35	2.23	2.48	−0.26
	Radio	1.53	1.24	1.72	−0.48**	2.04	1.63	2.30	−0.67***
	Internet‡	2.64	2.17	2.89	−0.72**	3.16	2.65	3.35	−0.70*
	Conferences, trade fairs, exhibitions	2.49	2.20	2.72	−0.52**	2.86	2.40	3.18	−0.78***
	Scientific journals and trade/technical publications	2.36	2.07	2.64	−0.57**	2.22	1.79	2.55	−0.75***
	Professional and industry associations	2.48	2.39	2.54	−0.14	3.30	3.00	3.43	−0.43

Note: Significance at the 10 per cent, 5 per cent and 1 per cent levels are indicated by one, two and three asterisks respectively. ‡ Information collected only from respondents with an internet access.

Table 4.12 *Importance of local sources of information for formal and informal firms in Tanzania (2015) (1 = insignificant, 5 = crucial, average values)*

		Technological Innovations				Management Innovations			
		Total	Informal	Formal	Diff.	Total	Informal	Formal	Diff.
Internal sources	Sources within the firm (colleagues)	4.48	4.45	4.50	−0.05	4.27	4.21	4.31	−0.10
	Sources within the group (if you have subsidiary)	2.06	1.67	2.34	−0.67***	2.00	1.50	2.32	−0.82***
Network	Member of cluster	2.27	3.20	1.61	1.59***	2.44	3.21	1.89	1.32***
	Member of associations	2.31	1.81	2.63	−0.82***	2.45	2.04	2.73	−0.68***
Market resources	Suppliers of equipment, material, components, software	3.79	3.92	3.71	0.22	2.88	2.78	2.94	−0.17
	Clients or customers	4.19	4.44	4.03	0.40***	3.80	3.76	3.83	−0.07
	Competitors or other enterprises in your sector	3.70	3.83	3.61	0.22	3.16	3.00	3.27	−0.27
	Consultants, commercial labs or private R&D institutes	2.73	1.90	3.28	−1.38***	2.84	1.95	3.40	−1.45***
Institutional sources	National universities or other higher education inst.	2.47	1.72	2.96	−1.23***	2.32	1.69	2.75	−1.06***
Other sources	Government or public research institutes	2.06	1.56	2.39	−0.83***	2.29	1.53	2.78	−1.24***
	Radio	2.37	2.45	2.32	0.13	2.44	2.33	2.52	−0.18
	Internet‡	3.51	2.82	3.96	−1.14***	3.39	2.78	3.82	−1.05***
	Conferences, trade fairs, exhibitions	3.41	3.08	3.62	−0.54***	3.33	3.06	3.52	−0.46**
	Scientific journals and trade/technical publications	2.39	1.46	3.00	−1.54***	2.26	1.49	2.78	−1.30***
	Professional and industry associations	2.53	1.74	3.04	−1.30***	2.32	1.45	2.90	−1.45***

Note: Significance at the 10 per cent, 5 per cent and 1 per cent levels are indicated by one, two and three asterisks respectively. ‡ Information collected only from respondents with internet access

knowledge sources is suppliers, clients and competitors; this highlights the importance of knowledge transfer within the market and the value chain that also occurs in LICs.

The internet, conferences, trade fairs and exhibitions are the third group of most valued sources of knowledge for innovations. In the case of Tanzania, these sources of knowledge are relatively more relevant for technological innovations. Scientific journals and industry associations are relevant sources of knowledge mainly for formal firms, and they are also valued almost equally for technological and management innovations. Finally, institutional sources (universities and public R&D institutes) and private consultants and R&D institutions are highly relevant for formal firms, but not for informal firms. These facts are in line with the information presented in the previous chapter, since informal firms engage less in technological innovations compared to formal firms.

4.9   Synthesis with Qualitative Evidence

Integrating the above findings with qualitative evidence leads us to identify two main categories of innovations: innovations that address cost savings and innovations aimed at increasing market opportunities. In the first category, we found several innovations aimed at improving the efficiency of the production system of firms, from the acquisition of new machinery to different ways of organizing the labour, and innovation that reduces the waste from production. In the second category, many firms introduced new products or implemented new marketing strategies. Notably, some of the firms surveyed seem to work at the intersections of the two categories. In some cases, the transformation of the waste from a production became a new line of products, giving value to something apparently valueless. For instance, Firm H uses waste fabric from cutting of the custom-designed clothes to create kids' wear. The production of kids' wear does not require large pieces of fabric and the design itself may include patchwork. In other cases, they developed new products to keep the labour force employed and the machines active all year round. A food-processing firm (Firm C) has introduced peanut butter and roasted peanuts to fill the production gap when peppers are not in season. This strategy does not only allow firms to enter new markets but also keeps the staff employed throughout the year.

Regardless of industries, a pattern emerged on the drivers of innovation for formal and informal firms. Innovation for formal firms is primarily for market expansion and ultimately increases the profits, while informal firms seem to innovate to survive with the aspiration of consolidating the business and eventually moving to a formal status. In any case, the innovation strategy is to adopt the appropriate technology – economically, socially and technically appropriate. This is predominant in the textile sector, although not exclusive to it. For example, Firm E had obtained a range of specialized machines with conversion kits that enable them to be used for different activities. Another firm had obtained some specialized machines that they were not previously using to enhance and improve efficiency and productivity (Firm H). Instead, Firm F had acquired new machinery to enhance the finishing and add value to the products. In the food sector, to expand the range of products or improve their current production, they introduced new technology. In several cases, firms constantly changed their recipes to improve not only the taste but also the production. For example, Firm A successfully substituted gum Arabic, which was previously imported from unstable countries, with acacia, which is supplied locally. They used the same firm to import filter papers for clarifying cocoa butter but when they found a local cloth to do the job, they fixed it to the machines, which was more efficient and enhanced the product. Some firms have made changes in the processes of production to ensure health and safety of their workers. For example, Firm C recently switched from coal pots to industrial gas burners for safety reasons and to improve efficiency in production.

Some innovations are simply adoptions of technologies or machinery, whereas in some cases the innovation requires modification to meet the adopter's needs. This is more common when innovations are developed abroad and are not designed to work in different contexts. For example, Firm F bought a sewing machine directly from China and they had to modify the engine for it to work with different electric voltage and better manage the blackouts that are frequent in Ghana. In some cases, the modifications can be so radical as to change the original purpose of a device and transform it to have a different purpose. For example, Firm B built a pasteuriser by modifying a metal tank which originally was a water heater and hence had a different purpose. Those kinds of innovations are born from the ingenuity of people and are kindled by the resource constraints that firms face in the context of developing countries. An interesting innovative practice observed was the usage of by-products to create new products. This was predominant in the informal sector and was aimed at optimizing production and reducing waste. For instance, Firm H uses waste fabric from cutting of custom-designed cloths to create kids' wear. Similarly, in the food sector, Firm D dries the unsold mushrooms and produces a line of dry mushroom powder (the same firm recycled the compost used for growing mushroom to fertilize gardens).

The innovations found are partly frugal innovations, and partly not, serving the relatively high end of the market. They are partly inclusive innovations that serve BOP, but there are also aims for structural change, though this is very limited. Most of those innovations are both created for the BOP and take place at the BOP. This allows firms to address the affordability constraints and the affordability issues of innovation in the context of LICs. Innovations tend to be cost-cutting and cost-efficient and are created to meet the diverse demands of consumers and customers in the market. There are also limited innovations in the high-tech sector, which do not necessarily aim at frugal innovation cost-cutting and resemble the inclusive innovation notion.

In summary, evidence from this chapter suggests that the innovation strategy implemented to overcome the constraints typical of LICs can be grouped into two categories:

- *Adopt and develop learning-based innovation:* Results show that most of the innovations happening in Ghana and Tanzania are learning based, without the traditional R&D activities that we normally observe in firms in industrialized countries. The firm-level survey indicates that the majority of these innovations are new to the firms, with a small proportion of the innovations being new to the country. A minority of innovations are thought to be new to the world. Imitation of other firms, with or without changes, is a way to become innovative. However, in some cases the adoption of innovation requires modification to meet the adopters' needs.

- *Emphasis on non-cost-intensive non-technology innovation:* Findings suggest that significant constraints in resources have pushed firms to employ a strategy of adopting financial resource-saving types of innovations, including non-technological innovation in management and marketing practices. Such type of innovation does not require heavy investment in laboratory-based research and development. In fact, in many cases it requires entrepreneurship, determination and leadership, which can be met by entrepreneurs' efforts.

4.10   Conclusions

This chapter analyses the scope and types of innovation reported in the surveys in Ghana and Tanzania. The chapter integrates in-depth qualitative research with a large-scale innovation survey to provide unprecedented and unique insights into innovation strategies in both countries. Our results show that innovation occurs just about anywhere in Ghana and Tanzania. Most research on innovation looks at the number of patents registered or R&D expenditure to see if innovation has occurred, but in LICs, such measures would not capture the fertile innovation scene currently under the radar. Entrepreneurial ingenuity leads to remodelling of old car-wheels into cooking-stoves, developing the capability to preserve fresh mushrooms with the help of local universities, designing fashions from local textiles, or making delicious food products from the most humble ingredients. These are just a few examples and they are more than just a local curiosity but new ways to turn a profit or, for some firms, to survive.

Using the *Oslo Manual* definition of innovation, which focuses on firms' self-assessment of the introduction of a new or significantly improved product (good or services) or process, a new marketing method, or new management practices, evidence from the three national surveys in Ghana and Tanzania also reveals that innovation occurs among a wide range of sectors, not only in the formal firms but also in the informal firms. These firms engage not only in technological product and process innovations but also engage actively, and to even greater extent, in non-technological marketing and management innovations. Our results also show that firms often engage in more than one type of innovation, which is likely to enable them to benefit from the synergy effects of the complementary innovations. In Tanzania, for instance, we found that more than half of the firms reported that they had implemented all the four types of innovation simultaneously. This is, again, not only in the formal sector, but also in the informal sector. Nearly all of the innovations are incremental, confirming the finding that innovations in Africa are mainly incremental.

The results from this study proved that the informal sector in Africa is dynamic and creative, despite the constraints firms in the informal sector face. The results suggest that although innovation was reported in every sector and in both the formal and informal firms, firms in Ghana and Tanzania still face substantial constraints in the innovation process. Firms are largely unsupported. In order to overcome the constraints typical of LICs, the innovation strategies that the African firms on the ground tend to favour are the development of learning-based innovations, with a focus on low-cost, non-technology innovations. The evidence also suggests that in Africa, knowledge spillover, imitation and adaptation are the main mechanisms of innovative knowledge transfer rather than licensing. This may be partly explained by the constraints in finance faced by the African firms and the difficulties in the pricing of technology in a way that both the buyer and the seller convincingly agree with each other.

5 Open Innovation as a Response to Constraints and Risks

The Role of Collaboration, Universities, Clusters and Value Chains

5.1 Introduction

'Learning by interacting' is a key source of knowledge and capability development at the firm level (Malerba, 1992). Specifically, interactions between firms and other agents have been shown in the empirical literature to not only generate and shape knowledge and the productive trajectories of firms (Malerba, 1992) but have also been found to be highly relevant for the innovation process (Chesbrough, 2003; Fu, 2012; Laursen and Salter, 2006; Katila, 2002; among others).

In developing countries where market failures such as information asymmetry exist, various learning-by-interacting strategies – collaboration, competition and networks, and so on – may serve as conduits through which both knowledge for innovation and information about markets flow. While interactions between firms, government institutions, research agencies and other actors are weak in developing countries (Kraemer-Mbula and Wamae, 2010; Oyelaran-Oyeyinka and Lall, 2006), strong interaction between firms, for instance, in clusters and in regional value chains, may help circumvent some constraints firms encounter in the innovation process. In other words, interactions are fundamental for 'free' and 'open' innovations. The importance of innovation in LICs is evident, given the relevance of innovation for technological upgrading and industrial diversification. However, questions related to how open innovation strategies affect the innovation performance of firms in LICs have received little attention. Few studies exist that examine open innovation strategies in LICs(Chen et al., 2011; Fu, 2012; Fu and Li, 2016). However, the literature has mainly focused on the study of open innovation in industrialized economies. Even less studied is the process of open innovation as a driver for innovation in the context of LICs (Karo and Kattel, 2011).

This chapter aims to investigate the role of openness in innovation performance of Ghanaian and Tanzanian firms. In particular, it focuses on the role of collaboration with other partners in the innovation system, the role of university–industry linkage and clusters, as well as the innovation and upgrading effect of the participation of regional and global production networks in promoting innovation capabilities and industrial upgrading and diversification of African firms. In the context of LICs, constraints to innovation are greater than in other contexts and therefore openness might be essential to the innovation process. For resource-rich or agriculture-based economies in Africa, these issues are crucial for their future development.

The rest of this chapter is organized as follows. Section 5.2 reviews the literature on open innovation in LICs. Section 5.3 describes formal collaborations that African firms had with a range of different agents. Section 5.4 analyses and discusses three main sources of external knowledge search: the role of universities and how firms collaborate (or do not) with them; the benefits of clusters and regional value chains; and the importance of regional product networks to SMEs' innovation. Section 5.5 concludes the chapter.

5.2   Open Innovation in LICs: Literature Review and Theoretical Framework

5.2.1   Open Innovation: The Concept and the Modes

The innovation process in a firm articulates different sub-processes which can be conducted inside the firm (intramural) or in collaboration with external partners (extramural). Knowledge and ideas to develop innovation processes can also come from internal and external sources (Cohen and Levinthal, 1989; Legros and Galia, 2011). Therefore, open innovation is 'a paradigm that assumes that firms can and should use external ideas as well as internal ideas, and internal and external paths to market, as the firms look to advance their technology' (Chesbrough, 2003). More recently, it is defined as 'a distributed innovation process based on purposively managed knowledge flows across organizational boundaries, using pecuniary and non-pecuniary mechanisms in line with the organization's business model' (Chesbrough and Bogers, 2014). Open innovation in practice took place decades ago when firms no longer focused only on internal R&D laboratories for innovation, and instead searched for or sourced external ideas, talents or resources for innovation. These may include formal or informal collaborations between the firm and various partners and collection of information from external sources.

The openness of a firm has been related to a firm's innovation, since linkages with external institutions increase a firm's knowledge base and innovation capacities (Freeman and Soete, 1997; Goes and Park, 1997; Hoffman et al., 1998; Powell et al., 1996; Tsai, 2001). External sources of information also help to expand the knowledge base and reduce the costs of developing solutions for the development of a new product (Fu, 2012; Laursen and Salter, 2006). The information search strategy of the firm impacts its innovation performance. Laursen and Salter (2006) found that both search strategies are positively related to innovation outcomes in UK firms, but for radical innovations new to the world, the depth of information from external sources was more crucial. Moreover, collaborations with different partners, particularly with clients, suppliers and even competitors, could lower the costs of placing a new product successfully into the market (Darby et al., 2003; Fu and Li, 2016).

5.2.2   Openness as a Response to Constraints to Innovation in LICs

Innovation in the context of LICs is very different from that in the developed countries. That is, innovations in LICs tend to be incremental and often aimed at solving specific societal problems (Kraemer-Mbula and Wamae, 2010). As a result, there are particular external and internal barriers to innovation in firms in LICs (Zanello et al., 2015). Although literature on the diffusion of innovations in developing countries is a recent field of study (Altenburg, 2009), evidence is growing on the main constraints that hamper the decisions and limit the choices of firms to innovate. Repeatedly, we find in the literature references to factors internal and external to the firm that can stand in the way of innovation and affect the competitive strategy of a firm, both in developed as well as developing countries. Literature of firms in middle-income countries focuses mainly on the lack of financial resources (cost barriers), technical knowledge and information (knowledge barriers), and management (management barriers) (Fu et al., 2014). However, those constraints are thought to have a stronger impact in LICs, where the financial and knowledge gap is greater. Limited financial resources of people living in developing countries narrow down the affordability of innovation, and the lack of technical knowledge may prevent some adoption of innovations that are too complicated or require technical adaptation.

The existing literature also suggests that factors outside the firms may prevent mechanisms of innovation creation and diffusion (Zanello et al., 2015). These include political factors, such as a weak political system and widespread corruption across society; economic characteristics, such as openness of an economy and level of economic development or inadequate infrastructure; institutional factors, such as the interaction between private (firms) and public sector (like research institutes and universities); and cultural and linguistic distances. Many of those barriers are country-specific and shape the economic environments in which all the firms work. Other barriers, such as market and infrastructure barriers, affect specific firms or sectors instead. Therefore, firms in every country have internal and external barriers to innovation (Fu et al., 2014), but firms in LICs face different, more restrictive, conditions to pursue innovation. Consequently, open innovation can be a response and strategy of firms in LICs to overcome constraints to innovation. We briefly discuss in the following sections some barriers to innovation in LICs.

Cost barriers: Technical innovations can be expensive, and firms cannot afford to implement them. In some instances, the financial and credit constraints could be obstacles more difficult to overcome than the lack of skill to adopt and use a new technology, such as the case of paper manufacturing firms in Northern Vietnam (Kimura, 2011) or manufacturing firms in Colombia (Kugler, 2006), India (Vishwasrao and Bosshardt, 2001) and China (Fu et al., 2014). In some cases, subsidies and grants could become a concrete support for innovation, even in advanced economies such as the United States (Darby et al., 2004) and emerging economies and LICs (Franco et al., 2011). Also, larger and older firms tend to have more capital to finance innovation (Chen et al., 2011; Fu et al., 2014; Robson et al., 2009). Open innovation strategies can reduce the cost of innovation. Some of the reasons why firms implement open innovation strategies are to gain access to external resources, to reduce uncertainties, to diversify risks and to learn from others (Chesbrough, 2003; Fu, 2012; Keupp and Gassmann, 2009).

Knowledge and skills barriers: Knowledge is critical in order to master a specific technology or implement a marketing strategy or managerial change. However, knowledge alone is not enough and must be supported by information (and vice versa). Bell and Albu (1999) argued that the diffusion of innovation in LICs should be assisted with systems of knowledge accumulation, rather than just production systems. They highlighted the critical role of external sources of knowledge, with a focus on cluster-learning dynamics. Back in 1992, Bagachwa studied the performance of small- and large-scale grain milling techniques in Tanzania to explain why some firms select inappropriate techniques and products. Besides the lack of financial capital, he found that an important factor was the lack of information on the appropriate technology. Similarly, studies have shown how the lack of comprehensive information and experience in larger-scale manufacturing seemed to be the largest impediment to improving Ghana's industrial capacity (McDade and Malecki, 1997) and in the manufacturing sector in India (Kumar and Saqib, 1996). Chinese manufacturing firms that face higher levels of knowledge and skill constraints to innovation have greater openness for innovation activities (Fu et al., 2014). Although the recent diffusion of ICTs (mobile phones and internet connections) in most areas of developing countries provides easier means to gather information, the lack of technical information is likely to be an important factor in hampering the diffusion and adoption of innovation.

Moreover, managerial skills have received increased attention as a factor explaining differences in firms' performance in LICs (Bruhn et al., 2010). Many empirical studies have found positive correlation between the level of education of managers and the innovation abilities of the firm, both in a multi-country (Wang and Wong, 2012) and single-country setting, such as Ghana (Robson et al., 2009), Tanzania (Hall et al., 2012), Uganda (Oyelaran-Oyeyinka and Lal, 2006) and Nigeria (Abereijo et al., 2007). The scarcity of local knowledge can lead managers to seek and value more external sources of knowledge, increasing the openness of a firm (Menon and Pfeffer, 2003). This fact is highly relevant in the context of LICs, given that the sources of local knowledge are far from the technological frontier. Also, it is possible that when a firm has more managerial rigidities which hinder innovation within the firm, the firm will search for external sources of innovation and will increase its openness (Fu, 2012).

Market barriers: The market structures in which a firm operates influence the innovation activities. Too little competition may not provide incentive for leader firms to innovate, given their consolidated dominant position. From a sample of 291 Indian manufacturing firms, Kumar and Saqib (1996) showed that the absence of competitive pressure in the market reduces the likelihood that firms would undertake R&D activities. At the same time, innovation capabilities can also be nurtured by market competition, pushing firms to innovate to stay in the market (Blalock and Gertler, 2008). Fu et al. (2014) find that firms' openness is positively affected by market constraints to innovate in the case of China.

In sum, through opening up the innovation process via collaboration and external knowledge search, firms in LICs may be able to overcome the cost, knowledge and market barriers that they face.

5.3   Collaboration and Innovation in Ghana and Tanzania

The innovation process is complex and expensive, and it comes with high risks. While innovations are usually done in collaborations with other firms and organizations, in Ghana, only a minority of firms report formal collaborations for innovation. Only 18 per cent of innovative firms in the sample (seventy-five firms) formally collaborate with others, with forty informal collaborative firms and thirty-five formal collaborative firms. On the contrary, in Tanzania 62 per cent of innovative firms in the sample (162 firms) collaborate formally in innovation activities. These suggest that sampled Ghanaian firms are less collaborative than Tanzanian firms. However, compared to the situation in 2010–2012 when only 41 Ghanaian firms reported formal collaboration, this is a significant increase by 83%.

Firms do not operate in isolation – they partner with other actors. Partners include other enterprises within the enterprise sub-sector, suppliers (e.g. equipment, materials, components or software), clients or customers, competitors or other enterprises working in the firm's sector, consultants or private R&D institutes, universities and government or public research institutes (e.g. research councils), ICT providers and other service companies. For each collaboration established, I also captured the importance of this cooperation in a 5-point Likert-scale (1 = less important and 5 = highly important collaboration). Table 5.1 presents the results for Ghana, and Table 5.2 presents the results for Tanzania.

From Table 5.1, one sees that most of the sampled Ghanaian firms collaborate with clients or customers, or with suppliers, identifying the importance of collaborations within the value chain for innovation. Informal firms seem to collaborate equally with clients and suppliers, while formal firms prefer collaborations with clients. Collaborations with clients, in particular, highlight the importance of user innovation in Ghana. The third most common partners are other enterprises within the group for informal firms and competitors for formal firms. Horizontal linkages are more common between formal firms.

Surprisingly, the importance of universities, the government or public research institutes is ranked only the 6th most important partner after all the other major players, for example, suppliers, customers, other firms in the company group, consulting companies and IT providers. They rank only ahead of the financial and marketing firms and competitors. This finding corroborates McCormick and Atieno (2002) and Oyelaran-Oyeyinka and Lal (2006), suggesting that weak linkages exist between formal institutions and firms in both countries' innovation systems. Informal firms' collaboration with ICT providers is almost non-existent. Lastly, only seven informal and eight formal firms partnered with consultants or private R&D institutes on innovation activities.

The different needs and capabilities of formal and informal firms are also reflected in the rankings of the most valuable types of co-operation for the two types of firms (Table 5.1). Informal firms most value suppliers, other

Table 5.1 *Formal collaborations in Ghanaian firms, by types of partners (2012–2014, number of firms)*

	All collaborative firms (75)		Informal (40)		Formal (35)	
	Total	Importance	Total	Importance	Total	Importance
Other enterprises within the enterprise sub-sector	35	4.17	25	4.44	10	3.50
Suppliers of equipment, materials, components	50	4.34	32	4.63	18	3.83
Clients or customers	61	4.25	33	4.39	28	4.07
Competitors or other enterprises in the firm's sector	23	3.48	5	3.60	18	3.44
Consultants, commercial labs or private R&D institutes	15	4.07	7	4.00	8	4.13
Universities, government or public research institutes	24	3.92	9	3.89	15	3.93
ICT and internet services providers	15	4.07	1	4.00	14	4.07
Other service enterprises e.g. financial, marketing firms	9	3.56	1	5.00	8	3.38

firms in the sub-sector and clients; formal firms favour consultants and private R&D institutes, followed by clients, ICT providers and suppliers. These findings suggest that there exists some level of interaction between actors in Ghana's innovation system. However, informal firms collaborate with limited number of actors as compared to formal firms.

Tanzania presents a somewhat different scenario. Sampled firms in Tanzania are much more open to innovation than Ghanaian firms. There are a higher number of sampled firms that collaborate for innovation than in Ghana. Most of these firms collaborate with clients or customers and with suppliers along the product value chain, which is observed in both informal and formal firms. Informal firms collaborate significantly less with consultants, universities and financial and marketing firms. However, for the few firms that do engage in collaboration, the importance of these external partners is regarded as more significant than with the formal firms. The same is the case in Ghana, where firms also ranked universities as the 6th most important partner, lagging behind all the other major types of potential collaborators.

Table 5.2 *Formal collaborations in Tanzanian firms, by types of partners (2012–2014, number of firms)*

	All collaborative firms (162)		Informal (48)		Formal (114)	
	Total	Importance	Total	Importance	Total	Importance
Other enterprises within the enterprise sub-sector	72	4.24	14	4.71	58	4.12
Suppliers of equipment, materials, components	141	4.48	41	4.51	100	4.47
Clients or customers	147	4.17	42	4.36	105	4.10
Competitors or other enterprises in the firm's sector	69	3.83	25	3.96	44	3.75
Consultants, commercial labs or private R&D institutes	90	4.20	14	4.50	76	4.14
Universities, government or public research institutes	82	4.09	5	4.60	77	4.05
ICT and internet services providers	86	4.16	12	3.50	74	4.27
Other service enterprises e.g. financial, marketing firms	87	3.90	25	4.36	62	3.71

Research partners, such as consultants, private R&D institutions, universities or public research institutions, are frequent collaborators of formal firms, but they do not interact much with informal firms. This may be because these are formal institutions providing formal services that are often not accessible to and, in some cases, 'irrelevant' for informal firms. ICT partners are also usual collaborators of formal Tanzanian firms. The contrary occurs with competitors, where informal firms collaborate more with them than formal firms. In fact, competitors are the third most common collaborator for informal firms, but they are the last for formal firms. Finally, other service companies are also a common collaborator for informal firms but are less relevant for formal firms.

Although the proportion of collaborators is less in the informal than in the formal firms, informal firms which engage with collaboration give more value to these collaborations than the formal firms do. Collaborations with other companies in the same sub-sector, with the universities and public research institutions, and consultants and private R&D institutes all scored high for informal Tanzanian firms in terms of innovation collaboration.

Suppliers are regarded as important collaborators in both the formal and informal firms. ICT providers, consultants and private R&D institutes also received high importance scores from the formal firms in Tanzania.

With respect to the importance of collaborations within the value chain and horizontal collaborations, the patterns observed are similar to Ghana on average. The most important collaborations are suppliers and other companies within the firms' sub-sector. In general, informal firms value more collaborations with any partner than formal firms. Overall, sampled Tanzanian firms appear to be more open to collaborations than firms in Ghana. Innovation collaboration is more widely adopted in Tanzania than in Ghana. This could be due to the fact that Tanzanian firms are more constrained in terms of resources (financial and human capital), and as a result, collaborate more to overcome some of these obstacles.

5.4   External Knowledge Search

Open innovation through external knowledge search often serves an important role in knowledge sourcing, especially for firms in developing countries. Compared to other forms of open innovation, such as collaboration or licensing, external knowledge search is financially less costly. A study examining firms' external knowledge search by Fu, Zanello and Contreras (2018) using the DILIC 2013 data finds that firms implemented open innovation to overcome the cost, skills and market barriers to innovation in the context of LICs. However, infrastructure barriers impede innovation and openness cannot overcome them. Moreover, they found that the degree of a firm's openness is positively associated with innovation. Further, the research finds that local knowledge is more relevant for innovation outcomes than foreign knowledge. This result emphasizes that the knowledge gap between LICs and the technological frontier is large; thus local knowledge is more appropriate to solve firms' problems in LICs. In the following sub-sections, we discuss three main sources of external knowledge search: university-industry linkage, clusters and regional value chains, and regional product networks, based on data collected in the DILIC 2013 surveys.

5.4.1   University–Industry Linkage and Innovation
in Ghana and Tanzania

Universities are an important player in national and regional innovation systems. The literature on national innovation systems has highlighted the role of universities in the innovation systems, not only in training and education, but also as an active player in knowledge creation and transfer (Fu and Yang, 2009; Nelson, 1986; OECD, 2008; Porter and Stern,

1999). Universities are also crucial players in the regional innovation systems and affect regional innovation capacities to a great extent (Braczyk et al., 1998; Cooke, 2001). Universities may contribute to an economy in a multifaceted manner through education, knowledge creation in the form of scholarly publications and patents, problem-solving activities and public space provision (Hughes, 2010; Kitson et al., 2009). They disseminate knowledge to the real economy by producing quality students and by interacting with firms through a number of channels such as consulting, licensing and co-operative research programmes (Eom and Lee, 2010). In the era of the knowledge economy, the importance of universities in contributing to economic growth has become an increasing focus of research (Etzkowitz and Leydesdorff, 2000; Sainsbury, 2007). Fast-paced global competition and technological change also link firms to universities not only through the discovery of knowledge but also by aiding industrialization (Etzkowitz and Leydesdorff, 1997; Hwang et al., 2003).

In developing countries, universities play a dual role in innovation. Researching into university and industry linkage in China in 2005–2008, Fu and Li (2016) find that collaborations with domestic universities have played a significant role in the promotion of the diffusion of advanced technology and the creation of innovation outcomes that are new to the country or firm in China. In contrast to the traditional view that collaboration with universities will lead to greater novel innovation, the contribution of domestic universities to the creation of groundbreaking innovations is limited in China at the early, catching-up stage of industrialization. In Ghana, evidence from the survey suggests that fifty firms (out of a total of 495 firms) reported that they have actively collaborated with universities or other higher education institutions in developing and adopting innovations in the past, including and beyond the 2012–2014 sampling period. Most of the collaboration was established proactively by the university, which is a significant change in comparison to the case in 2010–2012, when there was no collaboration initiated by a university. This is probably a result of the introduction of the government programme encouraging university–industry collaboration (UIC) in Ghana, following the publication of DILIC 2013 survey research results, and the increase of awareness of the importance of university–industry linkage in the country.

Personal networks remain an important cause of collaboration between firms and universities in Ghana. It accounted for 74 per cent of UIC in 2013, and still accounted for 44 per cent of the UIC in 2015. This suggests that a personal network and some trust between a staff member in a firm and an academic or researcher is an effective cause that leads to a UIC. One-third of the collaborations in 2015 in Ghana were initiated due to governmental initiative, showing a slight increase from 26 per cent in 2013.

In Tanzania, ninety-eight firms (out of a total of 274 firms) collaborated with universities and other higher education institutions for innovation in the past, including and beyond the 2013–2015 sampling period. Sixty-two per cent of collaborations were established upon personal connections; 35 per cent of the UICs were initiated proactively by the universities. This proportion is lower than that in Ghana, in 2015. But this is still a commendable outcome, suggesting universities are actively reaching out for collaborations with industry. As in Ghana, a third of the cases of collaborations between firms and universities in Tanzania are promoted by governmental initiatives.

Looking at the main reasons that firms provide for not collaborating with universities in Ghana and Tanzania, a large proportion of sampled firms in Ghana – 68 per cent in 2013 and 66 per cent in 2015 – mentioned the lack of connections. A total of 34 per cent of firms simply do not collaborate with universities, a significant reduction from 2013. Finally, about 22 per cent of firms reported that the universities 'are not interested' in having such collaboration, reflecting the lack of incentives for academics in the universities in knowledge transfer. Nonetheless, there are around 41 per cent of firms (185) that currently do not collaborate with universities but indicate that they have the intention of doing so, in the future.

Tanzanian firms do not collaborate with universities mainly because they do not identify a necessity for doing so or because they do not have the connections with universities to start such collaborations. About 30 per cent of firms reported that the universities 'are not interested' in collaborating. However, another 30 per cent of the firms that are not collaborating with universities are willing to start collaboration in the future.

In summary, the evidence from the Ghana and Tanzania surveys suggests that sampled Tanzanian firms are more open to collaborative innovation than sampled Ghanaian firms. Partners in the supply chain and in the same industry have been the main partners of innovative collaboration. Universities have not played an important role in either country, as suggested by the literature and when compared to other partners and in other countries. The situation in Ghana saw a significant improvement in 2015, especially in terms of more active outreach and participation by the universities in the UIC formation. In Tanzania, personal connection is the main cause of a UIC. In both countries, 'we are not connected' has been a major obstacle that hindered the development of a strong university–industry linkage in the national innovation system. These findings further highlight the perception that universities in developing countries are islands of knowledge that have limited interaction with the broader society. They point to an area of policy intervention required to build more platforms or bridges to link the two sectors (universities and industry) and match demand in the industry with the supply of skills from the universities.

5.4.2   Cluster Networks, Regional Value Chains and Innovation in SMEs and for Diversification

Clusters can be defined as a geographic concentration of interconnected businesses and suppliers that encompass an array of linked industries and other entities important to competition. Clusters can be characterized as being networks of production of strongly interdependent firms (including specialized suppliers), knowledge-producing agents (universities, research institutes, engineering companies), bridging institutions (brokers, consultants) and customers, linked to each other in a value-adding production chain (OECD, 1999). They are regarded as the 'reduced-scale innovation system' (den Hertog, Bergman and Charles, 2001).

Industrial clusters have long been recognized as important engines of economic growth through fostering enterprises' growth and boosting regional development (Markusen, 1996). Firms in clusters benefit from stronger knowledge transfers and spillovers from other firms in the cluster due to geographic proximity, supply chain linkages as well as economic considerations of the role of suppliers and customers in shaping innovations (Lundvall, 1998), or through social constructivist and actor-network accounts (Latour, 1996).

In LICs, clusters are often made up of small and informal firms that together can have a greater market power. Firms in the clusters may belong to different networks which bring in a diversity of knowledge and marketing networks, and they also benefit from being a member of the network and other externalities that the network may generate. In Ghana, more than half of the firms in the sample were part of a cluster in 2015 (54 per cent), and the percentage of informal firm members of clusters rose to 69 per cent (see Table 5.3). Differences between formal and informal firms are significant. Formal firms tend to be located in export processing zones and participate in vertical chains of production about twice as much as informal firms. The opposite is true with respect to participation in clusters for small firms.

The situation in Tanzania is similar. Table 5.4 shows that most of the sampled firms in Tanzania are part of a cluster of small firms

Table 5.3 *Participation in networks of firms in Ghana (2015, percentages of firms)*

	All	Informal	Formal	Difference
Firms located in a cluster consisting of small firms producing similar products	54.03	69.28	32.02	37.26***
Firms part of a vertical production chain consisting of SMEs	8.06	5.80	11.33	−5.53**
Firms located in an export processing zone or industrial park	11.69	8.53	16.26	−7.72***

Note: Multiple answers allowed. Significance at the 10 per cent, 5 per cent and 1 per cent levels are indicated by one, two and three asterisks respectively.

Table 5.4 *Participation in networks of firms in Tanzania (2015, percentages of firms)*

	All	Informal	Formal	Difference
Firms located in a cluster consisting of small firms producing similar products	46.18	70.43	28.75	41.68***
Firms part of a vertical production chain consisting of SMEs	23.27	39.13	11.88	27.26***
Firms located in an export processing zone or industrial park	17.45	6.09	25.63	−19.54***

Note: Multiple answers allowed. Significance at the 10 per cent, 5 per cent and 1 per cent levels are indicated by one, two and three asterisks respectively.

(46 per cent), with a higher proportion of informal firms (70 per cent) belonging to a cluster. Firms are part of a vertical production chain at a higher proportion than in Ghana (23 per cent in Tanzania and 8 per cent in Ghana). Informal firms are usually part of a cluster or a vertical production chain of SMEs more often than formal firms. Formal firms tend to locate in an export processing zone.

Comparing Ghana and Tanzania, the proportions of firms located in clusters are similar among both the formal and informal firms, with the proportion significantly higher in the informal than in the formal sector. In both countries, about 70 per cent of the sampled informal firms are located in a cluster, while this proportion is 30 per cent for the formal firms. However, the participation in vertical production chains (i.e. value chains) is significantly different in these two countries. In Tanzania, it appears that a significantly higher proportion of firms are part of a vertical production network (VPN) consisting of SMEs than the situation in Ghana – 23 per cent in Tanzania and 8 per cent in Ghana. This is mainly driven by a high participation ratio of the informal firms in VPNs in Tanzania. In the formal sector, the proportion of firms participating in vertical VPNs is similar in these two countries.

Clusters can provide different benefits to their members. Table 5.5 reports the benefits that firms receive from being a member of a cluster and provides a breakdown between formal and informal firms. Overall, the findings suggest that clusters as institutions provide greater support and assistance to informal rather than formal firms. The vast majority of the informal firms reported that clusters facilitate the exchange of relevant production and technology information and a greater collaboration on pricing. This may be due to the fact that informal firms face a higher number of constraints than their formal counterparts. Work- and resource-sharing are also important benefits for cluster members. One third of formal and informal members explicitly reported that clusters are environments that facilitate the diffusion and creation of innovations. Informal firms seem to have significantly greater benefits in collaborating on pricing and work-sharing, compared to formal firms. Markets are often fragmented in developing countries, and clusters may be enabling informal enterprises to easily access and share information about products and prices leading to lower transaction costs.

Table 5.5 *Benefits of being a member of a cluster in Ghana (percentages of members of cluster)*

	All	Informal	Formal	Difference
Easier to exchange or get relevant production and technology information	66.9	68.3	60.0	8.3
We can divide the labour	24.5	26.6	14.5	12.1
It provides a pool for resources	48.1	47.9	49.1	−1.2
Easier to collaborate in innovation	36.3	36.3	36.4	−0.1
Easier to collaborate in pricing	65.0	68.0	50.9	17.0*
Availability of specialist service and equipment providers	22.6	22.4	23.6	−1.2
Joint programmes to raise skills and enhance efficiency	38.9	39.0	38.2	−0.8
Work-sharing	51.0	53.7	38.2	15.5*

Note: *, ** and *** denotes statistical significance at the 10 per cent, 5 per cent and 1 per cent levels, respectively.

Qualitative evidence from field interviews also suggests that members of clusters are closely proximate with each other, with competitors, and suppliers. Labour movement within the clusters made these a very important environment of innovation diffusion. This is very important in LICs, where most of the firms are small or even micro firms. Being a member of a cluster made the diffusion of innovation much quicker. The contacts and relationships between members of the clusters allowed Firm G to sub-contract some work and borrow specific machinery for some others. This is consistent with the evidence of industrial clusters in Ghana (McDade and Malecki, 1997) and Tanzania (Murphy, 2007), in which the clusters do not seem to directly involve the creation of new products or processes. Instead, Firm H was involved in a participatory process in which members of the cluster shared the skills and expertise to produce and market a part of a garment. In this case, the dynamics among the members of the cluster and the shared risk resembled the functioning of a cooperative.[1]

5.4.3   Regional Production Network

The past three decades have witnessed a significant transition in production organization, which has become increasingly segmented and fragmented. The slicing up of value chains has also created opportunities for small manufacturing firms that specialize in producing a particular component or spare part or carrying out a specific task. While lead firms in global value chains (GVCs) are identified to exhibit monopoly behaviours by restricting upgrades, particularly by supply firms (Kaplinsky, 2018), firms that have successfully entered into and upgraded in GVCs have benefited through access to greater international markets and knowledge transfer, and spillovers from suppliers or customers or the coordinating MNEs through standards and quality requirements. Organising production through a chain or network of specialised firms may also offer other benefits to the participating firms and the industry as a whole. Exclusion from GVCs, therefore, could isolate firms in LIC countries to produce lower technological requirements, reducing firms' productivity and growth.

The DILIC survey has probed the causes of participation in a production network, the types of VPNs present, and the benefits of such engagement to African firms. It finds interesting benefits of forming and engaging in VPNs for Africa, not only for individual firms but also for the African industries as a whole, for upgrading and diversification,

---

[1] Characteristics of firms G and H are described in Table 4.1.

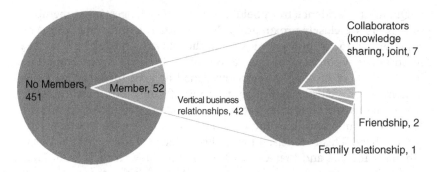

Figure 5.1 Number of firms in Ghana that are members of a vertical production network consisting of SMEs and origin of the network

especially in terms of regional value chains. In the case of Ghana, fifty-two out of a total of 503 firms are part of a VPN consisting of SMEs. This proportion is generally low, but it is higher for formal firms than for informal firms. While clusters are often established based on friendship relationships between members, vertical production chains including formal and informal firms are mainly initiated for business reasons. As Figure 5.1 shows, of a total of fifty-two sampled firms engaged in a VPN, forty-two of the firms were involved due to business relationships, e.g. brought into the VPN through their customers or suppliers. Seven of them were involved in a VPN through collaboration and knowledge sharing, two of them due to personal friendship and one due to family relationship.

Contrary to the literature on VPNs, our results show that very few vertical production chains in Ghana and Tanzania are led by a foreign firm. Small and large local firms are the leaders in most vertical production chains, suggesting that integrating local knowledge into VPNs is important for building the capabilities of firms. The geographical location of the network follows a similar pattern in both countries. In most cases, firms are part of regional or national production chains. Firms in LICs participate in GVCs only in exceptional circumstances. Vertical production chains in Ghana are mostly formed by family relationships, followed by business relationships. Most of the networks seem to be formed to make existing products cheaper or of better quality rather than to produce something that firms in Ghana would otherwise not be able to. Eighty-six per cent of sampled firms that are part of a network are able to reduce the price of the final output, thanks to the competitive advantage and lower transaction costs embedded in the network. By contrast, just less than 30 per cent of the members of a production chain produce new products for Ghana.

VPNs in Tanzania exhibit the same patterns as in Ghana. The networks are mainly led by small or large local networks, and in just 11 per cent of the networks, the leader firm is a foreign multinational. Geographically, the networks are also concentrated in different local regions, with only 5 per cent of them with locations in multiple African countries and 6 per cent with global locations.

Participation in GVCs is found to support economic growth, and better working conditions (Flanagan, 2005; Gereffi, 1994). If developing economies cannot supply a whole product or service competitively, they can at least capture part of the gains by specializing in particular segments of the value chain (Jones et al., 2005; UNECA, 2015). Therefore, integration into GVCs has been seen as a way to facilitate innovation transfer and human resources development (AfDB et al., 2014; Gereffi, 1999, 2014). In particular, vertical integration into GVCs has been associated with capacity building of peripheral suppliers through knowledge transfer from a more experienced lead firm (Gereffi, 1994; Humphrey, 2004; Schmitz, 2006). A recent empirical study by Fagerberg, Lundvall and Srholec (2018), based on the empirical analysis of 125 countries, found a contrary result suggesting that countries that increase their participation in GVCs grow just as much as countries that do not.

While the literature on the effect of entering a VPN or a GVC on economic growth and innovation remains mixed, evidence from the surveys confirms the benefits of being part of a VPN for individual firms. As Figure 5.2 shows, 35 per cent of the firms that participated in a VPN reported that such participation enables them to 'make existing products cheaper or better quality'. More importantly, 24 per cent of the firms reported that participation in a VPN enables them to 'produce something that firms in the country would otherwise not be able to produce'. This implies that by forming a VPN with firms in other countries in the region or in their own country, African firms can upgrade to produce much more sophisticated products which one single firm would otherwise not able to produce, or even diversify into a new industry by producing something different. This, no doubt, has significant implications for African industries. For many resource-rich countries or agricultural economies in Africa or other LICs, upgrading and diversification of their industries are of critical importance.

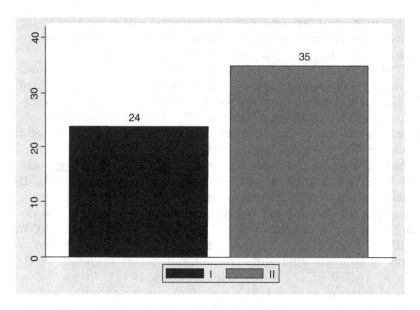

Figure 5.2 Benefits from being part of a VPN: (I) produce something that firms in the country would otherwise not be able to produce, (II) make existing products cheaper or better quality

5.5   Conclusions

Our findings from this chapter suggest that open innovation strategies seem to be an effective strategy to overcome internal constraints that formal and informal firms encounter in developing countries. Firstly, evidence from this chapter suggests that, overall, sampled firms in Tanzania appear to be more open than firms in Ghana. The findings also suggest that innovation collaboration is more widely adopted in sampled firms in Tanzania than in Ghana. Firms are also found to use external knowledge search to seek innovative ideas and technology that could help them improve their product design or quality, production process, or management or marketing practices. Such open innovation practices have been used by the surveyed African firms to overcome the cost, skills and market barriers to innovation in their economies. The degree of a firm's openness is positively associated with innovation. Further, the research finds that local knowledge is more relevant for innovation outcomes than foreign knowledge. This result emphasizes that the knowledge gap between LICs and the technological frontier is large; thus local knowledge is more appropriate to solve firms' problems in LICs.

Secondly, universities have not played an important role in either country as suggested by the literature and in comparison to other partners and other countries. The situation in Ghana has seen a significant improvement in 2015, especially in terms of more active outreach and participation by the universities in the UIC formation. In Tanzania, personal connection is the main cause of a UIC. In both countries, 'we are not connected' has been a major obstacle that hindered the development of a strong university–industry linkage in the national innovation system. This also points to the requirement of an area of policy intervention that would aim to build more platforms or other bridges to link the two sectors and match demand in the industry with the supply of skills in the universities.

Finally, the results show that Ghanaian and Tanzanian firms have a similar participation ratio in clusters, while Tanzanian firms have a significantly higher ratio of participation in VPNs. The findings suggest that clusters as institutions provide greater support and assistance to informal rather than formal firms. The vast majority of the informal firms reported that clusters facilitate the exchange of relevant production and technology information and a greater collaboration on pricing, providing evidence of close interaction between informal firms. Work- and resource-sharing are also important benefits for cluster members. One third of formal and informal members explicitly reported that clusters are environments that facilitate the diffusion and creation of innovations. Informal firms seem to have significantly greater benefits in collaborating on pricing and work-sharing, compared to formal firms.

Regional, instead of global, value chains seem to be more often observed among the surveyed firms, suggesting that using a regional value chain is a more realistic and feasible step for African firms to gradually upgrade and integrate into the global production network. Evidence from this chapter also suggests that by forming a VPN with firms in other countries in the region or in the country, African firms can upgrade to produce sophisticated products which one single firm would otherwise not be able to produce, or even diversify into a new industry by producing something different. This, no doubt, has significant implications for African industries. For many resource-rich countries or agricultural economies in Africa or other LICs, upgrading and diversification of their industries are of critical importance.

However, open innovation has not been effective in alleviating exogenous constraints such as infrastructure. The high cost of production in relation to utilities and the lack of reliability of electricity are often factors that undermine investments and future commitments. These difficulties are common to other LICs, where provision of utilities can be erratic. For firms in the informal sector that cannot afford electricity generators, the lack of electricity supply further hampers commitment to invest and innovate.

The findings of this study bear profound implications for the development of innovation capacity in Ghana. Open innovation strategies can be an effective engine and a suitable tool to overcome constraints and foster innovation activities. Policy efforts should, therefore, strengthen support to open innovation activities of both formal and informal firms in various forms. For example, firms with low innovation capabilities could benefit from inter-firm collaboration, external knowledge searching, stronger university–industry linkages, or forming regional production networks and participating in regional or global value chains. Again, in survival clusters, there may be situations where entrepreneurs and workers share capabilities to add value to their activities along the value chain of the products. The rich local environments of a cluster could prove to be a fertile setting to formalize and further support some of the collaborations and activities amongst firms that are already taking place under the radar.

The study of foreign and local sources of innovation provides a case for strengthening South-South collaborations. The knowledge transferred to LICs is likely to be more appropriate since it comes from countries with a similar factor endowment and at a similar development stage. The absorptive capacity of an LIC recipient may also be more effective in receiving and adapting more appropriate technologies.

6   Innovation and Growth of African Firms
Survival and Growth

6.1   Introduction

The economic growth of low-income countries (LICs) is a product of ideas, skills, capital and the organization of society and firms. It has not been different in the economic history of the current developed countries, where main industrial revolutions were all linked to an application and spread of an innovation – steam power, electricity and informatics – resulting in a remarkable increase in the total productivity, changes in the society and ultimately in the wealth and welfare of nations. The past also shows that the real impact of technologies and knowledge occurs when they are diffused and adopted by a large range of actors within a country and in other countries as well.

The level of technological innovation contributes significantly to economic performance, particularly at the firm and industry levels (see, e.g., Kleinknecht and Mohnen, 2002). Firms' growth is seen as a learning process in which firms grow and survive when they are able to adopt and create technologies and knowledge; firms that do not innovate decline and fail (Jovanovic, 1982). This is particularly relevant in the context of LICs in which the learning process is the major factor enabling innovation activities in firms (Bell and Pavitt, 1992; Lall, 1992). LICs face severe constraints and, as argued by Lundvall et al. (2011), technological capabilities in these countries are more than research and development (R&D). In such environments, learning-based innovations such as adoption or adaptation of both technological and non-technological innovations are significant factors for industrial development.

The chapter includes extracts reproduced from Fu X., P. Mohnen and G. Zanello, 2017. Innovation and productivity in formal and informal firms in Ghana, *Technological Forecasting & Social Change*, Vol 131, 315–325. I am grateful to Giacomo and Pierre and the publisher for kindly allowing a large part of the paper to be reprinted in this chapter.

While the role of innovation in the growth of firms located in developed countries is largely documented, its impact in developing countries is still only partially understood. Difficulties related to data availability and how to measure innovation have limited empirical studies on the link between innovation and firms' growth in LICs. This chapter aims to fill this gap by investigating the role of innovation in the survival, growth and upgrading of African manufacturing firms using case studies in Ghana, and survey evidence in Ghana and Tanzania.

The rest of the chapter is organized as follows. Section 6.2 briefly reviews the literature. Section 6.3 discusses the descriptive evidence from Ghana and Tanzania in 2013 and 2015, respectively. Section 6.4 presents an econometric analysis of the impact of innovation on labour productivity growth in Ghanaian firms using the DILIC 2013 survey data. Section 6.5 concludes and discusses policy considerations.

6.2   Related literature

6.2.1   Innovation and Firms' Productivity in Low-Income Countries

Fagerberg et al. (2010) review the literature and provide strong and ample evidence on how countries that are more active in innovation have higher productivity and income than the less innovative ones. Many scholars have argued that in developed economies, the growth of firms depends on their ability to learn about their environment, linking their strategies to the changing environment (Geroski, 1989; Klepper, 1996). This is even more relevant in LICs, where infrastructure is often poor, markets tend to be underdeveloped and potential local customers have limited disposable income. In such an environment, micro, small and medium-sized firms – many of them working in the informal sector – are particularly vulnerable because of the limited absorptive capacity and restricted access to financial and knowledge resources. Those firms in LICs that are able to successfully undertake innovation activities survive, and the innovating firms that are able to make the best use of the resources available have the potential to lead the market.

In recent years, an increasing number of studies have explored, in great detail, the role of innovation in LIC firms. Most of these studies have looked at the impact of product or process innovations on various performance outcomes. A survey of SMEs combined with in-depth case studies found a positive association between innovativeness and growth in small manufacturing firms in Tanzania (Mahemba and Bruijn, 2003). More recently, Gebreeyesus (2009) investigated the role of innovation in Ethiopian SMEs and found strong evidence that innovators grow faster than non-innovators in terms of employment. Using a rich dataset of SMEs operating in Sri Lanka, De Mel et al. (2009) find an association between innovation and profits.

Overall, the evidence emerging from the literature suggests a positive impact of innovation on firms' performance measured as either profit or employment growth. However, recent studies on the role of innovation on firms' productivity found a much weaker impact. Goedhuys et al. (2008, 2014) focused on the importance of various sources of productivity in developing countries. In Tanzania, they found that firm productivity is not enhanced by R&D, nor by product or process innovation, but business environment seems to play a more relevant role. Those conclusions suggest that the relationship between R&D, innovation and productivity is weaker in developing than in developed countries. In a subsequent study in which three sectors (food processing, textiles and garment and leather products) and five countries (Brazil, Ecuador, South Africa, Tanzania and Bangladesh) are considered, they conclude that the link between knowledge and productivity is sector- rather than country-specific. In the food processing sector, firms that import or license machinery and equipment are more productive, whereas no such evidence emerges in other sectors.

Especially in the context of developing countries, it is useful to differentiate between technological and non-technological innovations (often defined as the introduction of new organizational methods or new marketing methods). Although these are highly interconnected (the commercialization of product innovations often requires new marketing methods and new production techniques need to be supported by changes in the organization), the factors that drive the different types of innovation are likely to be different. A decade ago, Hausman (2005) highlighted how much of the existing research had examined product and process innovations and neglected non-technological innovation such as new management practices. Since then, management and managerial skills have received increased attention as factors explaining differences in firms' performance in developing countries with evidence spanning various geographical areas (Bloom et al., 2013a; Drexler et al., 2014; Karlan and Valdivia, 2011; Mano et al., 2012). Moreover, there is some qualitative and narrative evidence of the benefit of market innovations, mainly for firms in the informal sector (Hall et al., 2012; Ramani et al., 2012).

6.2.2   Informality, Innovation, and Firms' Productivity

Exploring the different ways in which formal and informal firms innovate and the impact this has on their growth is critical, given the size of the informal sector in developing countries. In addition, there is increasing evidence that the cure for informality is economic growth, as reported in La Porta and Shleifer (2014), and that innovation could play a key role in such a transformation. Although we have a fair knowledge of the characteristics of the informal sector, there is not a single widely accepted definition of informal firms. As reviewed in Benjamin and Mbaye (2014), scholars have used different criteria based on firm size, registration status, employer social security contributions, legal form of organization and character (sincerity) of financial accounts. However, a consensus has emerged on the fact that there are degrees of formality and informality along a continuum rather than mutually distinct sectors (Trebilcock, 2005). Therefore, using a single indicator is likely to capture only partially the formal character of the firm. Using various indicators to capture the informal sector, La Porta and Shleifer (2008) found that the informal sector accounts for 30–40 per cent of total economic activity in the poorest countries, and an even higher share of employment.

Limited empirical evidence is available specifically on the role of innovation and firms' growth in the informal sector of developing countries (Agyapong et al., 2017; De Mel et al., 2009; Gebreeyesus, 2009; Konté and Ndong, 2012; Mendi and Mudida, 2017; Wunsch-Vincent and Kraemer-Mbula, 2016). For example, Agyapong et al. (2017) established a positive relationship between the various types of innovation and performance in small and medium-sized enterprises in Ghana. Mendi and Mudida (2017) instead analysed data from informal firms in Kenya and found that past informality status negatively affected technological innovativeness. A few studies explore the determinants of innovation adoption, including firms' characteristics such as size and the entrepreneur's level of education. Firm size, which captures the scale of operations and has been recognized as one of the defining characteristics of informal establishments, has been identified as a barrier to innovation in various studies (De Mel et al., 2009; Gebreeyesus, 2009; Robson et al., 2009). The entrepreneurs' level of education is regarded as an important, although not a sufficient, condition for innovation. Bradley et al. (2012) advocate that capital is not a 'silver bullet' and that education and human capital are the major constraints for innovation in Kenyan small firms. The lack of resources in the education system in many LICs makes non-formal training the main source for learning, together with 'learning by doing' (Oyelaran-Oyeyinka and Lal, 2006).

Although ingenuity has been considered as an engine of innovation activities for informal businesses (Prahalad, 2012), most of the literature has tended to look at observable indicators (e.g. firm size, age, education of workers and entrepreneur) as determinants of innovation. In most cases, data constraints have prevented the inclusion of soft skills – such as entrepreneurship and management skills – which may be equally important in the adoption and impact of innovation. An exception is the work of De Mel et al. (2009), who use a range of indicators to provide evidence that the success of informal businesses in Sri Lanka is determined not only by the skills but also the acumen of entrepreneurs. Such findings reinforce the evidence that the entrepreneur's role is more evident in small enterprises in every strategic aspect, including innovation activities (Donckels and Fröhlich, 1991).

6.3 Innovation and Growth in African Firms: Evidence from the DILIC Survey

Figures 6.1 and 6.2 present the firms' self-assessment of the impact of innovation on different dimensions of firm performance. Formal firms obtained higher levels of success from their innovations, in all areas, than informal firms (Figure 6.1). For product and process effects, the average success level for formal firms is almost 1.5, while for informal firms it is about 1.0. This can be due to the fact that informal firms face higher constraints to innovate and therefore their innovations tend to be less risky and more imitative, reducing the potential benefits of product or process innovations. Compared to the results in 2013, the impact of innovations reported by Ghanaian firms in the year 2015 is lower than that in 2013.

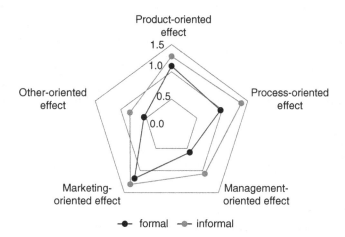

Figure 6.1 The success of the innovations introduced by informal (grey line) and formal (black line) firms in Ghana 2015 (irrelevant = 0 to high = 3, average values)

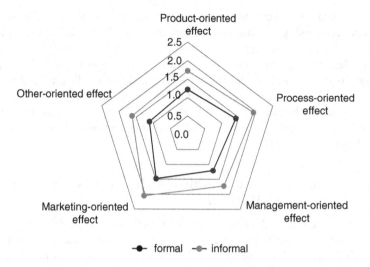

Figure 6.2 The success of the innovations introduced by informal (grey lines) and formal (black lines) firms in Tanzania 2015 (irrelevant = 0 to high = 3, average values)

Management innovations include the implementation of new managerial methods in the firm's business practices, internal workplace or external relations. This has a tendency to increase firm performance by reducing administrative and transaction costs, improving organizational efficiency and providing access to non-tradable assets such as non-codified external knowledge. Management success is higher for formal firms (1.1) than for informal firms (0.6).

Marketing-oriented innovations indicate the introduction of a new marketing strategy, for instance significant changes in product design or packaging, product placement, product promotion or pricing. The intention of adopting new marketing strategies is to address customer needs or open up new markets, which would eventually lead to increased firms' sales. Marketing innovations returned high levels of success for both formal and informal firms, although it is the most successful area for informal firms. This shows that informal firms are much closer to their customers, serving their needs directly.

In Tanzania, it is even clearer that formal firms benefit more from innovation in all areas (Figure 6.2). Also, average levels of success are higher than in Ghana. Formal firms consider marketing and process effects the most relevant, followed by product and management effects. Informal firms follow the same patterns of success of innovations;

however, the average levels of success reported are about 0.5 points lower than for formal firms.

A detailed analysis of the impacts of innovations on eighteen areas of firms is presented in Table 6.1 for Ghana and Table 6.2 for Tanzania. As mentioned earlier, for all the factors analysed, the level of success of innovations is lower in Ghana in 2015 than that reported in 2013 (Table 6.1). The larger reductions in benefits are evident in management and marketing innovations. For both formal and informal firms in 2013 and 2015, the major benefits obtained from being involved in product innovation were improving the quality and range of goods or services, although the differences between formal and informal firms are bigger and statistically different only in 2015. In a lower measure, new or improved products or services have also helped Ghanaian firms to gain access to new markets and increase their market shares, whereas their function in promoting exports is minimal. This finding suggests that product innovations drive expansions in the local market but not in foreign markets. This may be due to the fact that most of the product innovations intro-duced are only new to the firm and local market, and not new to the world. Success of process innovations is higher for formal firms. Formal firms identified that the introduction of process innovations led to the improvement of production efficiency. Yet such an effect was unsurprisingly found to be rather moderate for informal firms due to the fact that process innovations require some basic internal capability to introduce, which informal enterprises often lack.

Effects of management innovations were linked to the reduction in organizational costs, increased management efficiency, and improved supervision and accountability. With respect to management innov-ations, in 2013, informal firms gained more from them than formal firms did, while the opposite is found in 2015. For firms participating in marketing-oriented innovations, the greater success was in targeting new customers; however, formal firms entered new markets significantly more than informal firms in 2015.

Other studies of innovations explore the linkages between innov-ation and social challenges. These include impacts of innovation such as reducing environmental impacts, improving working conditions on health and safety, meeting governmental regulatory requirements and using less energy or generating less pollution. The results in Table 6.1 indicate that the impacts of innovation on the environment and gov-ernmental regulations were low in Ghana in 2013 and even lower in 2015, although formal firms gained more from addressing these issues.

Table 6.1 *Impact of the innovations introduced in Ghana, by nature of firm (irrelevant = 0 to high = 3, average values)*

		2013				2015			
		All	Informal	Formal	Difference	All	Informal	Formal	Difference
Product-oriented effects	Increased range of goods or services	2.29	2.24	2.33	-0.09	1.68	1.49	1.91	-0.42***
	Entered new markets	1.74	1.69	1.78	-0.08	1.37	1.23	1.55	-0.32***
	Increased market share	1.73	1.69	1.77	-0.07	1.35	1.21	1.54	-0.34***
	Improved quality of goods or services	2.40	2.32	2.48	-0.16	1.79	1.72	1.88	-0.16*
	Started to export	0.70	0.78	0.62	0.16	0.44	0.48	0.40	0.08
	Expanded export volumes or to new market	0.81	0.85	0.76	0.09	0.45	0.49	0.40	0.09
Process-oriented effects	Improved flexibility of production or service provision	1.80	1.64	1.99	-0.35**	1.13	0.98	1.32	-0.35***
	Increased capacity of production or service provision	1.89	1.80	2.00	-0.20*	1.31	1.12	1.55	-0.44***
	Reduced production costs per unit of labour, materials, energy	1.84	1.61	2.10	-0.50***	0.99	0.80	1.24	-0.44***
Management-oriented effects	Reduced organizational costs	1.82	1.95	1.66	0.29	0.70	0.50	0.97	-0.47***
	Increased management efficiency	2.07	2.19	1.93	0.26	0.87	0.66	1.14	-0.48***
	Improved supervision and accountability	2.15	2.34	1.93	0.42*	0.82	0.60	1.10	-0.49***
Marketing-oriented effects	Targeted new customers	2.34	2.35	2.33	0.02	1.54	1.53	1.55	-0.03
	Entered new geographical markets	1.51	1.47	1.56	-0.09	0.93	0.83	1.07	-0.24***
Other effects	Reduced environmental impacts	1.24	1.01	1.56	-0.55***	0.63	0.49	0.82	-0.33***
	Improved working conditions on health and safety	1.69	1.48	1.99	-0.51***	0.69	0.54	0.88	-0.34***
	Met governmental regulatory requirements	0.91	0.66	1.28	-0.62***	0.76	0.69	0.84	-0.15*
	Used less energy or generated less pollution	1.18	0.97	1.48	-0.51***	0.59	0.47	0.74	-0.27***

Note: Conditional on innovations introduced. Significance at the 10 per cent, 5 per cent and 1 per cent levels are indicated by one, two and three asterisks, respectively

Results for Tanzania (Table 6.2) show that formal firms benefit significantly more from innovations than informal firms, although the patterns and the levels of success of innovations presented for formal and informal firms are very similar. Higher gains are reported for product, process and

Table 6.2 *Impact of the innovations introduced in Tanzania, by nature of firm (irrelevant = 0 to high = 3, average values)*

		All	Informal	Formal	Difference
Product-oriented effects	Increased range of goods or services	1.85	1.62	2.00	−0.38***
	Entered new markets	1.81	1.44	2.06	−0.62***
	Increased market share	1.68	1.28	1.94	−0.65***
	Improved quality of goods or services	1.94	1.69	2.10	−0.41***
	Started to export	0.98	0.72	1.16	−0.44***
	Expanded export volumes or to new market	0.89	0.58	1.09	−0.51***
Process-oriented effects	Improved flexibility of production or service provision	1.78	1.43	2.01	−0.58***
	Increased capacity of production or service provision	1.88	1.58	2.07	−0.49***
	Reduced production costs per unit of labour, materials, energy	1.53	1.23	1.73	−0.50***
Management-oriented effects	Reduced organizational costs	1.44	1.18	1.61	−0.42***
	Increased management efficiency	1.57	1.22	1.80	−0.58***
	Improved supervision and accountability	1.55	1.21	1.76	−0.55***
Marketing-oriented effects	Targeted new customers	1.96	1.68	2.15	−0.47***
	Entered new geographical markets	1.69	1.28	1.96	−0.68***
Other effects	Reduced environmental impacts	1.42	1.07	1.64	−0.58***
	Improved working conditions on health and safety	1.42	1.18	1.57	−0.39***
	Met governmental regulatory requirements	1.51	1.14	1.75	−0.62***
	Used less energy or generated less pollution	1.33	1.07	1.50	−0.44***

Note: Conditional on innovations introduced. Significance at the 10 per cent, 5 per cent and 1 per cent levels are indicated by one, two and three asterisks, respectively

marketing innovations. The major benefits from product innovations are improvement in the quality of products, increase in the range of goods produced, entering into new markets and increase in market share. However, as in the Ghanaian case, product innovations do not seem to promote exports in LICs.

Benefits from process innovations are mainly obtained from increasing the capacity of production, followed by increasing flexibility in the production process and reducing production costs. In management innovations, most benefits come from an increase in efficiency and improvements in supervision and accountability. Lastly, marketing innovations allow firms to get new clients and enter new markets, which are important benefits for formal firms.

Finally, the benefits of innovations in reducing the environmental impact of firms' production or complying with governmental regulations are also significantly higher for formal firms and could be due to policy regulations. Most benefits for formal firms arise from meeting governmental regulations and reducing the environmental impacts. Informal firms benefit relatively more from improving working conditions with regard to health and safety, since these changes can increase labour productivity.

The findings from the above suggest that product innovations by sampled firms drive expansions in the local market but not in foreign markets. This may be due to the fact that most of the product innovations introduced are only new to the firm and local market, and not new to the world. The results also indicate that process innovations require some basic internal capability and are not easily imitated. As a result, informal firms are less process innovative as compared with their formal counterparts. Informal firms also have little regard for environmental sustainability, as they are also not covered under environmental regulations.

6.4   Innovation and Growth of African Firms: Evidence from Econometric Analysis

This section carries out an econometric analysis of the impact of innovation on the growth of both formal and informal firms in Ghana using the 2013 DILIC survey data.[1] It finds that firms in Ghana have characteristics very different to many firms in emerging countries and most of the firms in advanced economies and their work environment is also different. Many of the firms in Ghana are informal in nature; they employ a large proportion of the population but work extremely inefficiently and in

[1] The econometric specification is explained in the Appendix 6.6 at the end of the chapter.

a low-productivity regime. Moreover, the historical, socio-economic and political environment of Ghana provides strong challenges to firms, which face acute obstacles, from knowledge to market to resource constraints. The study found that in such an environment, innovation is a determinant factor for the growth of firms. Innovation positively impacts the labour productivity of firms – technological innovations more than managerial innovations. Formal firms do not tend to be more productive than informal firms but the role of innovation on productivity tends to be greater for formal firms.

6.4.1 Descriptive Statistics

Descriptive statistics of the firms in the sample are reported in Table 6.3. From our sample, we see how innovation is a widespread phenomenon in the private sector in Ghana, where between 2010 and 2013 most of the firms (78 per cent) were active in some innovation activity. When we break down the nature of innovations, we observe that most of the firms (70 per cent) are involved in some technological innovation, which includes process or product innovations. This may reflect the fact that often firms in LICs work far from the technological frontier and improvements are relatively easy or affordable to implement. Non-technological innovations, including management and marketing innovations, were implemented by 40 per cent of the firms. The vast majority of innovations introduced by the firms have an imitative and incremental nature, rather than being innovations that leapfrog or redefine value creation processes. Innovations that were born from a technology that was originally developed by others and licensed to the firm (with or without adaptation or modification) or developed in a formal R&D department within the company by scientists and engineers amounted to 6 and 2 per cent respectively.

Firms have been active, on average, for almost 16 years and employed 23 employees between 2010 and 2013. However, the distribution of the number of employees is heavily right-skewed with 73 per cent of the firms employing fewer than 9 workers (micro firms), 17 per cent with 10 to 29 employees (small firms) and the remaining 10 per cent is equally distributed between medium (30–99 employees) and large firms, with more than 100 employees. On average, firms have seven employees with a specialisation or university degree.

Most of the firms (63 per cent) are part of a cluster and tend to work predominantly in local markets (69 per cent). Access to subsidized loans is available for only 5 per cent of the firms in the sample. Finally, half of the firms sampled are located in the capital, Accra, or in Tema, a nearby industrial area with an active harbour on the Gulf of Guinea.

We capture entrepreneurship using a principal component analysis (PCA), a series of questions that aim to capture the skills and attitude of the entrepreneurs. Those are more common in the entrepreneurial psychology literature and go beyond the entrepreneur's level of education. A similar set of questions was used by De Mel et al. (2009) in a study of Sri Lankan firms. The variables included in the PCA are listed in Table 6.4 and include the degree of optimism, pro-active attitude, curiosity and tenacity. All these factors may influence the diffusion and creation of innovation. From the PCA, we identified one component (eigenvalue = 3.43) that captures the level of entrepreneurship with individuals that are ingenuous, pro-active, methodical and optimistic.

6.4.2   The Formal Character of Firms in the Sample

We do recognize that there is not a standard definition of formal and informal firms (Benjamin and Mbaye, 2012; Konté and Ndong, 2012).[2] We therefore collected a self-reported formal character of the firm by asking the respondents 'How do you define the nature of the firm?' and providing a spectrum of options that included different degrees of formality (informal, semi-informal, semi-formal, formal), in line with the idea that formality follows a continuum (Trebilcock, 2005). Moreover, during the survey administration, the local enumerators were trained to cross-check this specific information based on the visit to a firm's premises and the observation of its activity. For this study, we merged informal and semi-informal firms into one group ('informal firms') and formal with semi-formal ('formal firms') into another group. In our sample, most of the firms (64 per cent) are active predominantly in the informal sector, a figure in line with other estimations of the informal establishments in Ghana and sub-Saharan Africa (Institute of Statistical Social and Economic Research, 2013; Schneider et al., 2011).

Formal and informal firms differ in most dimensions. Informal firms are significantly less innovative than formal firms, both in technological and non-technological innovation activities. Informal firms also tend to have lower productivity and poorer entrepreneurial skills than formal firms, confirming the characterization of informal firms reported in La Porta and Shleifer (2014). Informal firms are on average younger than formal firms (13 years old as opposed to 19 years old) and smaller in size, with on average only five employees compared to an average work force of

---

[2] The World Bank in its Enterprise Survey defines informal firms as firms that are not formally registered when they start operations. Konté and Ndong (2012) define informal firms as 'all the production units with no statistical number and/or no formal, written accounting'.

55 workers in formal firms. Despite the difference in size, the Ghana Statistical Service estimated that 48 per cent of the population of working age (16–64 years old) is employed in informal establishments (GSS, 2008). Absorptive capacity is also greater in formal firms, with on average 19 employees with a specialization degree compared to less than one employee for the informal firms. Formal and informal firms also tend to be predominantly active in different markets, with half of the formal firms active in the national or international markets and three-quarters of informal firms in the local market.

Eight out of ten informal firms tend to work as part of a cluster as opposed to half of the formal firms. Clusters provide financial support, access to tools, bargaining power and access to larger markets. The relevance of clusters also hinges on the fact that, by nature, they provide information that is context- and sector-specific to their members. Finally, only fourteen formal firms and nine informal firms received government-subsidized loans during 2010–2013, accounting for a mere 4 per cent of the total sample.

6.4.3   Discussion of Results

6.4.3.1 Innovation Activities in Ghana   Table 6.5 reports the results from the first stage of the innovation model. The determinants of innovation, technological innovation and non-technological innovation are respectively reported in Columns I, II and III. The significance of the correlation coefficient (ρ) in every model suggests a significant correlation between the error terms across the two equations (the innovation and productivity equations) and justifies estimating them simultaneously.

Results show that formal firms are more likely to innovate than informal firms, yet when we distinguish technological and non-technological innovations, we find a significant difference only for technological innovations. This result highlights how even informal firms are equally able to adopt management and marketing innovations, which by nature are more likely to be affordable and determined by the entrepreneur's capacity. In fact, entrepreneurship is a critical factor fostering innovation activities across all the specifications in our model. This reinforces the view that innovation adoption and creation in developing countries is still greatly influenced by the acumen and skills of entrepreneurs, to an extent that we do not find in developed countries, where much of the innovation is driven by R&D activities. In less structured establishments, innovation is driven by people with characteristics that make them overcome the constraints distinctive of LICs. Entrepreneurial skills and attitude, including marked curiosity and inclination to form personal relationships, are important factors in the diffusion and adoption of innovations (Bruhn et al., 2010; De Mel et al., 2009).

Consistent with previous studies of firms in Ethiopia and Ghana (Gebreeyesus, 2009; Robson et al., 2009), firms that are more mature are more likely to engage in innovation activities. Firms located in the conurbation area, which comprises Accra and Tema (Greater Accra region), are also associated with innovation activities, particularly non-technological innovations. Large towns provide entrepreneurs the opportunities for personal interactions and exchange of information increases the likelihood that the entrepreneurs would be exposed to new ideas (Robson et al., 2009). Moreover, being part of a cluster is positively associated with greater innovation activities, particularly technological innovations. This result supports previous findings, both from Ghana (McDade and Malecki, 1997) and other LICs (Gebreeyesus and Mohnen, 2013; Murphy, 2007).

Other results are also in line with the previous literature. A larger number of skilled employees are associated with innovation activities and the correlation is significant for both technological and non-technological innovations. This supports the Bradley et al. (2012) study of Kenyan firms in which education and human capital were the main constraints to innovation. Competition seems to be a driver of innovation as well in the Ghanaian firms, pushing firms that work in competitive markets to innovate in order to remain in business. Market competition can nurture innovation capabilities in self-selecting firms that are able to thrive (Kumar and Saqib, 1996). Finally, access to subsidized loans is also correlated with innovation activities. This reinforces our a priori expectation that access to credit is one of the main constraints for innovation.

6.4.3.2 Informality, Innovation and Productivity   Labour productivity greatly varies across the different levels of formality (Figure 6.3 in Appendix 6.5). At the lower end, informal and formal firms have a similar distribution. However, at the upper end of the spectrum, we find only formal firms that have the highest labour productivity in the sample. Such a representation is in line with previous studies that highlighted differences in productivity levels between formal and informal firms (La Porta and Shleifer, 2014). It also shows that if we exclude some highly productive formal firms, the difference between informal and formal firms is not significant at the lower end of the distribution.

The estimates of the second stages of the innovation model are reported in Table 6.6. For each model, we separately introduced total innovation and its two components (techinnovation and non-technological innovation). We also report two specifications: column (A) reports results without an interaction term between the innovation and the formal nature of the firm, while column (B) reports results with interaction terms. Consistent with the mainstream literature on the role of innovation in emerging and developed countries (Fagerberg et al., 2010) and evidence from studies in LICs (Bloom et al., 2013a; Gebreeyesus, 2009), the models predict a positive relationship between innovation and firms' productivity. The econometric models support the conventional wisdom that more innovative firms experience greater productivity (Model I). For example, firms increasing innovation activities from the median to the third quartile are associated with an increase in labour productivity of 11.7 per cent. However, it also shows how technological innovations have a greater impact on productivity than non-technology-based innovations (Models II and III). Adoption of technological and non-technology-based innovations are respectively associated with a 14 and 7 per cent increase in labour productivity (assuming an increase in innovation activities from the median to the third quartile). In line with a growing literature on the relevance of management and managerial skills in firms in LICs (Bartz et al., 2016; Bloom et al., 2013a; Mano et al., 2012), these findings suggest that the low efficiency of firms in Ghana is partially due to poor management practices, from establishing standard procedures for operations and implementing quality control to efficiently managing the inventory and human resources.

Informality is a widespread phenomenon in LICs and a better understanding of the role of innovation in informal firms is critical for the support of economic activities that employ the vast majority of people in the non-agricultural sector. Formal firms tend to benefit more from innovation (Model I), in particular technological innovations (Model II). While informal firms tend to be characterized by modest absorptive capacity and limited resources, which may prevent them from adopting technological innovations, the role of non-technological innovation on firms' productivity is similar in formal and informal firms. The finding that innovation plays a crucial role for the productivity of formal and informal establishments may suggest that firms use innovation to survive. Market conditions, lack of financial resources and skills and limited support from the government may provide a Darwinian environment in which only firms that are able to innovate, from delivering new products or services to targeting market niches, survive.

Finally, across the various specifications we found a consistent pattern that smaller firms, those located in the Greater Accra region and those with a higher number of specialized employees and active in national and international markets tend to be more productive. Such results fit within the general literature providing evidence of the importance of location for the development of firms (Robson et al., 2009). Firms near the capital city have access to better infrastructure, a larger pool of skilled labour and market opportunities. Specialized labour force has also been found to be one of the contributing factors of firms' labour productivity (Blundell et al., 1999).

Our results show a more relevant role of innovation in firms' productivity than the recent findings from the work of Goedhuys et al. (2008, 2014), who found that supportive business environments have a greater influence on firms' performance than innovation activities. Three differences between their studies and ours can explain the dissimilar results. First, there might be some difference because of the industry composition of the samples in the two studies, although food and garments represent half of our sample. Secondly, we have corrected for the endogeneity of innovation, something Goedhuys et al. (2008, 2014) have not done. Given the measurement errors inherent in the technological indicators, not instrumenting innovation may lead to an attenuation bias. But most importantly, our setting focuses only on firms located in one country and, therefore, potential cross-country differences in business environments are not captured, only cross-industry differences.

6.5   Conclusion

Low-income countries rely on the transfer of technologies and knowledge from more advanced countries to increase the local wealth and welfare, reduce internal inequalities and ultimately accelerate the process of catching up. The current developmental state of most LICs suggests that the diffusion to and adoption of major technologies in LICs are likely to be faster than what we witnessed with the diffusion of major innovations such as the steam engine, which took a hundred years to be adopted in China. Economies nowadays are intrinsically more interconnected and lower-tech innovations have the potential to be adopted by LICs, favoured by trade and for collaborations between LICs and emerging countries. The rationale is that the knowledge transferred to LICs is likely to be more appropriate since it comes from countries with not too dissimilar factor endowments. The absorptive capacity of an LIC recipient may be more prone to receiving a similar level of technology. We are witnessing an initial process in which manufacturing industries will eventually be relocated to places – such as African countries – where labour is cheaper than in current manufacturing countries, where worldwide low-tech goods have been assembled and produced for decades. Nowadays, the diffusion of information and communication technologies holds the potential to promote the diffusion of information in places that until recently were disconnected and remote, and the increased capability with which people can move and travel is a powerful vector to support absorptive capacity of LICs with the injection of knowledge and skills.

In such a scenario, our results aim to provide a better understanding of the critical role of innovation on firms' growth in LICs. It finds that firms in Ghana have characteristics very different to many firms in emerging countries and most of the firms in advanced economies, and their work environment is also different. The vast majority of firms in LICs are informal; they employ a large proportion of the population but work extremely inefficiently and in a low-productivity regime. Moreover, the historical, socio-economic and political environment of LICs provides strong challenges to firms which face acute obstacles from knowledge to market to resource constraints. We found that in such an environment, innovation is a determinant factor for firms' productivity, with greater effect in formal firms.

6.5.1   Policy Considerations

Policies play a critical role in accelerating the diffusion and creation of innovation and in mitigating the obstacles LICs face. Findings from this research have important policy implications. Firstly, it should be more strongly emphasized among policymakers that innovation is not the outcome of development but a means for development. Too often in LICs, in the informal economy in particular, innovations are not recognized, and innovation efforts are not properly supported. Therefore, new thinking and policies to recognize and support innovation, for example by mitigating financial and labour skills constraints, are necessary in the context of LICs for long-term growth and development. In Ghana, recognizing the important role that knowledge and innovation must play in transforming the economy and reducing poverty, the Government of Ghana has placed science and technology (S&T) development high on its list of priorities (Amankwah-Amoah, 2016). This is reflected in various political and policy statements, including Vision 2020, the Growth and Poverty Reduction Strategy II and the medium-term development plan. These policies and strategies have emphasized that the absorption and application of much more S&T is a critical ingredient for successful growth. As with many other economies in sub-Saharan Africa, Ghana is still in the stage of 'factor-driven' growth. In the next decade, policy-makers in Ghana must address these issues in order to move from a 'factor-driven' growth into an 'innovation-driven' one.

Secondly, this study suggests that non-technological innovations also have a significant positive impact on labour productivity, although the size of their impact is smaller than that of technology-based innovations.

Poor management practices, poor standard of operations and poor quality control have been argued as important constraints for productivity growth in Africa. Therefore, government policies should also promote the diffusion and adoption of appropriate modern management practices, which may provide Africa with another engine of economic growth.

Our results show that innovation is the most important determinant of labour productivity for both formal and informal firms. Technological innovation makes a greater contribution to productivity than non-technological innovation. Innovation tends to be adopted and developed more when loans have low interest rates, when competition is higher in the markets, when more human capital and entrepreneurship are available and when firms are part of a cluster. Data also show that techno-logical innovation is more frequent in formal than in informal firms. As to non-technological innovation, its diffusion is equally spread in formal and informal firms.

Based on these pieces of evidence, managerial and government policies can be developed to support and enhance the innovation activities of formal and informal firms. First, innovation can be stimulated by govern-ment policies that aim at supporting firms financially, as financial con-straints show up as one of the major impediments to innovation (Kimura, 2011; Kugler, 2006). Such measures would benefit to a larger extent small and informal firms, for which the availability of cash flow is often a constraint in their activities (Nichter and Goldmark, 2009). Secondly, policies should be designed and implemented to provide platforms where potential employees can acquire and develop skills and firms assimilate technological progress and contribute to it. Finally, macro-economic policies and legislation should ensure a competitive environment, avoid-ing protected monopolies. Some competition in the market provides a conducive environment to innovate in order for firms to survive and succeed (Aghion et al., 2005).

Innovation should be supported by coordinated multi-sector policy actions that look at firms' needs (Borrás and Edquist, 2013). Targeted policy actions should also support non-technological innov-ation such as managerial innovation. Policies aimed at developing and supporting clusters and networks can provide fertile spaces for knowledge spillovers and information exchange. Moreover, policies should recognize the importance of promoting an entrepreneurial attitude, that is, a willingness to take risks and a determination to succeed. This can be developed by creating safety nets and nurturing the recognition of 'failures' as learning opportunities along the path to success.

Appendices

Appendix 6.1

Table 6.3 *Descriptive statistics*

	Description and unit	Mean full sample	Informal firms (n=321)	Formal firms (n=180)	Difference (informal-formal)
Dependent variables					
Innovation	Whether the firm implemented any innovation (dummy)	0.78	0.72	0.89	-0.18***
Technological innovation	Whether the firm implemented a technological innovation (dummy)	0.70	0.62	0.84	-0.23***
Non-technological innovation	Whether the firm implemented a non-tech innovation (dummy)	0.40	0.35	0.51	-0.16***
Labour productivity	Log (Turnover [in 1,000 GH¢] / Number of employees)	0.37	0.18	0.71	-0.53***
Independent variables					
Formal	Whether the firm is formal (dummy)	0.36	-	-	-
Capital / labour	Fixed assets [in 1,000 GH¢] / Number of employees (log)	39.38	2.14	105.81	-103.70***
Entrepreneurship	First component of entrepreneurship (PCA)	0.00	-0.26	0.46	-0.71***
Size	Number of employees (log)	23.14	5.35	54.88	-49.53***
Age	Age of the firm (log)	15.82	13.57	19.83	-6.26***
Conurbation	Whether the firm is located in Accra or Tema (dummy)	0.50	0.50	0.50	-0.01
Skilled employees	Number of employees with specialization or university degree	7.14	0.28	19.36	-19.08***
Competition	Degree of competition in the main market (from low (1) to high (5))	2.40	2.27	2.64	-0.38***
Local	Whether the firm predominantly marketed locally (dummy)	0.69	0.77	0.54	0.23***
Member of cluster	Whether the firm is member of a cluster (dummy)	0.63	0.81	0.30	0.51***
Subsidized loan	Whether the firm obtained a subsidized loan (dummy)	0.05	0.03	0.08	-0.05*

Notes: Statistics are reported for natural variables. Significance at the 10 per cent, 5 per cent and 1 per cent levels are indicated by one, two and three asterisks, respectively.

Appendix 6.2

Table 6.4 *Entrepreneurship: principal component (eigenvectors) and variable used*

	Mean full sample	Informal firms (n=321)	Formal firms (n=180)	Difference (formal-informal)	PCA Component 1
A. I plan tasks carefully	4.20	4.15	4.29	0.14	0.407
B. I will pursue my goal despite many failures and oppositions	4.27	4.20	4.38	0.18*	0.447
C. I am well organized and good at multi-tasking	4.02	3.93	4.17	0.23*	0.392
D. I am fully prepared to take risks	3.94	3.74	4.29	0.54***	0.392
E. I am always optimistic about my future	4.24	4.16	4.39	0.23*	0.411
F. A person can get rich by taking risks	3.75	3.57	4.08	0.51***	0.399

Notes: Responses to all questions are coded on a scale of one to five, with one indicating 'strongly disagree' and five 'strongly agree'.

Appendix 6.3

Table 6.5 *First stage of innovation model: determinants of innovation (Model I) and technological and non-technological innovation (Models II and III)*

	Model I: (Innovation)	Model II: (Tech innovation)	Model III: (Non-tech innovation)
Formal firm	0.117**	0.149***	0.007
	(0.053)	(0.049)	(0.047)
Entrepreneurship (PCA)	0.043***	0.053***	0.047***
	(0.012)	(0.009)	(0.008)
Capital/labour	−0.004	−0.001	0.022
	(0.015)	(0.012)	(0.010)
Firm size (log)	−0.027	0.001	0.031
	(0.023)	(0.021)	(0.019)
Skilled employees (log)	0.033***	0.024**	0.022**
	(0.010)	(0.011)	(0.012)
Age (log)	0.047**	0.043**	0.069**
	(0.029)	(0.022)	(0.019)

Table 6.5 *(cont.)*

	Model I: (Innovation)	Model II: (Tech innovation)	Model III: (Non-tech innovation)
Conurbation	0.087**	0.047**	0.171**
	(0.041)	(0.038)	(0.033)
Local	0.077*	0.061	0.091*
	(0.051)	(0.046)	(0.042)
Competition	0.044**	0.049**	0.039**
	(0.018)	(0.021)	(0.019)
Subsidized loan	0.221**	0.216**	0.265**
	(0.112)	(0.091)	(0.084)
Member of cluster	0.065*	0.077**	0.067
	(0.045)	(0.037)	(0.034)
Correlation (ρ)	−0.609***	−0.628**	−0.354*
	(0.236)	(0.248)	(0.184)
Pseudo R-Squared	0.19	0.16	0.14
Wald χ^2	99.39***	95.84***	91.75***
Correctly classified	82%	75%	70%
Ratio correct prediction[a]	1.26	1.29	1.31
Observations	501	501	501

Notes: Marginal effects are reported. For each model (I, II and III) are reported the estimates and statistics (R-squared, rho, prediction) of Model A. Estimates of the first stage Model A and B are not significantly different. Significance at the 10 per cent, 5 per cent and 1 per cent levels are indicated by one, two and three asterisks, respectively. Robust standard errors are in parentheses. ρ refers to the correlation between the error terms in the innovation and the productivity equations (tables 5.5 and 5.6, column A, respectively).

[a] The ratio of correct prediction is a measure of goodness of fit. It is computed as the sum of the fraction of zeros correctly predicted and the ones correctly predicted (McIntosh and Dorfman, 1992). The model is considered robust if the ratio is greater than one.

Appendix 6.4

Table 6.6 *Second stage of the innovation model: determinants of firms' productivity by innovation (Model I) and technological and non-technological innovation (Models II and III)*

	Model I: (Labour productivity)		Model II: (Labour productivity)		Model III: (Labour productivity)	
	A	B	A	B	A	B
Innovation	1.209*** (0.293)	1.221*** (0.256)				
Technological innovation			1.074*** (0.327)	1.110*** (0.308)		
Non-technological innovation					0.474* (0.276)	0.482* (0.291)
Innovation x Formal firm		0.722*** (0.249)				
Technological innovation x Formal firm				0.489** (0.248)		
Non-technological innovation x Formal firm						-0.018 (0.194)
Formal firm	0.158 (0.106)	-0.475* (0.247)	0.147 (0.112)	-0.261 (0.238)	0.323*** (0.101)	0.330*** (0.126)
Capital/labour	-0.003 (0.055)	-0.005 (0.055)	0.011 (0.057)	0.010 (0.058)	0.023 (0.052)	0.022 (0.052)
Firm size (log)	0.498*** (0.043)	0.503*** (0.044)	0.500*** (0.044)	0.502*** (0.045)	0.492*** (0.045)	0.492*** (0.045)
Skilled employees (log)	-0.356*** (0.062)	-0.360*** (0.063)	-0.388*** (0.062)	-0.392*** (0.064)	-0.407*** (0.063)	-0.407*** (0.063)
Age (log)	0.072*** (0.022)	0.062*** (0.023)	0.079*** (0.023)	0.072*** (0.023)	0.089*** (0.023)	0.089*** (0.023)

Conurbation	0.353***	0.370***	0.422***	0.444***	0.385***	0.384***
	(0.094)	(0.097)	(0.094)	(0.097)	(0.095)	(0.095)
Local	−0.258**	−0.301***	−0.233**	−0.268**	−0.215**	−0.215**
	(0.106)	(0.109)	(0.105)	(0.107)	(0.102)	(0.102)
Constant	0.087	0.071	0.275	0.246	0.815***	0.814***
	(0.299)	(0.289)	(0.298)	(0.295)	(0.223)	(0.224)
R-Squared	0.50	0.50	0.49	0.49	0.49	0.49
Wald χ^2	60.74***	54.43***	58.99***	52.55***	57.96***	51.42***
Observations	501	501	501	501	501	501

Notes: Significance at the 10 per cent, 5 per cent and 1 per cent levels are indicated by one, two and three asterisks, respectively. Robust standard errors are in parentheses.

Appendix 6.5

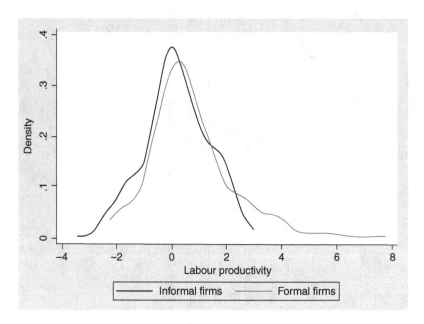

Figure 6.3 Distribution of labour productivity by level of formality of the firms

Appendix 6.6

ECONOMETRIC SPECIFICATION AND ESTIMATION

The literature review in Chapter 2 highlighted how most of the innovations in LICs have an adaptive or incremental nature and, therefore, innovations in such settings are unlikely to leapfrog or redefine value-creation processes. In fact, given the limited financial and knowledge resources and absorptive capacity of firms in LICs, R&D-based innovations are uncommon. The vast majority of innovation activities derive from the adoption (and adaptation) of innovations through the so-called 'technological capability', the firms' ability to employ existing technologies and knowledge in order to adopt, adapt and change existing technologies (Fransman, 1985; Lall, 1992). Therefore, in developing countries, innovation is a phenomenon that involves institutional and environmental factors as much as personal and entrepreneurial characteristics. Firm owners' entrepreneurial acumen is as critical as firms' characteristics for innovation adoption. Empirical evidence on this is limited but notably De Mel et al. (2009) control for both entrepreneurs' and firms' characteristics in the adoption of innovations. To suit these conditions, we had to take into account the lack of formal R&D activities[3] and the role of firm owners' entrepreneurial acumen in adopting innovations. We, therefore, decided to apply a structural model that recognizes the endogeneity of innovation, that is, a firm innovates based on certain characteristic of the entrepreneur and the firm and the role of innovation activity is a determinant of productivity.

The model, therefore, includes two equations. Let $i = 1, \ldots, N$ index the firm. The first equation captures the knowledge production function

$$I_i^* = z_i'\beta + \varepsilon_i, \qquad (6.1)$$

where I_i^* is an unobservable latent variable and where z_i is a vector of determinants of innovation effort, including the firm owner's entrepreneurial acumen, β is a vector of parameters of interest, and ε_i is an error term. We use a probit model to estimate (6.1), i.e.

$$I_i = \begin{cases} 1 \ if \ I_i^* > 0 \\ otherwise \end{cases} \qquad (6.2)$$

where I_i is the observed binary variable equal to 1 if a firm undertook any innovation activity in the past three years and I_i^* is the respective latent variable.

In the second step, we estimate a productivity equation

$$y_i = w_i'\alpha_1 + I_i^*\alpha_2 + v_i \qquad (6.3)$$

where y_i is labour productivity (log of total turnover (output) per worker), w_i is a vector of determinants of productivity and v_i is an error term. This measure of labour productivity is widely used in innovation studies to capture firm's productivity (Fagerberg et al., 2010). The rationale is that adoption of innovation can make workers more productive. In our estimation, we take care of the endogeneity of I_i by using in the estimation of (6.3) the predicted values from the knowledge production function equation as instruments using a two-stage least squares (2SLS) regression approach and correcting the standard errors accordingly.

In order to test our hypotheses, we expand the basic model in two directions to capture the different nature of innovations and the formal character of firms. First, we decompose the innovation activity

---

[3] In our sample, less than 6 per cent of the firms developed innovation through a formal R&D department.

(I_i) into technological (T_i) and non-technological (L_i) innovation. Technological innovation includes product and process innovations, while non-technological innovation includes marketing and management innovations. The first step of the estimation is expanded to include two knowledge production functions

$$T_i^* = z_{i1}'\beta_1 + \varepsilon_{1i} \tag{6.4a}$$

$$L_i^* = z_{i2}'\beta_2 + \varepsilon_{2i} \tag{6.4b}$$

where the starred dependent variables are latent variables and ε_{1i} and ε_{2i} follow a bivariate normal distribution. We jointly estimate models (6.4a) and (6.4b) with a bivariate probit

$$T_i = \begin{cases} 1 & \text{if } T_i^* > 0 \\ 0 & \text{otherwise} \end{cases} \tag{6.5a}$$

$$L_i = \begin{cases} 1 & \text{if } L_i^* > 0 \\ 0 & \text{otherwise} \end{cases} \tag{6.5b}$$

where T_i and L_i are observed binary variables equal to 1 if a firm undertook any technological, or respectively non-technological, innovation activity in the past three years.

The predicted values from (6.5a) and (6.5b) are then separately included as instruments in the productivity equation

$$y_i = w_i'\gamma_0 + T_i^*\gamma_1 + L_i^*\gamma_2 + v_i \tag{6.6}$$

Secondly, in order to capture the effect of innovation activities on the degree of formality of the firms, we estimate (6.3) and (6.6) interacting the two variables

$$y_i = w_i'\alpha_1 + I_i^*\alpha_2 + N_i\alpha_3 + (I_i^* \times N_i)\alpha_4 + v_i \tag{6.7}$$

$$y_i = w_i'\gamma_0 + T_i^*\gamma_1 + L_i^*\gamma_2 + N_i\gamma_3 + (T_i^* \times N_i)\gamma_4 + (L_i^* \times N_i)\gamma_5 + v_i \tag{6.8}$$

where N_i represents the degree of formality of a firm and I_i^*, T_i^*, and L_i^* are respectively the latent variables from models (6.2), (6.5a), and (6.5b).[4]

In the estimation, we rely on exclusion restrictions to identify the parameters of the innovation equation from those of the productivity equation, that is, at least one significant explanatory variable in the knowledge production function that does not appear in the productivity equation. This variable should affect innovation but affects productivity

---

[4] To simplify notation, we use the same notation for the error term in equations (6.3), (6.6), (6.7) and (6.8).

only through innovation. From an extensive qualitative research based on thirty-two in-depth interviews in ten formal and informal firms preceding the survey, it emerged that access to credit was one of the main constraints to innovation. In fact, at the time of the survey, the current loan interest rate (~20 per cent) was unaffordable for most of the firms. We, therefore, used access to subsidized loans as the exclusion restriction in our analysis, being confident that the impact of credit would affect productivity through investment in innovation.

In addition to the exclusion restrictions, we also need to consider that productivity and innovation are both endogenous. More productive firms may have higher profits and more opportunities for knowledge exchange with other firms, which may result in greater innovation activities. At the same time, innovation is a driver of productivity. In the original CDM model, innovation is instrumented in the productivity equation with the R&D expenses (Crepon et al., 1998). We use, instead, a measure of entrepreneurship. Entrepreneurship is likely to affect productivity through the implementation of innovations, both technical and non-technical.

7 Women Entrepreneurs and Innovation in Ghana

Xiaolan Fu, Mammo Muchie and Abiodun Egbetokun[*]

7.1 Introduction

Women account for half of the population in sub-Saharan Africa (SSA), and women entrepreneurs are increasingly playing an important role in the business sector. However, gender inequality and the discrimination that women face in education, access to finance, information and social networks are barriers not only to social and human development, but also to women's participation in economic activities (Branisa et al., 2013; Ekesinoye and Okolo, 2012). Yet, gender gaps in economic activities, particularly entrepreneurship and innovation, are rarely studied in the context of Africa, leaving gaps that have important implications for evidence-based policymaking in the literature. Hence, the aim of this chapter is to shed light on gender differences in firm-level innovation in SSA.

Studies have shown that women are significantly less likely to be involved in entrepreneurship than men (Global Entrepreneurship Monitor, 2017; Minniti et al., 2005; Minniti and Nardone, 2007; Shinnar et al., 2018). However, it is not yet understood if such differences are also reflected in firm-level performance. In other words, when women choose to start and/or manage firms, are there observable performance differences relative to firms owned by men? Of all aspects of a firm's performance, innovation is particularly crucial. Innovation is a key driver of long-term economic growth and sustainable development. Hence, promoting innovation capabilities of firms, which ultimately enhances the ability of a nation to exploit technology to its own advantage, has been an important subject for policymakers (Fagerberg et al., 2010). There is a wealth of studies investigating the factors that affect a firm's innovation behaviour, from innovation policy and ecosystem, innovation

---

[*] The authors are immensely grateful to Lene Foss for her expert comments on this chapter.

strategy, internal R&D management and external knowledge sourcing, leadership, top management characteristics, to incentives and corporate governance (see Cohen, 2005, 2010; Keizer et al., 2002, for comprehensive reviews). However, the gender dimension is rarely studied.

Most of the existing research on gender and gender inequalities focus on women's identity and inequalities in access to education, finance and social services (see, for instance, Abu-Ghaida and Klasen, 2004; Branisa et al., 2013; Klasen, 2002). Studies on women entrepreneurs have provided insightful findings on their strategy and performance (see, for instance, Bardasi et al., 2011; Ndemo and Maina, 2007; Morris et al., 2006). A few studies even compare men and women entrepreneurs in terms of how their human capital and networks affect their firms' growth potentials (e.g. Manolova et al., 2007). Yet, very little is known about the relative innovativeness of firms managed by female entrepreneurs. Considering the importance of firm-level innovation in economic empowerment and recent global efforts at creating and maintaining an inclusive society, this issue is of particular interest.

This chapter analyses how the gender of the entrepreneur is associated with firm-level innovation performance, both directly and in conjunction with other firm attributes and manager attributes. We use a firm-level dataset from a country in SSA – Ghana. The context of SSA is particularly interesting to study for a number of reasons. First, women in SSA face relatively higher institutional barriers to participation in economic activities (Ekesinoye and Okolo, 2012). Furthermore, the role of the entrepreneur's gender in firm-level innovative performance is under-researched. Several existing studies analyze women's role in economic activities in developing countries (Bardasi et al., 2011; Ekesinoye and Okolo, 2012; Wells et al., 2003)., There is also a rapidly expanding body of research on innovation in African firms (e.g., Adeyeye et al., 2015; Egbetokun et al., 2016). Nevertheless, to the best of our knowledge, there is hardly any research on whether firms managed by women entrepreneurs innovate differently from those managed by men; there is also a lack of studies that assess how policies addressing gender gap can encourage innovation in Africa.

The analysis uses the DILIC Project 2013 Ghana survey data set, of which just over a third of the firms are managed by women and a quarter are from the informal sector. All the firms in the sample have a manager who is also the largest shareholder, which, in effect, is another form of ownership. In other words, the manager is also the entrepreneur; hence, we use the terms manager (abbreviated MD) and entrepreneur interchangeably in the chapter. Apart from providing insight into the direct effects of gender, our data allow us to examine some interesting contingencies in the relationship between the manager's gender and innovation. Specifically, we explore the contingent effects of the business environment (in terms of formality) and the personal attributes of the entrepreneurs (education and risk attitudes) on this important relationship.

The results of our study show significant differences in innovation behaviour between women's and men's firms. The former are less likely to introduce technological innovation, but are more active in adopting non-technological, especially marketing, innovation. They are also less successful with innovation of higher originality, that is, new-to-market innovations. We find a striking contingency in the gender–innovation relationship: the effect of a manager's human capital on firm-level innovation depends on the manager's gender, and vice versa. Higher level of education increases the likelihood of product and process innovations as well as of product novelty in women-managed firms more than in men-managed firms. Compared to firms managed by men, women-managed firms experience a reduced likelihood of introducing a new product, but there are increased sales from new-to-market innovation if the manager is more risk averse. In moderating the gender–innovation relationship, formality plays no role even though it has a limited direct effect on innovation.

This chapter contributes to the literature in several ways. First, to the best of our knowledge, this is the first study that systematically analyses the differences in innovation behaviour between firms managed by women and by men in Africa, using a large firm-level data set. Secondly, this chapter sheds light on the different roles of the entrepreneur-manager's education and attitude to risk, in shaping the gender–innovation relationship. Thirdly, the analysis of the contingent role of formality in the gender–innovation relationship, using a large survey data set, provides a useful first step in our attempt to understand the difference in innovation in firms managed by women entrepreneurs in the informal and formal sectors.

The rest of the chapter is organized as follows. Section 7.2 briefly reviews the literature on gender and entrepreneurship, and develops the hypotheses. Section 7.3 describes data and methods. Section 7.4 describes our empirical specifications and results. Section 7.5 concludes and discusses policy implications.

7.2   Literature and Hypotheses

7.2.1   Gender Differences in Entrepreneurship and Firm-Level Performance

There has been a recent increase in the number of women entrepreneurs, particularly in developed countries like the United States, the United

Kingdom and Canada, where over 30 per cent of small companies are women-owned (Edelman and Brush, 2018). Yet, there is considerable evidence that women worldwide are much less likely to start new businesses. For instance, recent data from the Global Entrepreneurship Monitor (GEM) indicate that there are significantly fewer women entrepreneurs than men, despite the general increase in the absolute numbers of women entrepreneurs (Global Entrepreneurship Monitor, 2017).

Some researchers have argued that male and female entrepreneurs are not particularly different. For instance, Lefkowitz (1994) showed that men and women tend to react in the same way to the same set of incentives and that much of the difference across genders disappears after correcting for some socio-economic conditions. Other researchers have also noted fundamental similarities between male and female entrepreneurs, most notably in terms of key motives, such as the desire for independence or self-achievement or the tendency to have an internal locus of control (Morris et al., 2006). Such arguments leave unanswered the question of what explains gender differences in entrepreneurship.

Several explanations have been made for the observable gender differences in entrepreneurial activity. Minniti and Naude (2010) provide an overview of this literature. Greene (2000) identified differences between male and female entrepreneurs in human and social capital. Propensity for growth and overall performance may be lower among women's businesses due to female entrepreneurs' inferior aspirations, poorer prior relevant experience and insufficiently developed instrumental networks (Manolova et al., 2007). Women are also thought to generally have lower tolerance than men for risks and barriers (Jianakoplos and Bernasek, 1998). In addition, because women approach decision making differently than men (Ndemo and Maina, 2007), their management styles differ (Brush, 1990, 1992). For instance, Davis and Abdiyeva (2012) found women to show a tendency towards transformational leadership styles that were more collaborative, participative, team-oriented and centred on trust, harmony and building relationships.

Furthermore, women tend to be more sensitive than men are to a variety of non-monetary factors (Boden, 1999; Burke et al., 2002; Lombard, 2001), coupled with the fact that they feel the pressure of poor funding more. It has been reported that women are disadvantaged in terms of access to financial resources particularly in SSA (Asiedu et al., 2013). In many instances, women entrepreneurs get financial support from their spouses or partners and thereby become less independent in decision-making (Ndemo and Maina, 2007). This is much more of a problem in SSA, where most cultures expect women to be dependent on men (Schoepf, 2018). Such cultural institutions are also likely to bring about significant differences in the entrepreneurial motivations of women as well as their firms' performances. This points to the suggestion that differences in innovation between the genders is contextual, embedded in historical, structural and institutional factors. For instance, Ekesinoye and Okolo (2012) identified cultural restrictions as an important obstacle to women's empowerment and participation in economic activities in Nigeria.

7.2.2   Hypotheses

7.2.2.1   Gender Differences in Firm-Level Innovation   Clearly, the collective body of research on female entrepreneurs (see Jennings and Brush, 2013 for a review) has demonstrated that entrepreneurship is a gendered phenomenon. Thus, the effect of the entrepreneur's gender should be expected in many areas of a firm's existence, not only in its initiation but also in its management and performance. In fact, the specific areas in which women are believed to differ from men are those areas that influence the management and performance of firms, notably human capital, risk taking and access to resources (Ndemo and Maina, 2007; Morris et al., 2006; Wells et al., 2003). Thus, we expect that firms managed by women entrepreneurs will behave and perform differently from those managed by men. This is because existing research has established that firm ownership and management significantly influence innovativeness (van der Panne et al., 2003; Zheng et al., 2010). According to Bloom et al. (2012), management practices explain the astounding differences in performance across firms and countries.

Another notable difference between men and women entrepreneurs is in the conflict between home and family demands. In contrast to most developed countries, where women have access to long periods of paid maternity leave, subsidized childcare and part-time work opportunities, most African women face intense work–family conflicts. Consequently, the majority of women are pushed into starting their own businesses. Thébaud (2015) argues that where women's work–family conflicts are not mitigated through appropriate policies and institutional arrangements, the women tend to choose business ownership as a fallback employment strategy. Such entrepreneurs have a clear preference for a business environment that is predictable (Morris et al., 2006) and the self-employment strategy helps them escape the bureaucratic burdens of being an employee, while giving them the freedom to achieve a better work–life balance. Consequently, their businesses are likely to underperform compared with those of men. Indeed, performance differences between firms in developing countries owned by women and those owned by men have been reported (Bardasi et al., 2011). Therefore, we have a hypothesis as follows:

H1: Firms managed by women are less innovative than those led by men.

7.2.2.2 Manager's Risk Attitudes and Access to Resources

Entrepreneurship is inherently risky (Sine et al., 2005) and innovation is, by nature, a highly uncertain process (Dosi, 1988). Hence, successful entrepreneurs, whose firms are generally more innovative and productive, are typically characterized by a high level of risk tolerance (Djankov et al., 2005, 2007). But there is considerable evidence to suggest that, compared to men, women have lower tolerance for risk, barriers and ambiguity (Borghans et al., 2009; Ivanova and Alexandrova-Boshnakova, 2011; Jianakoplos and Bernasek, 1998) even in financial decisions (Wang, 1994).[1] For this reason, women may be less willing to commit to the extent of risk involved in innovation. Hence, we hypothesize that:

H2a: Firms led by a female top manager are less likely to embark on innovation activity due to risk aversion.

However, women's low risk tolerance may have a positive effect on their innovative success. A more risk-averse entrepreneur may be more selective in his/her decision to innovate such that he/she only does so when he/she has a considerably high probability of success. For instance, Ndubisi (2007) concluded that women entrepreneurs are outcome-oriented in their technology adoption decisions. They focus more on the beneficial outcomes rather than on ease or difficulty of use. Therefore, we suggest that:

H2b: Once a decision of innovation is taken, a female manager's risk aversion will have a positive effect on the level of success of this innovation activity.

7.2.2.3 The Role of Manager's Human Capital

One of the most important determinants of management quality is a manager's human capital. The availability of skilled people is an important difference between better-managed firms and the rest. Van Reenen and Bloom et al. (2007) showed that 84 per cent of managers in the best-managed firms were educated to degree level or higher, in contrast to only 53 per cent of managers of the worst-managed in a sample of 732 firms in selected industrialized countries. In addition, manufacturing firms with better

---

[1] Croson and Gneezy (2009) provide a comprehensive review of this literature. Not in refs.

management practices, including the introduction of modern techniques, attraction and retention of human capital as well as continuous performance management, have up to 69 per cent higher labour productivity (Bloom et al., 2012). In this regard, Gennaioli et al. (2013) ascribe a 30 per cent return to an extra year of a manager's education as against only 6–7 per cent return to an extra year of staff training. Thus, a positive relationship is to be expected between firm-level performance and the manager's level of education. But women differ from men in terms of human capital: in many developing countries, it has been noted that women lack human capital especially in the form of education (Mbaya and Estapé-Dubreuil, 2016). As a result, the relationship between a manager's level of education and performance will depend on a manager's gender, such that the marginal effect of higher educational attainment on firm-level innovation will be greater for female managers, since they are, on average, starting from lower levels of education. Hence,

H3: *Higher level of education has a greater effect on innovation if the manager is female.*

Of course, we need to note that it is not the gender per se, but institutional factors that make women start at a lower level of education.

7.2.2.4 The Role of Formality   It has been reported that firms in poor countries, especially the informal firms, are poorly managed – they are typically self-owned, managed by uneducated entrepreneurs and lack the desire to significantly innovate (de Mel et al., 2008; La Porta and Shleifer, 2014). While this may be true on aggregate, we suspect a gender contingency. Formalization is typically very costly in developing countries and it sometimes makes firms more visible to corrupt officials (Fisman and Svensson, 2007; Rand and Tarp, 2012). This is likely to be a much bigger problem for firms led by women entrepreneurs who, relative to their male counterparts, are disadvantaged in access to funding. For instance, Asiedu et al (2013) reported that the majority of women entrepreneurs in developing countries use their personal savings or family savings to start up their businesses. This is especially so in SSA where there is little collateral, limited financial information and high risks intrinsic to shock-prone economies. Palaniappan and Ramanigopal (2012) argued that though women have been successful in breaking their barriers within the limits of their homes by entering into varied kinds of businesses, finance remains their major problem. The above discussion can be summarized in the following hypothesis:

H4: In the context of Ghana, a manager's gender will moderate the effect of formality on firm-level innovation.

7.3   Methodology

7.3.1   *Key Variables and Descriptive Statistics*

7.3.1.1 Dependent Variables   To measure innovative performance in the selected firms, we employ two sets of variables. The first set includes four dummy variables related to different types of innovative output: product, process, management and marketing innovation. A product innovation is the introduction to market of a new or significantly improved good or service with respect to its capabilities, such as improved user-friendliness, components, software or sub-systems. Process innovation is the use or implementation of new or significantly improved process or method for the production or distribution of goods or services or supporting activity. A management innovation refers to the implementation of a new management method in a firm's business practices, workplace organization or external relations. A marketing innovation is the implementation of a new marketing method involving significant changes in product design or packaging, product placement, product promotion or pricing. The survey asked firms directly whether they introduced any of these during 2010–2013.

The second set of two variables captured the proportion of turnover derived from goods and services that were new to the market or new only to the firm. Similar variables have been used in previous literature on innovation in developed and developing countries (Adeyeye et al., 2015; Leiponen and Helfat, 2010; Mairesse and Mohnen, 2010). The two sets of variables allow us to analyze the innovation choices made by the firms and their innovative success in terms of market performance.

7.3.1.2 Independent Variables   Our data set includes information on the gender of the managers of the firms, which we coded as 1 if female and 0 otherwise. To measure risk attitudes of the firms' managers, we relied on categorical information contained in two survey items: *I am fully prepared to take risks* and *A person can get rich by taking risks*. Respondents rated their level of agreement with each of these statements on a scale of 1 (Strongly disagree) to 5 (Strongly agree). For the purpose of our analyses, this scale is reversed to ensure that higher scores correspond to a greater level of risk aversion. We then merge these two items by regression scoring, after subjecting the two items to a principal component analysis with varimax rotation, to obtain a single measure of risk aversion.[2] The primary advantage in doing so is keeping only one continuous measure for risk aversion, and consequently one interaction term in our regressions. In the univariate analyses, we use the full information in both items. The manager's educational attainment appears to be a good proxy of their human capital, as firms with highly educated managers tend to be better-managed (Bloom et al., 2007). We consider this aspect in our study, using information contained in a categorical variable that captured the highest level of schooling completed by the manager, that is, university degree, post-basic, basic or no education. Each of these levels was codified into a dummy variable so that we ended up with four indicators of each manager's educational attainment.

Recognising that there is no standardized definition of formal and informal firms (Benjamin and Mbaye, 2012), the survey collected a self-reported nature of firms, asking the respondents 'How do you define the nature of the firm?' and providing a spectrum of options that included different degrees of formality (informal, semi-formal, formal). This is in line with the idea that formality follows a continuum (Trebilcock, 2005). Using this information, we created three variables, each with a value of 1 if the firm is respectively in the formal, semi-formal or informal sector, and zero otherwise. This is important because semi-formal firms share attributes of both formal and informal firms, yet they have a unique profile.

7.3.1.3 Control Variables **Firm-level controls:** The number of employees (size) of the firm as well as the firm's age is relevant to our analyses. Both variables are known to be related to firm-level innovation (Balasubramanian and Lee, 2008; Cohen, 2010; Mairesse and Mohnen, 2010). The share of employees with at least a university degree is taken as a measure of staff quality, and a dummy variable captures whether the firm had on-the-job staff training during the survey period. These aspects are relevant because both the initial human capital stock of the firm, in the form of highly qualified staff (Jonker et al., 2006), and enhancing the human capital quality through continuous training (Caniëls and Romijn, 2003a) are important for sustained competitiveness. Existing literature has argued that a firm's ownership tends to affect its innovation potential, among other things (Aralica et al., 2008). Therefore, we include a dummy variable to indicate whether the firm belongs to a group of companies. The geography of the firm is captured through two dummy variables,

---

[2] One factor with eigenvalue above unity explains 65.2 per cent of variance. The Kaiser-Mayer-Olkin test value of 5, though rather low, is acceptable; and the Bartlett test of sphericity shows a significant chi-square at the 1 per cent level, suggesting significant inter-correlation between the two variables.

each indicating whether the firm is located in an export processing zone (EPZ) and/or in a cluster. By reducing transaction costs and creating collective efficiency gains, these locations are known to constitute important innovation milieux for the firm, particularly in a developing country (Caniëls and Romijn, 2003b; Oyelaran-Oyeyinka and McCormick, 2007).

Manager (MD)-level controls: In addition to the firm-level control variables just described, we control for some attributes of the entrepreneur-manager. To measure manager's experience, we use information from the survey on the age range in years and the number of years spent in the current position. The influence of the manager in terms of decision-making is also an important dimension. A manager who is the sole decision-maker is very likely to have a greater influence on firm-level strategies and performance. When only one individual is involved, strategic decision-making may be quicker, since the bureaucratic process tends to be simpler. However, the absence of dissenting voices as potential checks and balances may be detrimental to the firm, because the chances of errors are increased. To account for these aspects, we construct a dummy variable which equals 1 if the manager is solely responsible for making strategic decisions and zero otherwise.

Sector fixed effects: We consider sectoral heterogeneity by including fixed effects based on the Pavitt sectors, the baseline being the supplier-dominated sector (see Appendix 7.1 for details on the sectoral classification). Using this classification allows the inclusion of sectors that would otherwise be dropped from the analysis due to collinearity because they have too few cases. Besides, including fixed effects for every sector in the raw data set will lead to a considerable reduction in the degrees of freedom.

7.3.2   Descriptive statistics

Table 7.1 contains summary statistics of our data set. From our sample, we see how innovation is a widespread phenomenon in the private sector in Ghana, where between 2010 and 2013, most of the firms (about 80 per cent) were active in some innovation activity. When we break down the nature of innovations, we observe that most of the firms are involved in technological innovation, which may include product (45 per cent) or process innovation (61 per cent). This may reflect the fact that firms in developing countries often work far from the technological frontier, and improvements are relatively easy or affordable to implement. Learning innovations, including those related to management and marketing, were implemented by 50 per cent of the firms.

Table 7.1 *Description of variables*

Variables		Full sample		
Dependent	N	Median	Mean	SD
Product innovation (Yes=1, No=0)	496	0	0.452	0.498
Process innovation (Yes=1, No=0)	496	1	0.613	0.488
Management innovation (Yes=1, No=0)	496	0	0.238	0.426
Marketing innovation (Yes=1, No=0)	496	0	0.282	0.451
Total innovation (Yes=1, No=0)	496	1	0.796	0.403
Innovative sales, new to market (share of total sales)	224	0	0.081	0.171
Innovative sales, new to firm (share of total sales)	224	0.4	0.409	0.223
Total innovative sales (share of total sales)	224	0.5	0.49	0.25
Independent				
MD Gender (Female=1)	496	0	0.373	0.484
Risk attitude of manager	496	0.163	0.004	1.008
MD has at least a bachelor's degree (Yes=1, No=0)	496	0	0.129	0.336
MD completed only secondary school (Yes=1, No=0)	496	0	0.456	0.499
MD completed only primary school (Yes=1, No=0)	496	0	0.29	0.454
MD has no formal education (Yes=1, No=0)	496	0	0.125	0.331
Firm is formal (Yes=1, No=0)	496	0	0.248	0.432
Firm is semi-formal (Yes=1, No=0)	496	0	0.234	0.424
Firm is informal (Yes=1, No=0)	496	1	0.518	0.500
Controls				
Number of employees in 2013	496	5	27.47	114.347
Age of firm in 2013	496	13.5	15.78	10.261
Staff with university degree (% of total employees)	495	0	5.0	13.5
Formal/informal on-the-job training (Yes=1, No=0)	496	1	0.625	0.485
Part of a group (Yes=1, No=0)	496	0	0.095	0.293
Located in export processing zone (EPZ) or industrial park (Yes=1, No=0)	496	0	0.137	0.344
Located in cluster (Yes=1, No=0)	496	1	0.607	0.489
Firm has a written strategic plan (Yes=1, No=0)	496	0	0.298	0.458
Age of MD (categorical variable: [1] less than 19 years, [2] 19–25, [3] 26–35, [4] 36–50 and [5] over 50)	496	4	4.022	0.715
Tenure of MD in post	496	12	12.839	7.881
Strategic decision made by the managing director alone (Yes=1, No=0)	496	1	0.52	0.5

Imitative and incremental innovation (that is, new only to the firm) is substantially more prevalent than new-to-market innovation.

Just over a third of the firms in our sample have female managers. Average age of the entrepreneurs is in the range of 36–50 years and they have spent thirteen years, on average, as manager. Most of the firms

(52 per cent) are active predominantly in the informal sector. These figures are in line with other estimations of the informal establishments in Ghana and SSA (Institute of Statistical Social and Economic Research, 2013; Schneider et al., 2011). The remaining firms are divided between semi-formal (23 per cent) and formal (25 per cent). Average firm age in 2013 is sixteen years and average number of employees is twenty-seven. Absorptive capacity, viewed in terms of staff quality, is low among the sampled firms. Although 62 per cent of firms reported having implemented on-the-job training for their staff between 2010 and 2013, only an average of 5 per cent of the employees had a university degree. The firms' managers, however, are relatively well educated; 13 per cent of them have a university degree and 46 per cent have post-basic education.

7.3.2.1 Innovation in Male- and Female-Led Firms We compare the rate of innovation in firms managed by women entrepreneurs with those managed by men entrepreneurs. Some gender differences emerge. Women are less likely to implement product innovation and are less successful in terms of innovative sales. However, they are more likely to implement marketing innovation. This is partly consistent with the existing literature (e.g. Thébaud, 2015) that argues that women-owned firms are typically less innovative. Our evidence hints at the fact that female-led firms lag behind male-led ones only in product innovation and in the market success of their innovation. They are not necessarily worse in terms of process and management innovation, and they are, in fact, better off in the implementation of marketing innovation. These results are, however, univariate. In the next section, we examine the innovative differences between women's and men's firms in a multivariate setting, controlling for relevant characteristics of the firm and of the entrepreneur.

7.3.3 Model

The chapter aims to examine the relationship between a firm's innovation behaviour and the gender of its manager. To do this, we model the probability that a firm innovates, conditional on a set of firm and manager attributes. Similarly, we model innovative success, that is, the share of revenue accruing from the sale of new products, conditional on firm and manager attributes. Other firm and manager attributes are included as controls. Correlations are presented in Appendix 7.3, where we find no serious evidence of multicollinearity. Variance inflation factors are well within acceptable limits – maximum 3.63 and average 1.79.

Table 7.2 *Comparing innovation output in male- and female-led firms*

Variables	Male			Female			Comparison
	N	Median	Mean (SD)	N	Median	Mean (SD)	
Product innovation	311	0	0.49 (0.50)	185	0	0.39 (0.49)	**1.968**[a]
Process innovation	311	1	0.62 (0.49)	185	1	0.61 (0.49)	0.264[a]
Management innovation	311	0	0.25 (0.43)	185	0	0.22 (0.41)	0.874[a]
Marketing innovation	311	0	0.25 (0.43)	185	0	0.34 (0.47)	**−2.018**[a]
Total innovation	311	1	0.81 (0.39)	185	1	0.78 (0.42)	0.768[a]
Innovative sales, new to market	151	0	0.09 (0.19)	73	0	0.05 (0.13)	**1.612**[b]
Innovative sales, new to firm	151	0.4	0.43 (0.24)	73	0.3	0.36 (0.19)	**2.392**[b]
Total innovative sales	151	0.6	0.53 (0.25)	73	0.4	0.413 (0.23)	**3.287**[b]

Note: a. z-test of proportions; b. t-test; Bold figures are statistically significant at the 5% level

Our baseline specification is as follows:

$$Y_i = \beta_0 + \beta_1 \text{Gender} + \beta_2 \text{Formal} + \beta_3 \text{Semi−Formal}$$
$$+ \beta_m M_{j,i} + \beta_i X_i + \beta_j Z_{j,i} + u_{i,k} + v_i \quad (7.1)$$

where Y is either product, process, management or marketing innovation, or new-to-firm and new-to-market innovative sales. $\mathbf{M}$ contains the attributes of interest of manager j of firm i, that is, the manager's risk attitude and educational attainment. v is the error term and u is the sector's fixed effect for firm i in sector k, included because firm-level performance varies widely across sectors. $\mathbf{X}$ and $\mathbf{Z}$ are the vectors of control variables reflecting, respectively, other attributes of the firm and the manager.

To investigate the contingent role of formality and manager characteristics, we allow the slope of the variables measuring formality, manager's risk attitudes and educational attainment to vary across gender groups. The resulting specification, which is an extension of (7.1), is:

$$Y_i = \beta_0 + \beta_1 \text{Gender} + \beta_2 \text{Formal} + \beta_3 \text{Semi−Formal}$$
$$+ \beta_4 \text{Gender}^* \text{Formal} + \beta_5 \text{Gender}^* \text{Semi−Formal}$$
$$+ \beta_m M_{j,i} + \beta_n \text{GENDER}^* M_{j,i} + \beta_i X_i + \beta_j Z_{j,i} + u_{i,k} + v_i \quad (7.2)$$

We estimated the equations as a binary logit for the probability of a firm introducing each of the products, processes, marketing or management innovations. This is a straightforward choice because the respective variables have discrete zero-one values. In contrast, the innovative sales variables are proportions ranging from zero to one. For such variables, the fractional response estimator has been suggested as the most appropriate (Papke and Wooldridge, 1996). We applied the generalized linear model (*glm*) command in Stata with the binomial distribution and the logit transformation of the dependent variable. The logit transformation ensures that the conditional mean stays bounded between 0 and 1. The binomial distribution is a good choice because it is non-normal, and its variance tends to zero as the mean tends to zero or one, that is, the response variable approaches a constant. Maximum variance will occur when the mean is 0.5 (Baum, 2008). In other words, the variance, and hence the standard error of estimates, will depend on the conditional mean of the outcome variable. An obvious limitation of this approach is that it permits only a non-heteroskedastic analysis. It is, however, acceptable in our case since we do not specify a heteroskedastic equation (Wooldridge, 2011).

Recall that the survey elicited innovative sales only for firms that introduced a product innovation. This implies that the fractional logit estimation can only be performed for the sub-sample of product innovators. To avoid selection bias, we estimated a two-stage model. In the first stage, a probit model was estimated for the probability of a firm introducing a new product or service. Inspired by previous research (Molina-Domene and Pietrobelli, 2012; Vega-Jurado et al., 2009), this equation includes a set of firm-level variables like size and age as well as measures related to absorptive capacity (see Table 7.7 in Appendix 7.3 for results). The second stage estimation excluded the non-product innovators but included the inverse Mill's ratio (IMR) from the first stage model. This two-stage approach applied in earlier studies (Haas and Hansen, 2005; Vega-Jurado et al., 2009) is suitable when the selection outcome, in this case innovative sales, is observed.

7.4   Regression Results

Table 7.3 contains the results of the logit estimations for the probability of a firm implementing an innovation. For simplicity, we report only the results from equation (7.2). The results suggest that even when we control for other characteristics of the firm, there is a significant difference in innovation behaviour between firms managed by women and by men in Africa. The coefficient of the manager's gender is negative and significant for both product (Model 1) and process (Model 2) innovations but insignificant for both management (Model 3) and marketing (Model 4) innovations, though positive for the latter. Note that the positive coefficient is significant in the baseline model (results available from authors), suggesting that women-managed firms may be more likely to adopt marketing innovation. This is consistent with the difference found earlier in Section 7.3.2. Taken together, these results suggest that the innovation behaviour of firms led by women indeed differ from those led by men. Firms managed by women entrepreneurs are less likely to introduce technological innovation, but may be more active in implementing non-technological, especially marketing, innovation. In sum, our first hypothesis (H1) that women's firms are less likely to innovate is only supported for technological innovation. For non-technological innovation, we find no strong evidence that women's firms are less likely to innovate.

These results complement the literature that suggests that management characteristics influence firm-level innovation (van der Panne et al., 2003; Zheng et al., 2010). The new insight we deliver in this regard is that the difference in performance between firms managed by women relative to those managed by men is most observable in technological innovation. In particular, women's firms are indeed less innovative but only in product and process innovation. As far as non-technological innovation is concerned, there is no difference. Indeed, technological innovation requires significant human capital and experience, attributes that women often have less of (Mbaya and Estapé-Dubreuil, 2016). Moreover, women's struggle with work–life balance might make the pursuit of less risky non-technological innovation a more attractive strategy for them.

Some interesting moderation effects are observable in Models 1 and 2 in Table 7.3. These effects are plotted in Figure 7.1 and their statistical significance is reported in Figure 7.2. In Model 1, we see that the coefficient of the interaction term between gender and risk aversion is negative and significant. This suggests that the role of the entrepreneur's risk attitude in firm-level innovation is significantly affected by the gender of the entrepreneur. A firm is less likely to introduce a new product when a female entrepreneur who has a higher level of risk aversion manages it (top left plot in Figure 7.1). This difference becomes more substantial as the level of risk aversion increases (top left plot in Figure 7.2). Such difference is not found in the case of process, management and marketing innovation; albeit, the entrepreneur's risk aversion generally lowers the likelihood of process innovation (Model 2). Taken together, these results offer strong support for our hypothesis, but only in the case of product innovation, that a manager's risk aversion has a greater negative effect on the decision to innovate if the manager is female (H2a). This is an aspect in which women's preference for predictability plays out. Technological

Table 7.3 *The role of manager's gender in innovation (logit estimations)*

Independent variables	Innovation			
	(1) Product	(2) Process	(3) Management	(4) Marketing
MD is female (A)	-2.114***	-1.445**	-0.622	1.708
	(0.820)	(0.665)	(0.932)	(1.170)
Firm is formal (B)	0.318	0.933**	-0.685	0.023
	(0.413)	(0.445)	(0.497)	(0.477)
Firm is semi-formal (B1)	0.037	1.029***	-1.025**	-0.248
	(0.347)	(0.379)	(0.452)	(0.433)
MD's level of risk aversion (C)	0.061	-0.394***	-0.071	-0.665***
	(0.136)	(0.147)	(0.155)	(0.193)
MD has university degree (D)	1.413*	0.397	1.450	1.759
	(0.760)	(0.819)	(0.898)	(1.212)
MD completed second. school (E)	0.088	-0.383	0.716	1.504
	(0.512)	(0.550)	(0.688)	(1.072)
MD completed primary school (F)	0.263	-0.659	-0.081	1.469
	(0.537)	(0.572)	(0.743)	(1.096)
Interaction terms				
A × B	0.506	0.869	-0.264	-0.690
	(0.712)	(0.808)	(0.837)	(0.734)
A × B1	0.677	0.098	0.722	0.307
	(0.550)	(0.575)	(0.669)	(0.601)
A × C	-0.520**	0.091	-0.091	0.126
	(0.237)	(0.218)	(0.269)	(0.265)
A × D	2.764**	2.512*	1.521	-1.333
	(1.318)	(1.422)	(1.294)	(1.461)
A × E	2.468***	1.579**	1.171	-0.542
	(0.879)	(0.755)	(1.010)	(1.212)
A × F	1.067	1.729**	-1.803	-0.766
	(0.893)	(0.756)	(1.419)	(1.233)

Table 7.3 (cont.)

Independent variables	Innovation			
	(1) Product	(2) Process	(3) Management	(4) Marketing
Firm-level controls				
Log no. of employees in 2013	0.027	-0.042	0.200	-0.120
	(0.143)	(0.152)	(0.160)	(0.157)
Log age of firm in 2013	-0.176	-0.473*	0.208	0.698***
	(0.259)	(0.272)	(0.270)	(0.269)
Staff with university degree	-0.607	-1.689	0.808	1.089
	(1.252)	(1.293)	(1.283)	(1.258)
On-the-job-training	-0.398*	-0.456*	-0.520*	0.016
	(0.241)	(0.251)	(0.279)	(0.278)
Located in export processing zone	0.174	0.883*	0.359	1.412***
	(0.327)	(0.359)	(0.360)	(0.349)
Located in cluster	-0.083	0.331	-0.083	-0.240
	(0.258)	(0.278)	(0.297)	(0.283)
Part of a group	0.295	0.122	0.716	-0.251
	(0.478)	(0.439)	(0.485)	(0.458)
Has a written plan	0.456	0.419	0.350	0.870***
	(0.282)	(0.303)	(0.328)	(0.301)
MD-level controls	Yes	Yes	Yes	Yes
Sector dummies	Yes	Yes	Yes	Yes
Number of observations	495	495	495	495
Log likelihood	-287.470	-281.782	-218.518	-244.823
% correctly classified	67.68	70.10	80.00	75.76
McFadden's R-sq.	0.156	0.148	0.193	0.167
Chi sq.	**106.418**	**97.547**	**104.347**	**98.132**

Notes: Standard errors in parentheses. * $p < 0.1$, ** $p < 0.05$, *** $p < 0.01$

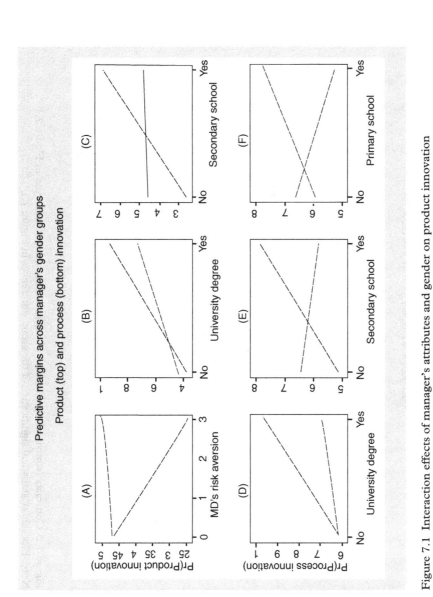

Figure 7.1 Interaction effects of manager's attributes and gender on product innovation

Note: Only significant interaction effects in Models 1 (top) and (bottom) are plotted

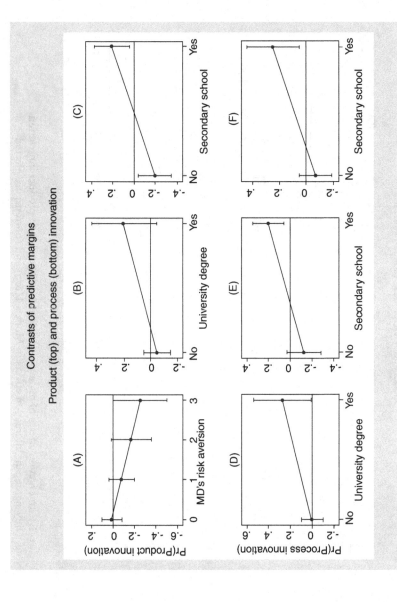

Figure 7.2 Contrasts (statistical significance) of the predictive margins reported in Figure 7.1

Note: Plots show statistical significance of the group differences in Figure 7.1

innovation is much less predictable, but women are known to prefer more predictable business environments (Morris et al., 2006). Moreover, women's lower risk tolerance (Ivanova and Alexandrova-Boshnakova, 2011) may cause them to be less committed to high-risk product innovation.

Most of the interaction terms between gender and the entrepreneur's educational attainment have significant parameter estimates in Models 1 and 2. The estimates tend to be larger for higher levels of educational attainment. The positive and significant coefficients suggest that the manager's level of education will increase the likelihood of product and process innovation in women-managed firms more than in men-managed firms. In other words, if a man and a woman with equal educational qualification each manage two different firms, the woman's firm is more likely to introduce a technological innovation than the man's, given other firm and entrepreneur attributes. Such effects do not appear for management and marketing innovation. The coefficients of $A \times D$ and $A \times E$ in Model 1 indicate that, compared to those with only basic education or no education at all, female entrepreneurs who have university or post-basic education will increase the probability of product innovation in their firms more than their male counterparts (top centre and top left plots in Figure 7.1). This difference is statistically significant for secondary education (top right plot in Figure 8.2) but not for university degree (top centre plot in Figure 7.2). Model 2 shows that even primary education, compared to having no formal education, makes a difference in the probability of process innovation, the coefficient of $A \times F$ also being significant (bottom row of Figure 7.1). The moderation effect sizes in this case are significant for all levels of educational attainment (bottom row of Figure 7.2). To sum up, our hypothesis that higher level of education has a greater effect on innovation if the manager is female (H3) is supported.

A practical connotation of the above results is that the returns from better education among women entrepreneurs may be higher than among men. The results complement existing evidence that an entrepreneur's and/or a manager's education is a key determinant of a firm's performance (Bloom et al., 2012; de Mel et al., 2008; Gennaioli et al., 2013). La Porta and Shleifer (2014) also suggest that better-educated entrepreneurs tend to start and/or manage enterprises that are more productive. What we add to this body of evidence is the gender gap that has so far been ignored: returns for entrepreneur-manager education are more pronounced if the manager is female. Whether or not this results in significantly better management practices is an open empirical question, but our evidence suggests that the association between a manager's human capital and firm-level technological innovation depends on gender. That is, if women entrepreneurs are at least as educated as men are, other things being equal, their firms may perform better in technological innovation.

The difference between Models 1 and 2 in the magnitude of the direct and moderated effects of a manager's gender is worth noting. When significant, the magnitudes of the parameter estimates are larger for product (Model 1) than process (Model 2) innovation. In order to test the statistical significance of the difference, we combine the estimation results into a one-parameter vector and a simultaneous variance-covariance matrix. This enables us to perform Wald tests of the hypothesis that parameter estimates across the two equations are statistically equal.[3] This hypothesis found no support, suggesting that though the likelihoods of a firm introducing product and process innovation are similarly affected by the manager's gender, the effect is significantly greater for product innovation.

With regard to the firm-level control variables, younger firms appear to have more process innovation while older firms are more likely to introduce marketing innovations. Firms located in export processing zones or industrial parks are more likely to have process innovation and marketing innovation. This suggests that industry policy through the development of export processing zones and high-technology industrial development parks does have some impact on firms' innovation, marketing innovation in particular. This is likely due to the market information spillover within the zone as found in Fu (2011). Firms that have a written strategic plan, which reflects more formality in management, are more likely to introduce marketing innovation. However, whether firms locate in a cluster, belong to a company group, or employ staff with university degrees do not seem to be significant predictors of firms' innovation outcome in Africa. This may be partly due to the very few university graduates working in African firms (5 per cent on average according to Table 7.1) and most of them are located in clusters (61 per cent on average according to Table 7.1). Interestingly, the estimated coefficient of the on-the-job training variable bears a negative sign, although it is only marginally significant at the 10 per cent level. Further research is needed to understand what type of training is provided, in what form, and why it does not make a significant difference in firms' innovation outcome in Ghana.

A particularly striking result in Model 5 is the positive and significant coefficient of A × C, the interaction between an entrepreneur's gender

---

[3] We used a combination of the *suest* and *test* commands in Stata to implement this procedure.

and level of risk aversion (Table 7.4). We find no such effect for new-to-firm innovation (Model 6). It suggests that a female-managed firm tends to be more successful with new-to-market innovation if the entrepreneur is more risk averse. This finding offers support to our hypothesis that a manager's risk aversion will have a positive effect on innovation success if the manager is female (H3b). This is striking, because the earlier result in Model 1 suggests that such enterprises are, in fact, less likely to introduce new products. However, upon closer look, one can see the logic behind this apparently contrasting result. Higher levels of risk aversion may discourage women entrepreneurs from product innovation more than it does men. A possible direct implication of this is that female entrepreneurs are more careful and selective, to the extent that when they choose to introduce a new product, their chance of success may be comparatively higher than that of men.

Throughout Tables 7.3 and 7.4, the study found no significant moderating effect of formality. Hence, the hypothesis that the effect of formality is contingent upon a manager's gender finds no support in our sample. However, compared to formal and informal firms, semi-formal firms show a unique profile. They are more likely to implement process innovation (Table 7.3, Model 2) but less likely to implement management innovation (Table 7.3, Model 3). Quite interestingly, the result in Model 5 (Table 7.4) suggests that formal firms may be less successful with innovation of higher novelty, at least in the Ghanaian manufacturing sector. This is interesting, considering the existing evidence that formal firms are superior to informal ones: they are more profitable (de Mel et al., 2008), significantly more productive and efficient (La Porta and Shleifer, 2008, 2014). Our evidence here suggests that as far as novel innovation is concerned, informal firms in the African context may be more efficient and successful. This particular result raises an important question for future research, but we can advance the business environment as a tentative explanation. Formalization is sometimes highly expensive in developing countries and it may expose firms to corrupt officials (Fisman and Svensson, 2007; Rand and Tarp, 2012). As a result, the formal firm may suffer a disadvantage relative to the informal one, in terms of innovation investment. Moreover, formal and informal firms may not necessarily operate in the same market, the market for the former likely being more sophisticated and competitive. The combined effect of consumer sophistication and competition may lead to lower aggregate innovative sales.

Table 7.4 *The role of manager's gender in innovative sales (fractional logit estimations)*

Independent variables	Innovative sales	
	(5) New-to-market	(6) New-to-firm
MD is female (A)	**−12.613**	−0.506
	(1.144)	(0.611)
Firm is formal (B)	**−0.917**	−0.078
	(0.548)	(0.264)
Firm is semi-formal (B1)	0.064	−0.238
	(0.409)	(0.173)
MD's level of risk aversion (C)	0.060	0.126
	(0.199)	(0.091)
MD has a university degree (D)	−0.737	0.107
	(1.297)	(0.480)
MD completed secondary school (E)	0.404	0.079
	(0.843)	(0.328)
MD completed primary school (F)	−0.749	0.253
	(1.071)	(0.348)
Interaction terms		
A × B	0.943	−0.384
	(1.042)	(0.420)
A × B1	−1.291	0.059
	(0.956)	(0.307)
A × C	**0.628**	0.068
	(0.302)	(0.139)
A × D	**12.732**	0.688
	(1.456)	(0.763)
A × E	**12.445**	0.510
	(1.238)	(0.665)
A × F	**12.861**	−0.280
	(1.564)	(0.647)
MD-level controls	Yes	Yes
Firm-level controls	Yes	Yes
Sector dummies	Yes	Yes
Number of observations	223	223
Log likelihood	−42.456	−104.053
Chi sq.	**970.750**	**153.279**

Note: Robust standard errors in parentheses; **Bold** figures are statistically significant at the 5% level

7.4.1   Robustness Tests

In this section, we test the robustness of our results with respect to the variables included. We investigate how the results are affected when the estimation equation changes. We first perform alternative estimations, wherein we include only one variable for formality, thereby treating semi-formal firms as informal. The main effects of formality discussed above do not appear in the results, but all other findings remain remarkably robust (Tables 7.8 and 7.9 in Appendix 7.3). It would seem that the lower level of aggregation of formality that we have used delivers deeper insight. It may be worthwhile for future research to keep with the notion that formality exists in a continuum, rather than as a discrete dichotomous event.

Next, following Barslund et al. (2007), this study runs a series of logit and fractional logit regressions to assess the sensitivity of the results to omission of specific groups of variables. Specifically, we organize the variables of Tables 7.3 and 7.4 into two groups. One group contains our main variables of interest and their interactions as well as sector's fixed effects. These are included in all subsequent regressions when we perform the fractional logit regressions and include the IMR in the first group of variables. The second group contains all other variables, namely the firm-level and manager-level control variables. Innovation is then regressed on all possible linear combinations of the control variables including, in all the regressions, the full set of main variables. In other words, if the group of control variables comprises x variables, we perform 2^x-1 regressions. As there are eleven control variables, 2,047 logit regressions and 2,047 fractional logit regressions are performed altogether.[4]

Table 7.10 in Appendix 7.3 shows the summary statistics from this analysis. The first three columns show the maximum, minimum and average of the point estimates over all possible regressions, as discussed above. Column 4 shows the average standard deviation of the point estimates. Columns 5–7 contain the main results from the analysis. They reflect, respectively, the share of regressions where the point estimate is significant at the 5 per cent level, the share with a positive point estimate (not necessarily significant) and finally the share of regressions with a negative point estimate. Column 8 gives the average t-value over all regressions.

Overall, our results are remarkably robust. In the case of product innovation, the signs on all parameter estimates and their significance remain consistent, irrespective of which control variables are included. With the exception of the dummy for whether the manager has a university degree, which is insignificant in only 27 per cent of the regressions, all significant

---

[4] The procedure was greatly simplified with the *checkrob* command developed for Stata by Barslund et al. (2007).

coefficients in Model 1 (Table 7.3) remain so at the 5 per cent level. Similarly, the parameter estimates for process innovation (Model 2 in Table 7.3) remain consistent in sign and significance, with the exception of the interaction between a manager's gender and possession of a university degree, which is insignificant many times, and the dummy for whether the firm is formal, which is significant in more than half of the regressions. In other words, both the gender-moderated effect of a university degree on the probability of process innovation and the direct effect of formality are sensitive to the inclusion or exclusion of some of our control variables. All the results for management and marketing innovation are consistent throughout. The results for innovative sales are also very robust to various specifications. In the case of new-to-market innovative sales, the signs and significance of the main parameter estimates are consistent with the results in Model 5 (Table 7.4). Only the direct effect of formality and the interaction of a manager's gender and risk attitudes are somewhat sensitive to the inclusion or exclusion of some of the control variables – their parameter estimates are insignificant in some of the regressions. We obtain robust results for new-to-firm innovative sales too – the parameter estimates are never significant, and their signs remain generally consistent with those in Model 6 (Table 7.4). In sum, the main results that we present and discuss in the paper are strong.

7.5   Conclusion

This chapter started with the observation that although half of the people in sub-Saharan Africa (SSA) are women, gender gaps in entrepreneurship and innovation are rarely studied in the context. Hence, there are important gaps in existing literature. Most of the existing research on gender-related inequalities and entrepreneurship focus on women's identity, inequalities in access to resources and performance in terms of firm size and growth (Bardasi et al., 2011; Branisa et al, 2013; Ndemo and Maina, 2007). The evidence from developed countries suggests that women's firms are less innovative than men's (Thébaud, 2015). We extend this literature with our study, which is arguably the first that rigorously examines firm-level innovation in the SSA context from a gender perspective. Considering the importance of firm-level innovation in economic empowerment, and recent global efforts at creating and maintaining an inclusive society, this issue is of particular interest. Our study context is the Ghanaian manufacturing industry from which we have a representative data set including approximately 500 firms. Similar to the United States, the United Kingdom and Canada, about a third of the firms are managed by women entrepreneurs. The results provide useful insight for research and policy.

Evidence from the data suggests that firms managed by women entre-preneurs are less innovative in product, process and management innov-ations than those managed by men. The average share of sales accruing from new or improved products is also significantly less in firms managed by women. The only exception is market innovation, for which the firms managed by women entrepreneurs did better than those managed by men.

Driving economic growth through entrepreneurship is a strategy that is needed in SSA due to pervasive and high levels of unemployment. It has been suggested that countries should implement deliberate strat-egies geared towards increasing the supply of highly educated entrepre-neurs and business managers who have a proven propensity to start high-growth firms and can better manage these firms (La Porta and Shleifer, 2014). Our results offer a specific novel insight regarding this. We have demonstrated that the marginal returns of higher levels of education in terms of firm performance are substantially higher among women entrepreneurs. This is particularly true for technological innovation and the success of new products. Hence, policies aimed at stimulating high-quality entrepreneurship may be even more successful if they incorporate a focus on women. Simultaneously, strategies aimed at the economic empowerment of women need to pay attention to women's education.

This chapter also deepens our understanding of the role of risk atti-tudes in firm-level innovation. The entrepreneurship literature highlights that women are typically more risk averse (Ivanova and Alexandrova-Boshnakova, 2011) and that successful entrepreneurs generally have lower risk aversion (Djankov et al., 2005; 2007). The results draw atten-tion to how these differences might be connected to the entrepreneur's gender. We find that compared to firms managed by men, risk aversion has a significantly bigger negative impact on the likelihood of product innovation in women-managed firms.

Furthermore, this chapter delivers some unique insights into formality. First, our study has an important implication for the research on formal-ity. In addition to the dichotomous classification of firms as formal or informal, this chapter also distinguishes semi-formal firms. This approach is consistent with the argument that formality follows a continuum (Trebilcock, 2005). Indeed, this chapter finds that semi-formal firms show a unique profile. Second, in contrast to the conven-tional wisdom that informal firms are poor performers (La Porta and Shleifer, 2014), the evidence in this chapter suggests that informal firms in the African context may be more efficient and successful in novel innovation. In moderating the gender–innovation relationship, formality plays no role even though it has limited direct effect on innovation.

Moreover, this chapter finds that in technological innovation, firms managed by women entrepreneurs are less innovative than those managed by men. This result is particularly relevant for policy and institution design. In an institutional approach to the analysis of gender gaps in entrepreneurship, Thébaud (2015) suggested that missing work–life balance or weak institutions are reasons behind the weaker innovative performance of firms managed by women. Indeed, institutional arrangements that help women to mitigate the challenge of work–life balance and to measure up to men in terms of human capital and work experience are generally weak or missing in Africa. To illustrate, consider a female entrepreneur who has a little child. The fact that the woman will allocate a significant amount of time to unpaid family-related work makes it difficult for her to attain the same performance levels as men who are allocating substantially less time to unpaid work (Asiedu et al., 2013). Institutional arrangements developed to address this gender gap in Europe, for instance, include long periods of paid maternity leave – up to two years in some countries – and subsidized childcare. Such arrangements are desirable in African countries, as well.

Appendices

Appendix 7.1

SECTORAL DISTRIBUTION – THE PAVITT TAXONOMY

There is considerable heterogeneity especially in innovation within and across sectors (Archibugi, 2001; Malerba and Mani, 2009; Srholec and Verspagen, 2012). For our analyses, we use a seminal sectoral classification scheme in the evolutionary economics literature, the Pavitt taxonomy (Pavitt, 1984), which categorizes firms according to sources of technology, requirements of the users, and appropriability regime, all of which affect performance, as listed here.

1. Supplier-dominated: mostly traditional manufacturing such as textiles and agriculture, which rely on external sources of innovation
2. Scale-intensive: mainly firms producing basic materials and consumer durables, for example, automotive sector. Sources of innovation may be both internal and external to the firm with a medium level of appropriability.

3. Specialized suppliers: specialized firms producing technology to be sold to other firms, for example, specialized machinery production and high-tech instruments. There is a high level of appropriability due to the tacit nature of the knowledge.
4. Science-based: high-tech firms that rely on R&D from both in-house sources and university research, including industries such as pharmaceuticals and electronics. New products or processes are rapidly developed, and there is a high degree of appropriability from patents, secrecy and tacit know-how.

Table 7.5 *Detailed sectoral distribution of the sampled firms*

SECTOR	Frequency (per cent of sample)
Supplier dominated	252
of which:	(50.81)
Manufacture of wearing apparel	102
Manufacture of furniture	75
Manufacture of wood and of products of wood and cork	51
Manufacture of textiles	23
Manufacture of leather and related products	1
Scale-intensive	224
of which:	(45.16)
Manufacture of food products	125
Manufacture of fabricated metal products, except machinery and equipment	65
Manufacture of paper and paper products	10
Manufacture of rubber and plastics products	9
Printing and reproduction of recorded media	9
Manufacture of basic metals	3
Manufacture of beverages	2
Manufacture of motor vehicles, trailers and semi-trailers	1
Specialized suppliers	15
of which:	(3.02)
Other manufacturing	12
Manufacture of electrical equipment	2
Manufacture of machinery and equipment	1
Science-based	5
of which:	(1.01)
Manufacture of chemicals and chemical products	3
Manufacture of basic pharmaceutical products	2

Appendix 7.2
CORRELATIONS

Table 7.6 *Pairwise correlations among independent variables*

	1	2	3	4	5	6	7	8	9	10	11	12	13	14	15	16	17
1 GENDER	1																
2 FORMAL	-0.2189	1															
3 MDDEGREE	-0.1572	0.5130	1														
4 MDPOSTBASIC	-0.1045	-0.0537	-0.3500	1													
5 MDBASIC	0.0568	-0.2425	-0.2446	-0.5871	1												
6 MDNOEDUC	0.2375	-0.1031	-0.1445	-0.3468	-0.2424	1											
7 RISKAVERSION	-0.0809	-0.1582	0.0098	0.0481	-0.0693	0.0129	1										
8 SIZE	-0.1076	0.4443	0.4835	-0.0909	-0.2482	-0.0094	-0.079	1									
9 AGE	-0.1239	0.2612	0.1749	0.0732	-0.1481	-0.0831	0.0267	0.2449	1								
10 STAFFQUAL	-0.1659	0.4937	0.7605	-0.1436	-0.2697	-0.1795	-0.0206	0.4466	0.1361	1							
11 TRAINING	-0.1421	0.2598	0.2337	-0.009	-0.2010	0.0541	0.1295	0.3170	0.0362	0.1972	1						
12 GROUP	0.0404	0.2206	0.2745	-0.1956	-0.1284	0.1942	-0.0048	0.3068	-0.0531	0.2472	0.2052	1					
13 EPZ	-0.1506	0.1667	0.2878	-0.083	-0.0876	-0.0446	0.042	0.2451	0.0262	0.2541	0.1400	0.0744	1				
14 CLUSTER	0.1497	-0.4531	-0.2522	-0.0368	0.1224	0.1413	0.0701	-0.2928	-0.2680	-0.2607	-0.1187	-0.0566	0.0198	1			
15 MDAGE	0.0501	0.083	0.0578	0.0573	-0.1334	0.0386	-0.0511	0.0751	0.2919	0.0205	-0.0796	-0.0129	-0.0175	-0.0131	1		
16 MDTENURE	-0.0372	0.0764	-0.1177	0.1135	-0.0384	0.0003	0.0226	0.0561	0.7038	-0.1429	-0.0332	-0.2279	-0.1049	-0.1369	0.3733	1	
17 PLAN	-0.1183	0.4798	0.5212	0.0434	-0.2897	-0.1925	-0.1490	0.4125	0.1640	0.5000	0.2030	0.1879	0.1388	-0.2028	0.057	-0.0101	1
18 DECISION_MAKER	0.055	0.0226	-0.1558	0.0017	0.0084	0.1428	0.0682	0.0743	-0.0153	-0.1278	0.3168	0.07	-0.1344	-0.0653	-0.1249	0.0947	0.0034

Note: Correlations greater than |0.1| are significant at the 5% level; Max (mean) Variance Inflation Factor = 3.63 (1.79); Condition number = 26.29

Appendix 7.3

SELECTION EQUATION AND ROBUSTNESS TESTS

Table 7.7 *Results of first-stage (selection) probit equation*

	Product
Log no. of employees in 2013	0.107
	(0.067)
Log age of firm in 2013	0.100
	(0.099)
% staff with university degree	0.824
	(0.619)
On-the-job training	−0.182
	(0.127)
Located in export processing zone	0.184
	(0.183)
Located in cluster	−0.154
	(0.129)
Part of a group	−0.342
	(0.229)
Has written strategic plan	**0.448**
	(0.151)
Number of observations	495.000
Log likelihood	−319.860
McFadden's R-sq.	0.061
Chi sq.	**41.638**

Note: Standard errors in parentheses; **Bold** figures are statistically significant at the 5% level

Appendix 7.4

Table 7.8 *Robustness test – logit estimations with semi-formal firms treated as informal*

Independent variables	Innovation			
	(7) Product	(8) Process	(9) Management	(10) Marketing
MD is female (A)	**−2.005**	**−1.521**	−0.435	1.799
	(0.805)	(0.654)	(0.925)	(1.160)
Firm is formal (B)	0.236	0.282	−0.112	0.156
	(0.360)	(0.389)	(0.427)	(0.406)
MD's level of risk aversion (C)	0.059	−0.436	−0.012	**−0.655**
	(0.135)	(0.144)	(0.152)	(0.193)
MD has university degree (D)	**1.392**	0.405	1.372	1.744
	(0.760)	(0.811)	(0.890)	(1.212)
MD completed secondary school (E)	0.082	−0.306	0.640	1.490
	(0.512)	(0.544)	(0.683)	(1.073)
MD completed primary school (F)	0.257	−0.649	−0.050	1.479
	(0.537)	(0.566)	(0.738)	(1.096)
Interaction terms				
A × B	0.202	0.782	−0.460	−0.826
	(0.683)	(0.793)	(0.752)	(0.674)
A × C	**−0.577**	0.090	−0.134	0.113
	(0.237)	(0.216)	(0.263)	(0.264)
A × D	**3.032**	**2.776**	1.503	−1.278
	(1.295)	(1.395)	(1.250)	(1.442)
A × E	**2.733**	**1.837**	1.203	−0.490
	(0.861)	(0.724)	(0.975)	(1.198)
A × F	1.066	**1.745**	−1.833	−0.780
	(0.887)	(0.748)	(1.416)	(1.233)
MD-level controls	Yes	Yes	Yes	Yes
Firm-level controls	Yes	Yes	Yes	Yes
Sector dummies	Yes	Yes	Yes	Yes
Number of observations	495.000	495.000	495.000	495.000
Log likelihood	−288.646	−287.764	−221.334	−245.005
% correctly classified	67.27	67.68	79.39	75.96
McFadden's R-sq.	0.153	0.129	0.182	0.166
Chi sq.	**104.066**	**85.584**	**98.716**	**97.767**

Note: Standard errors in parentheses; **Bold** figures are statistically significant at the 5% level

Appendix 7.5

Table 7.9 *Robustness test – fractional logit estimations with semi-formal firms treated as informal*

Independent variables	Innovative sales	
	(11) New-to-market	(12) New-to-firm
MD is female (A)	**−13.003**	−0.498
	(1.078)	(0.591)
Firm is formal (B)	−0.801	0.081
	(0.497)	(0.234)
MD's level of risk aversion (C)	0.047	0.143
	(0.196)	(0.088)
MD has university degree (D)	−0.643	0.107
	(1.291)	(0.472)
MD completed secondary school (E)	0.421	0.054
	(0.838)	(0.321)
MD completed primary school (F)	−0.758	0.255
	(1.050)	(0.343)
Interaction terms		
A × B	1.588	−0.382
	(0.970)	(0.360)
A × C	**0.661**	0.060
	(0.306)	(0.135)
A × D	**12.494**	0.651
	(1.387)	(0.717)
A × E	**12.108**	0.491
	(1.158)	(0.612)
A × F	**12.998**	−0.262
	(1.518)	(0.626)
MD-level controls	Yes	Yes
Firm-level controls	Yes	Yes
Sector dummies (Pavitt)	Yes	Yes
Number of observations	223.000	223.000
Log likelihood	−42.752	−104.183
Chi sq.	**1,049.543**	**144.139**

Note: Robust standard errors in parentheses; **Bold** figures are statistically significant at the 5% level

Appendix 7.6

Table 7.10 *Summary statistics of sensitivity analysis*

Main variable	Max	Min	Mean	Product innovation (logit)				
				AvgSTD	PercSig	Perc+	Perc−	AvgT
MD is female (A)	−1.90	−2.21	−2.07	0.81	1.00	0.00	1.00	2.56
Firm is formal (B)	0.56	0.22	0.39	0.38	0.00	1.00	0.00	1.03
Firm is semi-formal (B1)	0.16	0.00	0.09	0.33	0.00	1.00	0.00	0.26
MD's level of risk aversion (C)	0.07	0.02	0.05	0.13	0.00	1.00	0.00	0.34
MD has a university degree (D)	1.83	1.20	1.48	0.69	0.73	1.00	0.00	2.17
MD completed secondary school (E)	0.25	0.02	0.14	0.51	0.00	1.00	0.00	0.27
MD completed primary school (F)	0.35	0.17	0.26	0.53	0.00	1.00	0.00	0.49
A × B	0.57	0.33	0.46	0.70	0.00	1.00	0.00	0.65
A × B1	0.73	0.53	0.63	0.55	0.00	1.00	0.00	1.15
A × C	−0.48	−0.56	−0.52	0.24	1.00	0.00	1.00	2.21
A × D	2.89	2.53	2.74	1.30	1.00	1.00	0.00	2.11
A × E	2.58	2.30	2.42	0.87	1.00	1.00	0.00	2.79
A × F	1.32	0.94	1.12	0.88	0.00	1.00	0.00	1.28
				Process innovation (logit)				
MD is female (A)	−1.26	−1.67	−1.49	0.65	0.99	0.00	1.00	2.30
Firm is formal (B)	1.17	0.44	0.82	0.40	0.58	1.00	0.00	2.02
Firm is semi-formal (B1)	1.11	0.71	0.92	0.35	1.00	1.00	0.00	2.60
MD's level of risk aversion (C)	−0.34	−0.42	−0.39	0.14	1.00	0.00	1.00	2.71
MD has a university degree (D)	0.71	−0.44	0.18	0.74	0.00	0.78	0.22	0.32

MD completed secondary school (E)	-0.25	-0.59	-0.43	0.54	0.00	0.00	1.00	0.78
MD completed primary school (F)	-0.61	-0.99	-0.79	0.57	0.00	0.00	1.00	1.40
A × B	1.03	0.56	0.83	0.80	0.00	1.00	0.00	1.04
A × B1	0.35	0.00	0.16	0.57	0.00	0.99	0.01	0.28
A × C	0.15	0.00	0.08	0.21	0.00	1.00	0.00	0.38
A × D	2.99	2.29	2.58	1.40	0.10	1.00	0.00	1.85
A × E	1.73	1.37	1.54	0.74	0.91	1.00	0.00	2.08
A × F	2.24	1.70	1.94	0.74	1.00	1.00	0.00	2.63

Management innovation (logit)

MD is female (A)	-0.23	-0.89	-0.57	0.92	0.00	0.00	1.00	0.62
Firm is formal (B)	-0.08	-0.81	-0.47	0.45	0.00	0.00	1.00	1.05
Firm is semi-formal (B1)	-0.73	-1.09	-0.92	0.43	0.87	0.00	1.00	2.13
MD's level of risk aversion (C)	-0.03	-0.11	-0.07	0.15	0.00	0.00	1.00	0.47
MD has a university degree (D)	2.53	1.33	1.88	0.83	0.75	1.00	0.00	2.28
MD completed secondary school (E)	0.94	0.61	0.78	0.68	0.00	1.00	0.00	1.16
MD completed primary school (F)	0.12	-0.29	-0.07	0.73	0.00	0.22	0.78	0.12
A × B	-0.02	-0.57	-0.31	0.82	0.00	0.00	1.00	0.38
A × B1	0.83	0.49	0.66	0.66	0.00	1.00	0.00	0.99
A × C	-0.03	-0.19	-0.11	0.26	0.00	0.00	1.00	0.42
A ×D	1.68	0.72	1.25	1.27	0.00	1.00	0.00	0.98
A × E	1.48	0.81	1.12	1.00	0.00	1.00	0.00	1.13
A × F	-1.30	-2.21	-1.78	1.40	0.00	0.00	1.00	1.27

Table 7.10 (cont.)

	Marketing innovation (logit)							
MD is female (A)	2.04	1.30	1.65	1.15	0.00	1.00	0.00	1.44
Firm is formal (B)	0.67	-0.11	0.24	0.43	0.00	0.91	0.09	0.59
Firm is semi-formal (B1)	0.21	-0.30	-0.07	0.41	0.00	0.31	0.69	0.26
MD's level of risk aversion (C)	-0.53	-0.71	-0.62	0.19	1.00	0.00	1.00	3.31
MD has a university degree (D)	2.92	1.40	2.18	1.15	0.34	1.00	0.00	1.89
MD completed secondary school (E)	1.92	1.33	1.61	1.06	0.00	1.00	0.00	1.52
MD completed primary school (F)	1.71	1.22	1.45	1.09	0.00	1.00	0.00	1.34
A × B	-0.32	-0.77	-0.53	0.70	0.00	0.00	1.00	0.74
A × B1	0.40	0.10	0.26	0.59	0.00	1.00	0.00	0.44
A × C	0.15	-0.02	0.07	0.26	0.00	0.91	0.09	0.26
A × D	-1.04	-1.82	-1.50	1.43	0.00	0.00	1.00	1.05
A × E	-0.33	-0.86	-0.62	1.20	0.00	0.00	1.00	0.51
A × F	-0.48	-1.17	-0.80	1.21	0.00	0.00	1.00	0.66

	New-to-market innovative sales (fractional logit)							
MD is female (A)	-11.20	-16.37	-13.05	1.11	1.00	0.00	1.00	11.74
Firm is formal (B)	-0.09	-1.32	-0.72	0.55	0.10	0.00	1.00	1.33
Firm is semi-formal (B1)	0.26	-0.46	-0.02	0.46	0.00	0.56	0.44	0.27
MD's level of risk aversion (C)	0.30	0.01	0.16	0.21	0.00	1.00	0.00	0.74
MD has a university degree (D)	0.23	-1.46	-0.55	1.13	0.00	0.09	0.91	0.50
MD completed secondary school (E)	0.55	-0.31	0.15	0.82	0.00	0.67	0.33	0.29
MD completed primary school (F)	-0.42	-1.47	-0.89	1.00	0.00	0.00	1.00	0.90
A × B	1.46	-0.05	0.60	1.06	0.00	0.98	0.02	0.56

	Max	Min	Mean	AvgSTD	PercSig	Perc+	Perc-	AvgT
A × B1	−0.56	−1.78	−1.26	0.96	0.00	0.00	1.00	1.32
A × C	0.70	0.26	0.46	0.31	0.16	1.00	0.00	1.47
A × D	16.75	11.45	13.27	1.42	1.00	1.00	0.00	9.37
A × E	16.41	11.11	12.83	1.21	1.00	1.00	0.00	10.64
A × F	16.39	11.30	13.05	1.52	1.00	1.00	0.00	8.55
New-to-firm innovative sales (fractional logit)								
MD is female (A)	−0.38	−0.75	−0.59	0.62	0.00	0.00	1.00	0.96
Firm is formal (B)	0.13	−0.30	−0.07	0.26	0.00	0.24	0.76	0.39
Firm is semi-formal (B1)	−0.11	−0.34	−0.22	0.17	0.00	0.00	1.00	1.25
MD's level of risk aversion (C)	0.15	0.06	0.10	0.10	0.00	1.00	0.00	1.07
MD has a university degree (D)	0.22	−0.41	−0.02	0.47	0.00	0.49	0.51	0.21
MD completed secondary school (E)	0.18	−0.04	0.05	0.33	0.00	0.88	0.12	0.15
MD completed primary school (F)	0.37	0.07	0.20	0.35	0.00	1.00	0.00	0.59
A × B	−0.20	−0.47	−0.33	0.43	0.00	0.00	1.00	0.77
A × B1	0.24	−0.03	0.11	0.31	0.00	1.00	0.00	0.36
A × C	0.17	0.05	0.11	0.14	0.00	1.00	0.00	0.76
A × D	0.90	0.56	0.78	0.78	0.00	1.00	0.00	1.01
A × E	0.74	0.36	0.54	0.68	0.00	1.00	0.00	0.81
A × F	−0.07	−0.40	−0.20	0.66	0.00	0.00	1.00	0.31

Note: Max, Min, and Mean are, respectively, the maximum, minimum, and mean value of the point estimate over all regressions. AvgSTD and AvgT are, respectively, averages of the standard deviations and t-values. PercSig gives the percentage times the coefficient was significant, Perc+ indicates the number of times the coefficient had a positive sign and Perc− the number of times it had a negative sign.

8   The Role of the State in Innovation in Africa

Xiaolan Fu, George Essegbey and Bitrina Diyamett

8.1   Introduction

Government can effectively reduce the technological gap between LICs and advanced economies by strengthening the national and regional innovation systems to encourage indigenous knowledge creation, foster domestic and international knowledge transfers and promote the upgrading of technological capabilities. Since independence, stimulating a rapid social and economic development by using knowledge and tools derived from science and technology (S&T) has been the ambitious plan of the Government of Ghana. To date, however, the role played by S&T policy in Ghana's development has been limited. Similarly, Tanzania has had a long history of harnessing S&T for national development with the establishment of research institutes and the Tanzania Commission for Science and Technology, founded in 1958, with responsibility for S&T policy.

The question of what impact the research and development (R&D) system or even more specifically S&T policy has played in the national development in Tanzania is yet to be satisfactorily answered. Linked to the efforts to implement S&T policies are also the efforts to implement related policies; this implementation manifests the reality of successful harnessing of S&T. One such important policy is the industrial policy, which both Ghana and Tanzania have formulated in consonance with their S&T or science, technology and innovation (STI) policies. In reviewing some of the key elements of Ghana's and Tanzania's S&T policy from the perspective of local firms, this chapter seeks to offer an understanding of their current status and impacts. An examination of the innovation policies in these two countries also offers an opportunity to validate the findings and deepen our understanding of what innovation policies are valued by the firms in Africa, how effective they are and how they are implemented.

In this vein, the rest of this chapter is structured as follows. Section 8.2 discusses the role of the state in industrial and innovation policy. Section 8.3 presents evidence regarding firms' perception about different aspects of Ghana's innovation policy using qualitative data, while Section 8.4 compares the different changes in policy between 2013 and 2015 in Ghana and Tanzania. Concluding remarks are presented in Section 8.5.

8.2   The Debate on Industrial Policy, Innovation Policy and the Role of the State

8.2.1   Industry Policy and the Role of the State

Industrial policy has been the subject of a crucial debate regarding national economic policy for development. Generally, economic theories emphasize the role of market or the role of government, though each of them has its pros and cons. There are two competing theories in this regard. Neoclassical economists, who dominate the orthodox economic theory, believe that the market is generally efficient enough to maximize the total welfare of a society and that government intervention is needed only when a market failure occurs. Yet new institutional economists represented by Douglass North argue that institutions, or the setting of rules for players in the market, make a difference to economic development and that institutions can shorten the period of development if used wisely.

Traditionally, industrial policy is understood to be selective government policy of market intervention designed to stimulate economic growth that could not have happened in a free market (Pack and Saggi, 2006). Rodrik defines industrial policy slightly differently by acknowledging the engagement of private firms in the making of policy strategies (2004).[1] The reason why industrial policy comes into play largely originates from the sharp contrast of economic growth among late-industrializing countries in the second half of the twentieth century. The Washington Consensus, which takes neoliberal economics as its underpinning, failed in many countries in Latin America and in some countries in Africa. By contrast, an economic boom took place in East Asian countries such as South Korea (Amsden, 1989) and Singapore (Huff, 1994), where industrial policy was largely adopted and identified as a key factor that contributed to the success stories in East Asia (Amsden, 2001).

---

[1] This is consistent with the evolution of public policymaking, which suggests that for good policies, government has to involve all stakeholders, which include, especially, the private sector, when it comes to economic policies.

The debate on the role of industrial policy is still on-going. The theories supporting industrial policy include (1) technological externalities or knowledge spillovers, (2) information externalities and (3) coordination externalities (Rodrik, 2004). The technological externalities theory has developed into the infant industry protection policy, and the information externalities theory mainly contributes to the industrial targeting policy (Chang and Lin, 2009).

8.2.1.1 Infant Industry/Technology Externalities The infant industry argument goes as follows: production costs can be particularly higher at first for newly established industries vis-à-vis experienced foreign competitors with technological advantages. But the marginal cost will decrease very quickly as long as the domestic producers become skilled through 'learning by observing and doing' as a result of the presence of foreign firms with higher technological capabilities. However, learning from foreign firms presupposes some basic level of technological capabilities on the part of domestic firms; with an initial policy of infant industry protection, the domestic producers can mobilize such capabilities, and by learning from foreign firms, they can be as efficient as their foreign rivals or even perform far better because of the home-country advantage, such as familiarity with culture, language and the institutional set up that imposes additional costs on the part of foreign firms. This is beneficial not only for national development but also for world welfare (Wood, 2003). On the other hand, it is also argued by other scholars that the financial constraints on innovation should be solved by finance from capital markets, not by national governments (Pack and Saggi, 2006). Subsidies should go to research and development aimed at creating new knowledge and better technologies instead of publicly financing the competition based on production using existing technologies. For poor developing countries such as Ghana and Tanzania, however, Saggi's proposal might not be the best option for spending public resources; as will later become clear, innovation in these countries is largely achieved through learning by doing and using and interacting (DUI) rather than through R&D. Of course, this is not to say that R&D is not important in the DUI mode of innovation, but rather to put emphasis on the DUI itself.

8.2.1.2 Industrial Targeting/Information Externalities Admittedly, the static comparative advantage can make choices for the moment only but fails to have a long-term vision. In order to take an advantageous position in international specialization, Chang and Lin (2009) argue that developing countries should use industrial policy to promote capital/knowledge-intensive industries so that developing countries can learn in the process of the development of these industries. On the other hand, Pack and Saggi (2006) argue that it is very uncertain that industrial policy can be deliberately 'designed to encourage the "right" industries'. Moreover, Klimenko (2004) finds that learning through experimentation in the private sector without government assistance can actually yield better outcomes.

8.2.1.3 Coordination Failures   Some projects have to be invested in and operated simultaneously to be profitable, such as the steel and automobile industries. The market failure to coordinate two intertwined industries justifies a related industrial policy. However, Pack and Saggi (2006) argue that intertwined industries can, nevertheless, find ways to realize coordination, for example through supply networks in a free market.

8.2.1.4 The Drawbacks and Defence of Industrial Policy   However, industrial policy also has widely recognized drawbacks. Both Rodrik (2004) and Pack and Saggi (2006) agree that industrial policy brings more possibilities for corruption and rent seeking. Also, it can have negative impacts on the financial sector in the long run, taking the Asian financial crises in the late 1990s as an example (Pack and Saggi, 2006). Moreover, the government is not omniscient and can miss information that the private sector has about business opportunities, and therefore block diversification (Rodrik, 2004). Nevertheless, two counterarguments can be made against Pack and Saggi's criticisms of industrial policy. First, regarding industrial targeting in particular, developing countries can target technology in general instead of a specific sector as they are so limited in industrialization. Second, compared to allocation by market, industrial policy requires less time to achieve the goals and this is essential to international development. Moreover, in spite of the flaws of industrial policy that Pack and Saggi listed, Rodrik (2004) argues that industrial policy itself is not problematic; what is problematic is badly designed industrial policy. He further lays out institutional requirements for sound industrial policy, which should (1) have top-level political support, (2) coordinate and have smooth feedback processes between the public and the private, and (3) establish mechanisms of transparency and accountability to prevent corruption.

Recently, theories diverge on the question of whether industrial policy should conform to or defy a country's comparative advantage, between neoclassical economics and institutional economics; however, the two theories can find common ground – that 100 per cent conforming to the static comparative advantage is not the best policy to advance economic growth and that industrial policy is useful for economic development if adopted properly (Chang and Lin, 2009). Total and full conforming can only be idealistic and never realistic. Lin and Chang diverge in their theoretical interpretation of industrial policy. From the neoclassical economics perspective, Lin argues that industrial policy requires necessary government intervention when market failure occurs, including information externalities of innovation and infrastructure coordination problems. It conforms to the comparative advantage of a country on the ladder of the GVC; in particular, it agrees with the position that transition to capital/knowledge-intensive industries happens naturally, as the flying geese phenomenon happens and the human and physical capital are accumulated over time to develop capital/knowledge-intensive industries. From the institutional economics perspective, however, Chang argues that industrial policy is an essential institutional design for a country to compete in the international market. It defies the existing comparative advantage of a country and creates a new comparative advantage that is at a higher position along the ladder of the GVC. In particular, it argues that transition does not happen automatically due to imperfect factor mobility and asymmetric technological capabilities.

However, Lin and Chang's debate shows the convergent trend of recognition and understanding of industrial policy from two competing economic theories. The two theories converge as Chang admitted that industrial policy should not deviate too much from the country's comparative advantage because comparative advantage offers a 'useful guideline in telling us how much the country is sacrificing by protecting its infant industries'. On the other hand, Lin used the concept of adjustment costs to internalize the long-term benefits of transitioning from labour/resource-intensive industries to capital/knowledge-intensive industries and conceptualize comparative advantage as dynamic and able to be shifted by government intervention to reduce adjustment costs. Furthermore, Lin and Chang come to similar policy conclusions, which only differ in the degree to which a country's industrial policy should stretch from the static comparative advantage (Chang and Lin, 2009).

Empirically, there is mixed evidence on the effectiveness of industry policy. For example, evidence in Japan, Hong Kong, Korea, Singapore and Taiwan proves that capital accumulation was incentivized by government and led to investment in their economic development, which counters the then assumption that capital existed in East Asia in the pre-industrialization era (Akyüz and Gore, 1996). Also, the learning process set by the government boosted technological capability, or the ability to use technology, and helped developing countries move up along the GVC from resource-based manufacturing to technology-based manufacturing, which indicates the significance of building the national ability to master and use technologies as an industrial policy (Lall, 2000).

There is also evidence against industrial policy. For example, regarding capital accumulation, Beason and Weinstein (1996) find little connection between preferential policies in Japan and the rate of capital accumulation in the targeted sectors or the total productivity growth. Moreover, Pack (2000) finds that the learning process does not work well in Japan and South Korea as labour in the sectors that were encouraged did not flow to neglected sectors and transmit technology and knowledge elsewhere. In addition, a study of India's success in the software industry also refutes the cluster effect in Bangladesh as government-led industrial policy. The cluster came into being naturally as Indian information technology engineers received postgraduate education in the UK or the US and had an excellent reputation in the industry, which attracts investors and outsourcers; the Indian government simply ratified the success instead of creating it (Pack and Saggi, 2006).

In concluding, this section argues that industrial policy or not, the role of technology and innovation capabilities in industrial development cannot be overstated; and the major question is therefore: do we or do we not need innovation policy for industrial development? This is a major subject of discussion for the next section.

8.2.2   Innovation Policy and the Role of the State

Innovation policy has emerged as a new field of economic policy. During the last two to three decades, policymakers have increasingly become concerned about the role of innovation for economic performance and, more recently, for the solution of challenges that arise. The view that policy may have a role in supporting innovation has become widespread and the term innovation policy has become commonly used (Edler and Fagerberg, 2017). Innovation policy should be about national innovation capacity, that is, the generation of new knowledge as well as its absorption, diffusion and demand (Radosevic, 2012).

In recent years, the discussion on innovation policy research mainly focuses on the following aspects: (1) innovation policy rationale, (2) innovation policy instruments, and (3) innovation policy governance.

8.2.2.1 Innovation Policy Rationale The issue of innovation policy rationale departs from market failure to embrace several new types of failures (Laranja et al., 2008). Arnold (2004) expands the idea of failures to: capability failures (inadequacies in the ability of companies to act adequately in their own interest), failures in institutions (failures in social institutions such as universities, research institutes and patent offices to fulfil their NIS functions), network failures (innovation system interaction problems) and framework failures (framework policies with a negative effect on innovation). The most frequently used alternative type of failure is a system failure (OECD, 1998), which means a problem occurs when the system is not functioning well, that is, when one of these elements is inappropriate or missing: functions, organizations, institutions, interactions or links between the components of the innovation system. Moreover, the missing components or non-spontaneous interactions make the role of the state relevant within the system.

8.2.2.2 Innovation Policy Instruments   As innovation and its role in economic and social development have progressed, so have the number and types of innovation policy instruments. In the past decade, a number of different typologies of innovation policy instruments have been suggested to assist policymakers (Edler and Georghiou, 2007; Borrás and Edquist, 2013; Edler et al., 2016b; Gök et al., 2016). While the instruments considered so far may be seen as focusing mostly on the supply of innovations (e.g., fiscal incentives for R&D, direct support to firms' R&D and innovation, policies for training and skills, entrepreneurship policy, technical services and advice, cluster policy, policies to support collaboration, innovation network policies, etc.), recently the role of demand for innovation (e.g., public procurement policies, private demand for innovation, etc.) has gained more attention (Guerzoni and Raiteri, 2015; Edler, 2016) at national and regional levels (Kaiser and Kripp, 2010; OECD, 2011; UNU-MERIT, 2012).

This rather diverse set of innovation policy instruments reflects different theoretical rationales and political priorities. Johansson et al, (2007) argue that innovation policy instruments can have general or specific characteristics and some span over the two types of characteristics. Therefore, innovation policy instruments must be designed and combined into mixes in ways that address the problems of the innovation system (Borrás and Edquist, 2013; Fu, 2015). In other words, from the systemic nature of innovation – the instruments must represent both the supply and the demand side of innovation.

8.2.2.3 Innovation Policy Governance   The governance of innovation policy is critical to its success. Innovation policy normally lies within the remit of science and technology, education, industry, economy or trade ministries. Edler and Fagerberg (2017) mention that as policy-makers' attention to innovation and policies affecting it has increased, specialized public-sector organizations dedicated to innovation support have emerged in many countries. Another tendency is the increasing involvement of many different ministries in innovation policy governance. The many actors with stakes in the shaping of innovation policy point to the question of how to align the various interests (Kemp and Never, 2017) so that the initiatives of different stakeholders complement rather than contradict each other in coordinated policy mixes (OECD, 2010a; Magro et al., 2014). This good practice notwithstanding, however, Edler and Fagerberg (2017) argue that this is known to be challenging to achieve, as it tends to conflict with the established structures, practices and routines in public administration.

At the same time, the framing of policies for innovation needs to recognize that they operate in a more complex, dynamic, responsive and uncertain environment, where government action will not always get it right. In the view of Kuhlmann (2017), it needs to understand related governance failures and explore options for alternative, more efficient approaches. OECD (2015) put forward that a commitment to monitoring and evaluating policies, learning from experience and adjusting policies over time can help ensure that government action is efficient and achieves its objectives at the least possible cost.

8.3   Innovation Policy in Ghana

8.3.1   Participation in Training and Financing Programmes

The way public actors provide guidance and intervene in the innovation process is strongly associated with the determinants of innovation. For instance, policies to encourage open trade and investment would be suggested if trade and FDI were believed to generate knowledge spillovers. In Ghana, there is the National STI Policy, which the government revised in 2017. There is no standalone innovation policy and the STI policy presents a framework in which Ghana aims to 'build a strong STI capacity' to facilitate sustainable transformation of the economy (MESTI, 2017). As discussed in Chapter 6, an important determinant for LICs to effectively absorb advanced know-how is the local level of technological capability. In-house knowledge creation, external technology adoption and the process of translating knowledge into competitive advantage depend heavily on an adequate supply of engineering and management skills. In the situation that universities and institutions of education are not producing enough graduates with the required skills to spur technological innovation for economic growth, an inadequately skilled workforce has become one of the major barriers to improving the country's technological performance and growing a national system of innovation. Attempting to overcome this shortage, the Government of Ghana introduced various educational reforms and offered opportunities for improving training outside of the formal education system such as technical education, apprenticeships, in-service training and other means intended to ensure the workforce is appropriately skilled to absorb new technologies and to meet the local industry demands. The survey was carried out to gauge the extent to which Ghanaian firms took advantage of this policy, and to what effect. The bar graph on the left of Figure 8.1 shows that between 2010 and 2013, 107 firms (20 per cent of the total sample) had participated in government training programmes, among which the participation incidence for informal firms was nearly 43 per cent higher than for formal firms (63 versus 44). The first row of Table 8.1 presents the average extent to which formal firms and informal firms benefited from public training. In general, Ghanaian firms were aware of the advantages of taking part in a training service and the average

Table 8.1 *Benefiting from participation in training and subsidized rate loans programme for formal and informal firms: training (1 = insignificant, 5 = crucial, average values)*

	Total	Formal	Informal	Difference
Training opportunities	3.37	3.25	3.46	−0.21
Subsidized rate loans	3.17	3.14	3.22	−0.79

Note: Significance at the 10 per cent, 5 per cent and 1 per cent levels are indicated by one, two and three asterisks, respectively.

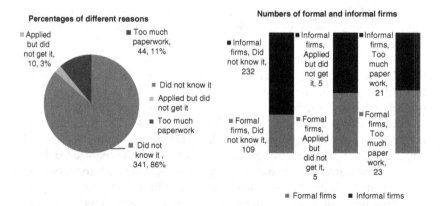

Figure 8.1 Reasons for not participating in training programmes for formal and informal firms: (left) percentages of different reasons and (right) numbers of formal and informal firms for each reason

beneficial rate was 3.37 out of 5. Despite the fact that informal firms had gained slightly more benefits compared to formal firms, there was no evidence that the benefits to two groups were significantly different from each other.

The government also aims to promote innovation in private firms via improving fiscal and legal incentives for domestic entrepreneurship. Given the 'supply-driven' nature of S&T systems in developing and least developed countries, direct funding subsidies have become one of the most commonly used incentives to encourage firms to adopt new technologies, innovate and raise productivity. Nevertheless, in Ghana the majority of domestic firms do not appear to have successfully gained benefits from the government financial support programme. Only 14 formal firms and 9 informal firms had received government subsidized rate loans during 2010–2013, accounting for a mere 4 per cent of the total sample. In line with the participants of training programmes, firms that received the subsidized loans responded positively to such financial incentives. The average beneficial rate evaluated in the 23 firms was 3.17 out of 5, among which informal firms tended to take more advantage than formal firms from the cheap rate loans. The t-test rejected the hypothesis that the difference between the two groups is statistically significant.

Among the various factors that caused Ghanaian firms to fail to participate in the public innovation programme, the survey listed the most common three categories for each firm to choose: did not know about it, too much paperwork or applied but did not get it. Figures 8.2 and 8.3 summarize the statistics in relation to training services and cheap rate loans respectively. The pie graph in Figure 8.2 demonstrates that many non-participants (almost 86 per cent) did not participate because they did not know about the existence of the training services. About 11 per cent of the non-participants pointed out that it was the bureaucracy of the procedures and the paperwork that kept them away, while only 3 per cent indicated that they applied for it but did not get it. The figures on the right in Figure 8.2 attempt to calculate the proportions of formal and informal firms indicating each of the reasons. There was clear evidence showing that the lack of effective channels to access the information was the main barrier for informal firms to participate in government-funded training programmes. This reason was less profound for formal firms as shown in the bar figure in Figure 8.2. For those who gave up because of the heavy load of paperwork or did not succeed with their application, the proportions of formal and informal firms were almost equal.

An analogous pattern was observed for firms that were absent from the subsidized rate loans programme, as exhibited in Figure 8.2. Owing to

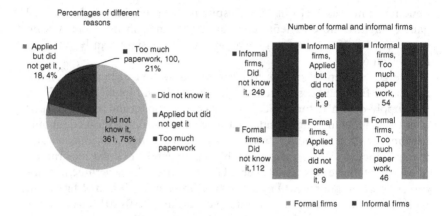

Figure 8.2 Reasons for not receiving subsidized rate loans for formal and informal firms: (left) percentages of different reasons and (right) numbers of formal and informal firms for each reason

the information asymmetry, nearly three-quarters of the firms missed the opportunity to take advantage of cheap rate loans. Compared to the training programme, more firms (21 per cent) were frustrated by the amount of paperwork involved with applying for the subsidized rate loans. The remaining 4 per cent of non-participation was due to the fact that non-participants were less qualified than applicants. In total, there were 249 informal firms that did not know about the subsidized rate loans, whereas 109 formal firms reported the same. Informal and formal groups are almost equally represented with respect to the reason 'applied but did not get it', while two more formal firms than informal ones gave up on their applications because of excessive paperwork.

Clearly, Ghanaian firms have not been responding to the existing incentives mainly because of the absence of information. Lack of effective means to gain access to innovation policy and information has prevented local firms, especially the informal ones, from participating in the government innovation programme.

8.3.2   The Role and Implementation of Innovation Policy in Ghana

Recognizing the important role that knowledge and innovation must play in transforming the economy and reducing poverty, the Government of Ghana has placed S&T development high on its list of priorities. This is reflected in various political and policy statements, including Vision 2020, the Growth and Poverty Reduction Strategy II, the Ghana

Shared Growth and Development Agenda (I and II) and the medium-term development plan. These policies, plans and strategies have emphasized that the absorption and application of much more S&T are critical ingredients for successful growth. The survey tried to better understand the role of the innovation policy in Ghana by inviting each respondent to assess the effectiveness and implementation of a series of government innovation incentives.

A 5-point Likert scale was used to index how effective each incentive was to the firm. The corresponding statistics are presented in Table 8.2. Ghanaian firms agreed that the ten listed innovation policy initiatives were, in general, beneficial for their innovation activities except for 'open the economy to foreign competitors and increase competition', which was rated below the median of 2.5. This is an indication that firms in Ghana are not mature enough for external competition from abroad. Fiscal incentives played a substantial role in stimulating knowledge creation and technology adaptation. Given that firms are often constrained financially, fiscal incentives received relatively higher rates of importance compared to other innovation policies. The top two important incentives for formal as well as informal firms were 'provide cheaper interest loans' and 'provide fiscal subsidies', suggestions for the two main constraints these firms face. Another important policy selected by entrepreneurs of formal firms was 'lower corporate taxes' whereas informal firms were more likely to benefit from 'government funding schemes: the MSME project of the Ministry of Trade and Industry'. Other policies such as allowing duty-free exports, developing high-technology industrial development zones, government procurement and the venture capital trust fund were also acknowledged by Ghanaian firms but considered less crucial to innovation than the ones mentioned above.

In addition, firms were also asked to evaluate the implementation of each policy on the same 5-point Likert scale. As the second column of Table 8.3 reports, the sampled firms, in general, agreed that there was still a great potential to improve the strength and coverage of innovation policies in Ghana. Except for government funding schemes, the implementation scores rated for other policies were all below 2 (2.5 being the median). In contrast to its relatively high score for its importance, fiscal-related policy was seen as having been less satisfactorily implemented. Informal firms seem to be slightly more satisfied than the formal firms with the finance-related policies, such as the MSME project, the venture capital trust fund and provision of fiscal subsidy. This is surprising given that informal firms do not often benefit from these funding policies. Neither the formal nor the informal firms are happy with the implementation of the 'development of high-technology industrial development

Table 8.2 *The importance of government policies for formal and informal firms (1 = insignificant, 5 = crucial, average values)*

	Total	Informal	Formal	Diff.
Provide fiscal subsidies	3.94	3.94	3.93	0.01*
Duty-free exports	3.71	3.65	3.82	−0.17
Impose higher duties for imported products	3.37	3.38	3.35	0.04
Develop high-tech industrial development zone	3.53	3.55	3.48	0.07
Lower corporate taxes	3.79	3.73	3.91	−0.18*
Provide cheaper interest loans	4.17	4.20	4.11	0.09*
Government procurement	3.57	3.57	3.56	−0.00
Open the economy to foreign competitors and increase competition	2.22	2.26	2.15	0.11
Gov. funding schemes, e.g. the Micro, Small and Medium Enterprise (MSME) Project of the Ministry of Trade and Industry	3.78	3.84	3.66	0.19
Government funding scheme, e.g. The Venture Capital Trust Fund	3.75	3.78	3.69	0.09

Note: More than one answer allowed. Significance at the 10 per cent, 5 per cent and 1 per cent levels are indicated by one, two and three asterisks, respectively.

Table 8.3 *The implementation of government policies for formal firms and informal firms (1 = insignificant, 5 = crucial, average values)*

	Total	Informal	Formal	Diff.
Provide fiscal subsidies	1.86	1.92	1.74	0.18
Duty-free exports	1.78	1.78	1.77	0.01
Impose higher duties for imported products	1.86	1.85	1.87	−0.02
Develop high-tech industrial development zone	1.77	1.85	1.64	0.22
Lower corporate taxes	1.79	1.82	1.73	0.09
Provide cheaper interest loans	1.88	1.91	1.83	0.08
Government procurement	1.88	1.89	1.87	0.01
Open the economy to foreign competitors and increase competition	1.93	1.98	1.86	0.12
Gov. funding schemes, e.g. the Micro, Small and Medium Enterprise (MSME) Project of the Ministry of Trade and Industry	2.02	2.12	1.85	0.27
Government funding scheme, e.g. The Venture Capital Trust Fund	1.99	2.07	1.86	0.22

Note: More than one answer allowed. Significance at the 10 per cent, 5 per cent and 1 per cent levels are indicated by one, two and three asterisks, respectively.

zones' strategy, suggesting a space in strengthening the industrial parks development in African countries.

As with many other economies in SSA, Ghana is still in the stage of 'factor-driven' growth. Inefficient innovation financing schemes, low capacity levels for innovation and weak international linkages are still severely constraining the development of innovation capability. Policymakers in Ghana, if they want to transform the economy from a 'factor-driven' one to an 'innovation-driven' one, must begin addressing these issues. The effective implementation of the innovation-oriented incentives is even more important than the formulation and enactment.

8.4   Changes in Government Policy: Comparing 2015 and 2013, and Comparing Ghana and Tanzania

8.4.1   Participation in Training and Financing Programmes

Firms in the sample were asked if they had taken advantage of training opportunities provided by the Ghanaian Government. Overall, 82 firms (16 per cent of the total sample) had participated in government training programmes in Ghana, among which the participation for informal and formal firms was about the same (38 and 44 respectively). The first row of Table 8.4 presents the average extent to which formal firms and informal firms benefited from public training. In general, Ghanaian firms increased their evaluation of training programmes in 2015, the average beneficial rate was 4.28 out of 5, larger than 3.37 in 2013. Formal firms had gained slightly more benefits of training compared to informal firms, and this difference is significant.

The government also aims to promote innovation in private firms via improving fiscal and legal incentives for domestic entrepreneurship. Direct funding subsidies have become some of the most commonly used incentives to encourage firms to adopt new technologies, innovate and raise productivity, given the emphasis on supply-side STI policy in LICs, as discussed earlier.

However, in Ghana, most firms have not successfully benefited from government subsidized rate loans during the years 2012–2014, for example. Only 12 firms reported they had received government subsidized rate loans, accounting for a mere 2 per cent of the total sample. This scenario did not change much from the position in 2013. In line with the participants in training programmes, firms that received the subsidized loans responded positively to such financial incentives. The average beneficial rate is 4.15 and formal firms value the incentive more than

Table 8.4 *Benefiting from participation in training and subsidized rate loans programme for formal and informal firms in Ghana (1 = insignificant, 5 = crucial, average values)*

	2013				2015			
	Total	Informal	Formal	Difference	Total	Informal	Formal	Difference
Training opportunities	3.37	3.46	3.25	0.21	4.28	3.95	4.57	−0.62***
Subsidized rate loans	3.17	3.22	3.14	0.08	4.15	4.00	4.20	−0.20

Note: Significance at the 10 per cent, 5 per cent and 1 per cent levels are indicated by one, two and three asterisks, respectively.

informal firms. The *t*-test rejected the hypothesis that the difference between the two groups is statistically significant.

Training opportunities provided by the government in Tanzania are used by 101 firms, about 36 per cent of the sampled firms. The value of these types of programmes is high, 4.3 points out of 5 (Table 8.5). Benefits from training programmes are higher for formal firms (4.4) than informal firms (3.9), and this difference is statistically significant.

Government policies and subsidized loans are more valued than training programmes by firms in Tanzania. However, very few firms actually use the benefit (19 firms which are 7 per cent of the sample). Informal firms value this benefit the most, given that they are more financially constrained; however, there are only three informal firms accessing these subsidies, showing the bias against informal firms. The difference in valuation of this policy by formal and informal firms is not statistically significant.

The survey asked the reasons that firms gave for not participating in the training and subsidy programmes. The survey listed the most common three categories for each firm to choose: did not know about it, too much paperwork, or applied but did not get it. Figures 8.3 and 8.4 summarize the statistics in relation to training services in Ghana and Tanzania respectively. Figures 8.5 and 8.6 present the statistics in relation to subsidised rate loans in Ghana and Tanzania.

The distribution of reasons for not participating in training opportunities is similar for 2013 and 2015. The pie graph in Figure 8.3 demonstrates that almost all non-participants (93 per cent) did not participate in training programmes because they did not know about the existence of the training services, a 7 per cent higher value than in 2013. This suggests that much needs to be done in terms of publicity for these opportunities. About 6 per cent of the non-participants pointed out that the application procedures were too

Table 8.5 *Benefiting from participation in training and subsidized rate loans programme for formal and informal firms in Tanzania (1 = insignificant, 5 = crucial, average values)*

	Total	Informal	Formal	Difference
Training opportunities	4.33	3.95	4.43	−0.47**
Subsidized rate loans	4.43	5.00	4.33	0.67

Note: Significance at the 10 per cent, 5 per cent and 1 per cent levels are indicated by one, two and three asterisks, respectively.

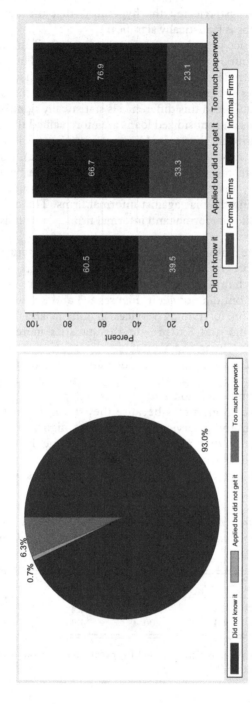

Figure 8.3 Reasons for not participating in training programmes for formal and informal firms in Ghana (2015): (left) percentages of different reasons and (right) numbers of formal and informal firms for each reason

bureaucratic, a reduction of 5 per cent from 2013. Only 0.7 per cent of the firms indicated that they applied for it but did not get it (in comparison to 3 per cent in 2013), which implies that there is a high success rate in the application process. The figure on the right in Figure 8.3 present the proportions of formal and informal firms accounting for each of the reasons for not participating in the programmes. Most of informal firms not participating in training programmes in Ghana consider the necessary paperwork for the application to be too costly. Also, information about the programme mostly reaches formal firms and informal firms tend to have less success if they apply to the programme, probably due to the fact that the informal firms are less capable in preparing the application documents. This is similar to the case even in the developed countries where the weakest SMEs are less likely to be successful in their application for government support than the strong and innovative SMEs (Cosh and Hughes, 2007).

A slightly different picture is found in Tanzania. Most of the firms not benefiting from training opportunities did not know about the scheme (76 per cent). This is somehow better than the situation in Ghana in which 93 per cent of the firms – as in Figure 8.3 – did not know about it. However, in Tanzania, the bureaucracy and paperwork necessary for the application are disincentives for firms to apply. Also, almost 5 per cent of the firms that apply do not get the benefit. This is most severe in informal firms. Formal firms complain more about the paperwork involved. Also, information about the training opportunities does not reach formal and informal firms in the same proportion.

A similar pattern was observed for firms that did not use the subsidized rate loans programme, as exhibited in Figure 8.5 for Ghana and Figure 8.6 for Tanzania. Eighty per cent of firms in Ghana did not have the opportunity to take advantage of cheap rate loans due to a lack of information about the scheme, an increase of 5 per cent from 2013. Compared to firms' feedback on training programmes, more firms (17 per cent) consider the heavy paperwork involved with applying for the subsidized rate loans as an obstacle for applying. This result shows a reduction with respect to 2013 statistics, indicating some improvement towards simplification of the application process. The remaining 3 per cent of non-participants were firms that applied and were unsuccessful, about the same as in 2013. For informal firms, the application process, the success in the rate of application and the information about the programme are all more restrictive limitations on the use of subsidies on rate loans than for formal firms.

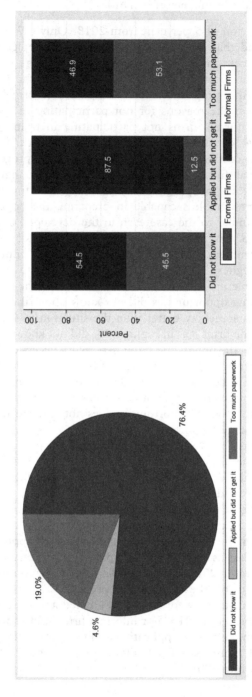

Figure 8.4 Reasons for not participating in training programmes for formal and informal firms in Tanzania (2015): (left) percentages of different reasons and (right) numbers of formal and informal firms for each reason

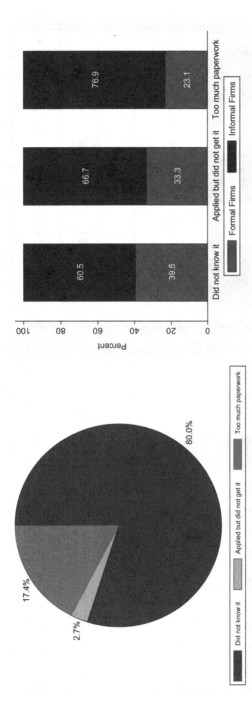

Figure 8.5 Reasons for not receiving subsidized rate loans for formal and informal firms in Ghana (2015): (left) percentages of different reasons and (right) numbers of formal and informal firms for each reason

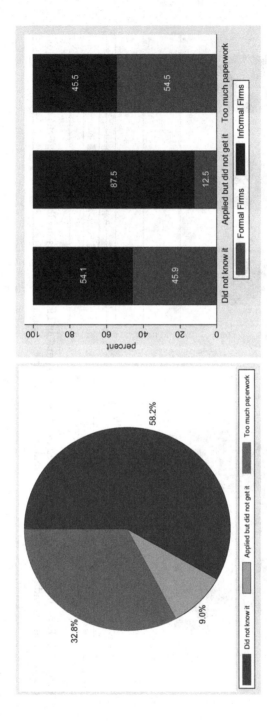

Figure 8.6 Reasons for not receiving subsidized rate loans for formal and informal firms in Tanzania (2015): (left) percentages of different reasons and (right) numbers of formal and informal firms for each reason

For Tanzanian firms, the lack of knowledge of the subsidies is less severe, where only 58 per cent of the firms argue they did not have knowledge of the incentive. Within the firms that have knowledge of the subsidized rate loans, the paperwork and bureaucracy associated with the application process affects 33 per cent of the firms. Nine per cent of the firms apply but get rejected and most of them are informal firms. Again, lack of information of the programme is found in about the same proportion of formal and informal firms, and the paperwork of the application procedures affects more formal firms.

There are two factors affecting the use of public programmes provided by governments in LICs that can be solved by the governments. Information about the programmes and the application procedures both need to be addressed if it is expected that there will be an increase in the number of firms participating in these programmes.

8.4.2   The Role and the Implementation of Innovation Policy in Ghana and Tanzania

Other policies related to innovations were also addressed in the survey. A 5-point Likert scale was used to index how effective each governmental innovation incentive was for the firm. The corresponding statistics for Ghana are presented in Table 8.6, and the statistics for Tanzania in Table 8.7.

In general, Ghanaian firms consider the measures implemented by the government as improved and as more important for them in 2015 than in 2013, although the pattern and distribution remain very similar. The ten listed innovation policy initiatives were perceived as important for firms, except for 'open the economy to foreign competitors and increase competition', which was rated the least important measure and affected the informal firms more. Fiscal incentives played a substantial role in stimulating knowledge creation and technology adaptation and received relatively higher rates of importance compared to other innovation policies. The three most important incentives for formal and informal firms were: 'provide cheaper interest loans', 'provide fiscal subsidies', and 'the Venture Capital Trust Fund'. Formal firms benefit more from 'lower corporate taxes' whereas informal firms were more likely to benefit from 'cheaper interest loans' and 'duty-free exports'.

Tanzania presents more significant differences in the average importance of public policies between formal and informal firms (Table 8.7). It is also possible to observe that the sampled Tanzanian firms value all innovation policies more than the sampled Ghanaian firms. For informal firms, the provision of fiscal subsidies is the most relevant policy, while

Table 8.6 *The importance of government policies for formal and informal firms in Ghana (1 = insignificant, 5 = crucial, average values)*

	2013				2015			
	Total	Informal	Formal	Diff.	Total	Informal	Formal	Diff.
Provide fiscal subsidies	3.94	3.94	3.93	0.01*	4.29	4.27	4.32	−0.05
Duty-free exports	3.71	3.65	3.82	-0.17	3.82	3.89	3.72	0.17*
Impose higher duties for imported products	3.37	3.38	3.35	0.04	3.62	3.63	3.62	0.01
Develop high-tech industrial development zone	3.53	3.55	3.48	0.07	4.11	4.09	4.13	−0.04
Lower corporate taxes	3.79	3.73	3.91	−0.18*	3.93	3.83	4.08	−0.25***
Provide cheaper interest loans	4.17	4.20	4.11	0.09*	4.53	4.58	4.45	0.14**
Government procurement	3.57	3.57	3.56	−0.00	4.03	4.07	3.99	0.08
Open the economy to foreign competitors and increase competition	2.22	2.26	2.15	0.11	2.15	2.01	2.36	−0.34***
Gov. funding schemes, e.g. the Micro, Small and Medium Enterprise (MSME) Project of the Ministry of Trade and Industry	3.78	3.84	3.66	0.19	4.33	4.33	4.33	0.00
Government funding scheme, e.g. The Venture Capital Trust Fund	3.75	3.78	3.69	0.09	4.29	4.28	4.30	−0.02

Note: More than one answer allowed. Significance at the 10 per cent, 5 per cent and 1 per cent levels are indicated by one, two and three asterisks, respectively.

Table 8.7 *The importance of government policies for formal and informal firms in Tanzania (2015) (1 = insignificant, 5 = crucial, average values)*

	Total	Informal	Formal	Diff.
Provide fiscal subsidies	4.63	4.83	4.49	0.35***
Duty-free exports	4.37	4.43	4.33	0.11
Impose higher duties for imported products	4.14	4.30	4.03	0.27**
Develop high-tech industrial development zone	4.30	4.50	4.16	0.34***
Lower corporate taxes	4.29	4.42	4.19	0.22*
Provide cheaper interest loans	4.61	4.60	4.63	−0.03
Government procurement	4.14	4.03	4.22	−0.19*
Open the economy to foreign competitors and increase competition	3.06	2.80	3.25	−0.45***
Gov. funding schemes, e.g. the Micro, Small and Medium Enterprise (MSME) Project of the Ministry of Trade and Industry	4.29	4.57	4.09	0.48***
Government funding scheme, e.g. The Venture Capital Trust Fund	4.36	4.60	4.19	0.41***

Note: More than one answer allowed. Significance at the 10 per cent, 5 per cent and 1 per cent levels are indicated by one, two and three asterisks, respectively.

formal firms put more value on the provision of cheaper interest loans. The data show that openness of the economy to competitors was the least relevant policy and affected informal firms more. Government funding schemes are also highly important for firms but particularly for informal firms. Formal firms benefit slightly more from government procurement. Other fiscal policies such as allowing duty-free exports, imposing higher duties on imported products and the development of technical industrial zones are also relevant for Tanzanian firms, but even more for informal firms.

In addition, firms were also asked to evaluate the implementation of each policy (on a 5-point Likert scale). Statistics are presented for Ghana (in Table 8.8) and Tanzania (in Table 8.9). In comparison to the results in 2013, Ghanaian firms considered that the implementation of the innovation policies improved in the country; however, there is still scope for improvement. Contrary to what is observed in 2013, formal firms tend to evaluate the implementation of policies better than informal firms in 2015. Strangely, the implementation of the less relevant policy (openness of the economy) was evaluated as the policy best implemented. Other policies evaluated properly were associated with the government funding schemes. Formal firms also rate the provision of cheap interest loans and fiscal subsidies as of average implementation quality.

Table 8.8 *The implementation of government policies for formal firms and informal firms in Ghana (1 = insignificant, 5 = crucial, average values)*

	2013				2015			
	Total	Informal	Formal	Diff.	Total	Informal	Formal	Diff.
Provide fiscal subsidies	1.86	1.92	1.74	0.18	2.22	2.06	2.45	−0.39***
Duty-free exports	1.78	1.78	1.77	0.01	2.09	2.07	2.13	−0.06
Impose higher duties for imported products	1.86	1.85	1.87	−0.02	2.31	2.24	2.42	−0.18*
Develop high-tech industrial development zone	1.77	1.85	1.64	0.22	2.19	2.05	2.41	−0.36***
Lower corporate taxes	1.79	1.82	1.73	0.09	2.25	2.12	2.44	−0.32***
Provide cheaper interest loans	1.88	1.91	1.83	0.08	2.24	2.03	2.54	−0.51***
Government procurement	1.88	1.89	1.87	0.01	2.18	2.13	2.25	−0.12
Open the economy to foreign competitors and increase competition	1.93	1.98	1.86	0.12	2.52	2.43	2.66	−0.23**
Gov. funding schemes, e.g. the Micro, Small and Medium Enterprise (MSME) Project of the Ministry of Trade and Industry	2.02	2.12	1.85	0.27	2.42	2.37	2.50	−0.14
Government funding scheme, e.g. The Venture Capital Trust Fund	1.99	2.07	1.86	0.22	2.44	2.40	2.50	−0.10

Note: More than one answer allowed. Significance at the 10 per cent, 5 per cent and 1 per cent levels are indicated by one, two and three asterisks, respectively.

When compared to Ghana, Tanzanian innovation policies present lower rates of satisfaction with respect to their implementation for firms. In general, formal firms provide better evaluation of the implementation of policies than informal firms. Again, the policy rated as the best implemented is 'open the economy to foreign competitors'. Other better-evaluated policies are the government funding scheme for small firms, the provision of cheap interest loans and the imposition of higher duties for imported products. The provision of fiscal subsidies, government procurement and lower corporate taxes are considered as relatively well implemented by formal firms only.

To note, although these policy instruments fall under the innovation policy instruments more generally, it is not clear to what extent these are conscious efforts of the government to spur innovation in these countries. In other words, these policies may be elements of the various existing economic policies issued by various government departments. Nevertheless, as innovation is an outcome of system engineering, innovation policy, in fact, includes policies issued by different government departments, which ideally would work coherently to promote innovation. Therefore, they may be introduced as part of a country's innovation policy or as economic or industry policy. Of course, this will have implications in monitoring and evaluation of policies.

Table 8.9 *The implementation of government policies for formal firms and informal firms in Tanzania (2015) (1 = insignificant, 5 = crucial, average values)*

	Total	Informal	Formal	Diff.
Provide fiscal subsidies	1.83	1.59	2.01	−0.41***
Duty-free exports	1.86	1.70	1.98	−0.28**
Impose higher duties for imported products	2.01	1.77	2.19	−0.42***
Develop high-tech industrial development zone	1.93	1.85	1.99	−0.14
Lower corporate taxes	1.83	1.64	1.96	−0.31**
Provide cheaper interest loans	2.06	1.90	2.17	−0.26**
Government procurement	1.80	1.51	2.01	−0.49***
Open the economy to foreign competitors and increase competition	2.82	3.01	2.68	0.33**
Gov. funding schemes, e.g. the Micro, Small and Medium Enterprise (MSME) Project of the Ministry of Trade and Industry	2.10	2.12	2.09	0.03
Government funding scheme, e.g. The Venture Capital Trust Fund	1.97	1.92	2.00	−0.08

8.5   Conclusion

This chapter examines innovation policies and their effectiveness and quality of implementation in Ghana and Tanzania. Findings from this chapter can be briefly summarized as follows;

Innovation is a key factor for long-term growth and development in Africa. However, research shows that market failure and system failure exist in the field of innovation, which can reduce the performance of innovation activities from all kinds of innovation bodies and the whole national innovation system. This provides the rationale for government intervention in the innovation process.

(1) Policy is a crucial measure and tool of government intervention. Facing market failure and system failure, policy can play a role in fixing these failures in local, regional or national innovation systems. Although there are different views on the necessity and appropriateness of policy intervention in specific industrial fields, policymakers are increasingly embracing the idea of using industrial and innovation policy to tackle the challenges facing innovation society.

Since public policies would greatly affect innovation, it is important that they are well designed and implemented to achieve the desired goals. The 2013 and 2015 survey results on formal firms and informal firms in Ghana and Tanzania suggest that the surveyed enterprises generally agree with the STI policies issued by domestic government departments but some are poorly implemented and ineffective; this problem should be given great attention. How to make the policy work better has become an important issue of policy governance in the innovation field. In the current situation of innovation policy development, aligning policy actions across different ministries, agencies and stakeholders, but also across different levels of governments is rather important. Dissemination of information on the instruments of policy actions such as training schemes and financial assistance is important for effective implementation. Policy monitoring and evaluation and learning from experience and policy improvements are still striving in this direction.

Part II

The Diffusion of Foreign Innovation into Africa

9   The Diffusion of Foreign Innovation to Africa
The Role of Trade, FDI and Diasporas

9.1   Introduction

The costly, risky and path-dependent nature of innovation pushes firms in LICs to seek external sources in order to compensate for the weak indigenous technological capability. Innovation activities carried out by them are characterized as learning and adoption of existing knowledge advances. Foreign sources of knowledge, complementing indigenous efforts, have become a substantial driver of economic growth in developing countries. Knowledge acquired from foreign channels not only helps the host economy fill gaps in indigenous technological capability but also upgrades the existing technologies to international standards.

Foreign direct investment (FDI) has long been recognized as a potential driver of economic growth in developing countries (Lall, 1996; Moran et al., 2005; Balasubramanyam, et al., 1998; Fu, 2004). Multinational enterprises (MNEs), firms that operate in more than one country, are the main sources of FDI (Dunning, 1993). Potential benefits of FDI for the host economy include an inflow of capital, job creation, and most importantly knowledge spillovers. Spillovers occur when the MNE cannot fully internalize its stock of knowledge (which embeds technology and management practices), and domestic companies are able to make use of it (Crespo and Fontoura, 2007; Görg and Greenaway, 2004). Theoretically, knowledge spillovers can increase domestic productivity, foster economic growth and ultimately lead to poverty alleviation in developing countries (Ghauri et al., 2017; Fu et al., 2019; UNCTAD, 2002 and 2003).

The current chapter reviews different types of foreign knowledge sources and the factors that ensure the success in adaption of foreign know-how to the local context.[1]

---

[1] This chapter contains extracts from Auffray and Fu (2013)

9.2   Countries of Origin of Innovation

Figure 9.1 reports the main countries of origin of the innovations adopted by firms in Ghana in 2015. The vast majority of technological innovations introduced during the three years 2012–2014 originated from within Ghana. In fact, in 2015, almost 58 per cent and 56 per cent respectively of informal and formal firms have adopted or created innovations with resources and information found in the country, which is similar to the patterns observed in 2013. Formal and informal firms behave differently regarding the adoption of innovation from abroad. Formal firms seem to be more likely to adopt innovations from abroad than informal firms – in particular, formal firms are more likely to adopt innovations from Europe, China, India and other countries. This may be due to differences in the capability of formal and informal enterprises.

It has been argued that technology transfer between non-industrialized countries, or what has been called South-South knowledge diffusion, is more appropriate for the adoption of new technologies and innovation by firms in these countries. Collectively, just 3.4 per cent of the innovations introduced came from a low- or middle-income country (other countries in Africa, India and China), an important reduction from the 13 per cent observed in 2013. Given this result, developing countries must do much in terms of South-South collaborations. The large rate of observations (35 per cent) without information about country of origin for techno-logical innovations might also be hiding the importance of technology transfer from 'Southern' countries.

For management innovations, most of the firms adopted new manage-ment practices that originated within Ghana (28 per cent). About 21 and 37 per cent of informal and formal firms respectively adopted manage-ment innovations developed in Ghana. The other main source of new managerial practices is Europe. About 6–7 per cent of management innovation came from a European country, in formal and informal firms. Again, the high rates of observations without information (63 per cent) are obscuring this analysis.

In Figure 9.2, it is possible to observe the country of origin of the technological and management innovations carried out in Tanzania. The vast majority of technological and non-technological innovations (71 and 77 per cent respectively) originated in Tanzania, indicating a high local content in innovations introduced in Tanzania. For the majority of informal firms (83 per cent), technological innovations ori-ginated within the country, while this is the case for only 62 per cent of formal firms, suggesting that informal firms use more local knowledge in their innovative activities than their formal counterparts. In technological

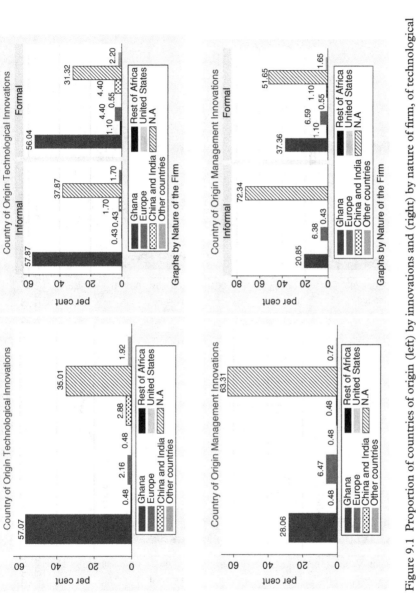

Figure 9.1 Proportion of countries of origin (left) by innovations and (right) by nature of firm, of technological and management innovations, in Ghana (2015). Note: More than one response allowed

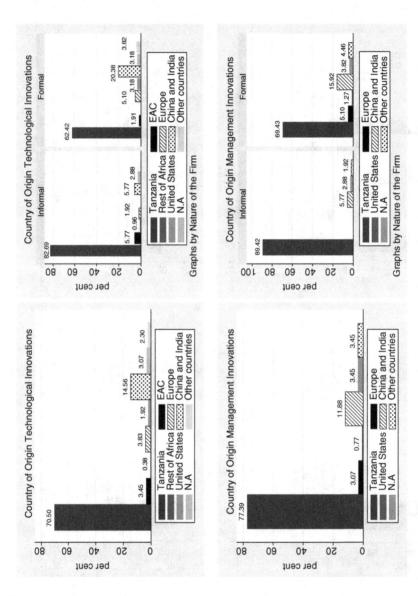

Figure 9.2 Proportion of countries of origin (left) by innovations and (right) by nature of firm, of technological and management innovations, in Tanzania (2015). Note: More than one response allowed

innovations, China and India are the second most relevant countries of origin for innovations (15 per cent), and particularly for formal firms (20 per cent). The increasing adoption of innovations from these countries is a sign of their growing influence in Africa. European countries are the origin of technological innovations for 4 per cent of the innovative firms, and again this is more evident in formal firms (5 per cent) compared to informal firms (2 per cent). The United States is a source for technological innovations for 3 per cent of formal firms, but no informal firms use American sources.

The relevance of South-South technology transfer is stronger in sampled Tanzanian firms than in Ghanaian firms. Almost 4 per cent of innovations originated in other African countries (East African Countries – EAC – or Rest of Africa). The technology and innovations from other African countries might be more suitable for the Tanzanian markets, especially for informal firms where 7 per cent of innovative firms adopted technology from Africa, while only 2 per cent of formal firms did the same. This may be due to the proximity to South Africa, a much-developed technological country. Technology that originated in low- and middle-income countries (African countries, together with China and India) was adopted by 18 per cent of firms in Tanzania to produce technology innovations.

With respect to management innovations, almost 9 out of 10 informal firms, and 7 out of 10 formal firms, adopt innovations from Tanzania. Again, the second most important origin for management innovations are China and India for 12 per cent of all firms, and these countries are more relevant for formal firms (16 per cent) than for informal firms (6 per cent). European countries and the United States are relevant as sources of management innovations only for formal firms (6 per cent). Other African countries are not present as sources of management innovations in Tanzania, which presents a challenge in understanding why the knowledge in these countries is important for technological innovations but not for non-technological innovations.

9.3   Channels for Acquiring Foreign Knowledge

Firms assessed how important different foreign knowledge sources are to their innovation activities (responding with a 5-point Likert scale measurement). Average results for Ghana are presented in Figure 9.3. The behaviour of formal and informal firms differs greatly; also, the importance of the sources of foreign knowledge is very different for technological and non-technological innovations. In general, informal firms consider foreign knowledge as less relevant for innovation activities than formal

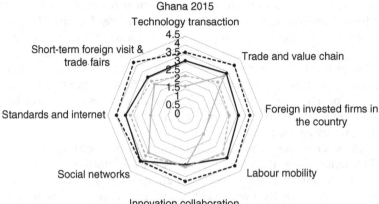

Figure 9.3 Importance of foreign sources of knowledge and innovation
for formal (dotted lines) and informal (solid lines) firms in Ghana 2015
(1 = insignificant, 5 = crucial, average values)

firms. This is understandable, considering the fact that informal enterprises have little direct access to foreign knowledge. As a result, informal
firms build their businesses on local knowledge. On the contrary, formal
firms engage with foreign firms in diverse ways, such as through trade and
collaboration, among others, that enable and increase their access to
foreign knowledge. Foreign sources of knowledge seem more relevant
for management innovations in both groups of firms.

Among the most important sources of foreign knowledge for technological innovations in formal firms are 'trade and value chain', 'standards
and internet', 'social networks' and 'labour mobility'. Other sources of
foreign knowledge are also highly valued with an average of 3 out of 5 points.
For technological innovations done in informal firms, the most relevant
source of foreign knowledge is 'trade and value chain', followed by 'social
networks', 'collaborations' and 'foreign visits and trade fairs'. This is
a surprising result, given that informal enterprises do not trade directly
with foreign firms. This could be due to acceptance bias where informal
firms may tend to agree to socially acceptable activities. Due probably to the
secluded nature of informal activities and the dominance of local knowledge
acquired through learning-by-doing, foreign knowledge obtained through

the mobility of skilled labour and foreign invested firms are perceived as the least important channels of foreign knowledge diffusion for informal firms.

For management innovations, the behaviour of informal and formal firms is similar. The main differences are in the valuation of the importance of foreign sources of knowledge, since it is lower for informal firms compared to formal firms. Variations in the valuation of sources of foreign knowledge are small, with a range of 3.5–4.5 for formal firms, and 2.3–3.3 for informal firms. The most relevant sources of foreign knowledge for management innovations in sampled formal firms are 'foreign visits and trade fairs', 'trade and value chains', 'labour mobility' and 'standards and internet'. For sampled informal firms, the main sources of foreign knowledge for management innovations are 'social networks', 'standards and internet' and 'labour mobility'.

As in Ghana, Figure 9.4 suggests that there are substantial differences between formal and informal firms' use of foreign knowledge sources in Tanzania. However, in Tanzania the importance of foreign sources of knowledge for technological and management innovations seems quite similar, except for the importance of information transmitted by 'trade and value chain', which is more relevant for technological innovations in formal and informal firms.

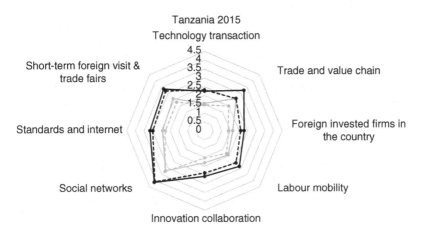

Figure 9.4 Importance of foreign sources of knowledge and innovation for formal (dotted lines) and informal (solid lines) firms in Tanzania, 2015 (1 = insignificant, 5 = crucial, average values)

In spite of evident gaps in the magnitudes of mean values, both formal and informal firms recognize spillovers through social networks as the most important channel for acquiring foreign knowledge for technological and non-technological innovations. Social networks are more relevant for formal firms than informal firms. Technology transactions, foreign invested firms and innovation collaborations are the least relevant source of knowledge for innovations.

Tables 9.1 and 9.2 show a detailed analysis of the relevance of foreign sources of knowledge in subcategories for the whole sample, formal and informal firms, for Ghana and Tanzania respectively. Differences between formal and informal firms were tested by t-statistics and the asterisks denote the significance level. In Ghana, the patterns of foreign sources of knowledge differ somewhat in 2015 from the ones observed in 2013. The top three important foreign sources reported in 2013 were all associated with importing activities, and the level of importance was found to be similar between formal and informal firms. In 2015, one of the top three categories, besides imports, is the information found via the internet.

Table 9.1 also shows that collaborations with foreign customers and competitors are highly relevant for formal firms in technological innovations. Collaborations with research institutions and suppliers are also important for the development of management innovations in formal and informal firms. In fact, collaborations are the most relevant source of foreign knowledge for management innovations. This is an indication that collaboration serves as a conduit through which knowledge exchange occurs between foreign and local firms. Labour mobility performs a different role for formal and informal firms. For formal firms, foreign knowledge for technological and management innovations is acquired from foreign workers employed in the firms, while informal firms rely more on workers who had previously worked for multinationals. Another relevant difference is the importance of international standards as a source of innovation. International standards force formal firms to innovate in products or processes due to the quality standard requirements, while they promote management innovations in informal firms leading to improvement in firms' internal management practices. Foreign firms in Ghana are an important source of knowledge for formal firms, in particular, MNE customers of formal firms. Finally, innovations introduced by informal firms are often imitated. Our results confirm that the imitation of products owned by competitors in export markets is relatively more important in the innovation process for informal firms than otherwise. Relevant learning can also happen via friends or relatives, foreign visits or trade fairs. In general, these knowledge-sourcing channels were

Table 9.1 *Importance of foreign sources of knowledge and innovation for formal and informal firms in Ghana (2015) (1 = insignificant, 5 = crucial, average values)*

		Technological Innovation				Management Innovation			
		All	Informal	Formal	Diff.	All	Informal	Formal	Diff.
Technology transaction	Foreign technology acquired through licensing	2.97	1.67	3.11	−1.44*	3.25	2.25	3.58	−1.33*
Trade and value chain	Imported goods in the same industry	3.46	3.60	3.43	0.17	3.63	2.75	3.92	−1.17*
	Imported goods that input as intermediate goods into your production	3.09	2.50	3.16	−0.66	3.69	2.33	4.10	−1.77**
	Imported machinery and equipment	3.67	4.20	3.58	0.62	3.86	3.00	4.09	−1.09
	Observing and imitating competitors in export market	2.91	2.40	3.00	−0.60	3.56	2.80	3.91	−1.11**
	New product or quality requirement raised by customers in export market	3.29	2.67	3.35	−0.69	3.81	2.80	4.27	−1.47***
Foreign invested firms in Ghana	Knowledge transferred from foreign suppliers	3.18	1.00	3.44	−2.44***	3.43	2.50	3.80	−1.03*
	MNEs in the same industry	3.06	1.40	3.37	−1.97***	3.54	2.25	4.11	−1.86**
	MNE suppliers	2.90	1.25	3.15	−1.90**	3.46	2.50	3.89	−1.39*
	In upstream industry but not direct suppliers	2.55	1.00	2.73	−1.73**	3.50	2.75	3.88	−1.13
	MNE customers	3.16	1.75	3.36	−1.61**	3.67	2.75	4.00	−1.25**
	In downstream industry but not direct customers	2.61	1.33	2.75	−1.42*	3.36	2.50	3.70	−1.20
Innovation collaboration	Foreign research institutions & universities	2.73	1.67	2.87	−1.20	3.75	3.25	4.00	−0.75
	Foreign competitors	3.33	1.00	3.59	−2.59***	4.09	3.33	4.38	−1.04
	Foreign suppliers	2.96	1.00	3.22	−2.22**	3.92	3.33	4.11	−0.78
	Foreign customers	3.41	2.33	3.54	−1.21*	3.87	3.20	4.20	−1.00
Labour mobility	Returnees employed in your firm	2.52	1.00	2.67	−1.67	3.58	2.67	3.89	−1.22
	Foreign workers/managers employed in your firm	3.18	1.50	3.35	−1.85*	3.79	2.67	4.09	−1.42*
	Local workers who have worked in MNEs before	2.80	2.33	2.86	−0.53	3.64	3.50	3.70	−0.20
Social networks	Relatives or friends working/living abroad	2.54	3.25	2.40	0.85	3.73	2.75	4.29	−1.54*
	Information found via internet	3.59	3.00	3.68	−0.68	3.59	3.25	3.69	−0.44
Standards and internet	International standards that your firm has to meet	3.29	2.00	3.48	−1.48**	3.75	3.20	4.00	−0.80
Short-term foreign visit & trade fairs	Attending international trade fairs	2.83	2.50	2.86	−0.36	3.71	2.50	4.20	−1.70**
	Visits to foreign production sites	3.08	2.50	3.14	−0.64	3.92	3.00	4.33	−1.33**

Note: More than one answer allowed. Significance at the 10 per cent, 5 per cent and 1 per cent levels are indicated by one, two and three asterisks respectively.

Table 9.2 *Importance of foreign sources of knowledge and innovation for formal and informal firms in Tanzania (2015) (1 = insignificant, 5 = crucial, average values)*

		Technological Innovation				Management Innovation			
		All	Informal	Formal	Diff.	All	Informal	Formal	Diff.
Technology transaction	Foreign technology acquired through licensing	2.01	1.56	2.25	−0.69***	2.03	1.48	2.32	−0.84***
Trade and value chain	Imported goods in the same industry	2.41	2.23	2.52	−0.28	2.02	1.99	2.05	−0.06
	Imported goods that input as intermediate goods into your production	2.68	2.20	2.94	−0.74***	1.93	1.78	2.01	−0.23
	Imported machinery and equipment	4.45	4.17	4.60	−0.43***	3.09	2.54	3.39	−0.85***
	Observing and imitating competitors in export market	2.71	2.23	2.97	−0.74***	2.30	1.94	2.49	−0.55***
	New product or quality requirement raised by customers in export market	2.81	2.73	2.86	−0.14	2.47	2.14	2.65	−0.51**
Foreign invested firms in Ghana	Knowledge transferred from foreign suppliers	2.70	2.03	3.09	−1.06***	2.35	1.58	2.79	−1.21***
	MNEs in the same industry	2.10	1.36	2.53	−1.18***	1.99	1.57	2.22	−0.65***
	MNE suppliers	2.48	2.00	2.76	−0.76***	1.83	1.23	2.17	−0.94***
	In upstream industry but not direct suppliers	1.75	1.59	1.85	−0.26	1.71	1.38	1.89	−0.52***
	MNE customers	2.26	1.96	2.44	−0.48**	2.12	1.55	2.45	−0.90***
	In downstream industry but not direct customers	1.66	1.29	1.88	−0.59***	1.59	1.20	1.81	−0.61***
Innovation collaboration	Foreign research institutions & universities	2.06	1.34	2.47	−1.13***	1.97	1.43	2.27	−0.83***
	Foreign competitors	2.47	1.99	2.75	−0.76***	2.35	1.94	2.58	−0.64***
	Foreign suppliers	2.70	2.04	3.08	−1.04***	2.36	2.04	2.54	−0.50**
	Foreign customers	2.73	2.37	2.95	−0.58***	2.43	1.84	2.77	−0.93***
Labour mobility	Returnees employed in your firm	2.07	1.68	2.29	−0.61***	1.84	1.26	2.17	−0.91***
	Foreign workers/managers employed in your firm	2.39	1.66	2.80	−1.14***	2.23	1.57	2.60	−1.03***
	Local workers who have worked in MNEs before	2.41	1.63	2.86	−1.23***	2.16	1.41	2.61	−1.20***
Social networks	Relatives or friends working/living abroad	2.18	2.27	2.13	0.15	1.97	1.93	2.00	−0.07
Standards and internet	Information found via internet	3.79	3.21	4.12	−0.92***	3.79	3.26	4.08	−0.82***
	International standards that your firm has to meet	2.90	2.44	3.16	−0.72***	2.73	2.28	2.99	−0.72***
Short-term foreign visit & trade fairs	Attending international trade fairs	2.76	2.25	3.05	−0.80***	2.43	1.70	2.83	−1.14***
	Visits to foreign production sites	3.36	2.93	3.59	−0.66***	3.29	2.89	3.50	−0.61***

Note: More than one answer allowed. Significance at the 10 per cent, 5 per cent and 1 per cent levels are indicated by one, two and three asterisks respectively.

more important for formal firms in management innovations, while they were relatively more important for informal firms in technological innovations.

As Table 9.2 shows, in Tanzania, there are four main groups of sources of foreign knowledge for technological and management innovations. These are: knowledge from importing machinery and interactions with foreign suppliers and customers; collaborations with foreign suppliers and clients; standards and internet; and foreign visits and trade fairs. As noted above, the behaviour of formal and informal firms is very similar, although the valuation of each channel is significantly higher for formal firms.

The most important channel for knowledge transfer is the import of machinery and equipment, followed by information found via the internet, visits to foreign production sites, and international standards. Foreign machinery and equipment are embodied with knowledge and, as a result, the adoption and adaption of these into the production processes of firms automatically results in some knowledge transfer. This ranking holds for formal and informal firms, as well as for technological and management innovations. Imitative innovations from foreign competitors in export markets are relevant for formal and informal firms in technological innovations and relatively important for informal firms in management innovations.

New product or quality requirements by foreign customers are, relatively, the fifth most important source for informal firms. Formal firms consider the knowledge transfer from foreign suppliers important for technological innovations, and attending international trade fairs as more important for management innovations, suggesting that backward and forward linkages are important for knowledge transfer to domestic firms.

Collaboration with foreign customers for innovation is also valued; however, it is valued relatively more by informal firms in technological innovations, and by formal firms for management innovations. The contrary is true with respect to collaborations with foreign suppliers, where formal firms consider it more important for technological innovations and informal firms consider it more important for management innovations. Collaborations with foreign competitors are important for informal firms in management innovations.

9.4 Factors Ensuring Foreign Knowledge Adoption and Adaptation

Foreign technology usually needs to be adapted to local conditions in firms and in the market to be useful for local firms. The adaptation of technology is more relevant if the new technologies and innovations that have been adopted come from developed and industrialized markets, and where conditions are significantly different from LICs. The different ways firms adapt to foreign technologies change over time. As observed in Ghana, the main change is in the form of assistance that national universities and public research institutions offer. In 2013, the average importance of this factor in adapting foreign knowledge was just 1.3 for formal and informal firms, while it is valued between 3 and 4 points in 2015. As the radar pattern in Figure 9.5 depicts, informal firms consider all factors for adapting foreign technological innovations as equally important in Ghana with an average rate of 4. Formal firms consider 'the adaptation of the technology to be used' and 'the corresponding capacity to carry out the adaptation' as the most important determinants in foreign knowledge adaptation for technological innovations. In addition, assistance from suppliers for the adaptation would also encourage local formal firms to acquire more advanced knowledge for technological innovations. Our results evidence that assistance from suppliers and from national universities and research centres was more crucial to informal firms.

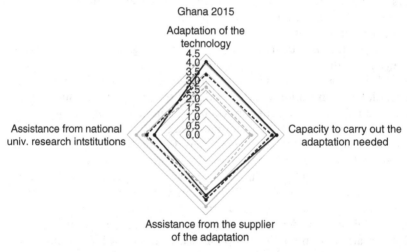

Ghana 2015

Adaptation of the technology

Assistance from national univ. research intstitutions

Capacity to carry out the adaptation needed

Assistance from the supplier of the adaptation

--- TANZANIA 2015 Technological Innovation Informal Firms
--- TANZANIA 2015 Management Innovation Informal Firms
·•· TANZANIA 2015 Technological Innovation Formal Firms
·•· TANZANIA 2015 Management Innovation Formal Firms

Figure 9.5 Factors in ensuring the success of foreign knowledge absorption and adaptation for formal (dotted lines) and informal (solid lines) firms in Ghana 2015 (1 = insignificant, 5 = crucial, average values)

The importance of the factors of adaptation of foreign technology between formal and informal firms is different for management innovations in Ghana. Formal firms consider the internal capacity to adapt the knowledge more important, while informal firms rely more on the assistance of universities or public research institutes. Also, adaptation of the technology, internal capacities to adapt the technology and the assistance of suppliers of the technology are valued as more relevant for formal firms than informal firms. These suggest that while formal firms look inward to adapt new foreign technologies, informal firms seek the assistance of other actors in the national innovation system such as universities.

Tanzania presents a more even valuation of three adaptation factors for formal and informal firms in technological and management innovations (Figure 9.6). The internal capacity of firms to conduct the adaptations needed to the foreign technologies is the most relevant factor for all firms

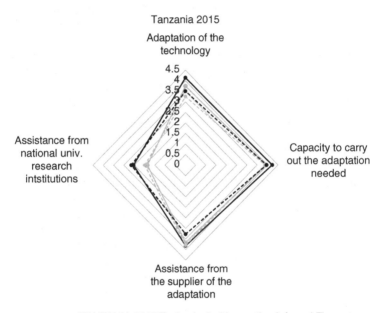

-•- TANZANIA 2015 Technological Innovation Informal Firms
-•- TANZANIA 2015 Management Innovation Informal Firms
-•- TANZANIA 2015 Technological Innovation Formal Firms
-•- TANZANIA 2015 Management Innovation Formal Firms

Figure 9.6 Factors in ensuring the success of foreign knowledge absorption and adaptation for formal (dotted lines) and informal (solid lines) firms in Tanzania 2015 (1 = insignificant, 5 = crucial, average values)

in any type of innovation. This is followed by assistance from the suppliers of the foreign technologies, and then by the general adaptation of the technologies.

Assistance from universities and public research centres could be fundamental in adapting foreign knowledge to local conditions. In Tanzania, formal firms value the assistance from research institutions in adapting foreign knowledge for technological and management innovations significantly more than what is observed in informal firms. However, assistance from universities and research centres is valued as the least relevant factor in the adaptation of foreign technologies. This can explain the low rate of collaboration between firms and universities observed before.

9.5   Factors Affecting Foreign Knowledge Transfer from MNEs: Evidence from the Construction Sector

MNEs face a number of difficulties when investing abroad – for instance, linguistic issues, cultural distance or unfamiliarity with the local market (Lall and Streeten, 1977). For their foreign investments to be profitable, MNEs must therefore possess a substantial advantage over their local competitors, for example, cheaper access to capital, advanced management skills or new technology (Lall and Streeten, 1977). With the shift to a knowledge-based economy in the twenty-first century, managerial and technological capacities are now the main assets of MNEs (Powell and Snellman, 2004). When MNEs invest abroad, they are not always able to fully internalize their stock of knowledge, and domestic firms can then benefit from these assets; this is a knowledge spillover (Crespo and Fontoura, 2007). Demonstration effects are perhaps the most obvious spillover channel: domestic firms can observe new practices and techniques in MNEs and reproduce those they perceive as productive (Blomström and Kokko, 1998; Crespo and Fontoura, 2007). Local firms interacting with the MNE (suppliers, subcontractors, clients) are the most likely to benefit from demonstration effects (Lall, 1980). Labour mobility, domestic firms employing workers trained by the MNE, is a second possible channel (Motta, 1999). Finally, knowledge may also circulate through informal social networks by word of mouth (Fu, 2012b; Inkpen and Tsang, 2005).

The empirical evidence of knowledge spillovers from FDI is, 'at best', mixed (Görg and Greenaway, 2004: p. 171), and suggests they are highly dependent on the investment context. There is strong evidence that absorptive capacity, understood as the level of human capital in the FDI-recipient country, is a positive determinant of spillovers (e.g. Durham, 2004; Fu, 2008; Girma and Görg, 2003). Host-country institutions and policies also impact knowledge spillovers, although there are considerable debates on which are most suitable. The source country of FDI can affect its potential for knowledge spillovers. For instance, Keller (2001) shows that knowledge spillovers decrease with geographical distance between source and host countries. This is due to increasing costs of communication between headquarters and subsidiaries, but can also be a consequence of cultural and linguistic distance. Others argue that cultural distance could actually favour knowledge spillovers by exposing domestic firms to more diversity (Rodriguez-Clare, 1996; Zhang et al., 2010).

Finally, the level and type of knowledge embedded in the investment significantly determine the extent of spillovers. The literature emphasizes the importance of the 'technological gap' between MNEs and local firms (Findlay, 1978; Kokko, 1994; Wang and Blomström, 1992). If the knowledge of the MNE is too far ahead or too close to that of domestic firms, spillovers risk not taking place: either domestic firms will lack the ability to assimilate foreign knowledge, or the amount of knowledge they will be able to grasp will be insignificant for productivity improvements. This argument is close to the 'appropriate technology' (AT) theory. The AT hypothesis argues that technology from developed countries might only lead to limited productivity gains in developing countries because it would not match their specific endowments in skills, labour and capital. AT fits the socio-economic characteristics and the technological level of the recipient country (Fu et al., 2011; Stewart, 1983; Willoughby, 1990). Following this argument, MNEs from emerging economies, such as China, could bring more AT to other developing countries (Fu, 2012a; Fu and Gong, 2011; Fu, 2012a).

A case study based on evidence from thirty-nine interviews in seven foreign construction companies (including four Chinese MNEs and three European MNEs) in Ghana suggests culture and language barriers are also at play and that they affect the knowledge diffusion from MNEs to local firms in Ghana. This chapter analyses the key channels for innovation diffusion, their determinants and major barriers.

9.5.1   Inter-organizational Knowledge Transfer Mechanism in the Construction Sector

9.5.1.1 Suppliers Local suppliers' managerial capacity may also improve as a consequence of foreign contractors' activities. In this case, the most important element seems to be the development of a long-term business relationship involving multiple interactions between the supplier and the foreign contractor. A long-term relationship with frequent interactions creates a pressure on the supplier to upgrade its services to keep clients satisfied. Foreign contractors generally observed an improvement over time in the services of their regular suppliers, such as more timely deliveries and better quality of products purchased. Though this pressure to upgrade, or disciplining factor, is not exactly a managerial knowledge spillover (the supplier is not necessarily adopting the practices of the foreign firm), it is an efficient driver for managerial capacity-building in suppliers. Additionally, a long-term business relationship with a foreign contractor can be a factor of financial stability for local suppliers. Regular cash entries can provide an opportunity for a local company to expand and upgrade its management system. Finally, in terms of training, only one foreign contractor mentioned organizing formal training sessions for its suppliers, though others indicated that they provide suppliers with more informal guidance.

The extent of these positive externalities remains limited. Given the low development of the Ghanaian manufacturing sector, local suppliers are often import companies: they are generally small in size and may simply not have the space or the need for a more complex management system.

9.5.1.2 Subcontractors   The dynamics of managerial knowledge spillovers for local subcontractors are similar to those of suppliers. Again, the development of a long-term business relationship is essential to an upgrading of subcontractors' managerial capabilities, and most contractors noted an amelioration of subcontractors' services over the time of their collaboration. Given the high turnover in subcontractors (the type of works subcontracted varies from project to project), the incentive for foreign contractors to provide them with managerial training is low.

However, subcontractors have more opportunities than suppliers for learning through observation of the contractor's management practices. Indeed, subcontractors work on-site for the duration of their contract, often under the direct supervision of the foreign contractor's project manager. Additionally, subcontractors are more likely than suppliers to pick up new managerial practices, as the core of their work is more closely related to that of the contractor's.

9.5.1.3 Competitors   Local competitors can theoretically benefit from knowledge spillovers, through pressures to upgrade, demonstration effects and labour mobility (Cheung and Lin, 2004). Fieldwork findings were inconclusive in that regard – time and budget constraints did not allow for a thorough examination of the sources of managerial knowledge for local construction companies.

Nonetheless, a few careful hypotheses can be suggested. Firstly, local and foreign contractors do not seem to compete on the same level: local contractors bid on smaller contracts reserved for Ghanaian companies, while foreign contractors have a de facto monopoly on larger works. Direct observation of foreign competitors is therefore limited. Secondly, the capacity gap between foreign and domestic contractors might be too wide for efficient knowledge spillovers through demonstration effects. The management systems used by foreign companies might simply be inappropriate for smaller local firms. Finally, labour mobility could be strongly limited by budget constraints: local contractors might not be able to afford foreign-trained employees.

9.5.1.4 Construction Consultancies The specific case of construction consultancies is interesting. These firms do not categorize as local linkages – they are usually brought in by the client rather than the contractor; they also do not qualify as local competitors to foreign contractors. However, the research highlighted possible managerial knowledge spillovers from foreign construction firms to local construction consultancies through labour mobility. Whereas domestic contractors' development is constrained by a lack of access to finance, consultancies can be set up more easily and require a lower start-up capital. Technical experts (e.g. civil engineers, quantity surveyors) exposed to advanced management practices in foreign construction firms are therefore in an ideal position to start or join a local consultancy firm.

Figure 9.7 summarizes the different channels of managerial knowledge spillovers in the Ghanaian construction sector, emphasizing the most effective ones.

9.5.2 Key Determinants of Knowledge Spillovers

Table 9.3 presents a summary of determinants of managerial knowledge spillovers in the Ghanaian construction sector, for each of the potential knowledge recipients. The discussions of the main determinants of knowledge spillovers in the Ghanaian construction sector we identified are discussed in the following section.

9.5.2.1 Absorptive Capacity Educational achievement rates are high in Ghana compared to other SSA countries, and they have been improving rapidly. But they remain low, and as a labour-intensive industry, the construction sector attracts many more unskilled workers than university-educated ones. Assuming that knowledge spillovers can only impact

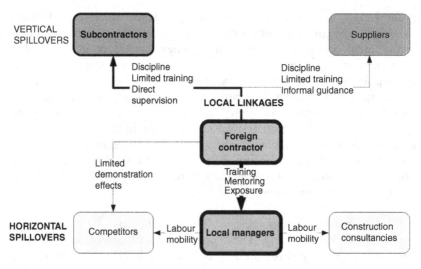

Figure 9.7 Channels of managerial knowledge spillovers in the Ghanaian construction sector
Source: Authors' elaboration

individuals over a certain threshold of human capital,[2] it is likely that they will be restricted to the most educated individuals interacting with the foreign entity. In addition to the limited labour mobility from foreign to domestic firms, this implies that the broader impact of those managerial knowledge spillovers on domestic productivity could very well be insignificant in absolute terms.

9.5.2.2 Tacit Knowledge and the Central Role of Personal Interactions   Research findings suggest that tacit knowledge is particularly present in the construction sector, with exposure and mentorship being two key ways of transferring managerial knowledge onto local employees. This makes interpersonal and cross-cultural relationships within the foreign company a strong determinant of managerial knowledge spillovers. Frequent and fluid communication, as well as cross-cultural understanding, appear to be important elements favouring knowledge spillovers. This means the extent of managerial knowledge spillovers will vary depending on the quality of

---

[2] This assumption has been tested successfully at the firm (Girma, 2005) and country levels (Falvey et al., 2007) with absorptive capacity measured in terms of R&D investments (rather than human capital).

Table. 9.3 *Determinants of managerial knowledge spillovers in the Ghanaian construction sector for selected recipients*

Recipient	Determinants of managerial knowledge spillovers
Ghanaians employed in foreign construction firms	• Absorptive capacity • Quality of communication with foreign managers • Quality of interpersonal relationships with foreign managers • Formal training opportunities • Mentoring relationship
Subcontractors	• Absorptive capacity • Scope of knowledge gap with foreign firms • Quality of communication with foreign firms • Quality of interpersonal relationships with foreign managers • Quality of foreign supervision while working on-site • Duration of business relationship with foreign contractor
Suppliers	• Absorptive capacity • Scope of knowledge gap with foreign firms • Quality of communication with foreign firms • Quality of interpersonal relationships with foreign managers • Frequency of interactions with foreign managers • Duration of business relationship with foreign contractor
Competitors	• Absorptive capacity • Scope of knowledge gap with foreign firms • Appropriateness of foreign managerial knowledge • Poaching capacity • Structural constraints (access to capital)
Consultancies	• Absorptive capacity • Scope of knowledge gap with foreign firms • Quality of communication with foreign firms • Quality of interpersonal relationships with foreign managers • Poaching capacity • Structural constraints (access to capital)

the learning environment within the foreign construction firm and on the personalities of the individuals involved.

9.5.2.3 Structural Constraints to Further Transfers   Finally, some of the structural features of the Ghanaian construction sector limit the extent of managerial knowledge spillovers. For instance, labour mobility from foreign to local contractors is constrained: local managers trained in foreign companies are a scarce resource, and local contractors can rarely afford to poach them. Limited access to capital also means that foreign-trained managers wishing to start their own firm may not be able to expand their companies and to transfer their managerial knowledge onto their own employees. Construction consultancies do not face the same structural constraints and could be more successful at keeping alive the managerial knowledge acquired.

9.5.3   The Language and Cultural Barriers to Knowledge Transfer from MNEs

9.5.3.1 The Language Barrier   The language barrier can be defined as the loss of rhetorical skills (including negotiation, persuasion and motivation) caused by a limited competency in the working language, resulting in difficulties in 'achieving and sustaining effective communication and a productive, collaborative relationship' (Harzing and Feely, 2008). To limit the effects of the language barrier in the HQ–subsidiary relationship, MNEs with headquarters operating in a 'minority language' (i.e. not spoken at the global level, such as Chinese) tend to rely more heavily on expatriates in subsidiaries (Feely and Harzing, 2003).

This is the case for Chinese contractors operating in Ghana. To achieve fluent communication with the parent company in China, the top management of the subsidiary needs to be Chinese. But as senior expatriates struggle the most with language, they naturally prefer a middle-management team who also speaks Chinese, which, in turn, favours Chinese entry-level managers over Ghanaian ones. This results in the exclusion of Ghanaians from the management ladder. This is not simply a question of personal preference: linguistic unity leads to more effective communication, resulting in time and economic gains (Bolton and Dewatripont, 1994). This is not something that can be solved by the presence of an interpreter. Real-time interpretation reduces the clarity and the spontaneity of exchanges; it is also extremely time-consuming.

Furthermore, the language barrier can cause feelings of exclusion, confusion and frustration (Harzing and Feely, 2008). This is a major impediment to trust-building, which could affect knowledge transfers by altering the quality of interpersonal relationships and restricting the opportunities for formal training and informal learning within the firm (Henderson, 2005).

9.5.3.2 The Cultural Difference   In addition to linguistic issues, a deeper cultural clash between the Chinese and Ghanaians could explain the lack of local managers in Chinese firms. Culture is a blurry concept that can be understood here as 'a collective phenomenon . . . about shared values and meanings' (Hoecklin, 1995: p. 24). Cultural factors are difficult to discuss because people tend to take them for granted (Pun et al., 2000). Indeed, though half of participants cited cultural difference as a barrier to increased local employment in Chinese firms, few were able to give specific examples. Nonetheless, two main points of tension seemed to emerge from cultural conceptions of work and of time.

For instance, while Chinese workers are lauded for their hard-working attitude, Chinese managers complained that their Ghanaian employees did not have the same working efficiency and did not express the same commitment to work. This can be explained by different cultural relations to work, rather than by an intrinsic Chinese capacity to work hard. There is a high work centrality in Chinese culture (Westwood and Lok, 2003). While anthropological studies of the meaning of work in Ghanaian culture are lacking, some studies suggest that it places an emphasis on interpersonal relationships, rather than increased productivity (Dzobo, 1992). Traditionally, work is not supposed to take time from important social, familial and religious activities, which may explain the reluctance to do overtime and weekend work. However, globalization and the associated capitalistic transformation of the Ghanaian economy may have reduced the prevalence of these traditional values. Ghanaians could simply lack a reason to work hard under Chinese management (wages too low, limited perspectives of professional evolution). Similarly, divergent Chinese and Ghanaian conceptions of time seem to foster mutual misunderstandings. While the Chinese seem attached to a strict, mechanical conception of time, Ghanaians traditionally construct time more flexibly (Mbiti, 1990). This issue hinders effective communication not only within the company but also with suppliers and subcontractors, resulting in delayed deliveries and works.

This cultural clash has a direct impact on the decision to employ, or not employ, locals in managerial positions in Chinese construction firms. These cross-cultural misunderstandings add to the language barrier in preventing the emergence of trust relationships. Previous research has emphasized repeatedly the role of culture in creating trust (Doney et al., 1998; Gelfand et al., 2007; Joynt and Warner, 2002; Yuki et al., 2005). Trust is especially necessary in uncertain legal environments, such as in developing countries, to act as an additional safeguard to formal contracts (Haglund, 2009). In this case, mistrust can explain the Chinese reluctance to include Ghanaians at decision-making levels.

9.5   Conclusions

While diffusion of innovation from leading domestic sources is still the largest source of innovation in African firms, North-South innovation transfer is still the main external source of knowledge for Ghanaian firms. However, in Tanzania, China and India are the second most relevant countries of origin for technological innovations (15 per cent), and particularly for formal firms (20 per cent). Overall, the role of foreign innovation is not as significant as suggested by the literature. There is a greater space for foreign technology transfer to play a more significant role in African innovation. Formal firms seem to be more likely to adopt innovations from abroad than informal firms; particularly, formal firms are more likely to adopt innovations from Europe, China, India and other countries.

The behaviour of formal and informal firms differs greatly, and also the importance of sources of foreign knowledge is different for technological and non-technological innovations. Foreign sources of knowledge seem more relevant for management innovations in both groups of firms. The pattern and the importance of knowledge diffusion channels also differ between Ghana and Tanzania. Ghanaian firms appear to experience greater effectiveness of foreign knowledge than firms in Tanzania. On the other hand, there are some common characteristics between these two countries. Social network appears to be regarded as the most effective source of foreign knowledge in both countries. However, the impact of knowledge transfer from foreign-invested firms in the country is different in these two countries. They are important sources of foreign knowledge in Ghana, especially from customers and competitors, but are less important in Tanzania.

Importing activities have been the most important foreign knowledge transmission mechanisms in both Ghana and Tanzania in both 2013 and 2015, and the level of importance was found to be similar between formal and informal firms. Interestingly, in 2015, the information found via the internet has also risen to be one of the top three foreign knowledge sources. In fact, collaborations are the most relevant source of foreign knowledge for management innovations. Collaborations with foreign customers and competitors are highly relevant for formal firms in technological innovations. Collaborations with research institutions and suppliers are also important for the development of management innovations in formal and informal firms. For the success in the adoption and adaptation of foreign knowledge, firms' internal capacity to adapt knowledge is identified to be important in both Ghana and Tanzania. Assistance from local universities and research institutions is regarded as an important factor affecting the success in adoption, while their role in Tanzania is limited.

Evidence from the case study of the construction sector in Ghana emphasizes the central role of personal interactions in the transmission of managerial innovation. However, Chinese MNEs were found to face constraints that other investors do not face – or at least not with the same intensity: linguistic and cultural distance, fuelled by historical factors, makes local communication and trust-building a difficult endeavour. The absence of strong economic incentives does not encourage them to tackle these issues urgently. Whereas these firms are often regarded as being unwilling to integrate and to hire local labour, empirical findings indicate that they employ most of their unskilled labour locally and seriously consider the issue of managerial localization.

Findings from the case study also suggest that the emergence of managerial localization strategies in Chinese construction firms is likely to become a pressing matter in the near future. Meanwhile, localization could benefit FDI-recipient economies by fostering knowledge spillovers, creating local employment and encouraging linkages with domestic firms. For Africa, the learning potential from Chinese firms is therefore very real. Unlike most Western firms operating in Africa, Chinese construction firms have had recent experience of a rapid build-up of capacity in a developing country context. Domestic African firms willing to take their business to the next level can certainly draw lessons from that experience. But knowledge-sharing is not a one-way street: just as Africa can learn from China, China may very well learn from its experiences in Africa. Indeed, Chinese firms operating on the continent face challenges unmet in their domestic market. To be successful, they have to take into account higher CSR considerations, accept more intense public scrutiny and engage with local civil societies (trade unions in particular). Above all, they have to address cross-cultural management issues urgently, and design systems that are able to integrate the culture and working practices of their local employees. Localization strategies are a very important step in that direction. Not all Chinese companies in Africa will solve these challenges – but those who do may become global leaders.

10 Social Networks and Knowledge Diffusion within MNE Subsidiaries

10.1 Introduction

Individuals are important agents in the economy as they undertake learning, creation and production activities. Despite this, the existing literature on FDI and knowledge transfers mostly focuses on inter-organisation transfer and spillovers at the firm, regional or national level (e.g. Fu and Gong, 2011; Javorcik and Saggi, 2003; Kokko et al., 1996). How knowledge is transferred at individual level is under-researched. Moreover, MNEs in Africa from other emerging (E) economies such as China have grown rapidly in the past decades. Do these new EMNEs have different characteristics and hence a different impact on the host economies, especially in terms of knowledge transfers to the local communities? These are new research questions that await exploration.

Using a unique survey of employees and managers in eight MNEs in Ghana in 2015, this chapter analyses the transfer of knowledge at the individual level using social network analysis. It systematically examines the various work and social links between employees at these MNEs and the channels for the diffusion of knowledge. We mapped out the network structure and calculated the network properties for the firms and individuals. We then tested whether the knowledge transfer within the MNEs is influenced by the social network structure and compared the social network and the knowledge transfer in MNEs from different backgrounds, that is, the European and Chinese MNEs.

The research finds that decentralized networks of the MNEs enhance knowledge transfer in the firms. In addition, more channels of communication mean more knowledge transfer. We also find that the Chinese

This chapter includes extracts reproduced from Fu and Xu (2019) and Auffray, C. and Fu, X. (2013) 'MNEs and Managerial Knowledge Transfer: The Case of the Construction Sector in Ghana'.

MNEs and European MNEs have no significant difference in knowledge transfers except that subordinates of Chinese MNEs benefit more from knowledge transfers. The rest of the chapter is structured as follows: Section 10.2 reviews the literature on FDI, social network and knowledge transfer. Section 10.3 introduces the data. Section 10.4 presents the quantitative analysis and Section 10.5 presents a qualitative case study of knowledge transfer within MNEs. Section 10.6 concludes the chapter.

10.2   MNEs, Social Network and Knowledge Transfer Within the Subsidiaries

10.2.1 FDI and Knowledge Transfer

In academic research, there are traditions of studying the diffusion and spillover of knowledge in different areas, focusing especially on technology, innovation and growth (see Barro and Sala-i Martin, 1997; Jaffe, 1986, and a review for international technology diffusion in Keller, 2004). Recent studies include Bloom et al. (2013) studying technology spillover using US firm-level panel data, Aghion and Jaravel (2015) studying the R&D and knowledge spillover in the economic growth process. FDI impacts the development and economic growth of the host developing countries in many aspects. As stated in Fu and Buckley (2015), the Chinese FDI impacts the host developing countries in the following ways: development financing, knowledge transfer and spillover, and competition and crowding-out effect.

This chapter focuses on the knowledge transfer and spillover. Literature on knowledge spillover always focuses on technology diffusion. Glass and Saggi (2002) model the technology transfer. They assume that workers employed by the MNEs acquire knowledge of superior technology, and find that the host country would attract FDI due to technology transfer to local firms. Singh (2007) uses patent citation data and studies the knowledge spillover between MNEs and host-country firms. The research finds that knowledge inflows from foreign MNEs to host-country organizations and also knowledge outflows back from the host countries to foreign MNEs. Liu (2008) uses a panel data of Chinese manufacturing firms to study the FDI externalities in the form of technology transfer. He finds a positive increase in the productivity of domestic firms in the long run. Driffield et al. (2010) study FDI and the knowledge flows in Italy. They conclude that investment in R&D and capital-embodied technology plays a significant role in intra-firm technology flows. Some studies investigate the conditions for knowledge transfer. Fu et al. (2011) find that emerging countries can only benefit from international technology diffusion with parallel indigenous innovation, modern institutional and governance structures and conducive innovation systems. However, some studies find different results. Aitken and Harrison (1999) find that the net gain from FDI is quite small and FDI negatively affects the productivity of domestically owned firms in Venezuela. García et al. (2013) find that FDI inflows into Spain are negatively associated with the ex post innovation of local firms.

Some papers address workers' mobility as an important channel of knowledge transfer from MNEs to local firms. For instance, Fosfuri et al. (2001) study the technological spillover through workers' mobility and find that spillover from FDI happens when the previously MNE-trained worker is hired by the local firms. Poole (2013) finds that in Brazil, when workers leave MNEs and are rehired in local firms, their wages increase. High-skilled former MNE workers are better able to transfer information, and high-skilled incumbent local workers are better able to absorb knowledge. Görg and Strobl (2005) empirically investigate the spillover from FDI via worker mobility and find that firms run by owners with previous MNE experience in the industry are more productive than other local firms.

Some papers study the mechanism of knowledge transfer. For example, Park and Choi (2014) study what accounts for acquisition of knowledge from MNEs in subsidiaries. They find absorptive capacity in learning firms and daily interactions with knowledge possessors are essential to learn from parent MNE firms. More importantly, support from parent firms is particularly important for knowledge acquisition. Park et al. (2016) study the mechanisms of intra-industry knowledge spillovers in South Korea. They find that the demonstration effect is an efficient channel of knowledge transfer from MNE subsidiaries to local firms, and also worker mobility and local firms' absorptive capacity are important roles in learning foreign knowledge.

Some studies also focus especially on the managerial knowledge transfer. Fu et al. (2012) study the impact of management capabilities of foreign firms on management capabilities and performance of domestic firms using UK survey data. They find that, overall, the management capabilities of local firms have a significantly positive effect on their own productivity, while foreign management capabilities have no direct efficiency effect on local firms. Fu (2012) studies the nature and extent of managerial knowledge spillovers from FDI through the diffusion of management practices. The author finds evidence of the existence of the intra-industry linkage and non-linkage based inter-industry managerial knowledge transfer from foreign to local firms using US firm-level panel data.

This chapter uses unique worker and manager-level survey data about managerial knowledge in eight European and Chinese MNEs in Ghana to study the managerial knowledge transfer in MNEs. Different from Fu (2012), this study uses a combination of social network approach and qualitative case study to explore the managerial knowledge transfer within the MNE subsidiaries and between them and the local communities.

10.2.2 Social Network and Knowledge Transfer

Social network is important in knowledge diffusion. However, real network data of MNEs is rare. This chapter uses survey data of 231 individuals in eight multinational firms based in Ghana to implement the social network analysis of the diffusion of managerial knowledge and practices.

A social network in the firm is a structure of individuals (workers, managers and CEO) of the firm with connections and interactions among the individuals. Social network has been popular across disciplines, such as economics, psychology and computer sciences. The study of the impact of individual-level ties within MNEs is rare in economics, business and management studies. This study examines how social networks affect knowledge transfer of MNEs and contributes to the field by providing evidence that decentralized social networks of MNEs improve knowledge transfer.

Some papers in economics, business and management explore social network analyses. For example, Banerjee et al. (2013) study how participation in a micro-finance loan programme diffuses via social network in Indian villages. Ellis (2000) finds that the inter-personal links are important for foreign market opportunities. Ghoshal and Bartlett (1990) especially conceptualize the MNE as an inter-organizational network which is embedded in an external network consisting of organizations such as customers, suppliers and so on. Joshi et al. (2003) use a social network of an MNE to study the workflow, communication patterns and the informal social interactions within the firm.

Some papers particularly focus on the social network and knowledge transfer. Reagans and McEvily (2003) study how different features of an informal network affect knowledge transfer. Inkpen and Tsang (2005) study three different network types: intra-corporate network, strategic alliances and industrial districts. They examine how the social capital dimensions of different networks affect the transfer of knowledge. Capaldo (2007) looks at how the network ties impact the innovative capability of firms. Kaše et al. (2009) develop a conceptual model and examine the relationship among human resource (HR) practices, interpersonal relations, and intra-firm knowledge transfer in knowledge-intensive firms. Fritsch and

Kauffeld-Monz (2010) study how the network structure influences the knowledge transfer using German regional innovation networks with about 300 firms. A recent paper which focuses on the network and knowledge transfer of MNEs is Haas and Cummings (2015). They analyse a large social network of an MNE to examine the barriers to knowledge seeking between MNE team members.

Adding the social network into the analysis of knowledge diffusion of FDI is a major innovation of this chapter. More specifically, we study the diffusion of a typical knowledge: managerial knowledge, which is important for MNEs but has not been given much academic attention over the years. To our knowledge, this is the first study examining the diffusion of managerial knowledge in MNEs using detailed individual-level social network data. The information from 61 managers and 170 workers would give us the opportunity to construct social networks of the MNEs. Thus, we can examine how managerial knowledge diffuses within firms and how the knowledge diffusion process differs across firms of various network structures and different backgrounds such as industry, nationality and other dimensions. Do the centralized or decentralized/hierarchical organizations communicate more effectively and does the knowledge diffuse quickly and sufficiently? The empirical evidence from this study would have direct implications for MNEs to reshape their organizational structure.

The interpretation of the social network analysis needs some attention because the social network in our data is quite incomplete. The complete networks of the firms are not available. Given the large size of some firms in the survey, it is difficult to infer the whole network based on the incomplete network we observed. Thus, the network analysis would mainly rely on characteristics of a part of the network.

10.2.3   Chinese FDI in Ghana and Africa

According to Okon (2016),[1] MNEs operating in Africa do not differ significantly from MNEs from the rest of the world. For example, African MNEs have many foreign affiliates or subsidiaries in foreign countries; they are involved in much more than merely establishing sales office and incorporate a full range of manufacturing, research and development activities. MNEs in Africa come from around the world. According to the 2018 world investment report, the top investors in Africa come from the US, the UK, France and China. As shown in Figure 10.1, there is a sharp increase in FDI stock from China in Africa, jumping from USD 16 billion

---

[1] Okon, E. E., Operational Structure of Multinational Enterprises in Africa, in Multinational Enterprise Management Strategies in Developing Countries, 2016 IGI Global.

Figure 10.1 Major investors in Africa, 2011 and 2016, by UNCTAD, World Investment Report 2018. Data (billions of dollars) based on the FDI stock of partner countries

in 2011 to USD 40 billion in 2016. During the same period, the top 3 investors in Africa – the United States, the United Kingdom and France – have experienced either a slight increase or decrease in the total amount of FDI stock in Africa.

In 2009, China surpassed the United States as Africa's largest trade partner and the Sino-Africa trade volume hit a new historical high of USD 221.88 billion in 2014. According to statistics of the Chinese Ministry of Commerce, the outflow of China's FDI to Africa reached USD 3.5 billion in 2014, making the total stock nearly USD 30 billion with a yearly average growth rate of 46 per cent over the last decade. China has also become Africa's second largest overseas project contracting market, with a total of USD 46 billion contracting projects completed in 2014, and more than 2,500 Chinese enterprises operate their business in Africa across a broad range of sectors such as agriculture, telecommunications, energy, manufacturing, etc.[2]

---

[2] Data obtained from Ministry of Commerce of the People's Republic of China (2015). Website: www.mofcom.gov.cn/article/i/dxfw/gzzd/201503/20150300910506.shtml

Chinese FDI penetrates different layers of Africa's economy with diverse strategies. State-owned enterprises mainly invest in strategic sectors such as infrastructure, oil or ores. The improvement of infrastructure, one of the fundamental needs in Africa's path to industrialization, directly serves and stimulates economic development. Large-sized Chinese enterprises from the private sector are mainly involved in non-infrastructure projects such as manufactured goods, telecommunications and wholesale trade. Through linking local partners, their presence is expected to induce positive spillovers that enhance the technological and managerial capability of local industries. Some SMEs are dominant in light industry and superior technologies mastered by them are acknowledged to be more appropriate for African engineers to learn, compared to the technologies initiated in advanced countries.

Tsikata et al. (2010) analyse the impact of Chinese outward FDI (COFDI) in Ghana qualitatively and descriptively. They find that Chinese FDI 'helps reduce import dependency, contributes to export expansion, contributes in terms of value addition and helps improve the competitiveness of local industries'. Auffray and Fu (2015) use a case study of Chinese FDI on the managerial knowledge transfer in Ghana and suggest that the progressive replacement of Chinese managers by local ones can help to overcome the culture and linguistic barriers of managerial knowledge spillovers. Kernen and Lam (2014) study the work localization in Chinese state-owned enterprises in Ghana, saying 'Chinese SOEs have gradually localized workforce, and the localization experience is similar to those of Western companies'. Some argue that 'China's increased engagement with Africa could generate important gains for African economies' (Renard, 2011).

Knowledge transfer of MNEs from China can be different from the MNEs from Western countries due to differences in cultural backgrounds. According to the Western models of international expansion, advanced countries' MNEs already possesses the technology and required knowledge which they transfer to create new market opportunities abroad (Aulakh, 2007). On the other hand, MNEs originating from developing countries have different motivations and paths for internalization. For example, Cuervo-Cazurra (2012) finds that Latin American multinationals with strong domestic location advantages are more likely to set up international marketing subsidiaries. Another example is Aulakh (2007), who finds that Chinese multinationals in the consumer electronics industries have paths to multinationality which are derived from domestic dominance and product diversification, which are precursors to accelerated globalization. Thus, knowledge transfer is expected to differ between MNEs from China and EU due to differences in their motivations for market seeking and dealing with constraints.

Another important difference between Chinese and EU MNEs is the cultural background. Social factors beyond economic principle often play an important role in the managerial knowledge transfer in MNEs. As for Chinese MNEs, an important barrier to developing linkages with local companies is language (Auffrey & Fu, 2015). Language barrier may enhance relational distance of the Chinese MNEs with local employees as well as the relational distance of Chinese and local employers within the Chinese MNEs. Thus, with the larger relational distance, the communication and interaction of individuals in these Chinese MNEs may weaken knowledge transfer. In addition, Chinese traditional culture makes Chinese people humble and shy to communicate with co-workers, especially co-workers from other cultural backgrounds. This is totally different from the EU MNEs – where people from Western backgrounds are always open, adapt easily to work environments of diverse cultural backgrounds, and are more likely to make contacts or communicate with local workers. Above all, we predict different patterns in knowledge transfer between CMNEs and EMNEs and we test this in this chapter using a unique individual-level firm social network data set.

10.3   Data

Empirical analysis in this chapter uses a worker-manager-level survey carried out by the MNEmerge project in Ghana. This survey focuses on the impact of MNEs on development and poverty reduction through building of local managerial capabilities. By conducting an individual survey, it intends to uncover the linkages through which knowledge is transferred to local firms and people, how this contributes to capability building at firm and individual level, and how this empowers local employees and changes their personal skills, career future and aspirations in life.

10.3.1   Survey and Sampling

The collection of data was carried out by researchers from Oxford University and CSIR-STEPRI during the period of March to June 2015. A pilot survey was first conducted in two pharmaceutical MNEs (EU and Chinese MNEs) and then feedbacks were used for refining the questionnaires and interview techniques. Before carrying out the individual interviews in each MNE, we obtained a name list that helped us ensure variation in terms of education, age, gender, any physical disability and department. In total, we carried out 30 interviews per MNE which provide in-depth understanding of the linkages and

Table 10.1 *Distribution of participants in the survey*

Company	Ghanaian	Non-Ghanaian	Managers	Workers	Chinese Firm?	High-Tech Firm?
Action	20	7	7	20	0	0
Akosombo	27	2	6	23	1	0
Gokals	23	2	5	20	0	1
Huawei	22	8	9	21	1	1
Sanbao	26	3	8	21	1	1
Texstyle	28	4	11	21	0	0
Topint	21	8	5	24	1	0
Vodafone	29	1	10	20	0	1
Total	196	35	61	170	4	4

interactions. Therefore, the sample size covers 8 MNEs with about 30 interviews each, amounting to 231 observations (170 workers and 61 managers) in total. Table 10.1 shows the sampling frame of the data.

Management knowledge is likely to spillover from MNEs to indigenous firms through several channels. One of the key channels is through the demonstration effect induced by regular interaction among employees within the organization. The concept and routines of explicit management practices embedded in MNEs' culture can be observed and learned by their workers through demonstration-by-implementation and word-of-mouth. These will not only allow industry-specific managerial knowledge to diffuse, but also provide local employees with the opportunity to learn some generic management knowledge which can be useful in other firms or even other industries.

Firm-level sampling method is purposive sampling. Purposive sampling was used to select eight companies according to: nationality, technology intensity, sector and market size, and power. We choose eight multinational enterprises (4 Chinese, 4 EU); there are 2 high-tech (ICTs, pharmaceuticals) firms and 2 low-tech (textiles, construction) firms. The 4 EU firms are Vodafone (ICT), GoKals Laborex (pharma), Textiles Ghana Ltd (Vlisco being the main company) (textiles), Acticon (construction), and the 4 Chinese firms are Huawei (ICT), Sanbao (pharma), Akosombo (textiles), Top International (construction).

The aim was to include the major players in each of the four low-tech and high-tech sectors. Nationality was split into Chinese and EU. MNEs were compared along this dimension and the technology intensity dimension to draw conclusions as to whether transfer of knowledge differed according to investors' nationality or technological intensity of activities.

Sectors such as oil, gas, and mining were excluded as they are predominantly extractive and less representative of the 'transfer of knowledge' model.

Individual-level sampling is as follows. We aimed to interview between 5 and 10 managers plus the CEO or deputy CEO. Among the managers, we tried to always include at least one manager dealing with the main coordination functions such as HR and marketing; for workers, in each firm, we aimed to interview around 20 workers, with a mix of skills and abilities (which varied sector by sector).

10.3.2 Measurement of Variables

The main information this chapter describes is the survey on knowledge transfer as well as the channels of communication. Knowledge transfer comes from the following questions:

(1) I learn from and (or) transfer my personal knowledge to subordinate workers;
(2) I learn from and (or) transfer my personal knowledge to managerial staffs at a higher level;
(3) I learn from and (or) transfer my personal knowledge to colleagues of the same level.

This chapter firstly uses the principal component analysis (PCA) technique to combine the information into a knowledge transfer index. Then it uses this detailed information as knowledge transfer with subordinate workers, managers or colleagues.

The channels of communication can be diverse and they come from the following information:

(1) I learned, tutored and (or) supervised within the firm through the telephone;
(2) I learned, tutored and (or) supervised within the firm through emails;
(3) I learned, tutored and (or) supervised within the firm through manuals;
(4) I learned, tutored and (or) supervised within the firm through technical advice;
(5) I learned, tutored and (or) supervised within the firm through training sessions;
(6) I learned, tutored and (or) supervised within the firm through external experts;
(7) I learned, tutored and (or) supervised in the firm through joint team work;
(8) I learned, tutored and (or) supervised within the firm through industry associations;

(9) I learned, tutored and (or) supervised within the firm through social events.

On average, males have more knowledge transfer compared with females, but the channels of communication are similar. High-tech firms have more channels of communication but fewer knowledge transfers than low-tech firms. Chinese firms have more channels of communication, but fewer knowledge transfers compared with EU firms. Ghanaian individuals have fewer channels of communication but more or less the same knowledge transfer as non-Ghanaians.

10.4   Empirical Results

The analysis in the chapter starts with a traditional econometric analysis as a benchmark. After this, we construct the network from the survey data and analyse how social network characteristics work in the knowledge transfer in the MNEs. We also apply the propensity score matching methods to find out the treatment effects.

10.4.1   The Base Model

We considered the following linear model:

$$Know_{ij} = \alpha + \beta 1 Ghana_i + \beta 2 Channel_i + \beta 3 X_{ij} + \varepsilon \qquad (10.1)$$

where $Know_{ij}$ is the knowledge transfer of individual i in firm j, $Ghana_i$ is a dummy variable indicating whether individual i is Ghanaian or not. $Channel_i$ is the number of communication channels of individual i, and X_{ij} is a set of controls of individuals and firms. The lists of the dependent and independent variables and their meanings and measurements are presented in Table 10.8 and Table 10.9 respectively in the Appendix, together with the correlation coefficients of the control variables in Table 10.10.

The regression results in Table 10.2 show the estimation of the model in two specifications. Model 1 and Model 2 are different as Model 2 has extra control variables; both models include firm fixed effects and robust standard errors clustered at firm level. The R squared of the models is about 0.3, which suggests the linear model fits well with the data. There are 231 observations in total, which may be challenged, as a small sample size would hardly provide a good statistical reference for the population. However, we argue that, firstly, the objective sampling that allows us to study typical and representative firms would make our findings more meaningful in the case of MNEs in Ghana. Second, the sample size is not actually small. Macro economists always do carry out regression analysis for about 200 observations. For example, in economic growth,

Table 10.2 *Base model*

	(1)	(2)
	Knowledge transfer	
Ghanaian	0.5076*	0.5369**
	(0.2321)	(0.2250)
Channel	0.2181**	0.2208**
	(0.0823)	(0.0834)
ChinaMNE	−0.2706	−0.3087
	(0.3004)	(0.3114)
Worker	−0.1675	−0.1026
	(0.2586)	(0.2305)
Reward	−0.0716	−0.0601
	(0.0680)	(0.0653)
MNEs Exp		−0.0106**
		(0.0039)
Field Exp		0.0191**
		(0.0080)
N	231	231
R^2	0.3270	0.3330

Standard errors in parentheses, $* \, p < 0.10$, $** \, p < 0.05$, $*** \, p < 0.01$

papers choose a number of countries as their study sample. Finally, we tried many different specifications to show that the findings are consistent; these include the study of different outcomes, different sub-samples and different methods. Overall, the sample size is not an issue in this study and should not lead to a major bias of the estimators.

Model 1 and Model 2 both give straightforward and expected results, suggesting that more channels of knowledge transfer would have more knowledge transfer in MNEs. The channels, which are descried in part 10.3.2, are important ways for individuals in the MNEs to gain information and knowledge. Model 1 and Model 2 both show that Chinese MNEs have no significant difference with traditional EU MNEs with regard to knowledge transfer within the firm. Considering the fact that managerial knowledge in the Chinese and EU firms is high, both transfer knowledge to local firms and individuals, and they perform similarly in knowledge transfer, Model 2 shows that a Ghanaian employee would have significantly more knowledge transfer. This shows that the knowledge in MNEs would spread to local individuals. The direction of the knowledge flow goes from the expatriates to local workers or managers. Model 2 also shows that work experience in the relevant sector would enhance the knowledge transfer, while work experience in the MNEs would have a negative effect on knowledge transfer. It may be the case that individuals who have longer experience in a similar field would have stronger absorptive ability, such that they adapt to the managerial knowledge in MNEs. As for the experience in MNEs, it may be possible that people who have had enough exposure to knowledge in the MNEs would have obtained a certain level of managerial knowledge, such that they would be reluctant to learn and transfer new knowledge.

From the baseline results, we find evidence that Ghanaian workers benefit from knowledge transfer and the channels of knowledge flow would increase the knowledge transfer in the firm. The results show that there is no cultural difference regarding knowledge transfer in Chinese and EU MNEs, while the knowledge in both types of MNEs flows from the expatriates to the local workers or managers. The other specifications and robustness checks in this study also support these findings. Network analysis and matching in the subsequent sections are based on Model 2, which includes more relevant controls and dummy variables and provides evidence that local individuals benefit from knowledge transfer in MNEs, while Chinese MNEs have no difference in knowledge transfer compared with EU MNEs.

10.4.2 Social Network

Network analysis is a growing modelling method in many subjects: sociology, computer science and epidemiology among others. In economics, some model the learning behaviour in social networks, the spread of innovation in social networks and the network effect of job searching, migration and micro-finance in development and labour economics. However, there is a lack of empirical evidence about the effect of network structure on knowledge transfer.

Information on social networks in MNEs comes from the following information in the survey: Name of first person you interact most often with; Name of second person you interact most often with; Name of third person you interact most often with; Other information on the contacts, such as the position and department of the three contacts, is also obtained.

We firstly construct a network for each MNE based on the above information and compute the network properties for firms and individuals. A network or a graph is a collection of vertices jointed by edges. Vertices are nodes, sites and actors denoted by i. Edges are links, bonds and ties denoted by ij between vertex i and vertex j. Number of vertices is n and number of edges is m. $Aij = 1$, if there is an edge between vertices i and j. The construction of a social network of managers, workers and firms comes from work and relationship questionnaires of managers and workers where they are asked to report their three most important linkages in the firm. Each individual is treated as a node and an arrow-directed linkage shows the information paths amongst individuals. We combine the workers and managers, directed and undirected networks and construct the network adjacency matrix. For instance, if individual i describes individual j as a contact, the ij entry in the matrix is then denoted as 1; otherwise it is 0. After constructing the typology of social network structure, we can then calculate the network characteristics of the individuals and firms following Jackson (2008). Given the networks are incomplete, we focus on the degree centrality of the individuals and firms (position of individual within the networks, overall network characteristics). However, other characteristics of the network are also presented in the results for robustness reasons.

The network graphics of the eight firms are presented in Appendix 10.2. The nodes are the surveyed individuals while the links show the contacts of the individuals and the structure of the firm's network. The blue nodes are Ghanaian while the pink nodes are for non-Ghanaian workers. This study includes the network properties of the firm and individuals as extra control variables in Model 2 in the benchmark model and shows how the network structure impacts the knowledge flow in the MNEs.

The network analysis results are presented in Table 10.3 and Table 10.4. The results show that the network of the firm matters and the firm network structures have a significant impact on the knowledge transfer in the MNEs. The firm network characteristics such as centralization index, average degree of connections, eigenvector degree and betweenness have a significantly negative impact on the knowledge transfer. As the networks are not complete, these results should be examined with caution. However, the degree centrality, for example, shows the number of connections, which reveals the average degree or the eigenvector degree connection of the firm and is a better indicator in this case. The results suggest that the decentralized firm network would enhance the knowledge transfer. Different from the bureaucratic organizations, the decentralized firms are easier and more flexible and are able to communicate among workers, between workers, managers and CEO.

The decentralized firms are also more open and friendly to new ideas and managerial knowledge. Decentralized does not mean 'not organized'. However, it means that the firms are organized in a more flat and flexible way, rather than the traditional bureaucratic and hierarchical firms. Thus, it makes sense that the more decentralized MNEs in Ghana would help to transfer knowledge in the firm. Table 10.3 provides consistent results with the baseline model, which shows that sampled Ghanaian workers

Table 10.3 *Firm network*

	(1)	(2)	(3)	(4)
		Knowledge Transfer		
Ghanaian	0.5369**	0.5369**	0.5369**	0.5369**
	(0.2250)	(0.2250)	(0.2250)	(0.2250)
Channel	0.2208**	0.2208**	0.2208**	0.2208**
	(0.0834)	(0.0834)	(0.0834)	(0.0834)
ChinaMNE	−0.5256*	−0.4629	−0.2439	−0.5050
	(0.2661)	(0.2981)	(0.1432)	(0.2703)
Worker	−0.1026	−0.1026	−0.1026	−0.1026
	(0.2305)	(0.2305)	(0.2305)	(0.2305)
Central Index	−0.1136***			
	(0.0293)			
Average Degree		−0.4048***		
		(0.0474)		
Eigen Degree			−0.0139***	
			(0.0019)	
Between				−0.0862***
				(0.0222)
N	231	231	231	231
R^2	0.3330	0.3330	0.3330	0.3330

Notes: Standard errors in parentheses. * $p < 0.10$, ** $p < 0.05$, *** $p < 0.01$

benefit from knowledge transfer, there is no culture difference in knowledge from Chinese or EU firms and more channels of communication means more knowledge transfer.

A decentralized structure of the firm helps the knowledge transfer within the firm. This evidence is also provided in Table 10.4, the same model but only for worker sample, thus reducing the number of observations to 170. The findings on network structure of MNEs have positive implications, especially for China, where we could predict more outward FDI in the future. Traditionally, Chinese firms are centralized. They have multiple levels of management and various company rules that may restrict the productivity of the workers or employees. Chinese firms may have to reform their organization structure so as to embrace the enhancement of knowledge flow in the firm and thus the increase the productivity of the firm. Chinese MNEs in Africa, such as the four observed in this study in Ghana, could also consider the reformation of their firms in order to improve their knowledge as well as help adapt more to the local economy.

Table 10.4 *Firm network for worker sample*

	(1)	(2)	(3)	(4)
		Knowledge Transfer		
Ghanaian	0.8118*	0.8118*	0.8118*	0.8118*
	(0.3559)	(0.3559)	(0.3559)	(0.3559)
Channel	0.1718*	0.1718*	0.1718*	0.1718*
	−(0.0841)	(0.0841)	(0.0841)	(0.0841)
ChinaMNE	−0.0999	0.0676	0.1277	−0.0755
	(0.3539)	(0.4037)	(0.1288)	(0.3600)
Central Index	−0.1340***			
	(0.0357)			
Average		−0.2325***		
Degree		(0.0570)		
Eigen Degree			−0.0131***	
			(0.0025)	
Between				−0.1017***
				(0.0271)
N	170	170	170	170
R²	0.3539	0.3539	0.3539	0.3539

Notes: Standard errors in parentheses. * p < 0.10, ** p < 0.05, *** p < 0.01

10.4.3 Robustness Check Using Matching Technique

In order to check the robustness of our results, we used propensity score matching technique as an alternative estimation method. The idea behind it is that for each observation in the treatment group, we look for one observation in the control group that has the same observable characteristics in the data such as age, education, gender, position, experience and communication channels among others.

One important assumption about the matching method is the 'common support'. We draw the overlap graph for the propensity scores for the treatment and control group. Although the treatment group and control group do not overlap perfectly (they are of course very different and hard to match), their propensity scores both extend from 0 to 1 (see details in Figure 10.2). This study also implements two other sets of propensity score matching by matching not only the individual and firm characteristics, but also the firm and individual network properties.

The estimation results are presented in Table 10.5, and the results show that, on average, compared with the non-Ghanaians, Ghanaian individuals

Table 10.5 *Estimation results from the propensity score matching*

	Knowledge Transfer
Average Treatment Effect Ghanaian vs Non-Ghanaian	0.6417***
	(0.2444)
N	231

Standard errors in parentheses, * $p < 0.10$, ** $p < 0.05$, *** $p < 0.01$

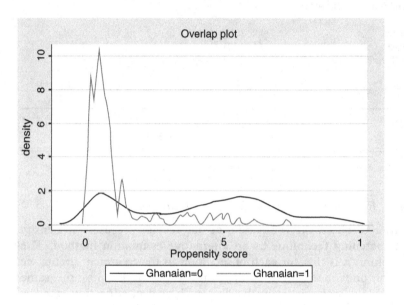

Figure 10.2 Overlap plot of the propensity score

have about 0.64 units more knowledge transfer. This result is significant at the 1 per cent level. Compared with the results in the baseline and the network analysis (0.54), the matching method shows slightly larger coefficients. The small change in the magnitude of the coefficients may be due to some factors that may lead to a bias in the estimation and is eliminated by the fixed effect, but not in the matching method. However, the propensity score matching method shows a slightly different but consistent result with the previous analysis and shows that local individuals in MNEs benefit more from knowledge transfer.

Table 10.6 *Propensity score matching with firm network*

	(1)	(2)	(3)
		Knowledge transfer	
Average Treatment Effect	0.3106	0.7246**	0.5062**
Ghanaian vs Non-Ghanaian	(0.3357)	(0.3542)	(0.2003)
N	231	231	231

Standard errors in parentheses, * $p < 0.10$, ** $p < 0.05$, *** $p < 0.01$

10.4.4 Robustness Check Using Matching With Network Properties

It is built on the matching method of Section 10.4.3. What we have done for this robustness check is to introduce the network properties as an extra matching criterion. The results are presented in Tables 10.6 and 10.7, where Table 10.6 uses firm network structure and Table 10.7 uses individual network properties. The models are different as different network characteristics are included separately in the models.

The results in the two tables are consistent with the main matching results in Table 10.5. The average treatment effects are around 0.5 to 0.6. Most of the coefficients are significant. The results show that the average treatment effect by matching method is robust to different matching criterion of social network.

10.5 Case Study Evidence of Intra-firm Knowledge Transfer Within MNEs

Qualitative evidence from case studies and interviews in the MNEs' subsidiaries in the construction sector in Ghana provides valuable information that supplements the above social network analysis. Details of these eight sampled European and Chinese construction MNEs under case study and the research methods for data collection and analysis are explained in Chapter 9.

Because of their direct integration in the MNEs' management systems, Ghanaian employees in foreign construction firms are the primary recipients of foreign managerial knowledge. Interviews with foreign contractors highlighted three vectors of managerial learning: experience (1), formal training (2), and mentorship (3).

10.5.1 Demonstration, Imitation and Learning-by-doing

Locals employed in managerial positions in foreign companies accumulate foreign managerial knowledge through observation and experience. As

Table 10.7 *Propensity score matching with individual network*

	(1) Knowledge transfer	(2) Knowledge transfer	(3) Knowledge transfer	(4) Knowledge transfer
Average Treatment Effect	0.4397*	0.5545**	0.6421**	0.6134**
Ghanaian vs Non-Ghanaian	(0.2422)	(0.2481)	(0.2909)	(0.2779)
N	231	231	231	231

Standard errors in parentheses, $* p < 0.10$, $** p < 0.05$, $*** p < 0.01$

foreign companies undertake the biggest contracts in Ghana, their local managers have the opportunity to be exposed to complex projects involving large budgets, tough time and quality constraints and to the correspondingly advanced management practices. Employees in non-managerial positions also have limited learning opportunities through observation and interaction – they are also included in a foreign management system – but how much knowledge they will be able to assimilate and reuse will depend on their prior experience and education, as well as on the time they spend with the foreign contractor.

10.5.2   Formal Training

Local managers in foreign construction firms can also benefit from a more active form of managerial knowledge transfer through formal training programmes. Most foreign companies interviewed reported having training sessions for their local managers. Training content is usually tailored to the development level of the employee and targets specific skill gaps. Examples of training modules included time, quality and cost management, as well as more general sessions on project management. Training locations vary, and sessions can be internal to the company and conducted by local employees' own foreign managers or delegated to an external consultancy. MNEs may also send their local employees abroad for training.

10.5.3   Mentorship

Mentorship can be defined as a formal or informal dyadic relationship between a foreign senior manager (the 'mentor') and a more junior local employee working for the same company. Mentorship supposes the development of a long-term professional relationship between two individuals with the implicit purpose of building the capacity of the local employee. Among the seven companies interviewed for this research, only one indicated having a formal mentorship scheme, but in at least one other foreign firm, interviews revealed the existence of similar dyadic relationships, though at a more informal level.

10.6   Conclusion

This study uses unique firm survey data to study the knowledge transfer in MNEs in Ghana, a typical country in West African that welcomes FDI for development. This chapter is the first empirical study using the network approach to study the managerial knowledge diffusion in MNEs. It contributes to the literature on the impact of FDI on the knowledge diffusion in host countries, and to the emerging literature that uses social network in international business studies.

The baseline model which controls for the firm's fixed effects shows that first, local workers benefit more from knowledge transfer compared with expatriates. This makes a lot of sense and shows that the knowledge in the MNEs flows from the expatriates to local people. In other words, knowledge transfer is unidirectional and tends to flow from expatriates to local workers. Second, more channels of communication mean more knowledge transfer. Finally, at the aggregate level, Chinese MNEs and EU MNEs show no significant difference in terms of knowledge transfer. However, grouping local employees into managers and workers, there are differences in knowledge transfer between Chinese and European MNEs in different groups. These MNEs have different network structures, partly due to different culture of the country of origin. The network analysis shows that the firm network structure, then, influences the knowledge transfer within a firm. The more decentralized MNEs tend to perform better in knowledge transfer. The decentralized organizations tend to be more flexible and more flat in organizational structure. Such firms may be more open to new ideas and knowledge. The flow of information and knowledge in these firms would be smoother and quicker within the firms and between different departments and positions.

The propensity score matching method provides more evidence that local workers benefit more from knowledge transfer compared with expatriates, who are supposed to have more managerial knowledge and are sent to MNEs' overseas branches in Africa to help the establishment, maintenance and expansion of the local business of the MNEs. The finding suggests that the FDI does not only bring the capital and technology that are needed for Ghana's economic growth, but also the human capital, particularly the managerial knowledge embedded in the expatriates coming together with capital and technology. This evidence shows the FDI would help improve the local development in the case of knowledge spillover to local workers.

In the more detailed outcomes, we find evidence to show that subordinate workers in Chinese MNEs get more knowledge transferred from their managers. This is in line with the finding that knowledge in the MNEs flows from the expatriates to local people. As for the detailed role and position of the local people, local sub-ordinates in Chinese MNEs benefit more from knowledge transfer. This is the only cultural difference we observed in the knowledge transfer in MNEs in Ghana.

This study has interesting policy implications. MNEs may have to reform their organizational form in order to enhance the knowledge transfer within the firm. At a macro level, developing countries have to consider FDI not only for technology and capital, but also for human capital, which is important for economic growth. At the policy level, African countries should consider human capital policy together with FDI policies.

The findings also have important practical implications for policymakers and managers of MNEs. Local employees do benefit from the managerial knowledge transfer from the MNEs through various channels. Therefore, trade policies should continue to encourage the inflow of FDI into the country. Moreover, if network structure and basic individual characteristics are controlled for, there is no significant difference between Chinese and European MNEs in terms of managerial knowledge transfer, in general. The cultural difference appears mainly in the knowledge acquired by the subordinates in the Chinese MNEs who reported having learned more from their managers. Finally, decentralized MNEs' subsidiary structure appears to be more of a conduit to the knowledge transfer. Therefore, adopting a more decentralized structure will facilitate more knowledge transfer between foreign and local employees in the MNE subsidiaries.

This study bears some limitations. Our analysis is based on a cross-sectional data for only eight firms. A follow-up survey to create panel data to study the dynamic properties of knowledge transfer of workers in the firms would provide additional insights and extension of the current paper.

Appendices

Appendix 10.1

VARIABLES

Table 10.8 *Dependent variables*

Variable Name	Meaning	Measure
Knowledge Transfer	Knowledge transfer between individuals	PCA to combine the 3 variables
D2a CKT Subordinate	Knowledge transfer to or with subordinate	0 for no transfer, 1 for learn, 2 for tutor, 3 for both
D2b CKT Managerial	Knowledge transfer to or with manager	0 for no transfer, 1 for learn, 2 for tutor, 3 for both
D2c CKT Colleagues	Knowledge transfer to or with colleagues	0 for no transfer, 1 for learn, 2 for tutor, 3 for both
Know ML	Whether transfer with managers	Binary

Table 10.9 *Independent variables*

Variable Name	Meaning	Measure
Ghanaian	Whether the individual is Ghanaian or not	Binary
Channel	Number of channels for knowledge transfer	PCA to combine the 9 channels
China MNE	Whether the firm is Chinese MNE	Binary
Worker	Whether the individual is a worker	Binary
Male	Whether the individual is male	Binary
Education	The education level of individual	Education level for basic, secondary, tertiary
Age	The age level of individual	Age level for <30, 30 to 40, 41 to 50, >50
Ht MNE	Whether the firm is a high-technology MNE	Binary
MNEs Exp	Individual's years of experience in current MNE	Number of years in current MNE
Field Exp	Individual's years of experience in the relevant field	Number of years in relevant field

Table 10.10 *Correlation among controls*

	Ghanaian	Channel	ChinaMNE	Worker	Male	ht MNE	Age	Education	MNEs Exp	Field Exp	Reward
Ghanaian	1										
Channel	-0.0981	1									
China MNE	-0.079	0.2617	1								
Worker	0.4316	-0.0797	0.0569	1							
Male	-0.0512	0.0336	0.2048	0.0595	1						
Ht MNE	0.079	0.0947	0.0218	-0.0372	-0.1166	1					
Age	-0.1759	0.219	0.5256	-0.0676	0.1634	-0.238	1				
Education	-0.1657	0.3012	-0.1307	-0.3961	-0.2355	0.3973	-0.1346	1			
MNEs Exp	0.0306	0.1982	0.2312	0.0715	0.1887	-0.1597	0.5768	-0.109	1		
Field Exp	-0.122	0.119	0.0995	-0.149	0.1921	-0.259	0.6026	-0.0833	0.6963	1	
Reward	0.0496	0.2197	0.114	-0.0521	0.0387	0.1588	0.1565	0.2073	0.2738	0.1402	1

Appendix 10.2

SOCIAL NETWORK STRUCTURE OF SURVEYED FIRMS.

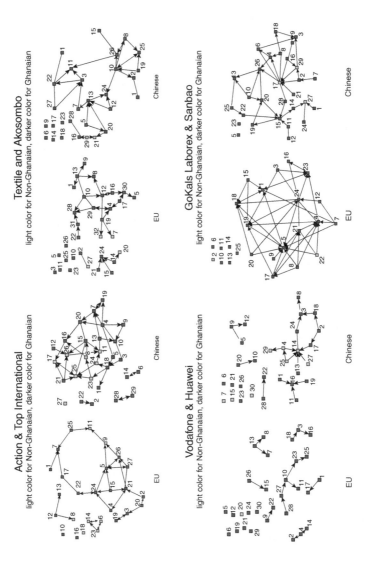

Figure 10.3 Social network

Part III

Emerging Technologies and Innovation
in Africa

11 ICT Adoption and Innovation in Ghana

Xiaolan Fu and Jun Hou

11.1 Introduction

Innovation in the context of developing countries becomes a more complex system in which, for the majority of firms, R&D is no longer considered as the only core input among various innovation inputs. Due to the lack of internal resources and technological experience, various external inputs emerge as equal or more important contributors to the innovativeness of firms in low-income countries. Although firms in low-income countries actively engage in various innovation activities, the innovating process remains uncertain and the outcomes vary widely due to the different levels of absorptive capacity and environmental settings (Cohen and Levinthal, 1989).

The most recent empirical evidence confirms the positive effect of information and communication technologies (ICT) on firm performance, not only in terms of economic growth (Bakhshi and Larsen, 2005; Brynjolfsson et al., 2002; Brynjolfsson and Hitt, 1995, 2000; Brynjolfsson and Yang, 1998; Lee et al., 2005) and the nature of ICT itself (Corrocher et al., 2007; Shin and Park, 2007; Sorenson et al., 2006), but also innovation and diffusion patterns of a specific ICT (Chen et. al., 2007; Greenan and Mairesse, 2000; Vicente and Lopez, 2006). ICT has always been acknowledged as one of the main instruments in upgrading a firm's technological capability, while many studies have uncovered its critical role in pushing the technology catch-up in developing countries. Yet evidence regarding the mechanism by which ICT contributes to innovation outcomes is inconclusive. Moreover, many previous studies have been limited by focusing only on the presence of ICT, instead of further investigating the innovation effects of ICT by considering its interactions with knowledge input factors.

There is also considerable policy interest in the implications of different sources of innovation inputs in low-income countries (LICs). Traditionally,

267

in-house innovation would be targeted mainly at new and significantly improved product innovation (following the results of much earlier surveys, such as Mansfield, 1968). In the context of developing countries, innovation would be transformed into different formats of behaviours by which not only invention would happen, but imitative innovation also could take place. In addition, other sources of innovation inputs such as ICT investment have frequently been found to be accompanied by innovations in processing and the organization of work within the firm. To our knowledge, studies that jointly investigated the effects of innovation activities and ICT adoption are scarce in the developing country context. There are few articles in the literature, and they are mainly focused on developed economies and have produced conflicting results. For example, while Cerquera and Klein (2008) find that a more intense use of ICT brings about a reduction in R&D effort in German firms, Polder et al. (2009) find a complementarity effect of ICT with respect to innovation in the service sector only in the Netherlands, albeit one that is small in magnitude.

This chapter attempts to highlight the critical role of ICT in the complex system of innovation in LICs. Various elements interact and complement each other in the system to reach the goal of becoming an innovator. Several questions remain unanswered. For example, among different knowledge assets in an organization, does ICT adoption play a significant role in enhancing innovation? How do the impacts vary for different types of innovation? And how is ICT likely to yield the instrumental effects of facilitating innovation? We use an augmented knowledge production function in which ICT is treated in parallel with other innovation sourcing activities as an input to innovation performance. Not only does this uncover the role of ICT, such specification also takes into account the potential interactive effects between innovation-oriented ICT adoption and different types of knowledge sources.

The next section reviews the previous literature on innovation in developing countries and the adoption of ICT in innovation. Section 11.3 introduces the model specification and the data used in the empirical analyses. The next section (11.4) discusses the empirical results and summarizes the findings. The last section (11.5) provides the conclusion to the chapter.

11.2   Innovation in LDCs and the Adoption of ICT

11.2.1   Knowledge Creation in LDCs

Innovation in least developing countries is gaining increasing mention in the literature, as a mechanism to achieve economic development goals.

Due to their specificities, firms in LDCs show a particular behaviour with regard to the creation, learning, development, sharing, and transmission of knowledge. Cooper (1989) explained the differences in characteristics between innovation in industrialized economies and developing countries. At a low stage of development, firms normally face obstacles such as inadequate human capital and poor infrastructure. In-house innovative activities are severely constrained for a majority of firms. Freeman (1989) suggested that external knowledge and compatible innovation infrastructure supports have significant influences on the learning process. Aggarwal (2000) explained that external technological sourcing plays two important roles in developing economies: filling gaps in domestic technological capability and upgrading the existing technologies to international standards. By enhancing the technological capability, external technology sourcing benefits in-house activities.

However, acquiring external knowledge per se does not guarantee that a firm will achieve successful learning (Matusik, 2000). For external knowledge to be exploited effectively, it has to be combined with a compatible innovation infrastructure and complementary assets within the firm. Cooper (1989) mentioned that failure to learn is in fact quite common in developing countries because the firms there that receive technology via external sources are quite often unconcerned about how to develop and appropriate this internal technological support. Cohen and Levinthal (1989) define 'absorptive capacity' to describe the substantial role of a stock of prior knowledge in order to absorb external know-how. They argue that the in-house R&D process would at the same time assist firms to build up their own technological capability. This technological infrastructure and absorptive capability within firms is needed in order to understand the tacit components of the technology (Desai, 1989; Lall, 1989; Mowery and Oxley, 1995).

The paradigm of open innovation demonstrates that firms should make the best use of internal and external knowledge (Chesbrough, 2003). This perspective not only emphasizes the significant value of external knowledge, it also indicates that firms organize their internal activities in part in order to absorb the wealth of available external information. Such a mutual interaction implies the possible complementarity between their own and external sources of knowledge.

11.2.2 Adoption of ICT and Innovation

Firms can use ICT for different, but compatible, uses. These are related to acquiring information, facilitating communications and offering the automation of internal business processes. ICT (e.g. the internet) also performs as a knowledge acquisition channel through which firms in developing countries can get access to advanced technological information and transfer back and share with inter-organizational stakeholders without time and geographical boundaries. In this sense, ICT can be used as a corporate channel for one-way information acquisition, dissemination and data access across organizational levels (Bafoutsou and Mentzas, 2002; Huzingh, 2000). The literature argues that the amount of information and knowledge in a modern organization that needs to be stored and shared, and the dynamic evolution of information make the use of technology support not an option, but a necessity. Even in developing countries, no firm nowadays can afford to ignore new ICTs which radically reduce the time needed to create and communicate knowledge (Nonaka and Nishiguchi, 2001). Besides, ICT is also an effective way to leverage codified knowledge that is acquired externally (Zack, 1999). Empirically, even if based on different indicators, the relationship between ICT and innovation and firm performance, at the firm level, is generally positive (Black and Lynch, 2001; Bresnahan et al., 2002; Castiglione, 2009; Greenan et al., 2001).

In the knowledge creation process, ICT adoption also serves as an instrumental factor, which contributes to innovation outcomes through both direct and indirect interactions with the innovation inputs' activities (Adamides and Karacapilidis, 2006). Organization learning theory suggests that ICT adoption is a process of accumulating an organization's capabilities, such as absorptive capability, integration, organization learning, and knowledge development (Wiseman and Anderson, 2012). Therefore, it has become an essential component to reinforce the innovation return of R&D investment (Hicks and Katz, 1996), suggesting that the adoption of ICT practices may increase the effectiveness of internal and external innovation activities, and hence upgrade innovation outputs. Sambamurthy and Subramani (2005) have also defended the critical role of ICTs in shaping organizational efforts for knowledge creation, acquisition, integration, valuation and use. Ruiz-Mercader et al. (2006) find, from a sample of ICT businesses, that these companies are likely to use ICT tools more frequently, and they conclude that knowledge creation can be boosted through investing in ICT. In addition, ICT allows cost reduction in communication when compared to traditional communication tools. It effectively facilitates exchange of information, collaboration and the possibility of establishing close relationships among various actors within a firm (Kalakota and Robinson, 2000). ICTs, and especially web technologies, provide great opportunities for the automation of processes (Fischer, 2004).

However, ICTs used to support knowledge creation present some limitations, since they reduce the very richness of knowledge when it is codified, and management and sharing of tacit knowledge through technologies is problematic (Flanagin, 2002). Some of the previous studies have pointed out that ICT alone is not enough to lead successful innovation and affect a firm's productivity. Black and Lynch (2001) and Bresnahan et al. (2002) focus on the interaction between ICT and its complementary assets (human capital, in this case) and discover their impact on organizational innovation. Meanwhile, the ability to use ICT to support knowledge creation in a meaningful manner depends on the types and natures of knowledge (Flanagin, 2002). Therefore, the acquisition of technological-oriented information via the internet would not necessarily induce positive innovation effects.

In summary, the benefits derived from ICT implementation, which include efficient information and knowledge sharing as well as working with no distance limitations, are expected to be positively related to knowledge creation, which, in turn, may affect higher levels of innovation. However, ICT cannot improve innovation performance in LICs if it is not used appropriately. We argue that the orientation in the implementation of ICTs can also have an impact on the different processes for creating knowledge. The innovation-oriented ICT as a source of innovation increases the likelihood that firms will become an innovator. For knowledge acquisition purposes, the adoption of these practices seeks the interaction with innovation inputs in response to the growth of new product sales.

11.2.3 Innovation and ICT Adoption in Ghana

Since the early 1990s, Ghana has considered the use of ICT as a means to leverage the country's development process. To this effect, a first five-year plan for accelerated development was launched in 1994. More recently, Ghana has developed its ICT for Accelerated Development (ICT4AD) policy statement, which was officially adopted in 2004. The ICT4AD took into consideration Ghana's Vision 2020 Socio-Economic Development Framework, the Ghana Poverty Reduction Strategy (2002–2004) and the Coordinated Programme for Economic and Social Development of Ghana (2003–2012). The ICT4AD is a product of the National ICT Policy and Plan Development Committee set up by the Government to develop an ICT-led socio-economic development policy for the country. It aims to help Ghana formulate a number of socio-economic development policy frameworks. The ICT4AD has over the years identified a number of key developmental objectives to address the developmental problems facing the country. Of these policy frameworks, promoting investment, innovation, R&D and diffusion of ICTs within the economy are among the priorities. As a result, there has been a rapid growth of ICT adoption in local businesses and it has also been widely used to facilitate innovation activities.

In the developing country context, a strand of literature has emphasized ICT's capability and its impact on firm performance (Bhagwat and Sharma, 2007; Bresnahan et al., 2002; Brynjolfsson and Hitt, 2000; Dewett and Jones, 2001). Although ICT has evolved to support new business strategies (Henderson and Venkatraman, 1999), the adoption of ICT in Ghana still plays a major role in traditional back office. Given the lack of internal technological capability and limited innovation resources, the adoption of ICT does not guarantee knowledge creation within the firm.

11.3   Methodology

11.3.1 Model Specification

11.3.1.1 Innovation Performance: Dichotomous Measures As discussed in the previous chapters, innovation in LDCs is more of an imitative behaviour rather than an invention or knowledge creation process. Various sources could contribute to innovation performance besides investing in R&D. Given the limited strategic resources to invent new products or services, innovations are primarily developed in response to customer needs and they emerge and are developed in accordance with customer requirements. In such circumstances, firms in LICs seek alternative sources, such as through directly acquiring from the internet, collaborating with other actors and obtaining technology. Meanwhile, innovation performance will also be captured by different measures. First, we are interested in whether a firm is an innovator or not. The dichotomous variable will be used to denote if a firm is an innovator as given below:

$$Y_i = \alpha + \beta_{inno}Inno_{activities} + {}_i\beta_{int}Internet_i + \beta_{int's}Int\_source_i + \beta_c Control_i + \varepsilon \tag{11.1}$$

$$\beta_{inno}Inno_{activitesi} = \beta_1 inhouse_i + \beta_2 Collaborate_i + \beta_3 Imitate_i \tag{11.2}$$

where Yi is a dichotomous variable that takes the value 1 if a firm is an innovator (product, process or management innovation). '*Internet*' equals 1 if a firm has reported using internet facilities within the firm. '*Int_source*' is a binary variable taking the value 1 if a firm reports that the internet has been adopted as an important channel to achieve innovation. '*Innoactivities i*' captures a set of innovation inputs, including conducting in-house innovation activities, modifying existing products or processes, collaborating with other actors, licensing and imitating existing technologies. The detailed definitions of innovation variables and their corresponding summary statistics are given in Table 11.1. '*Control*' denotes a vector of control variables: age, scale, ownership, industry dummies etc. ε is the disturbance term. In equation (1), '*Int_source*' enters as an explanatory variable which directly influences the propensity of a firm to become an innovator. It is different from the ICT adoption '*Internet$_i$*', which is expected to take an instrumental role to complement other innovation inputs in the knowledge creation process. Equation (11.1) will be estimated with multivariate probit in which correlations between residuals from each type of innovation are taken into account.

11.3.1.2 Innovation Performance: New Product Sales   Another indicator used to measure firms' innovation performance is new product sales. New product sales denote the ratio of sales of new product in total sales, and it is recorded in a continuous manner. The ratio of new product sales is a function of knowledge inputs, ICT adoption and a set of firm characteristics, while controlling for size, industry and location specificities. Given the censored nature of new product sales, Tobit estimation will be adopted in estimating the innovation function. Additionally, by including the interactions between ICT and knowledge inputs' variable, it also systematically examines the potential complementarities existing among the variables.

$$PD_i^* = a + b_{inno}Inno_{activites_i} + b_{int}ICT\_source_i + b_{rnd}\left(Inno_{activites_i^*}\right.$$
$$\left.ICT\_source_i\right) + b_c Control_i + e$$
$$PD_i = \begin{cases} PD_i^*, if\ PD_i > 0 \\ 0,\ otherwise \end{cases} \tag{11.3}$$

where PD_i^* indicates the ratio of new product sales in total sales. PD_i^* is a latent variable and observed only if PD (new product sales) is positive. '*Innoactivities i*' is defined as in equation (11.2) and it captures a set of innovation inputs. Two implications regarding the use of ICT in LIC firms will be given by estimating equation (11.3). First, the direct effects of '*ICT_source*' in determining the level of innovation outcome will be captured by the coefficients b_{int}. Second, with controlling for the potential interaction between the adoption of the internet and innovation inputs,

Table 11.1 *Summary of variables*

Variable	Definition	Mean	S.D.	Min	Max
Dependent variables					
Product dummy	Value 1 if a firm reports having product innovation in the past three years	0.44	0.50	0	1
Process dummy	Value 1 if a firm reports having process innovation in the past three years	0.60	0.49	0	1
Management dummy	Value 1 if a firm reports having management innovation in the past three years	0.40	0.49	0	1
Product inno. sales in %	Percentages of sales due to new product innovation	21.35	29.41	0	100
Product inno. sales new to firm in %	Percentages of sales due to new product innovation, new to firm.	3.60	12.36	0	80
Process inno. sales new to market in %	Percentages of output due to process innovation new to market	17.75	25.02	0	100
Independent variables					
In-house	Value 1 if a firm reports conducing in-house innovation activities, dummy	0.64	0.48	0	1
Collaboration	Value 1 if a firm reports conducing collaborated innovation activities, dummy	0.44	0.50	0	1
Imitation	Value 1 if a firm reports conducing imitative innovation activities, dummy	0.44	0.50	0	1
ICT_source	Value 1 if a firm reports using the internet as a source to acquire innovation, dummy	0.12	0.32	0	1
Controlled variables					
No. Employee	Number of total employees, in logarithm form	1.87	1.34	0	7.55
Ln.age	Logarithm of firm's age	2.65	0.65	0	4.16
Foreign, dum.	Value 1 if a firm is shared with foreign ownership	0.07	0.25	0	1
Competition, dum.	Value 1 if a firm perceives the competition in the local market is fierce	0.49	0.50	0	1
Technician ratio	Ratio of employees who completed technical training	0.07	0.18	0	1

we will be able to uncover the intrinsic role of ICT in facilitating innovation by interacting with different types of knowledge sourcing activities.

11.3.2   Data and Variables

Table 11.1 gives the definition of all variables used in the empirical analysis and reports the descriptive statistics. Innovation performance is measured using two indicators: a dichotomous and a continuous term. As given in equation (11.1) and equation (11.3), innovation is a function of innovation inputs and a set of controlled variables. Although taking various forms in LICs, knowledge sources are still the main contributors to innovation performance. Without engaging in effective knowledge acquisition or creation activities, firms may fail to achieve innovation goals given the unavoidable uncertainties and risks of innovation. Therefore, it is essential to distinguish different types of knowledge sources and evaluate their innovation effects.

The dependent variable in the innovation equation (11.3) is product innovation and it is a continuous variable, in logarithm form. The explanatory variables are the set of innovation inputs. Firms are asked to report if they have engaged in any of the indicated innovation activates during the survey period. The knowledge input variable will be given the value 1 if a firm reported engaging in the corresponding activity. As an innovation-oriented ICT practice, 'ICT_source', a binary measure specifies that a firm has adopted the internet as a channel to acquire innovation-related information. The descriptive statistics in the table show that innovators, regardless of the types of innovation, are, in general, more likely to engage in innovation activities, and they also tend to use the internet more frequently than non-innovators.

The survey contains information on a set of firm and industry specifics. We control for several variables that capture the firms' competitiveness and technological capability. The natural log of the number of employees serves as an indicator of the capital intensity. Firm size is measured by the natural log of the mean of number of employees. We also control for industry and year specificities by using industry and year dummies. The first Schumpeter hypothesis claims that innovation activity increases proportionately more than firm size; larger firms are expected to have more resources to allocate to innovation, which leads to better innovation performance. Hence, firm size has been included as a control variable. Scale in logarithm form is measured by the total number of employees by the end of 2013, and it is used to capture the scale effect of innovation. Company ownership can be a crucial variable in innovation performance in the case of Ghana, as it affects the motivation to innovate and the continuity of business strategy. Foreign-owned firms are characterized by higher capital intensity, high quality of human capital and efficient management. Many previous studies suggest that foreign-owned firms are more innovative (Kimura and Kiyota, 2007). Studies also suggest that foreign-owned firms are more innovative and productive compared to domestic-ownership firms (Doms and Jensen, 1998; Globerman et al., 1994; Kimura and Kiyota, 2007). 'Foreign' indicates if a firm is shared with foreign ownership. 'Age' is calculated as the number of years since the enterprise started production, up to 2013. Young firms are expected to be more dynamic and innovative, all other things being equal (Katrak, 1997a), and therefore a negative effect is expected. 'Competition' is measured by the scale of competition in the domestic market perceived by interviewed firms. We also control for industry and year specifics by using industry and year dummies.

To get some preliminary implications regarding the relationships between different types of knowledge inputs, Table 11.2 reports the mean values of the major variables by types of innovation. Table 11.3 presents the pairwise correlation matrix results. Two issues are worth mentioning here. First, innovation is not a single-path process. Multiple activities can be conducted simultaneously to achieve innovation. The positive correlation between in-house activities and other types of innovation sources suggests that in-house creation, modifying existing technologies and collaboration with other actors are positively associated. Such associations between various innovation inputs imply the potential interdependent relationships among them. Second, not all the innovation inputs and ICT practices conducted in a firm will be treated as complementary elements. Some of them may enter the innovation process as substitute inputs. This is particularly true for firms making innovation investment decisions in LICs, where financial, technical and other strategic resources are limited. Increasing the investment of these substitutive inputs would result in a decrease in the investment of other inputs such as in-house R&D. In such circumstances, positive correlation will not appear. As one of the major channels to acquire knowledge externally, innovation through imitative activities does not appear to have strong associations with other types of knowledge inputs. This may be caused by the hard budget constraints of the firm. Without enough investment to allocate to multiple knowledge inputs, optimizing the inputs regarding the innovation performance becomes difficult. The negative association between 'ICT_source' and 'Imitate' may reflect this point.

Table 11.2 *Descriptive statistics: knowledge sourcing strategies across firms reporting different innovations, mean values*

	In house	Collaboration	Imitate	ICT_source	Size	Age	Foreign	Compete	Uni.
Product									
No	0.427	0.308	0.319	0.054	1.646	2.606	0.054	0.437	0.041
Yes	0.917	0.605	0.588	0.202	2.149	2.716	0.088	0.548	0.119
Process									
No	0.378	0.239	0.191	0.048	1.682	2.592	0.091	0.344	0.040
Yes	0.815	0.570	0.599	0.166	1.987	2.696	0.054	0.580	0.098
Management									
No	0.468	0.334	0.341	0.057	1.703	2.588	0.057	0.411	0.049
Yes	0.900	0.593	0.579	0.211	2.108	2.753	0.086	0.598	0.113
Total	0.641	0.438	0.436	0.119	1.865	2.654	0.069	0.486	0.075

Int_source: Internet was reported as an important source of innovation.

Table 11.3 *Correlation matrix: innovation sources*

	Product Inno.	Process Inno.	Management Inno.	In-House	Collaboration	Imitation	ICT_source
Product Inno.	1						
Process Inno.	0.32	1					
Management Inno.	0.22	0.22	1				
In-House	0.51	0.45	0.44	1			
Collaboration	0.30	0.33	0.26	0.53	1		
Imitation	0.29	0.46	0.26	0.21	0.09	1	
IT_inno. source	0.23	0.18	0.23	0.23	0.17	0.02	1

11.4   Empirical Evidence

Table 11.4 presents the multivariate probit estimation results. The estimated results indicate that, having relatively more capital, human and strategic resources, large firms tend to be more innovative than otherwise. Such effect is reflected by the positive estimates of log employees, although the innovation effects only appear in product and process innovation. Given the simple structure and smaller number of employees, management innovation may take place more easily among small-sized firms in Ghana. The foreign ownership variable included in the process innovation exerts a significant negative impact on the likelihood of process innovation. Such finding suggests that firms with foreign ownership tend not to be innovative. This may be because most innovation activities are conducted back in their home countries (OECD, 2010). More vigorous competition exerts discipline on firms. It therefore tends to strengthen their efficiency and push the firm to be more innovative in order to survive, and the estimated coefficient of competition shows a positive innovation effect in process and management innovation.

Regarding the knowledge acquisition activities, in-house innovation activities are found to have significant positive effects on the likelihood to become an innovator, regardless of the types of innovation. 'Imitation' of competitors is a significant innovation input strategy for all three types of innovation, whereas process innovators are more likely to adopt collaboration as their innovation input. Among the three types of innovations, in-house innovation activity has the highest coefficient for process innovation, which reflects its significant role in increasing the likelihood of becoming a process innovator. The direct innovation effects of acquiring knowledge via the internet are exhibited in the results, suggesting ICT as a source of innovation increases the likelihood of firms to become product innovators.

We now turn to the results of the econometric analysis regarding how ICT affects the intensity of innovation. We estimate ICT's interactive effects on innovation performance and the estimated coefficients are presented in Table 11.5 for product innovation and process innovation, with standard errors given in parentheses. Acknowledged as one of the most crucial sources of innovation, in-house activities drive innovation of Ghanaian firms by means of directly improving the innovation performance regardless of product or process innovation. The estimated coefficients for 'in-house' are all positive and significant at the 99 per cent level. The same innovation effect has also been observed for imitative activities, despite the magnitudes being much smaller. Although both internal creation and external imitation are essential to product innovation, it is

Table 11.4 *Probit results: the role of ICT in determining the likelihood of becoming innovators, without and with internet interactions*

VARIABLES	Product inno. (1)	Process inno. (2)	Management inno. (3)
In-house	1.364***	0.851***	1.274***
	(0.182)	(0.169)	(0.191)
Collaboration	0.078	0.533***	0.209
	(0.149)	(0.159)	(0.150)
Imitation	0.616***	1.039***	0.610***
	(0.146)	(0.152)	(0.146)
ICT_source	0.473*	0.374	0.211
	(0.252)	(0.283)	(0.233)
No. employees	0.196***	0.166**	−0.004
	(0.067)	(0.072)	(0.067)
Ln.age	−0.010	0.051	0.161
	(0.114)	(0.117)	(0.112)
Foreign	−0.074	−0.958**	−0.152
	(0.342)	(0.375)	(0.346)
Competition	0.243*	0.440***	0.416***
	(0.141)	(0.146)	(0.141)
Technician ratio	0.640	1.280**	0.687
	(0.423)	(0.498)	(0.431)
Constant	−1.952***	−2.866***	−2.965***
	(0.748)	(0.788)	(0.786)
Observations	523	523	523

Note: Standard errors in parentheses *** p<0.01, ** p<0.05, * p<0.1; industry dummies are included.

confirmed in our results that in-house R&D investment plays a more important role in increasing innovation sales compared to buying technology externally. The scale effects have also been observed for innovation intensity, as shown in Table 11.5. Larger-size firms are expected to have more resources to support innovation. In terms of new product sales, firms with a large number of employees have performed significantly better than those with fewer employees. Competition effects are also shown to enhance the intensity of innovation. Neither 'ln.age', nor 'foreign' coefficients are significant.

The estimated coefficients of ICT suggest that, without taking into account the potential interactive effects, ICT significantly contributes to innovation performance, and the adoption of ICT increases the ratio of sales due to both product and process innovation. Turning to the models with interaction terms, the variables of '*ICT_source*inhouse*' are

Table 11.5 *Tobit estimation results: the role of ICT in fostering innovation intensity*

VARIABLES	Product inno. Total (Model 1)	Product inno. new to market (Model 2)	Product inno. new to firm (Model 3)	Product inno. total (Model 4)	Product inno. new to market (Model 5)	Product inno. new to firm (Model 6)
In-house	0.574***	0.694***	0.488***	0.542***	0.548**	0.469***
	(0.071)	(0.226)	(0.062)	(0.074)	(0.224)	(0.065)
Collaboration	0.059	0.045	0.036	0.053	0.081	0.043
	(0.051)	(0.104)	(0.045)	(0.059)	(0.131)	(0.051)
Imitation	0.231***	0.084	0.216***	0.273***	0.149	0.255***
	(0.052)	(0.106)	(0.045)	(0.057)	(0.127)	(0.050)
ICT_source	0.205***	0.286**	0.167**	0.164	0.072	0.200**
	(0.078)	(0.134)	(0.069)	(0.103)	(0.178)	(0.092)
ICT_source *inhouse				0.198	0.532*	0.106
				(0.144)	(0.280)	(0.127)
ICT_source* collab				−0.001	−0.124	−0.041
				(0.121)	(0.211)	(0.107)
ICT_source* imitate				−0.216*	−0.214	−0.198**
				(0.114)	(0.221)	(0.100)
No. employees	0.065***	0.012	0.062***	0.058**	−0.009	0.061***
	(0.023)	(0.045)	(0.020)	(0.023)	(0.045)	(0.021)
Ln.age	−0.005	−0.039	−0.004	−0.006	−0.045	−0.004
	(0.040)	(0.079)	(0.035)	(0.040)	(0.079)	(0.035)
Foreign	0.006	0.196	−0.036	−0.052	0.099	−0.074
	(0.110)	(0.184)	(0.099)	(0.115)	(0.189)	(0.103)
Competition	0.082*	0.177*	0.055	0.080	0.165	0.051
	(0.049)	(0.102)	(0.043)	(0.049)	(0.102)	(0.043)
Technician ratio	0.067	−0.098	0.121	0.074	−0.090	0.132
	(0.133)	(0.249)	(0.117)	(0.133)	(0.247)	(0.117)
Constant	−0.660***	−0.909**	−0.737***	−0.677***	−0.916**	−0.736***
	(0.246)	(0.448)	(0.222)	(0.252)	(0.455)	(0.225)
Sigma	0.428***	0.538***	0.375***	0.426***	0.530***	0.372***
	(0.022)	(0.065)	(0.020)	(0.022)	(0.064)	(0.019)
Observations	523	523	523	523	523	523

Note: Standard errors in parentheses *** $p<0.01$, ** $p<0.05$, * $p<0.1$; industry dummies are included

significant in Model 5, suggesting that there is a moderate effect of innovation-oriented ICT adoption on in-house innovation. Hence, information acquired from the internet is treated as a complementary source to in-house innovation, in yielding innovation sales new to the market. In contrast to innovation new to the market, different patterns are exhibited for innovation new to the firms. There is a replacement effect exhibited between '*ICT_source*' and 'imitate', as shown by the corresponding coefficient (Model 6). This finding suggests that information acquired from the internet replaces imitative innovation activities to enhance the innovation sales new to the firm.

11.5   Conclusion

The lack of advanced technological competencies in LICs requires innovation to occur through the absorption of existing knowledge and the adoption of existing technologies. Due to the inadequate experiences and limited resources allocated to technology development, innovation in developing countries normally faces greater risks and uncertainties compared to developed countries. A well-designed and optimal investment level for innovation is therefore needed in order to achieve technological catch-up. In LICs, the low levels of technological infrastructure and lack of competent R&D personnel severely inhibit firms in their efforts to build up their own knowledge stock. Meanwhile, the presence of hard budget constraints requires firms in these countries to seek a balance point between internal and external innovation inputs to optimize their investment, which results in the failure of benefiting from the potential complementarity. Hence, firms in countries where the income level is low and technological capability is weak are more likely to rely, instead, on alternative knowledge acquisitions such as imitative behaviours and ICT technologies. The returns of the technological acquisition via the internet verify the substantial contribution of ICT to innovation performance in Ghanaian manufacturing firms.

The empirical findings reveal that the adoption of ICT does not only contribute to innovation directly by influencing the innovation output, but also seeks interaction with innovation inputs in response to the growth of new product sales. It is important to emphasize the role of the internet as a vector of innovation information, especially in regard to product innovators. Among the sample firms that have access to the internet, the internet is considered a significant source of information. This is relevant, considering the potential of the internet to overcome the lack of information in LICs and allow users to find specific knowledge sources. Besides getting access to strategic information, ICT serves as an instrumental factor and its function of facilitating in-house innovation is acknowledged by Ghanaian manufacturing firms. The adoption of ICT offers a unique and integrated opportunity for interacting with innovation activities. In this regard, ICTs facilitate the in-house innovation (as potential innovation infrastructure) and become part of the integrated innovation resources to affect innovation performance. By differentiating the innovation sales new to the market and new to the firm, we found that the presence of the 'internet' as a knowledge source has helped firms utilize the effect of in-house innovation activities and eventually yield high innovation sales, which are new to the market. Ghanaian manufacturing firms, in particular those who achieve innovation mainly by relying on imitating competitors, adopt the internet as a replacement for their imitative activities.

Obtaining information via the internet and pairing international standards with local production were acknowledged as important channels by the Ghanaian manufacturing firms. Therefore, it is important for host-country governments to differentiate between the policy needs of firms which target different types of knowledge sources and also different types of innovation. ICTs are tools that allow knowledge flow and information exchange. The adoption of ICT can break geographic boundaries and help firms gain access to the global knowledge pool. To ensure the success of international technology transfer, a fundamental challenge for developing countries is to improve the local innovation environment and climate to encourage domestic firms to open up various channels (e.g. internet knowledge sourcing) that allow them to access the international stock of knowledge and strengthen the interactions between ICT practices and innovation activities that foster knowledge creation.

12 The Diffusion and Adoption of Digital Finance Innovation in Africa
The System Dynamics of M-PESA

Xiaolan Fu and Anne Kingiri

12.1 Introduction

There is an increasing recognition of the potential role of digital financial innovations to revolutionize economic growth in developing countries. In addition, there is a growing agreement by a wide range of stakeholders on the potential of these technologies to promote inclusive access to finance in Africa. The rapid growth in the mobile money industry, in particular, has led to increased access to affordable financial services for the less privileged and the disadvantaged population (GSMA, 2015; World Bank, 2014). Considering the opportunities this provides, any effort to persuade these rapidly developing technologies to impact the economic growth in emerging economies must be harnessed. It is thus crucial to understand the underlying mechanisms influencing the diffusion and adoption of new technologies. Consequently, this would enhance the design of appropriate strategies for policy and practice intervention.

Analysis of emerging innovations and their diffusion and adoption process reveals that they have taken different paths. The contemporary innovation scholars propose an evolutionary approach and systems thinking to understand the dynamics and function of innovation systems from a national, regional, sectoral and technological standpoint. The current study attempts to show that emergence and diffusion of dynamic emerging innovations take a systematic path. This trajectory embraces both the economic and technological factors as well as an institutional context in which technologies and actors in the supply and demand side operate.

This study reviews the evolution of M-PESA mobile money transfer, which is claimed to be the most advanced mobile money transfer platform in developing countries (*The Economist*, 2014). The analysis of its functionality using the technology innovation system framework (TIS) shows that institutional functioning around emerging technologies explains the potential success factors to a large extent. The study contributes to the on-going scholarly discussion about the prospects of a digital financial revolution in emerging economies. The chapter is structured as follows; first is the presentation in Section 12.2 of the framework that has informed the study. Second is a critical review of functions associated with M-PESA development, diffusion and adoption in Section 12.3; and lastly, policy- and practice-oriented lessons are drawn in Section 12.4 to contribute to the discussion about emerging innovation and diffusion in emerging economies.

12.2 Analytical framework

12.2.1 Analytical Approaches for Analysing Innovation and Diffusion

The first Sussex Manifesto focused on research and development (R&D) and stressed the importance of institutional changes associated with science and technology for innovation and long-term economic development. It emphasized the R&D capacity building as opposed to building the requisite competence of users to apply innovations and harness technological benefits in developing countries (Clark et al., 2009; Kaplinsky, 2011). The appropriate technology discourse, on the other hand, was technology-focused, where diffusion was dependent on its characteristics and appropriateness to the developing countries' local contexts (Kaplinsky, 2011). The response was technology-focused project planning and implementation approaches, which over time proved to be a failure (Kaplinsky, 2011).

The contemporary innovation scholars have moved the debates on innovation and diffusion to a notch higher. They propose an evolutionary approach and systems thinking to understand the dynamics and function of innovation systems from a national, regional, sectoral and technological standpoint. The national innovation system (NIS) domain pursues a nation's boundary view (Lundvall, 1992). The sectoral innovation system (SIS) pursues an industrial- or economic-sector approach (Malerba, 2005). The technological innovation system (TIS) is organized around a technology or product of technology or knowledge field (Bergek et al., 2008; Hekkert et al., 2007).

The innovation systems' framework (having roots in evolutionary, institutional economic and interactive learning theories) recognizes that technology development with a diffusion and adoption process is determined by the key basic structures, actors, their activities and interactions, and institutions (Jacobsson and Johnson, 2000; Negro et al., 2008). According to Freeman (1987: p. 1), an innovation system is a *'network of institutions in the public and private sector whose activities and interactions initiate, import and diffuse new technologies'*. This innovation system framework also takes note of absorption capacity, historical and political contexts and path dependency as instrumental to development, diffusion and use of new technologies. In addition, interactions amongst the system's actors generate requisite knowledge and interactive learning (Edquist and Johnson, 1997; Freeman, 1987; Lundvall, 1992). Overall, it proposes that the diffusion and adoption process of technologies is determined by the broader socioeconomic and institutional environment in which firms and consumers are situated (Jacobsson and Bergek, 2004; Negro, 2007).

The innovation system concept has received acceptance from strategic organizations like the OECD and the World Bank as a framework to inform the dynamics embedded in innovation, industrial transformation and economic growth. Despite this recognition, this framework is perceived by some scholars to be weak because it fails to expose the underlying factors influencing performance of the innovation system (Bergek et al., 2008). The proponents of the functional TIS dynamic approach have gone further to address the shortcomings inherent in the innovation system framework.

12.2.2 The TIS Approach

The TIS is technology-focused and its simplicity in scope makes it easy to explore the dynamics associated with the characteristics, performance and evolutionary transformation of the system (Hekkert et al., 2007). According to Carlsson et al. (2002), analysts need to focus on the system's ability to identify, absorb and exploit global technological opportunities. Bergek et al. (2008), Hekkert et al. (2007) and Hekkert et al. (2011) provide an outline of how to operationalize the TIS framework. They largely adopt a functional-based approach to the analysis of activities and processes in a system (see Figure 12.1). Bergek et al., (2008) outline seven system functions that can be used to map the functional pattern of a TIS. These are (i) knowledge development, (ii) diffusion, (iii) influence of knowledge on the direction of search, (iv) entrepreneurial experimentation, (v) market formation, (vi) creation of legitimacy/legitimation and (vii) resource mobilization. Mapping the respective functions and embedded interactions over different phases in a given time helps to expose the nature of a TIS as well as the determinants of technological change. It is important to note that different functions tend to reinforce one another positively or negatively resulting in virtuous cycles (Hekkert et al., 2007).

Proponents of the TIS framework attempt to operationalize these seven functions or activities that significantly influence development, diffusion and adoption of new technologies. For instance, the TIS approach has been applied in analysing the dynamics of renewable energy technologies

M-Pesa dynamics of learning and capabilities

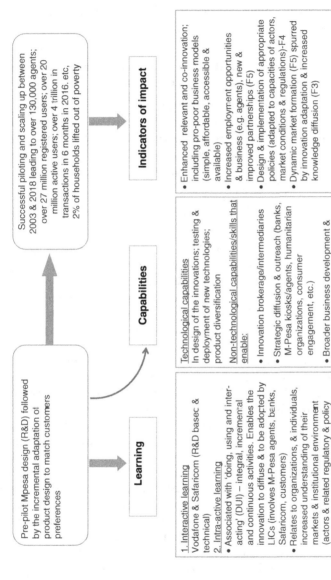

Figure 12.1 Learning, knowledge flow and capabilities in M-PESA TIS

in European countries (Bergek et al., 2008; Hekkert and Negro, 2009), renewable energies in African countries (Tigabu, 2017), mobile data TIS in Sweden (Lindmark and Rickne, 2005; quoted in Bergek et al., 2008). The TIS framework is used to map the performance of M-PESA thereby describing empirically the success narrative that has advanced over the years.

12.3   Functioning and Diffusion of Mobile Money Technology in Emerging Economies – The Case of M-PESA

The narrative informing this case study is supported by secondary materials (literature and grey materials), complemented by subtle experiences observed and encountered (real-time transactions on a daily basis in money payments and remittances as an M-PESA user) and interactions with the service providers (M-PESA agents). The analysis takes five steps derived from Bergek et al. (2008).

12.3.1   Step 1: Defining the TIS in Focus

TIS-focused studies' unit of analysis may either be knowledge field or product. The TIS is also defined by the range of application and spatial focus. In the current study, the analysis is focused on a technological knowledge field (digital or mobile money transfer). The application in question is M-PESA mobile money transfer platform, which defines the boundaries of the system. It has a global outlook although localized in the Kenyan/East African context.

M-PESA ('M' for mobile and Pesa is Swahili for money) is a mobile-phone-based money transfer and micro-financing service launched in Kenya in 2007 by Vodafone-UK and Safaricom, the largest telecommunication company in Kenya. A year later, it was introduced in Tanzania. Ten years after its market launch in 2007, the M-PESA platform has evolved tremendously in design to allow different functionalities. Cell phone users can use this service to deposit, send and withdraw funds, pay bills, do shopping, make banking transactions and receive social disbursements and international remittances. It is also used to offer loans and savings products, among other services. The reliability of this mobile money transfer platform has stimulated the growth of business start-ups in Kenya and East Africa, while also opening up international money transfer opportunities (Appendix 12.1). M-PESA has since grown rapidly in terms of users, transactions and functionalities. As of September 2016, there were 24.8 million registered customers and 17.6 million active users. The M-PESA transactions are facilitated through a growing network of agents or service providers (114,000 as of September 2016) spread out across Kenya that has grown alongside the growing number of customers.

12.3.2 Step 2: Identifying the Structural Components of the TIS

12.3.2.1 Actors and Networks From the available secondary resources, which include published papers, organizational websites and profiles, a wide range of actors and networks critical to the development and diffusion of this TIS can be identified.

M-PESA is primarily a public–private partnership (PPP) between the government and the industry. The role of non-state actors (industry) stands out in technology design and deployment. Vodafone-UK had the initial technological idea and partnered with Safaricom, a voice and text telecommunication company, for testing and launching purposes. A win-win inspired negotiation with Faulu Kenya as a micro-finance institute (MFI) and the Commercial Bank of Africa (CBA) brought in the initial requisite competencies for the piloting of the innovation. Sagentia, a blue-sky British software development company designed the functionality of the money transfer platform. In the early phase of M-PESA, its integration benefited from an initial pool of Safaricom retail agents established throughout the country (Sadana et al., 2011). These outlets were then used as M-PESA stores and later grew into a vibrant M-PESA agent network. The M-PESA service could be accessed at 114,000 M-PESA retail outlets nationwide, in both urban and rural areas, as of September 2016.

12.3.2.2 Institutions Institutions here refer to cultures, norms, laws, regulations and routines (North, 1994). The authorization of M-PESA by the Central Bank of Kenya (CBK) was done under a policy vacuum. The launch in 2007 signalled the actual process of formulation and implementation of the digital financial policy. This culminated in significant policy and regulatory innovations (the National Payment System (NPS) Act, 2011, & NPS Regulations, 2014). In addition, a collaborative working culture emerged between CBK and the Communications Commission of Kenya (CCK), born out of their experience engaging in the M-PESA case (Muthiora, 2015: p. 14). The NPS regulations actually promote a healthy competition and collaboration amongst Kenya's digital financial actors which has been institutionalized in the Kenyan setting.

12.3.3 Step 3: Mapping the Functional Pattern of the TIS

12.3.3.1 Knowledge Development and Diffusion The original M-PESA concept was an innovative R&D technology designed by Vodafone-UK around provision of low-cost financial services to the unbanked poor (Mas and Radcliffe, 2010). This scientific/technological idea diffused downstream when Safaricom agreed to test its viability in the Kenyan context. New design concepts and functionalities have since evolved and been launched by Safaricom, enhancing an upstream technological knowledge flow to low- and middle-income consumers (LICs and MICs). This upstream trend is characterized by consolidation and expansion of the knowledge base as a result of practical learning and capabilities building witnessed around M-PESA today. The dynamics of this function can be measured by a range of indicators, including the multiple values and functionalities that have been tested and adapted since the launch of M-PESA (see Appendix). In addition, the significant learning and capabilities built around M-PESA TIS denote the dynamism of knowledge generation and diffusion (Figure 12.1).

Figure 12.1 above demonstrates intra-active and interactive learning, including capabilities emerging from M-PESA TIS at multiple levels. The outcome of the knowledge diffusion is perceived enhanced social and economic growth.

12.3.3.2 Influence on the Direction of Search   A functional TIS depends on enlisting interested firms and other actors who must be persuaded that the venture is profitable. The collective force and strength must be significant to influence the direction of search within the TIS in terms of competing technologies, business models, markets and applications (Bergek et al., 2008: p. 415). The unprecedented revolution in the ICT sectoral innovation system both globally and nationally has presented a promising and changing 'landscape' for entrepreneurs and innovators (Geels, 2004). This landscape and the conducive policy environment in telecommunication and digital finance innovation in Kenya (Muthiora, 2015) had implications. This may have provided a prospective mobile money actors' assessment of present and future technological opportunities in this sector.

According to Bergek et al. (2008: p. 415), this function can be measured by qualitative factors: (i) Beliefs in TIS' growth potential (which has been the case with Vodafone-UK, Safaricom and Kenyan entrepreneurs), (ii) Extent of regulatory pressure (The M-PESA case demonstrates a dynamic PPP approach to formulation of digital financial regulations (Muthiora, 2015)) and (iii) Articulation of demand or interest by leading customers in the digital innovation. This can be attributed to the increased capabilities and learning built around M-PESA TIS (Figure 15.1).

12.3.3.3 Entrepreneurial Experimentation   The early phase of M-PESA was characterized by uncertainty around technology, applications and markets, which is normal for a TIS according to Bergek et al. (2008). This uncertainty attracts what the authors call 'entrepreneurial experimentation', resulting in the entry of firms and diversification of functions; some fail and exit while others become established. According to Hughes and Lonie (2007), who were instrumental in the M-PESA piloting phase, the successful piloting is credited to the entrepreneurial nature of the Kenyan formal (industry) and informal business sector (risk takers and explorative/innovative). The generation of crucial process innovation by the entrepreneurs was critical in lifting M-PESA from the grassroots during the formative phase (Foster and Heeks, 2013). After the M-PESA launch in 2007, there has been an increased growth in Kenya's digital entrepreneurship (FinAccess National Survey, 2009; GSMA, 2014).

12.3.3.4 Market Formation   The early phase of an emerging innovation is challenged by many factors, including uncertainty, regulatory vacuum and articulation of demand by potential investors and inadequate capabilities which may stifle market formation. Navigating around these non-technical factors calls for institutional change (policies, attitudes, norms, practices, etc.), which is critical for markets to develop and get established (Hughes, 1983, quoted in Bergek, 2008: p. 416). To understand the dynamics of market formation along the 'nursing, bridging and mature phases', it is critical to expose the factors that drive or hinder market formation (Bergek, 2008: p. 416). In the M-PESA case, we can track several qualitative and quantitative indicators of development along this market-transition continuum (see Figures 12.2 and 12.3). These are the high adoption of mobile phones by Kenyans, the actors' strategies (in negotiating policies, business strategies and contracts) and the growing trend in the mobile money TIS.

The formative stage of M-PESA revealed that the product was leading to an unexpected 'something big' or to unexpected business ventures for Safaricom (Hughes and Lonie, 2007: p. 77). This was characterized by an expanded market – including other telecommunication companies in the mobile money transfer TIS (global and local) as well as numerous formal and informal actors (Jack and Suri, 2011; Onsongo and Schot, 2017). In addition, other successful financial innovations have been launched as partnerships between different financial institutions (See Appendix 12.1). Among these, M-Shwari has been quite successful.

12.3.3.5 Legitimation   A new technology must receive social acceptance and be regulatory and policy compliant. The M-PESA legitimization process involved a wide range of stakeholders in the digital finance sector. The two regulators, CBK and CCK, played a critical role in the M-PESA

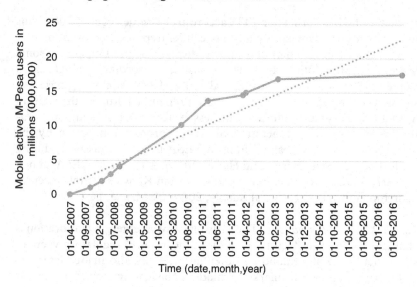

Figure 12.2 Number of M-PESA active users
Source: Safaricom website, as of Dec 2017

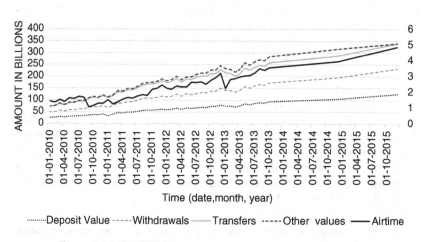

········Deposit Value ·····Withdrawals ——Transfers ·····Other values ——Airtime

Figure 12.3 M-PESA output
Source: Safaricom website, as of Dec 2017

case. However, CBK, which is mandated under the CBK Act to regulate mobile banking and banking services, played a major role in aligning the mobile money TIS and existing legislation, and establishing a value base within this industry and the society.

At the formative stage, there were discussions between the private sector (Safaricom, Vodafone Group and CBA) and relevant government authorities (Ministry of Information and Communication, Ministry of Finance, CBK and CCK). Under the leadership of CBK, the stakeholders assessed the benefits and risks of M-PESA to the financial system. According to the then Governor of the Central Bank, there was a degree of flexibility and innovativeness that was required to arrive at a positive decision to support the digital financial sector despite the regulatory vacuum that existed.

When regulators embrace a leadership role in developing the market, they become innovative and take reasonable risks inherent in making the changes needed to create a more inclusive financial sector. Although regulators' main concern is always the safety and soundness of financial systems, those that have made the most progress have been willing to explore new routes or to use new tools to enhance traditional financial activities. (Governor, Central Bank of Kenya, quoted in Muthiora, 2015: p. 9)

The M-PESA case demonstrates how different factors, including politics and interests, play out in the legitimization process. Despite the distinct role of each player in the value chain, the uncertainty and suspicion surrounding the economic and social impact of M-PESA needed to be managed. Intense lobbying by Kenya Bankers Association almost killed the M-PESA service, citing favouritism from CBK and possible fears of instability following the controversy around pyramid schemes. The CBK audited the service, giving it a clean bill of health (Okoth, 2009). The facilitative role of government was clear while the different interests of non-state actors were declared, thus enhancing transparency and trust.

Safaricom was allowed to operate as both a telecommunications company and a mobile banking company, which involved trust (Sultana, 2009). Nyaoma (2010, cited in Muthiora, 2015: p. 10) noted 'CBK went a step further, seeking assurances from Safaricom that it had taken appropriate measures to ensure sufficient system security, maintain business continuity plans and risk management programme'.

Ultimately, Safaricom in collaboration with CBK developed a simple business model that met the requirements of the regulator and interests of the private actors (Ntara, 2015). In this business model, the agents are paid by Safaricom on a commission basis. The money generated from transaction fees is used to pay operational costs, for example, transfer channels and banking services. The model ensures that the service platform is secure and that users' money is deposited in a well-structured financial institution. There was an agreement between the service provider and the regulator that the profits earned from cash deposit balances would be directed to a trust (non-profit). To prevent money laundering, restrictions were put in place relating to the size of cash transactions (Mas and Radcliffe, 2010).

12.3.3.6 Resource Mobilization Innovation scholars have attributed establishment of successful TISs to mobilization of resources that include financial, competence and human capital (see for instance Edquist and Johnson, 1997; Lundvall, 1992). The M-PESA TIS demonstrated the ability to undertake this function. The M-PESA journey to success started in 2003. Vodafone-UK, which partly owns Safaricom, had just won a £1 million matched grant from the Department for International Development (now FCDO), supported by the Financial Deepening Challenge Fund (FDCF). This donor support was instrumental in initial awareness creation and capabilities building (competence and human capital) amongst different value chain actors. It was also crucial to the establishment of critical partnerships and networks, collection of relevant context-specific information and subsequent overall piloting. In the later phases of M-PESA development, human and competence building targeted M-PESA agents and consumers. The resource mobilization function is embedded in Safaricom's capacity building and branding strategy pursued through different avenues, including social, voice and print media (Hughes and Lonie, 2007; Sadana et al., 2011; Safaricom, 2018). Safaricom has expanded its competence-building portfolio to include seed and venture capital initiatives directed through its M-PESA platform. For instance, 'Safaricom roll out ready business platforms' targeting small and medium-sized enterprises (SMEs) is an example of a solution-and competence-building oriented initiative (Wainaina, 2016).[1]

12.3.3.7 Development of Positive Externalities This function of development of **positive externalities** is informed by the systemic nature of the innovation and diffusion process in an evolving TIS spurred by enlisting of new entrants (including firms). The new actors bring different

---

[1] This initiative helps SMEs measure their level of readiness and what they need to improve their competitive advantage. The Ready Business Index is a simple step-by-step test that benchmarks a business's processes against global best practices. By taking the Index, businesses have access to a consultant who can offer further advice on identified gaps and solutions.

contributions to the other six functions of the TIS, thereby generating positive externalities. This is an indicator of a dynamic system (Bergek, 2008: p. 418). The M-PESA case, as alluded to elsewhere, is characterized by consistent enlisting of new entrants by Safaricom as new products and functionalities are launched (Appendix 12.1). M-PESA on the other hand has opened up the digital money transfer platform to other actors who would otherwise have been locked out of this innovation by a number of factors, including cost and regulation (Bergek and Jacobsoon, 2003; Muthiora, 2015).

12.3.4 Step 4: Assessing the functionality of the TIS and setting process goals – The phase of development

12.3.4.1 Piloting or Formative Phase Hughes and Lonie (2007) give a detailed account of the piloting phase characterized by non-technological-related undertakings that shaped the ecosystem that made the launch of M-PESA possible. Muthiora (2015), on the other hand, chronicles the evolution of the mobile money policies in Kenya that was triggered by M-PESA. Thus, a review of the available resources during this period of uncertainty helps us to understand the dynamics involved in charting a roadmap for deployment of M-PESA. These lessons demonstrate the importance of local context, learning, knowledge and cumulative capabilities in the diffusion of emerging innovation.

12.3.4.2 Post-Launch or Growth Phase After the pilot phase, the product was perceived to be ready technically and commercially, and profitable to the developers. In addition, it could meet the needs of Kenyans and other emerging economies with a similar institutional context. The launch eventually took place in March 2007 and ten years of M-PESA product in the market have recorded tremendous growth (see Figures 12.2 and 12.3). As well as enabling traditional services that include withdrawal, deposits, transfers and airtime, the platform has evolved to include other values or functionalities (Figure 12.3 and Appendix 12.1).

12.3.4.3 Comparison between TIS The proponents of the TIS framework recommend the comparison of the TIS under analysis with other TISs across regions or nations as a way of informing policy directions with regard to success or failure (see Bergek, 2008; Tigabu, 2017). Tigabu (2017), analysing the functions of renewable energies in East Africa, identified weak market formation as a major contributor to the uptake of these technologies. The M-PESA platform has been launched in other countries, but the Kenyan context is the most advanced mobile payment TIS in the world (*The Economist*, 2014; Heeks et al., 2013; Foster and Heeks, 2013; ADB, 2013; Onsongo, 2013; World Bank, 2014; Onsongo and Schot, 2017; Meagher, 2018). According to *The Economist* (2014), Kenya leads the world in mobile money based on active accounts followed by Tanzania. Arguably, the explanation of the Kenyan success story lies in the analysis of the functionality of the TIS in question (M-PESA in Kenya at different phases), taking cognizance of other similar TISs. Depending on policy goals (for instance, economic growth, financial inclusion and sustainable development), process goals can be drawn that inform attainment of a targeted higher functionality (Bergek, 2008: p. 420) in a given TIS. To promote adoption of M-PESA in other contexts, for instance, a process goal may entail expanding the number of stakeholders in the TIS in order to enhance positive externalities. Process goals provide to the policymakers an easier way to evaluate the suitability of available policy options (*Ibid*).

12.3.5   Step 5: Identifying Inducement and Blocking Mechanisms

In recent studies focusing on renewable technologies, new or emerging TISs have been found to have weak functional dynamics (see, for instance, Tigabu, 2017). This is attributed to a number of blocking mechanisms which may be internal or external to the system. Some of these can be institutional alignment failure, poor networks and underdeveloped capabilities that ultimately affect the other functions, thereby affecting attainment of advanced functionality (Bergek et al., 2008). On the other hand, a system may have inducement mechanisms that support the growth and diffusion of a technology. In the case of M-PESA, blocking mechanisms were experienced at the formative phase in the form of an anti-technology lobby group in the banking sector that almost killed the M-PESA initiative (Okoth, 2009) and a regulatory vacuum (Muthiora, 2015). The latter, however, was reversed to become an inducement mechanism, promoting market formation and legitimization when the relevant regulatory policies were passed. Other inducement mechanisms include the belief in the upward growth of the ICT sector in Kenya and, in particular, mobile money transfer (FinAccess national survey, 2009).

More than ten years of M-PESA, up-scaling and re-design have contributed to significant learning and capabilities building that have informed the M-PESA G2 platform upgrading (Figure 12.1). This is an inducement mechanism which could turn in to a blocking mechanism, if not sustained.

12.3.6 *Step 6: Identifying Key Policy Issues*

Policy issues should be informed by mechanisms that block or induce diffusion or adoption of an innovation. The intention is to provide policy interventions that target 'system failure' rather than market or structural failure (Bergek et al., 2008). In the M-PESA case, the inducement mechanisms supersede the blocking mechanisms, perhaps the reason why the TIS has been quite successful. A few policy issues are recommended which largely re-enforce the inducement mechanisms more generally.

12.3.6.1 Support Inclusive Capabilities for Sustained Demand Articulation To maximize the productive application of advanced features and functionalities on the M-PESA TIS, essential capabilities are required. These should target both systems developers and users, including low-skilled consumers.

12.3.6.2 Strengthening Chain Linkages Informed by Cumulative Learning It is clear that M-PESA, based on its design and organizational structures, has largely met the needs of the LICs and MICs. As a consumers' need-oriented innovation, it embraced the entrepreneurial experimentation culture. This attracted multiple intermediaries to Safaricom product development and its service delivery chain. To improve functionality of M-PESA and thereby enhance sustained growth, Safaricom must invest in resource mobilization (capital, competence and human). This is one way of strengthening and sustaining chain linkages to and from users. It also provides opportunities for consumer-driven learning to inform the incremental improvement of M-PESA products and diversification. This would also enhance demand articulation more generally. According to Meagher (2018), the users of innovation are important actors who contribute to the innovation process by providing relevant product information, based on their respective needs and context of use.

12.4 Conclusion and Discussion

This chapter examines the emergence and diffusion of new digital technology-based innovation in Africa through a case study of the M-PESA in Kenya. It finds that the success of M-PESA can be attributed to its overall dynamics, as demonstrated through the mapping of the seven functions.

M-PESA has led to fundamental changes in the organization of roles and structures in mobile money transfer in what would be perceived to be an emerging-business-oriented production paradigm (Kaplinsky et al., 2010). Although the re-organization is social, technological and institutional in nature, it is strongly linked to re-designing of the M-PESA platform to accommodate new entrants or improved functionalities that allow increased business opportunities (sustained market formation). Even with the milestones to date, this question posed by the Central Bank Governor is still relevant: 'how can we make sure solutions are sustainable, systems built are credible and also reach deeper and especially to the poorest?' (Ndung'u, 2010). M-PESA TIS helps in reflecting on the future of the digital financial revolution from an inclusive and innovation perspective.

M-PESA TIS has demonstrated that profits driven by innovations below the radar, targeting LICs and MICs, are no longer elusive. Safaricom has successfully integrated large numbers of small disaggregated actors into the M-PESA design and delivery chain through a process of entrepreneurial experimentation. This has been made possible by entrepreneurs' ability to adapt business models, supply chain production methods and delivery systems that suit the prevailing environment. Whether the gains attributed to this collaboration are genuinely inclusive has become a subject of discussion by development scholars (Foster and Heeks, 2013; Meagher, 2018). Prahalad and Hammond (2002) have emphasized the importance of LICs and MICs as providing a market for emerging innovations that benefit multinationals. The M-PESA TIS has demonstrated that this market is crucial for the growth of the informal sector, which in a way denotes some degree of financial inclusion. M-PESA has largely accommodated the unbanked low-income earners, including those living in rural areas, allowing them to be 'financially included' (Hinz, 2014). It has further enhanced their ability to manage their lives, since they can send money, store money and make payments at cheap rates and low risk (Kimenyi and Ndung'u, 2009).

According to Deb and Kubzansky (2012), financial inclusion is a combination of three aspects: active participation, financial capability and financial services accessibility. As Hinz (2014) argues, using the service promotes inclusion but also creates different opportunities that eventually lead to inclusion (see Appendix 12.1 for different emerging outputs attributed to M-PESA). From a TIS perspective, M-PESA has exhibited these aspects through legitimization and enhanced capabilities that have promoted interest among different actors. Empirical evidence should be generated to qualify the financial inclusion claims and further determine whether and how the social and economic benefits meet Kenya's developmental and sustainability goals agenda as a growing economy.

It is noted that the original idea for M-PESA capitalized on low-value mobile money activity (sale of airtime to facilitate communication) and the embedded conversion of airtime (from scratch cards) to money that would be shared out via mobile phones (van der Boor et al., 2014). This evolved later to a micro-credit facility. During the formative phase, the local informal actors and airtime retailers were highly involved in entrepreneurial experimentation (Foster and Heeks, 2013; Onsongo and Schot, 2017; Maurer, 2012). According to Meagher (2018: p. 27), this informal community was critical to M-PESA growth because it shaped the 'local familiarity with agent based financial pooling and transfer system … providing infrastructure and practices that underpinned the rapid expansion of M-PESA'. These practices, subsequently perpetuated additional product and process innovation (knowledge development and diffusion) characterized by different outputs and value derived from diverse product applications (Foster and Heeks, 2013; Table 12.1 in Appendix). The dynamic practices around informal and formal integration form an important research area to generate evidence about how to improve the different functionality of mobile money TISs.

The mobile money innovation and the regulatory infrastructure in the setting of Kenya have co-evolved, which is the major reason why M-PESA was officially launched in a regulatory vacuum. This co-evolution process generated useful institutional innovation and learning attributed to key regulatory policies that have guided the sector to date (Muthiora, 2015). The Kenya mobile policy evolution provides an excellent public–private partnership whereby the M-PESA case presented a learning platform for both product developers and the policy actors. Financial service regulation is just developing in many emerging economies and formulation of appropriate policies may be a delicate terrain. This process is prone to politics especially in a situation of uncertainty, competition and diverse interests (Njiraini and Anyanzwa, 2008). According to Muthiora (2015), a facilitative but firm regulatory role of the state is critical for effective legitimization. The Central Bank of Kenya played multiple but very critical policy-oriented roles but remained an honest broker throughout the formative phase and beyond.

Appendix

Appendix 12.1 *Selected values derived from the M-PESA platform within ten years (between 2007 and 2018)*

Type	Example
Cash payments and transfers	- M-Pesa money transfer among friends and relatives
	- Lipa na M-Pesa for shopping and bill payments (from Oct 2010)
	- M-Pesa outlets at fuel stations started with Caltex in 2008
	- Lipa Kodi for rent payment (since Aug 2013)
	- Bank to M-Pesa transfers and vice versa
	- International money transfer
	• Western Union transfer from UK in Dec 2008;
	• Western Union international transfers from 45 countries from Mar 2011
	• Moneygram International transfers in over 90 countries from Nov 2014
	• M-Pesa & Vodacom Tanzania -3/2015
	- MTN & Vodacom for inbound and outbound money transfer across EA (since 12/2016)
	- Lipa Karo for school fee payment support from Jan 2011 (about 4,500 schools as of 2016)
	- Bulk payments (e.g. salaries)
	- Utility payment – Electricity started with KPLC in April 2009); and M- Grundfos Lifelink project for safe water access in Sep 2009
	- Okoa Stima – Kenya power bills payment by dialling *885# from the mobile (04/2015)
	- M-Ticketing (for concerts, events, galas and other sports since Dec 2010)
	- M-Pesa Prepay Visa card. Started in Dec 2011 with I&M Bank International Prepay Safari Visa Card from
	- PesaPoint for ATM money withdrawal services directly mobile (from 2008)
	- M-Pesa services at commercial banks (started with Postbank in 2008)
	- Trade in unit trusts and shares (started with Old Mutual Unit Trusts in 2008)
	- E-Citizen platform for payment of Government of Kenya services using paybill number 206206 (April 2015)
	- Real-time settlement (RTS) – 17 commercial banks boarded for the RTS service (07/2015)

Microfinance services	Housing Finance mortgage financing with Housing Finance (since 2008) SMEP – Small and Micro Enterprise Programme in May 2009 Equity Bank – M-Kesho (from May 2010) M-Shwari (since Nov 2012) Kenya Commercial Bank (KCB). Started with M-Pesa agents' access to E-float from May 2009 M-Akiba (allows buying Central Bank bonds since 2015)
Payments for specific use services	M-Kopa* (energy) Grundfos* (water kiosks) Shupavu 291 (education)
Social support ventures	Kenyans for Kenya fundraising platform to avert starvation (Safaricom Foundation and KCB Foundation partnership launched in July 2011) Short Term M-Pesa Pay Bill for short term fundraising (used for education, weddings, medical or funerals). Initiated between 2012 & 2013 M-Tiba (blocked mobile wallet for health expenses since 12/2015) Linda Jamii health insurance wallet targeting uninsured Kenyans – since Jan 2014 Sema Doc (health) iCow (agriculture) Shupavu (education) Kilimo Salama' agricultural insurance product (Since 2009) Tibu – platform to monitor, evaluate and manage TB & other infectious diseases Daktari-1525 (medical tele-triage service)
Diversified ventures	- Little cab (ride-hailing services integrated with M-Pesa) - Sendy (last-mile package delivery and logistics services) - FarmDrive (farmer information for credit rating) - mSurvey (a mobile research platform leveraging SMS technology) - Lynk (connects informal market artisans with employers) - Eneza (provides education support to primary school pupils through mobile phones) - iProcure (Provides farmers with quality farm inputs at affordable prices) - NEW Kenya Co-operative Creameries (KCC) cashless solution. Service targeting over 200 KCC sales and milk distribution agents (since 11/2015)

Appendix 12.1 (cont.)

Type	Example
Enhanced functionality of the platform	- M-Shwari Application Programming Interface (API) upgrade in Nov 2012 for efficient money transfer e.g. M-Shwari lock savings - Lipa na M-Pesa service functionality (from June 2013) becomes available on M-Pesa Menu under 'Lipa na M-Pesa'. Merchants acquire a 6-digit number where customers make payments to at no extra cost - M-Pesa sure pay – Service allows organizations like World Food Programme (WFP) to track funds sent to beneficiaries via M-Pesa (from 03/2015) - M-Pesa G2 Platform – allows secure Application Programming Interfaces (APIs) integrating third-party applications including Business to Customers – B2C, Customer to Business – C2B and Business to Business – B2B (since 04/2015) - Hakikisha Service allows customers to confirm the name of the recipient before any transaction (since 10/2015) - M-Pesa statements – Customer access M-Pesa statements by dialing *234# from their handsets or via email (since 01/2016) - Bill manager. A new service enabling customers to manage and pay bills all in a single transaction, by dialing *234*1*3# (since 06/2016) - Information of each transaction received sent to M-Pesa Customers (since 02/2017) - Reverse transaction – M-Pesa users to reverse wrong transactions by sending the transaction code, via text message, to the number 456 (since 10/2017) - Safaricom, Airtel and Telecom interoperability – interoperable mobile money wallet that allows transactions across Safaricom, Airtel and Telecom networks at no extra cost (since 04/2018)

Source: Safaricom website, 2018; media resources and insights from Lashitew, Bals, and van Tulder (2018)

13 Opportunities and Challenges of the Fourth Industrial Revolution for Africa

13.1 Introduction

Disruptive technologies can be either a new combination of existing technologies or new technologies that can dramatically shift the technology product paradigm or create entirely new ones (Kostoff et al., 2004; Manyika, et al., 2013); they are advances that will transform life, business, and the global economy. First came mechanical production, then mass production, then automated production, and now we are entering the age of the Fourth Industrial Revolution. The Fourth Industrial Revolution (4IR) is characterized by the convergence of a mix of new technologies that interface across the physical, biological and digital worlds. Currently, it covers the fields of technology breakthroughs, including artificial intelligence, robotics, the Internet of Things, 3D printing, autonomous vehicles, biotechnology, nanotechnology, materials science, energy storage, quantum computing, and distributed ledger, among others. These disruptive technologies are revolutionizing the various industry sectors and provide a basis for a new competitive paradigm.

Such rapid and wide-ranging disruptions may further transform the entire systems of production, management and governance; hence they make revolutionary changes in the way production is organized, how profit is produced, and even how public and private services are provided. This will further affect the demand for labour in production and services provision, how income is distributed and how global division of labour is restructured as a result of business model innovation triggered by disruptive technological innovations. They also have profound implications for development and cross-country income inequalities (Korinek and Stiglitz, 2017).

These profound expected ramifications of the 4IR may be greatest in Africa, for several reasons. The 4IR technologies, if properly adopted and adapted, can drive Africa's renewed (re-)industrialization agenda. Second, Africa as a continent remains far from the global technological frontier, and the 4IR technologies present a window of opportunity for Africa to leapfrog on the technological ladder. Fourth, the continent remains bewildered with low industrial and agricultural productivity, increasing unemployment, increasing inequality, and food and water insecurity among others. Expected changes to the production system could help resolve some of these economic issues on the continent. These leave us with several unanswered questions rather than answers: What are the opportunities and challenges of this new wave of industrial revolution for African countries? And how can policies help Africa develop its innovation and technological competences to benefit from the 4IR? How can policies make these disruptive technologies a leading force for inclusive growth in Africa? While there has been some research on the significant ethical implications, and there have been concerns on the impact of robotics on job opportunity, there is little systematic analysis with regard to the impact of the 4IR on Africa, and the required policy responses to ensure these countries can maximize the benefits from it. This chapter contributes to this field of research.

The remainder of the chapter is structured as follows: Section 13.2 presents an overview of the 4IR, followed by a discussion of the opportunities the 4IR holds for developing countries, specifically Africa, in Section 13.3. Section 13.4 discusses the challenges the 4IR holds for Africa, while Section 13.5 focuses specifically on the opportunities and challenges for women and youth. The last Section (13.6) concludes the section.

13.2   The Fourth Industrial Revolution: An Overview

Modern technologies are fuelling economic growth and changing the way we communicate, transport, live and work. With the coming of the 4IR, new technologies such as the Internet of Things (IoT), artificial intelligence (AI), autonomous vehicles and 3D printing are becoming embedded into everyday life. The emerging technologies in the 4IR have transformed and continue to rapidly transform the very way individuals live and work, and are also expected to revolutionize the industrial sectors and services, including but not limited to manufacturing, agriculture, health and finance.

While the 4IR technologies' development and their adoption in the production systems are well advanced in developed countries, the pace of 'adoption' of these technological innovations is rather slow in developing countries, specifically Africa. This may be due to the existing gaps in knowledge, infrastructure, human capital, R&D investment and innovation rates between these two regions. As a result, Africa lags behind developed countries in designing, adopting and applying new technologies. For instance, Figure 13.1 shows the number of operational industrial robots globally in 2016, compared with the change in installation of industrial robots between 2010 and 2016. The figure shows that developing countries lag behind developed countries in the number of operational robots. There has, however, been leapfrogging in the number of robots operational in the industrial sector in developing countries, due mainly to China. China has registered an increase as high as 550 per cent, while the whole developing world increased by 251 per cent, Germany increased by 28 per cent and the United States by 46 per cent. While China has improved remarkably in terms of the number of operational robots between 2010 and 2016, the same cannot be said of Africa. The number of operational robots in Africa remains insignificant globally, with very marginal change between 2010 and 2016. The figure shows Africa to have increased its number of operational robots from 921 in 2010 to 3,381 in 2016, whilst mostly concentrated in South Africa and countries in North Africa.

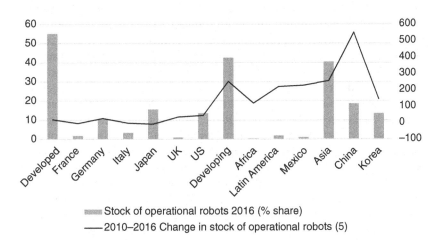

Figure 13.1 Stock of operational robots in 2016 and changes in 2010–2016
Source: International Robots Federation.

13.3   Opportunities for Africa

The 4IR and its new technologies, arguably, offer a new window of opportunity for Africa to industrialize (Naude, 2017) as well as achieve the sustainable development goals (SDGs). The disruptive technologies that underpin the 4IR can also be the engine of inclusive growth through the creation of decent employment. According to Schwab (2016), the 4IR holds and has the potential to make the world more prosperous with higher global income levels and improved quality of life for populations around the world. Empirical evidence by Graets and Michaels (2015) of robots in 17 countries shows that robots added an estimated 0.4 percentage points on average to countries' annual GDP growth between 1993 and 2007, accounting for just over one-tenth of those countries' overall GDP growth during that time. The potential impact of 4IR technologies, specifically robots, may be much higher in Africa, giving the low productivity levels and low capital intensity, particularly in the manufacturing and agricultural sectors. Not only do these disruptive technologies have the potential to increase Africa's output, they hold the prospects to also create completely new ways of consuming goods and services in the process, and can also level the playing field, enabling small and medium-sized enterprises (SMEs) in Africa to challenge large industry incumbents from developed economies.

The 4IR also offers other direct benefits to the continent. Digitalization of production processes and services in Africa may lead to the collapse of barriers between digital and physical spaces, leading to the reduction in the costs of transportation and communications. This may have direct impacts on logistics, and the effective integration into and upgrade in supply chains. The 4IR technologies also hold the potential to improve the quality of lives on the continent through the provision of remarkably cheaper products and services that may be obtained conveniently. Healthcare access and quality healthcare delivery remains one of Africa's challenges. The use of 4IR technologies for healthcare has the potential to transform how doctors diagnose and treat diseases, potentially extending lives in Africa. Adoption and use of drones, for example in Rwanda and Ghana, for delivery of urgent medical supplies have greatly influenced the health conditions of the citizenry, particularly those living in villages with limited access to health facilities. Instead of using trial and error, scientists can systematically test how genetic variations can bring about specific traits and diseases with rapid sequencing and advanced computing power. Moreover, desktop sequencing machines could be used in routine diagnostics, significantly improving treatments by matching treatments to patients (Manyika et al., 2013).

Africa's economic growth has, for the last decades, been driven by the exportation of natural resources such as gold, crude oil, diamond and bauxite, among others. Due to the fluctuation of prices for these products in the international market, African economies tend to experience unstable growth. The 4IR technologies offer the continent an opportunity to automate and add value to exports. This is essential, given that refined gold and crude oil, for example, have higher value than when they are exported in their raw forms. These could be essential in addressing Africa's quality of growth problem.

Another important feature of the 4IR is the presence of an 'on demand' economy. 3D printing, for instance, enables an idea to go directly from a 3D design file to a finished product by skipping many traditional manufacturing steps. It has critical implications for supply chains as well as for stocking spare parts, which is a major cost for manufacturers. Moreover, 3D printing can reduce the amount of material wasted in manufacturing and create objects that are difficult or impossible to produce with traditional techniques (Manyika et al., 2013). As a result, diffusion of 3D printing not only enables on-demand production, it also will lead to the restructuring of the global production network and global value chain, leading to business model innovation. In particular, much of the production will be distributed and/or localized. That is, mass production factories and large-scale assembly lines will be replaced by distributed local production stations allocated in scattered communities. This disruptive innovation offers a change of the landscape of the global production system, with critical benefits for Africa. African firms face diverse barriers in their daily lives, preventing them from exploiting and reaching their full potential. The lowering of barriers for these firms through the restructuring of 'monopolized' production networks, for example, could enable further creation and redistribution of wealth, as well as improvement in the professional and personal environments of workers. Consequently, this can help enhance the inclusiveness of economic growth by reducing both unemployment and inequality in Africa and the world as a whole.

13.4   Challenges for Africa

Most technology innovations are not neutral and are biased towards certain directions: some are biased towards capital, some favouring labour. When technologies favour workers, technology advances are more likely to benefit labour forces that have skills but disadvantage those without digital competencies. Thus, the result of technology changes might be advantageous to some essential productive factors, and disadvantageous to other factors. Many of the technological innovations that are emerging in the 4IR, such as automation and AI, are significantly biased towards capital and certain groups of skilled labour whose work is creative and does not follow repetitive and routine patterns. These have significant implications for Africa, in terms of employment and income distribution, not only between capital and labour, but also skilled versus unskilled labour. We discuss here some of these implications in the context of Africa and developing countries as a whole, where possible.

13.4.1 Employment Effect

Technological progress is often not neutral. Technological unemployment, which is derived from John Maynard Keynes' prediction of widespread technological unemployment 'due to our discovery of means of economizing the use of labor outrunning the pace at which we can find new uses for labor' (Keynes, 1933: p. 3), remains a concern. The empirical literature, for example, has found that computerization of production processes and services leads to the decline of employment in routine intensive occupations, that is, occupations mainly engaging in tasks following well-defined repetitive procedures that can easily be performed by sophisticated algorithms (Frey and Osborne, 2013).[1]

Globally, the 4IR is found to be more rapid and wide-ranging with possible fundamental technological shifts than the previous waves. In particular, the breakthrough in AI, the wide diffusion of industrial robotics, and the combination of AI, robotics and the rapid development in infrastructural technology such as information technology, cloud technology and big data further spreads the impact of the 4IR. Hence, these sophisticated technologies are expected to disrupt global labour markets by making workers redundant in almost every industry and every country (Brynjolfsson and McAfee, 2011). As automation increases, for instance, smart machines will soon be able to replace workers across a vast spectrum of industries, from accountants to drivers and from estate agents to insurance agents handling routine insurance claims. In other words, blue-collar jobs will continue to be automated, and this trend will increasingly spread to white-collar jobs. Frey and Osborne (2013), for example, estimate that about 47 per cent of US jobs are at risk from automation. This ratio is expected to be much higher in developing economies because there are proportionally more routine-intensive jobs which can be more

---

[1] Computerization refers to job automation by means of computer-controlled equipment (Frey and Osborne, 2013).

easily substituted by computers and machines in these countries than in the developed countries like the United States.[2]

This expectation is in line with the recent argument of the United Nations Conference on Trade and Development (UNCTAD, 2016). They argue that the increased use of robots in developed countries erodes the traditional labour-cost advantage of developing countries because developing countries have a higher share of occupations that could experience significant automation than their developed counterparts. This is even more unnerving in Africa given the dominance of routine tasks, increasing levels of unemployment and the impending demographic 'curse'. As discussed above, the 4IR holds great prospects for Africa's development and industrialization agenda. However, for the continent to truly benefit from the 4IR, it needs to make deliberate policy efforts to shape the 4IR in terms of what it means to the continent, and how the continent can not only optimize the benefits but also mitigate the short-term consequences of the 4IR. These pose a new challenge for new pragmatic policies at the continental, regional and national levels.

13.4.2 Distributional Effect

Another major concern about the wide spread of disruptive technologies is greater inequality. As documented in Autor and Dorn (2013), computerization could also lead to a structural shift in the labour market. They argue that workers are reallocating their labour supply from middle-income manufacturing sectors to low-income service sectors because the latter require a higher degree of flexibility and physical adaptability and consequently are less susceptible to computerization. Meanwhile, a substantial employment growth in occupations involving cognitive tasks is witnessed because problem-solving skills are becoming relatively more productive due to falling prices of computing. This gives rise to labour market polarization, with growing employment in high-skill/high-pay jobs and low-skill/low-pay jobs, accompanied by a hollowing-out of middle-income routine jobs.

The 4IR featuring the pervasiveness of digital technologies could exaggerate inequality in a rapid and widespread manner. Disruptive technologies are no longer confined to routine manufacturing tasks. Rather, they are penetrating almost every industry and making transformational changes. It is naive to believe that the wealth created by this new industrial

---

[2] The fact that the potential replacement is higher in developing countries may reflect that more of such occupations continue to exist in developing countries, while they have already been replaced in developed countries. This is, to a certain extent, a result of different levels of development of these countries.

revolution would be distributed equally between rich and poor, and that those displaced could just walk into another job with a similar salary. In fact, the largest beneficiaries of the ongoing disruptive innovations tend to be a small elite group, including people who own intellectual or physical capital and people with more creative and technical skills. This will continue to exacerbate the current trend towards greater levels of inequality.

13.4.3   The Skills, Resources, Infrastructure and Institutional Gaps between Africa and the Developed Countries

The development of the digital economy requires the necessary skills, in particular digital skills, financial resources, availability of necessary digital infrastructure and relevant regulations and institutions to provide an enabling environment for firms and members of a society. As shown in Chapter 3, in the year 2017, the secondary school enrolment ratio in Ghana and Tanzania was 69.95 per cent and 25.84 per cent, respectively. For tertiary education enrolment, the ratio for Ghana was 15.84 per cent, while that in Tanzania was only 3.92 per cent. There exists a significant gap between Africa and the developed countries (which had higher than 100 per cent secondary school enrolment rate in 2017), and many of the other developing countries such as Thailand, Mexico, Peru and Colombia whose rates were 117 per cent, 100 per cent, 99 per cent and 99 per cent in the same year, respectively.[3]

While the above listed 'framework' conditions are largely missing in developing countries, the digital competencies required to benefit from the digital revolution is even scarcer. The digital competencies required to take advantage of the 4IR include: (1) digital competencies for all such as skills for the adoption and basic use of technologies; and (2) digital competencies for ICT professionals such as skills for adaptations and creation of technologies. More specifically, the skills needed include: (1) Technical and professional skills which directly relate to the operation of industrial technologies, for example, how to install and operate industrial robots, or how to interpret received codes on the interface display. Workers in developing countries need to be equipped with technical backgrounds in training programmes to understand how robots work, and these workers require the skills to train robots to accomplish tasks, to detect systematic errors or to facilitate inter-departmental collaborations. (2) Generic ICT skills, which include skills to understand, use and adopt new technologies, are fundamental to the digital transformation in Africa. The speed of technological innovations is rapidly accelerating and

---

[3] Data source: World Development Indicator, World Bank.

workers need technical skills that enable them to do life-long learning. Teaching young people in Africa about the ability to cope with emerging technologies is particularly important. (3) The labour force in Africa needs ICT-complementary 'soft skills', which refer to human skills that cannot be replaced by machines, computers or robots. Empirical evidence shows that professions involving a higher degree of creativity and innovation are less susceptible to digitalization and computerization, for example, science and engineering (Frey & Osborne, 2017).

However, due to the existing gaps in infrastructure and equipment, software and platforms, and teaching staff and resources, people living in developing countries can rarely enjoy the benefits of technology-assisted training on digital skills. For example, according to International Telecommunication Union (ITU), in 2017, in developed countries, 81 out of 100 individuals use the internet, while this figure was only 41.3 out of 100 in developing countries (see Figure 13.2). Moreover, although digitalization offers important opportunities for women (e.g. 73.9 per cent of e-business owners on Chinese e-shopping website Taobao are women), there is a wider gender gap in internet use in the developing countries (ITU, 2017). In 2016, the percentage of men using the internet was 12 per cent higher than that for women worldwide, while this gap was 31 per cent in developing countries. Women are also less represented in the ICT workforce. Women are 31 per cent of Google's overall workforce, yet they occupy only 20 per cent of technical positions (Google, 2017), and women comprise 17 per cent of the Facebook workforce (Williams, 2016). Compared to the developed

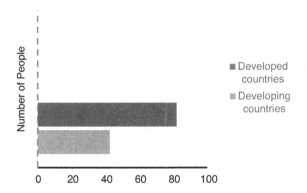

Figure 13.2 Individuals using the internet per 100 inhabitants (2017)
Note: Estimated 2017 or latest year available.
Source: ICT access data from ITU available at www.itu.itn.

countries, the percentage of youth using the internet in developing countries is also lower. In 2016, 70 per cent of young people had access to the internet in the world on average. This share was 94 per cent in developed countries; but it was only 67 per cent in developing countries and only 30 per cent in LICs. Nearly nine out of ten young individuals are not using the internet live in Africa or Asia and the Pacific. Digitalization is integral to the 4IR. As a result, there is the need for developing countries to close these digital gaps in order to be able to take full advantage of the digital revolution.

Infrastructure and Equipment gap

The disparity in electricity supply and broadband availability, which are essential for big data, IOT or any other digital technology to work properly, between Africa and the developed countries is also substantial. This is in addition to their differences in the availability in the infrastructure for large-scale data collection, storage, processing and analysis, and the capabilities in using them for business and policymaking, as well as in supervision and policy regulation.

Training on digital competencies has a relatively high requirement for well-established ICT infrastructures such as broadband and 3G or 4G mobile networks, and for ICT equipment such as computers, tablets and mobile phones. The availability of ICTs varies in African countries. As shown in Chapter 3, although the past fifteen years have witnessed a rapid diffusion of mobile phone technology in Africa, the gap between Africa and the rest of the world persists while it did not enlarge. In Tanzania, for example, the rate of mobile cellular subscription per 100 people has been around 70 per 100 people since 2015. Internet coverage at school falls below 20 per cent on average in developing countries (ITU, 2014). In terms of more advanced digital technology, such as high-speed internet, which is critical for the use of IoT and big data technology, the availability and access in Africa still significantly lags behind that in the developed countries or some of the emerging economies such as China. Current software and platforms developed for digital skills learning are predominantly designed for social and cultural contexts in developed countries. More open-sourced software and online platforms need to adapt and be localized to fit into classrooms for students in developing countries (UNCTAD, 2019).

13.5   Opportunities and Challenges for Women and Youth

The 4IR is also accompanied by demographic changes, especially since a more diverse population in the global South is increasingly adopting emerging technologies. The diffusion of ICTs, such as mobile phones, first started with the young, urban, rich and male population, and later was adopted by a more diverse population that includes middle-aged and the elderly, rural and female groups, owing to the decreased manufacturing cost of ICT devices (Aker & Mbiti, 2010). In this section, we will mainly focus on youth and women in developing countries, to explore how technologies are bringing new opportunities and challenges for them.

As many countries are now becoming ageing societies, improving the education and employment of the young is becoming particularly important in policymaking. Developing countries are witnessing an increase of young people in the labour market. About half a million young Indian and Chinese are joining the workforce per year in the coming decades. In Africa, it is expected that around 11 million young Africans will join the labour market every year for the next decade (World Bank, 2016).

Technologies are both empowering the youth and displacing them in the job market. On the one hand, ICTs such as mobile phones and computers enable young people to have convenient access to diverse information sources and provide them with platforms to expand social networks, acquire knowledge and engage in public spheres.

Young people in developing countries are in an advantageous position compared to other social groups when adapting to the digital transformation. The multimedia interface on computers and mobile phones allows young people with a lack of traditional literacy skills to understand content on digital devices and exploit various functions via new technologies. On the other hand, some emerging technologies like robotics and machine-learning algorithms are replacing workers, leading to the shrinkage of blue-collared job opportunities for young people with low or medium educational backgrounds. The competition with modern technologies pressurizes the young to enhance their creative, cognitive and critical-thinking skills. It also creates pressure on educators and policymakers to design curricula that equip young people with essential skills in the face of digitalization and automation in all industries.

13.6   Conclusion

We are living at a crucial moment in history – we are entering the age of the 4IR that features a fusion of disruptive technologies blurring the lines between the physical, biological and digital worlds. In Africa and the world as a whole, this new industrial revolution can be considered as a double-edged sword that can generate both positive and negative impacts under the concept of social inclusivity. Like the revolutions that preceded it, the 4IR has the potential to raise the unemployment rate by replacing routine tasks and also deepen the increasing inequality in Africa. By contrast, the 4IR also has the potential to transform Africa by creating economic opportunities through industrialization, fostering social inclusion and ultimately contributing to shared prosperity for the continent.

These challenges and opportunities pose several policy issues. As revealed by Dutta et al. (2015), only widespread and systematic use of the disruptive technologies by all stakeholders – individuals, firms and government – can trigger the transformation. Therefore, efforts must be made to formulate policies that enable the 4IR to benefit all and not only the richest people in Africa. In addition, since we are living in a time where the norms and regulations of technological systems of the 4IR are being established, the African Union (AU) and governments must take the opportunity to shape this new industrial revolution with a far-sighted system approach and guide it toward the kind of inclusive and prosperous continent that is desired. On the other hand, tax to redistribute income to those who are negatively affected or who lose their jobs in the new wave of industrial revolution should also be considered in the continent.

Moreover, as highlighted in Fu and Akter (2016), a system of well-used technology that is assisted by trained village youths can serve as a valid tool for inclusive development. Therefore, it is important for African governments to adopt a systematic approach in developing the proper policies concerning disruptive technologies, as both connectivity and education play a vital role in achieving inclusive growth. The argument of UNCTAD (2016) also confirms that developing countries, like those in Africa, should redesign education policies and embrace the digital revolution. Such an approach should be combined with supportive macroeconomic, industrial and social policies for the purpose of inclusive growth. As Philip Jennings, general secretary of the global UNI union, said: 'We need some governance to ensure a democratic evolution and that requires public policy discussion. There is the opportunity to shape technology to improve people's lives; through connectivity, education, health. We shouldn't be fearful and fatalist about it.'

14   Conclusions
Can Africa Leapfrog the Innovation Gap?

Coming to the twenty-first century, the global community worked together to achieve the Millennium Development Goals (MDGs). From the year 2015, this shared set of goals has been expanded to the 2030 Sustainable Development Goals (SDGs), which aim to promote socially, economically and environmentally sustainable global development. Amongst the seventeen goals of the SDGs, innovation plays a key role to 'Build resilient infrastructure, promote inclusive and sustainable industrialization and foster innovation' (SDG9), 'Ensure sustainable consumption and production patterns' (SDG12), 'Promote sustained, inclusive and sustainable economic growth, full and productive employment and decent work for all' (SDG8). In fact, science, technology and innovation contribute to the implementation of all the seventeen SDGs, in different ways and to different degrees. Accompanying this progress in development policy and practices, the development of technology and innovation capabilities of the developing countries has moved to the centre of the field of development studies. The emergence of digital technology and the 4IR have made the task of building innovation capabilities in the developing countries even more urgent. This book makes an attempt to address a couple of important and under-researched questions in this pursuit.

In order to achieve this objective, three national surveys of innovation creation and diffusion were carried out in Ghana and Tanzania. They are the first surveys in Africa that are dedicated to the origin and diffusion of innovation within and into these countries. The unique design of the surveys provides valuable insights into the transmission mechanisms of innovation, expanding our understanding and going beyond the traditional input and output indicators. Such efforts are not only unique for Africa but also for the other low- and middle- income developing countries where transmission mechanisms have not been receiving the

This chapter benefits from valuable private discussions with Raphie Kaplinky and Bengt-Åke Lundvall.

315

attention they deserve. Through a combination of the valuable insights from these three national innovation surveys and qualitative case studies in Ghana and Kenya, as well as survey evidence at the individual level from within the foreign-invested firms in Ghana, the book offers distinctive evidence on the form and nature of innovations in the African context, the origins and the effective channels for the diffusion of innovation within African countries and from foreign sources to these countries, the barriers to innovation creation and diffusion and the space for innovation policy in these economies.

This chapter summarizes the findings of this book, outlines the characteristics and origins of the under-the-radar innovation prevailing in Africa, examines whether Africa can leapfrog the innovation gap with the current type of innovation and discusses the policy implications learned from the research and the policy interventions which would transform the innovation system to empower and enable Africa to harness innovation and technical progress for inclusive and sustainable development.

14.1   Innovation under the Radar: The Nature and Impact of Innovation in Africa

Firms in Africa are innovating. They innovate in the context of LICs. The traditional measures such as the number of patents granted or R&D expenditure have proved inadequate to capture the fertile innovation scene currently under the radar. Using the *Oslo Manual* definition of innovation, which focuses on firms' self-assessment of the introduction of a new or significantly improved product (good or services) or process, a new marketing method or new management practices, evidence from the three national surveys in Ghana and Tanzania reveals that innovation occurs among a wide range of sectors, not only in the formal firms, but also in the informal firms. More than 90 per cent of the sampled formal firms reported to have implemented innovation in both countries. In addition, 80 per cent and 89 per cent of the sampled informal firms reported to have introduced innovation in the 2012–2014 period in Ghana and Tanzania, respectively. They engage not only in technological innovation in product and process but also engage actively, or even more, in non-technological marketing and management innovations. Innovation occurs in a wide range of sectors, and in both the formal and informal firms, but formal firms are evidenced to innovate more.

Evidence from Chapter 4 suggests that these innovations are mostly in the form of low-cost non-R&D innovations. Most firms in Ghana innovate in marketing, and most firms in Tanzania innovate in management. All these non-technological innovations do not involve the more expensive or risky activities such as R&D. Within product and process innovations, firms tend to adopt and imitate innovations from others. Most of the innovations observed are based on learning and are incremental in nature. Nearly all of the innovations are incremental, diffusion innovations that are new to the firms or new to the country. These accounted for more than 97 per cent of the total innovations in the surveyed countries. The new-to-the-world novel innovations accounted for less than 3 per cent of total innovations in Tanzania and Ghana. Using the normal indicators of innovation such as R&D investment or number of patents applied or granted to search for innovations in the economy, these innovations – defined as innovations under-the-radar – are not detectable.

Overall, most of these under-the-radar innovations (URIs) take place at the base of the pyramid. They are about diffusion technology or management and marketing practices which are technically and economically appropriate to the local context. The fact that these learning-based innovations do not require heavy investment into R&D suggests that the firms in Africa see feasible survival opening for them to reduce costs or increase productivity and be more competitive. Such a model of innovation enables the African firms to address the resource, skill and institutional constraints and meet the affordability and accessibility of local consumers.

These URIs in LICs share some common characteristics with frugal, '*jugaad*' or inclusive innovations. For example, most of these innovations are cost-efficient and are created to meet the diverse demands of consumers in the market. Yet, there are differences between them. URIs are not purely frugal. Nor are they all the so-called inclusive innovations that serve the base of the pyramid. This assertion is based on three main reasons and/or characteristics of URIs.

Firstly, there are also URIs in the high-technology sector or targeting the higher end of the market which pursue higher-quality and greater variety of products or services, and do not necessarily aim at cost-cutting, frugality in function, or serving the base-of-the-pyramid market. Upgrading the technological and production capacities is also an important objective of the innovation policies of the LIC governments and entrepreneurs.

Secondly, URIs are clearly not the R&D-based versions that are often observed in industrialized countries; although there are some frugal or inclusive innovations developed in R&D labs in both developed and developing countries. Most of the URI activities are incremental in nature and based on organizational or individual learning and adaptation, practice or individual creativity in the countries under study. They are often demand-led, learning- and non-R&D-based, low-cost innovation as a result of the constraints that the African firms face and the responses that they make to survive and grow.

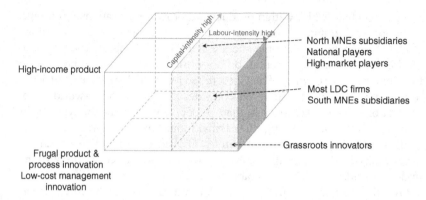

Figure 14.1 Types and players of under-the-radar innovation

Thirdly, URI innovations are visible in new or significantly improved products or processes, but more than that, they are just everywhere in non-technological areas such as management and marketing practices followed by the African firms. They do exist in African and other LICs, but they are not detectable by the traditional innovation indicators such as R&D investment and patent applications/grant numbers.

Figure 14.1 summarizes the type, nature and major innovators of the URIs. They are mostly highly labour-intensive, low-cost (low capital-intensive) innovations. While most of them are frugal product or process innovations, or low-cost management or marketing innovations, some of them may also serve the high-income segment in the LICs. The firms in Africa, most of which are SMEs, are the major innovators of URIs. The grassroots innovators also contribute to URIs, in particular those low-capital-intensive, social-demand-driven URIs. The MNEs also contribute to the URIs. While the Northern MNEs contribute more to the medium-capital-intensive URIs through the adoption of new machineries and equipment in LICs, the Southern MNEs contribute more to the labour-intensive URIs by bringing the URIs in emerging markets to the LICs.

All these characteristics of the URIs discovered in this study in the low-income or lower-middle-income African countries share some of the characteristics of the 'innovation below the radar' that Kaplinsky (2011) identified in the Asian drivers, which focuses on consumers at the bottom of the pyramid. Yet, the nature, origin and diffusion of the URIs discussed in this book in the socio-economic and physio-technical context of the LICs is broader than the below-the-radar innovations documented in the literature.

14.2   Origin of Innovations in LICs

14.2.1   The Context and Constraints for Innovation in LICs

Inevitably, firms in developing countries encounter significant obstacles during the process of knowledge adaptation and innovation. This research also reveals the substantial challenges to innovation in Africa. The main bottlenecks for innovation in these countries include the lack of funding and skills as well as market constraints. Innovation is costly and often requires substantial financial support. Most of the innovations in Africa are incremental and learning-based, hence skills actually determine the capacity to learn. Therefore, the lack of skills is a very important factor. In Ghana, these factors present about the same level of constraints for formal and informal firms; however, in Tanzania the same factors are more relevant for informal firms.

In addition to the lack of finance and skills, and the lack of political will and leadership are another constraint to innovation. Innovation is not only risky and costly, it also takes time. In contrast, the pressure to win elections often makes politicians prefer introduction of policies that could deliver quick changes in the short run. As a result, the political will to prioritize innovation in policymaking is weak. This is further exacerbated by the traditional perception that innovation is the business of somebody else or the business of advanced countries. The fourth challenge comes from weak protection for intellectual property rights (IPR) in LICs. In many African economies, overall institutional development still lags behind, and so protection of IPR is still weak. This has clear implications for the creation and diffusion of innovation.

14.2.2   Origins of Innovation in LICs

The majority of innovations introduced during the three years, 2012–2014, originated from within the countries, both for technological and non-technological innovations. In fact, 57 per cent of firms in Ghana and 70 per cent of firms in Tanzania adopted or created technological innovations with resources and information found in-country, while this is the case for 28 per cent of Ghanaian firms and 77 per cent of Tanzanian firms involved in non-technological innovations.

Given the context and constraints to innovation in Ghana and Tanzania, the sources of innovation in these countries exhibit the following characteristics:

(1) *In-house versus extra-mural innovation sourcing:* Overall, African firms rely mainly on their own capacity for innovation. They are not very

open to external sources of innovation. Internal sources such as colleagues in the firm comprise the most important domestic knowledge source. 'Internal sources such as colleagues' was ranked the most important source in Ghana and second most important in Tanzania.

(2) *Customer demand as a major inspiration of innovation:* Findings from Chapter 6 demonstrate that innovations are primarily responses to customer needs. Customer requirements have been the major driver of innovation in the surveyed African countries. The importance of internal sources and market sources such as customers is consistent in both Ghana and Tanzania.

(3) *Technological learning versus traditional R&D:* Most of the innovations observed in these two countries are of a different nature than those in more developed countries. Research and development (R&D) departments are available only in the larger and formal firms in Ghana and Tanzania, and most of the firms need to rely on different ways to innovate. Instead, the contribution of skilled workers to the innovation process is highly relevant, mainly for formal firms. More than half of the firms in Ghana and Tanzania introduced technological innovations that came from skilled workers who had found a better way for the production process after some experiments, in a trial-and-error approach.

(4) *Technological learning through spillovers versus formal licensing:* An important mechanism for the introduction of innovation in surveyed firms is imitation and adaptation of innovations implemented in other firms. According to the surveys, imitation and adaptation account for 41 per cent of innovations in Tanzania and 59 per cent of innovations in Ghana over the 2012–2014 period. Besides adaption and modification, many firms innovate simply by imitating other companies. This is normal behaviour in a situation in which R&D departments are extremely rare.

(5) *Entrepreneurial ingenuity:* Entrepreneurial ingenuity drives firms to remodel old car wheels into cooking stoves, develop the capability to preserve fresh mushrooms with the help of local universities, design amazing fashions from local textiles or make delicious food products from the most humble ingredients. These are just a few examples and they are more than just a local curiosity – they are new ways to turn a profit or, for some firms, to survive.

There are, however, also some differences in the pattern of internal sources between these two countries – for example, the use of network and other external knowledge sources. The Ghanaian firms have made good use of networks to search external knowledge for innovation. However, the importance of a network, such as being a member of clusters and associations, is not valued highly by Tanzanian firms. Other sources such as the internet and journal papers appear to be an important knowledge source for the formal firms in Tanzania but were not regarded as an important knowledge source for Ghanaian firms.

14.3   Diffusion of Innovations within LICs

14.3.1   Collaboration and External Knowledge Search

Evidence from Chapter 5 suggests that, overall, sampled Tanzania firms appear to be more open than sampled firms in Ghana. Innovation collaboration is more widely adopted in Tanzania than in Ghana. Partners in the supply chain and in the same industry have been the main partners of innovative collaboration. Firms also used external knowledge search for seeking innovative ideas and technology that can help them improve their product design or quality, production process, or management or marketing practices. Such open innovation practices have been used by the surveyed African firms to overcome the cost, skills and market barriers to innovation in their economies. The degree of a firm's openness is positively associated with innovation. Further, the research finds that local knowledge is more relevant for innovation outcomes than foreign knowledge. This result emphasizes that the knowledge gap between LICs and the technological frontier is large, thus local knowledge is more appropriate to solve firms' problems in LICs.

14.3.2   Universities

Universities have not played an important role in either of the countries, as suggested by the literature and in comparison to other partners and in other countries. The situation in Ghana saw a significant improvement in 2015, especially in terms of more active outreach and participation by the universities in the UIC formation. In Tanzania, personal connection is the main cause of a UIC. In both countries, 'we are not connected' has been a major obstacle that hindered the development of a strong university–industry linkage in the national innovation system. This also points to a possible area of policy intervention to build up more platforms or other bridges to link the two sectors and match demand in the industry with the supply of skills in the universities. Lundvall (2016) identifies that one way to build and enhance the university–industry interaction would be to reduce the 'cultural distance' between universities and the more traditional industries, and also develop the traditional industries' 'capability to communicate with the academic community'.

14.3.3 Clusters and Regional Value Chains

The Ghanaian and Tanzanian firms have similar participation ratios in clusters, while Tanzanian firms have a significantly higher ratio of participation in regional vertical value chains. The findings suggest that clusters as institutions provide greater support and assistance to informal, rather than formal firms. The vast majority of the informal firms reported that clusters facilitate the exchange of relevant production and technology information and a greater collaboration on pricing. Work- and resource-sharing are also important benefits for cluster members. One third of formal and informal members explicitly reported that clusters are environments that facilitate the diffusion and creation of innovations. Informal firms seem to have significantly greater benefits in collaborating on pricing and work-sharing compared to formal firms.

Regional instead of global value chains seem to be more often observed among the surveyed firms, suggesting that using a regional value chain is a more realistic and feasible step for African firms to gradually upgrade and integrate into the global production network. Evidence from the study not only confirms the benefits of being part of a vertical production network for individual firms; it enables the participating firms to 'make existing products cheaper or better quality'; it also enables them to 'produce something that firms in the country would otherwise not be able to produce'. The importance of regional versus global value chains in benefiting the studied African economies also echoes the findings by Fagerberg, Lundvall and Srholec (2018) that small countries with weak capabilities do not benefit from participation in global value chains, while participation in regional value chains may benefit them. This has significant implications for the upgrading and diversification of the African industries. Overall, the sources of innovation in these countries appear to present a 'flying geese' model, with some (mainly formal) firms having sourced innovations directly from a range of foreign countries, adapting and localizing them, and then being imitated by other local firms.

14.3.4 Women Entrepreneurs and Innovation

Research in Chapter 7 finds that sampled firms managed by women entrepreneurs are less innovative in product, process and management innovations than those managed by men. The average share of sales accounted for by new or improved products is also significantly less in firms managed by women. This is to a large extent due to the lack of finance and skills in the surveyed countries, as found in Chapter 7, and that women entrepreneurs experience discrimination in access to finance and education. The only exception is market innovation, in which the firms managed by women entrepreneurs did better than those managed by men. This fact that women entrepreneurs have a stronger performance in marketing innovation is a result of African women entrepreneurs' struggle to innovate in the face of the constraints in finance, and also a reflection of the culture in African society where women and men have different divisions of labour regarding domestic and external work. Similar to the findings in other countries, risk aversion has a significantly bigger negative impact on the likelihood of product innovation in women-managed firms in comparison to firms managed by men.

14.3.5 The Role of the State

Although there are different views on the necessity and appropriateness of policy intervention in a specific industrial field, policymakers are increasingly embracing the idea of actively tackling the challenges facing innovation using policy tools. The 2013 and 2015 survey results on formal firms and informal firms in Ghana and Tanzania suggest that in both countries, firms reported having benefited from government subsidy and training programmes. They value almost all of the listed policy measures to a high degree, more than four out of a total of five score points, except they give a lower score (more than two only) to openness to imports and competition.

Nevertheless, firms in both countries are not happy with the quality of implementation of these policies. The surveyed enterprises regarded most of the issued S&T policies as poorly implemented and ineffective. How to make the policies work better must become an important issue of policy governance in innovation policy study. In the current status of innovation policy development in Africa, it is important to align policy actions across different ministries, agencies and stakeholders, and also across different levels of government. Policy monitoring and evaluation, as well as learning from experience and policy improvement are still striving in this direction.

14.4 Diffusion of Innovations to LICs

The findings identified that most of the innovations in Ghana and Tanzania emerged from domestic sources; however, we have seen some innovation being imported from abroad or resulting from spillovers emanating from multinational companies. International knowledge is mainly acquired via networks, labour mobility, and imports and exports.

324   Emerging Technologies and Innovation in Africa

Trade is a critical channel for local firms to come across and potentially adopt innovations. In addition, formal firms can engage in the global value chain via the downstream manufacturing sectors, which is a very effective way to obtain innovation from abroad. Spillovers from multinationals are an increasingly relevant source of innovation diffusion.

Not only technology transfers but also non-technological innovations occur between multinationals and local firms. Multinationals often provide training for local employees, and knowledge can be transferred via the mobility of labour. Skilled workers in multinationals often move to another company or start their own business at some point in their career. Some technological and non-technological innovation transfer processes occur deliberately, but most are spontaneous. Using the internet as another important way to obtain knowledge information and establishing vertical linkages with local firms that received foreign investments tended to be more essential to firms in the formal sector.

Due to inevitable technological plus social and cultural differences, foreign technologies developed in advanced economies may not fit well into the local conditions of developing countries. Therefore, external conditions such as assistance from linked partners and universities can foster and support the adaptation of foreign knowledge. Our results are in general terms similar for Ghana and Tanzania. The most relevant factors in ensuring the success of foreign knowledge acquisition for both formal and informal firms are the adaptation of the technology to be used and the corresponding capacity to carry out the adaptation. In addition to internal capacity building, assistance from suppliers for the adaptation would also encourage local firms to acquire more advanced knowledge. Our results confirm that assistance from suppliers was more crucial to formal firms, while the assistance from the Ghanaian universities and research institutions was more meaningful to the informal group. The exact opposite is observed in Tanzania, evidencing the relevance of local context in the behaviour of firms.

We captured a different behaviour of formal and informal firms towards the adoption of innovation from abroad, and this behaviour is different in the countries studied. Therefore, it is important for host-country governments to differentiate between the policy needs of formal and informal firms. Meanwhile, the efficiency of the knowledge flow responds to factors such as effective infrastructure, investment regime and, most importantly, the capacity to absorb and assimilate technology. To ensure the success of international technology transfer, a fundamental challenge for host LICs is to improve the local environment and investment climate to encourage domestic firms to participate in international activities that allow them to access the international stock of knowledge and strengthen the interactions between foreign and domestic firms that foster international knowledge diffusion.

As the leading players in global economic integration, foreign firms bring key knowledge resources to host countries and facilitate knowledge diffusion across national borders. From the comparison between foreign-owned and formal local firms in Chapter 9, it is found that foreign firms are slightly more oriented towards innovation, in particular the process and management innovation, and relatively less towards product innovation, probably because of the product innovation process being developed in their home country or a developed country. In Ghana, the behaviour of foreign firms regarding sources of knowledge is different from local firms, while in Tanzania foreign firms behave in a similar manner to formal local firms. Foreign firms in Ghana tend to rely more on internal resources and collaboration with government or public research institutes for innovation activities.

Collaborations with foreign institutions are mainly found in formal firms, which often are closer to the local technologies' frontier and have the local capacity to support such relationships. Firms in the food sector have sought collaborations in developing new products, while firms in the textile sector have benefited from the international initiative of South-South collaborations that focused on process and managerial models. The former included collaborations aimed at developing new products and supported the local firm in critical phases of the production (i.e. increasing the shelf life) and access to foreign laboratories to test the composition of the product, since advanced equipment is not available in Ghana. The latter showed how a South-South collaboration has been extremely beneficial for Firm E in improving the production line. Although this initiative is observed in only one case, it shows how training courses funded and organized by international cooperation programmes can strengthen local capabilities (Sawada et al., 2012).

Overall, Tables 14.1 and 14.2 summarize the drivers of and channels for the diffusion of URIs in the studied African countries.

14.5   Innovation Strategies of African Firms

Based on the studies of the nature of domestic and foreign sources of innovation in Ghana and Tanzania, a strategy employed by the African firms to innovate despite the constraints typical of LICs can be summarized as follows:

Table 14.1 *Drivers of under-the-radar innovation*

Drivers	Explanation or examples
Customer demand	Domestic market International market (Exports, GVCs, Regional VCs)
Competition to survive	Cut cost Improve quality New product New management/marketing practices
Entrepreneurship	Both men and women Women more low-cost management/ marketing innovations
Characteristics of infrastructure	Forced innovation, e.g. unstable energy supply, so use solar power, or manual operation instead of automation
Inspiration of innovations & knowledge spillover	Both horizontal in the same industry and vertical in other industries.
Big change in the industry	Induced innovation, e.g. e-commerce
Regulatory environment, policy push	E.g. grassroots innovation in agriculture to address climate change
Social needs	E.g. NGO-driven innovation for the poor
Factor prices	E.g. capital shortage and increase of interest rates. Adoption of more labour-intensive technology from the South

(1) *Adopt and develop learning-based innovation:* All economies and firms are 'learning economies' and 'learning organizations' (Lundvall, 2016: p. 110). Results from our analyses corroborate this assertion and show that most of the innovations taking place in Ghana are learning-based, without the traditional R&D activities that we normally observe in firms in industrialized countries. The firm-level survey indicates that the majority of these innovations are new to the firms, while a small proportion of the innovations are new to the country. A very small minority of innovations are thought to be new to the world. However, in some cases the adoption of innovation requires modification to meet the adopters' needs.

(2) *Emphasize low-cost, non-technology innovation:* Findings suggest that significant constraints in resources have pushed firms to employ a strategy of adopting financial resource-saving types of innovations, including non-technological innovation in management and marketing practices. Such type of hidden innovation does not require heavy investment in laboratory R&D. In fact, in many cases, it requires entrepreneurship, determination and leadership, which can be met by entrepreneurs' efforts.

Table 14.2 *Routes of under-the-radar innovation*

Routes	Sub-routes	Notes
Customer requirement	Domestic customer	Learning-based, not lab-based
	International customer	New player: South and BRICs
Regional VC /GVC	Quality requirement	
	Training	
Imitation	Without adaptation	
	With adaptation	
On-the-job experiment / trial	Individual creativity	
University–Industry collaboration	Commercialization of new technology, or help firms to absorb and make adaptation of acquired external technology	
Knowledge transfer & spillover	FDI	
	Export	
	Diaspora	

(3) *Adopt an open innovation approach, albeit not knowing the concept, especially relying on external knowledge search and imitation:* Firms collaborate with a range of actors, customers, workers and other firms to develop and adopt innovations. Imitation of other firms, with or without changes, is a way to become innovative. These initiatives are critical not only for the innovation activities of firms, but also to increase their competitiveness and, for some, their survival.

(4) *Synergies in innovation:* Evidence from Chapter 4 finds that in Ghana and Tanzania, if a firm innovates in product, it will also innovate in all the four types of innovation, that is, product, process, management and process innovation. As found in Battisti and Stoneman (2010), such synergies enable the innovating firms to maximize the benefits of innovation. This is also due to the advantage of small business. In large and formal companies, such coordination is much more difficult due to the organizational rigidity and coordination costs, which are much higher.

If we compare the URIs and the above-radar-innovations (ABIs), there are substantial differences between them in terms of strategy of and pathways to innovation. URIs focus on various methods of learning (learning from customer, learning by imitation, learning by doing, learning by collaboration) and individual creativity and entrepreneurship, all

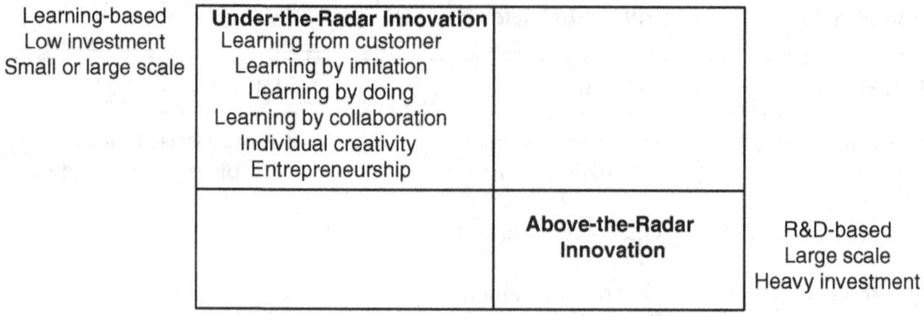

Learning-based Low investment Small or large scale	**Under-the-Radar Innovation** Learning from customer Learning by imitation Learning by doing Learning by collaboration Individual creativity Entrepreneurship	
		Above-the-Radar Innovation	R&D-based Large scale Heavy investment

Figure 14.2 Strategies of under-the-radar innovation in comparison to that of above-the-radar innovation

of which need only low investment. ABIs rely mostly on investment-intensive R&D and large-scale commercialization. However, they also share some common strategy such as collaboration (Figure 14.2).

14.6   Innovation in the Informal Firms

The informal sector is a very important part of the LICs. It is often regarded as a static part of an economy that has nothing to do with innovation. Results from this study proved that the informal sector in Africa is dynamic and creative, despite the constraints it faces. These African firms often engage in more than one type of innovation, which is likely to enable them to benefit also from the synergy effects of the complementary innovations (Battisti and Stoneman, 2010). In Tanzania, more than half of the firms reported having implemented all the four types of innovation simultaneously. This is, again, not only in the formal sector, but also in the informal sector.

We also observe differences between formal and informal firms. Internal and market sources of knowledge are most relevant for techno-logical innovations in formal firms, while informal firms value more the knowledge acquired from internal sources with the firm and network channels. Another characteristic of the informal firms is that they are significantly more likely to introduce only marketing innovation or only marketing and management innovations, which do not require heavy investment in R&D or even experiments and are often driven by entre-preneurs' innovativeness and determination.

Formal and informal firms behave differently regarding the adoption of innovation from abroad. Informal firms seem to be more likely than formal firms to adopt innovations from nearby countries and Africa in general. The latter instead are more likely to adopt innovations from China, India, Europe and the United States. In recent times, there has been an emphasis on the relevance of South-South collaboration and technology transfers. The rationale is that the knowledge transferred to Ghana is likely to be more appropriate if it comes from countries with similar factor endowment and at a similar development stage. The absorptive capacity of Ghana may also be more able to adopt technologies of a similar level to its own. Collectively, 3 per cent of the technological innovations introduced in Ghana and 18 per cent of the technological innovations introduced in Tanzania came from a developing country (other countries in Africa, India and China). Formal firms seem to have a greater share of innovation from those countries, highlighting the fact that adoption of innovations from a country at a similar development stage may be easier for firms with lower absorptive capacity.

14.7   Innovation as a Means for Development

Importantly, the chapters found that innovation is not the outcome of development but a means for development. Innovation is not a characteristic of rich countries; rather, without innovation of the type we captured, there will be no transition from low income to middle income. Empirical studies in Chapter 6, for example, found that in such an environment, innovation positively impacts the labour productivity of firms, and technological innovations are more effective than managerial innovations. Formal firms do not tend to be more productive than informal firms, but the role of innovation on productivity tends to be greater for formal firms. On the one hand, innovation is a factor that may push developing informal firms into the formal economy. On the other hand, the survival of some informal firms may be linked to their ability to innovate. 'I survive because I innovate', a comment made by an entrepreneur in Ghana, presents vividly the role of innovation in LICs.

14.8   Opportunities and Challenges of the Fourth Industrial Revolution

14.8.1   Opportunities and Challenges

The rapid development and wide applications of digital technology and the emergence of the 4IR offer both opportunities and challenges to the African economies. On the one hand, digital technologies such as mobile internet, 5G, Cloud and big data will greatly enhance connectivity and efficiency, and therefore empower people and businesses in Africa through greater connectivity and bridging the digital divide. African people and businesses will be able to access knowledge, information and services at much faster speed, with more convenient access and lower costs. There will also be great efficiency gains to business and government. The lower costs and greater variety of products will also benefit consumers in Africa.

However, this wave of technical change, which is biased towards capital and skilled labour – highly creative skilled labour in particular – will also have significant impact on the job opportunities in Africa and increase income inequalities within Africa, and between Africa and the middle- and high-income countries. A significant challenge for Africa is that to benefit from this new wave of industrial revolution requires the relevant infrastructure and digital competencies in the African economy and society. These include electricity supply, not only connectivity but also broadband connection, digital skills in creative use of emerging technologies in the business sector and basic IT literacy in the society, including both youth and elderly, men and women, plus the capacity to create new or make adaptations of external digital technology. It also requires the capacity and digital infrastructure for big data collection, storage, analysis, and ability to use all these to help economic and business decision-making, as well as an enabling environment fostering new business in the digital economy to grow and prosper. All these require financial investment and take time to build.

14.8.2 ICT Adoption and Innovation

Findings from this book indicate that the adoption of ICT does not only contribute to innovation directly by influencing the innovation output, but also seeks the interaction with innovation inputs in response to the growth of new product sales. It is important to emphasize the role of the internet as a vector of innovation information. Among the sample firms that have access to the internet, the internet is considered a significant source of information.

The adoption of ICT offers a unique and integrated opportunity for interacting with innovation activities. In this regard, ICTs facilitate in-house innovation (as potential innovation infrastructure) and become part of the integrated innovation resources to affect innovation performance. By differentiating the innovation sales new to the market and new to the firm, we found that the presence of 'internet' as a knowledge source has helped firms utilize the effect of in-house innovation activities and eventually yield high innovation sales which are new to the market. Ghanaian manufacturing firms, in particular those who achieve innovation mainly by relying on imitating competitors, adopt the internet as a replacement for their imitative activities.

14.8.3   Lessons from Kenya's Digital Financial Innovation

The in-depth case study of the success of a digital financial innovation in Kenya, the M-PESA, from its origin to scale-up, not only proves that Africa is able to seize the opportunity of digital revolution, but also suggests that Africa can succeed with acquisition and localization of a foreign idea, and scale it up successfully through open innovation. In this process, a vertical production chain of services and user community has developed; this is further legitimated and strengthened though an excellent public–private partnership (PPP).

Findings from Chapter 12 suggest that Safaricom has successfully integrated a large number of small, disaggregated actors into the M-PESA design and delivery chain through a process of entrepreneurial experimentation. It also built up an informal community of service providers and users, which was critical to M-PESA growth because it shaped the 'local familiarity with agent-based financial pooling and transfer system ... providing infrastructure and practices that underpinned the rapid expansion of M-PESA'. These practices subsequently perpetuated additional product and process innovation (knowledge development and diffusion) characterized by different outputs and value derived from diverse product applications. Moreover, the Kenyan mobile policy evolution provides an excellent public–private partnership, whereby the M-PESA case presented a learning platform for both product developers and the policy actors. A facilitative but firm regulatory role of the state is critical for effective legitimization. The Central Bank of Kenya played multiple and very critical policy-oriented roles but remained an honest broker throughout the formative phase and beyond.

Such a digital financial innovation did make a valuable contribution to financial inclusion and inclusive development. M-PESA has largely accommodated the unbanked low-income earners including those living in rural areas, allowing them to be 'financially included' (Hinz, 2014). It has further enhanced their ability to manage their lives, since they can send money, store money and make payments at cheap rates and low risk (Kimenyi and Ndung'u, 2009).

14.9   Policy Implications

Several policy implications emerge from the findings in this book.

(1) *Changing mind-set and supporting innovation in Africa:* Even though firms in Africa can be innovative, we also found that they are very largely unsupported. Policies play a critical role in accelerating the diffusion and creation of innovation and mitigating the many obstacles that African firms face. Too often in Africa, and in the informal economy in particular, innovations are not recognized and innovation efforts in the firms are not properly supported. The results in this volume challenge the opinion that supporting these innovations is not what is needed to propel Africa's development. The volume suggests the need for new thinking, and formulation of new policies to recognize and support innovation – mitigating the constraints of financial and labour skills, for example – necessary in the context of LICs for long-term growth and development. Some efforts are being made in this regard. For example, in the Ghanaian case, there has been an increase in the number of firms benefiting from public policies in training and subsidies on loan rates, from 3–4 per cent of surveyed firms. Also, in Tanzania, 4 per cent of firms participated in training and subsidies on loan rate programmes. Innovation policies must not be formulated and implemented in a vacuum, but should be followed by a strong commitment from the government. Incentivizing external transfer of innovation, facilitating cluster participation, easing access to credit, and further strengthening education and the capacity to use research are all critical actions that can mitigate some of the current constraints and drive innovation and economic growth in the long run.

(2) *Development of open national and firm innovation systems:* Developing countries can develop their innovation capability and catch up at a faster pace through the development of an open national innovation system (Fu, 2015). Findings from this study attest to this argument, to some extent, in the context of Africa. Firms in Ghana which are more open to external knowledge search have a stronger innovation performance. Trade and customer demand from international markets are the sources that serve the African firms with the highest importance. However, the level of the benefits from openness in African firms is far from allowing them to fully realize their potential, especially with regard to the roles that MNEs and collaboration played in technology transfer and spillover.

Africa has to build up Open National Innovation System (ONIS) that is opened up to international knowledge, resources and markets. The fact that trade, the internet, people flow and FDI have all played some role in facilitating international innovation diffusion at either firm or worker levels suggests these channels can possibly work in the African context while there is more to do. In order to develop the NIS in Africa to an ONIS, greater openness should be promoted through trade and investment policy. This is easy to say but requires great determination to implement. Investment policies should also encourage the type of FDI that has the potential to generate technology spillovers and create substantial linkages with the local economy. Moreover, a dedicated migration policy should also be introduced to encourage the international flow of talents, including some changes in relevant law and regulations.

At the same time, complementary policies in education, technology capacity upgrading, and infrastructure development should be strengthened to enhance the indigenous technology capability and absorptive capacity in the domestic economy. Given the fact that market institutions in Africa are not mature at this stage, and that the state is an important player in the innovation system, the state should play an active role through appropriate and competition-neutral innovation policies in the development of innovation capacities in Africa.

(3) *Enhancing capacity for innovation leapfrogging:* The study finds that under-the-radar innovations are everywhere in Africa. There are learning-based, non-R&D and incremental innovations that are new to the organization or new to the African countries. Given the rapid technical change in the global economy, it is important to develop Africa's capacity in science and engineering and build the necessary research infrastructure in order to keep Africa moving forward together with the rest of the world. This is even more important for enhancing Africa's capacity for innovation leapfrogging. In order to achieve this, improving the quality of education, developing the higher education sector and increasing investment in research institutes in Africa are important tasks for the science, technology and innovation policy in each African country and for the African Union. This should be started now and not wait for the day Africa becomes a high-income continent.

(4) *Strengthen university–industry linkage and encourage regional value chains:* While it is widely recognized that university–industry linkage is important for the commercialization of new technology, in

developing countries universities can play a dual role in their national innovation system (Fu and Li, 2016). On the one hand, they serve the traditional role of knowledge creation; on the other hand, through university–industry collaboration, they help firms to assimilate, decipher the transferred foreign technology and make necessary adaptations for local application. Findings from the book suggest that university–industry linkage is still weak in African countries. Lack of incentives and lack of institutions to bridge the demand and supply information to both sides are the key reasons. The Ghanaian government introduced a dedicated programme in 2014/ 15 to strengthen the linkage between research institutions and industry. This is found to have motivated and supported more collaboration between universities/research institutions and industry in Ghana. Government policies should continue to incentivize, support and facilitate university–industry linkage in Africa, not only using financial policy tools, but also combining them using non-pecuniary policy tools, such as project evaluation and talent appraisal policies.

(5) *Supporting African women entrepreneurs:* Firms managed by women entrepreneurs should be supported by breaking the skills and finance barriers that they face. Evidence from this volume suggests that the marginal returns of higher levels of education are substantially higher among women entrepreneurs (Chapter 7). This is particularly true for technological innovation and the success of new products. Hence, policies aimed at stimulating high-quality entrepreneurship may be even more successful if they incorporate a focus on women. Simultaneously, strategies aimed at the economic empowerment of women need to pay attention to women's education.

(6) *Recognizing and supporting innovation in the informal sector:* The majority of the chapters in this book are based on data from the first large-scale firm-level survey of innovation in the informal sector in developing countries. The findings suggest that firms in the informal sector are innovative in both Ghana and Tanzania. These are, however, not recognized in the literature and in practice. Informal firms are struggling to survive and grow without support and are being discriminated against in their access to finance. With respect to the limited government support in training and subsidy, the informal firms are significantly less likely to have access to these support programmes, and the paperwork required in the application process is regarded as too burdensome for informal firms who do not have enough resources to spend on this. Therefore, special programmes should be introduced that are dedicated to the informal firms and simplifying the application process.

(7) *Improving state capacity in designing and implementing innovation policy:* The 2013 and 2015 survey results on formal firms and informal firms in Ghana and Tanzania suggest that the surveyed enterprises generally agree with the STI policies issued by domestic government departments, but some are poorly implemented and ineffective; this problem should be given great attention. How to make the policies work better has become an important issue of policy governance in the innovation field. In the current situation of innovation policy development, aligning policy actions across different ministries, agencies and stakeholders, and also across different levels of government is rather important. Dissemination of information on the instruments of policy actions, such as training schemes and financial assistance, is important for effective implementation. Policy monitoring and evaluation and learning from experience and policy improvements are important aspects which would strengthen the intended impact of the policy tools.

(8) *Developing innovation community through partnerships between state and private sector and between domestic and foreign players:* The success of the M-PESA mobile money transfer service in Kenya suggests that African countries can make an innovative application of modern technology pushed forward by a dynamic local innovation community that involves broad stakeholders in the relevant experimental, entrepreneurial, sectoral innovation ecosystem. In this regard, the private sector should actively engage with the regulatory body. At the same time, government policies and regulations should be responsive and engaging so that they co-evolve with the technological change to facilitate the progress. In the case of M-PESA, a facilitative but firm regulatory role of the state is critical for effective legitimization. The Central Bank of Kenya played multiple but very critical policy-oriented roles but remained an honest broker throughout the formative phase and beyond.

(9) *Building digital competencies through training, international cooperation and enabling environment building:* ICTs are tools that facilitate knowledge flow and information exchange. The adoption of ICT can break geographic boundaries and help firms gain access to the global knowledge pool. Obtaining information via the internet and pairing international standards with local production were acknowledged as important channels by the Ghanaian and Tanzanian manufacturing firms. Therefore, it is important for host-country governments to prioritize the investment in ICT infrastructure and skills development to facilitate internet knowledge-sourcing in the African economy.

Given the rapid development of technology and the 4IR in the world economy and the opportunities and challenges it may present to African countries, preparing societies with adequate digital competencies to understand, adopt, use and create new technologies, particularly ICTs, all are key to sustainable development in a digital world. Therefore, emphasizing the improvement of digital competencies in national policy and strategy is of high importance. These policies include the following four aspects.[1]

Firstly, building digital competencies through education is critical. This includes reforming of the course curriculum and incorporating digital skills training at school, providing digital skills training for the labour force and embedding digital skills in lifelong learning.

Secondly, an enabling environment through investment in infrastructure, institutional development and entrepreneurship has to be created. While direct interventions through education and training are critical for the development of digital competencies of the workforce, the creation of an environment that nurtures digital competencies of a country indirectly through investment in infrastructure, institution development and entrepreneurship is also crucial. This includes investment and development of digital infrastructure, such as data resources and the facilities and capabilities in collecting, analysing and using big data, such as the facilities building national big data centres, realizing full broadband coverage in developing countries and regional high-speed computing and processing facilities for big data analysis. Moreover, the creation of an enabling environment also means the development of institutions and environment to nurture digital competencies and the establishment of initiatives that promote entrepreneurship in the digital economy.

Thirdly, promoting international collaboration to facilitate technology adoption and knowledge exchange. Like many other areas of international development, enhancing digital and other technological skills requires international collaboration between countries that possess infrastructure, human resources and knowledge to work together with countries lacking these resources to equip their future workforce with necessary digital skills. While a few international collaborations already exist in the development of infrastructure, such as telecommunication networks and ICT centres between South Korea, China and some African countries, for example (UNCTAD, 2017), much more work is needed. In particular, there are several areas in which international collaboration can contribute to the strengthening of

---

[1] Discussion in this section includes some extracts from a technical document prepared for UNCTAD (2017).

digital competencies in countries. These include (a) Training of researchers and educators; (b) Collaborative development of digital skills programmes; (c) Collaborative development of international digital competencies education platforms; for example, Code Club provides training materials for educators and volunteers around the world to teach children to code, in collaboration with institutions in over 100 countries (Code Club, 2017).

Finally, fostering PPP in delivering digital skills and building digital infrastructures. PPP can support training provision, infrastructure development, and data facility building. There is also a tendency that the public and private sectors become involved in the delivery of digital skills training and education. Close partnership between government and companies leads to more frequent information and knowledge exchange on digital competencies and thus could narrow the employment gap between the education system and the job market, designing more practical and career-oriented curricula for students. There are examples of large private sector technology companies partnering with the public sector in training programme delivery; these include Apple and Microsoft (UNCTAD, 2017). But more of such partnerships should be encouraged, involving wider participation, instead of the limited corporate social responsibilities programmes of some MNEs.

14.10 Limitations and Areas for Future Research

Although the study tried to be as comprehensive and in-depth as possible, the book still bears some limitations. First, the book uses data from two countries in East and West Africa, respectively, to provide a wider description of the phenomenon. It tries to identify common characteristics and sources of innovation that these countries share. Future research could compare these countries to further understand what economic, institutional and cultural factors underline the differences between the countries identified in this book, in respect to the sources and diffusion process of technologies and the policy implications for other African economies.

Second, although Ghana and Tanzania represent good examples of countries in West and East Africa, and the case study in Kenya brings in another country context and perspective, future research could benefit from including more countries, for example Nigeria, the largest economy on the continent, and a landlocked country such as Uganda or Zimbabwe, to capture the great diversity of the economies in the African continent.

Third, given the country and topic coverage of the book, and the fact that innovation is a system outcome, a thorough understanding of innovation in Africa requires broad and in-depth knowledge of the history, economy, society and evolution of the institutions and policy. Interpretations of some of the results may be constrained by our limited knowledge of the continent, its rich but different histories, and cultural, economic and social diversity.

Fourth, protection of intellectual property provides important incentives to innovators and hence serves as an important driver of innovation. A balanced IPR system is needed to drive innovation in Africa (NPCA, 2014). More research is needed on what type of IP system will achieve this balance that stimulates innovation and encourages technology transfer, and at the same time facilitates the maximum diffusion of the necessary technology to the widest community, so as to enable African countries to achieve the SDGs and greater development.

Fifth, findings from this book suggest that African universities have fallen short in their contributions to the economic development of the continent. What are the reasons that underline such shortfall? What are the roles that African universities can play in the promotion of innovation in the continent? How can policies incentivize and facilitate the university–industry linkage? These are some questions future research could focus on.

Sixth, findings from this book suggest that firms engaged in vertical regional value chains (RVCs) are able to produce not only something of higher quality, but also something that is much more sophisticated that one single firm could not produce otherwise. This suggests that such a vertical RVC may play a significant role in the industry upgrading and diversification in Africa. Therefore, it is important for future research to further investigate the types of such vertical RVCs, and in what industries they are more likely to succeed. How can vertical RVCs be fostered in Africa? What are the roles of the state, the private sector, the MNEs and international organizations in this pursuit?

Finally, findings from the research suggest that firms reported that they have moderate gains from government training programmes and subsidized loans. It will be interesting to further explore whether a combination of these policies, that is, if training when used together with subsidized loans, would offer better results than otherwise. In other words, our understanding of policy packages, including the sequence and the pace and intensity, is still limited in regard to delivering the best innovation results.

Appendix 1 The Diffusion of Innovation in Ghana Survey

▌About This Survey

This questionnaire asks for information relating to innovation activities during the three-year period – 2010 to 2012 inclusive. For the purpose of this survey,

Innovation is defined as major changes aimed at enhancing your competitive position, your performance, your know-how or your capabilities for future enhancements. These can be new or significantly improved goods, services or processes for making or providing them. The innovation (new or improved) must be new to your enterprise, but it does not need to be new to your industry, sector or market. It does not matter if the innovation was originally developed by your enterprise or by other enterprises.

The University of Oxford, working in strong collaboration with the Council for Scientific and Industrial Research, commissioned the Science and Technology Policy Research Institute (CSIR-STEPRI), which is the lead local partner, to perform this survey as part of the Diffusion of Innovation in Low Income Countries Project.

▌Confidentiality

All information gathered by this survey will be held in strictest confidence. Under no circumstances will the STEPRI, Oxford University or the DILIC project publish, release or disclose any information on, or identifiable with, **individual** firms or business units.

▌Scope

The statistical unit for the survey is the **enterprise**. An enterprise refers to a unit that has autonomy in decision making regarding innovation and can range from a very small concern with only one or two employees to a much larger and more formal business or firm.

Screen Questions

[To be filled beforehand by the survey assistant – check the company name, industry and number of employees at the start of the interview.]

Interview Details

Company ID	
Company name	
City/region	
Sector (see code below)	

Industry Code (SIC Codes 1987 – www.osha.gov/pls/imis/sic_manual.html) TO BE EXPANDED

Food processing		Lumber And Wood Products	24
Meat Products	201	Chemicals	28
Dairy Products	202	Rubber And Miscellaneous Plastics Products	
Canned, Frozen, And Preserved Fruits, Vegetables, and Food Specialties	203	Tires And Inner Tubes	301
Grain Mill Products	204	Rubber And Plastics Footwear	302
Bakery Products	205	Gaskets, Packing, And Sealing Devices And Rubber	305
Sugar And Confectionery Products	206	Fabricated Rubber Products, Not Elsewhere	306
Fats And Oils	207	Miscellaneous Plastics Products	308
Beverages	208	Non-metallic mineral products	26
Miscellaneous Food Preparations And Kindred	209	Basic metals	27
Textile Mill Products		Electronics	36
Broad woven Fabric Mills, Cotton	221	Machinery and equipment	35
Broad woven Fabric Mills, Manmade Fibre And Silk	222	Other manufacturing	2
Broad woven Fabric Mills, Wool (including Dyeing and Finishing)	223	Construction	15
Narrow Fabric And Other Smallwares Mills, Cotton, Wool, Silk, and Manmade Fibre	224		
Knitting Mills	225	Wholesale trade	
Dyeing And Finishing Textiles, Except Wool Fabrics	226	Wholesale Trade-durable Goods	50
Carpets And Rugs	227	Wholesale Trade-non-durable Goods	51

(cont.)

Food processing		Lumber And Wood Products	24
Yarn And Thread Mills	228	Finance, Insurance, And Real Estate	6
Miscellaneous Textile Goods	229	Services	7
Apparel And Other Finished Products Made From Fabrics And Similar Materials			
Men's And Boys' Suits, Coats, And Overcoats	231		
Men's And Boys' Furnishings, Work Clothing, And Allied Garments	232		
Women's, Misses', And Juniors' Outerwear	233		
Women's, Misses', Children's, And Infants'	234		
Hats, Caps, And Millinery	235		
Girls', Children's, And Infants' Outerwear	236		
Fur Goods	237		
Miscellaneous Apparel And Accessories	238		
Miscellaneous Fabricated Textile Products	239		

Part 1.General Information About Your Enterprise

1. When was the enterprise registered (*year of registration*)?	

	2010	2012
2. Number of Employees		
3. Turnover	GH₵	GH₵
4. Fixed Asset	GH₵	GH₵

5. Approximately what percentage of your total employees had a university degree or diploma in 2010?	%
6. Approximately what percentage of your total employees had a technical specialization degree in 2010?	%

	Yes	No
7. Is formal training provided for any occupational groups?	☐	☐
8. Is on-the-job informal training provided for any occupational groups?	☐	☐
9. Is the firm a sub-contractor?	☐	☐
10. Is the firm part of a company group?	☐	☐
11. Is your firm invested by a foreign investor?	☐	☐

⌐→ 11. A. If yes, which country? _____

12. Infrastructure: Does the establishment have any of the following facilities?	Yes	No
A. Access to public electricity grid	☐	☐
B. Access to an electricity generator	☐	☐
C. Access to public provided water system	☐	☐
D. Access to borehole water	☐	☐
E. Access to landline telephone	☐	☐
F. Access to mobile phone	☐	☐
G. Access to internet connectivity	☐	☐

13. Did the establishment, during the past year, experience the following?	Often	Seldom	Never
A. Insufficient power for production	☐	☐	☐
B. Insufficient water supply for production	☐	☐	☐
C. Unstable internet connection	☐	☐	☐

	Not competitive	Moderate competitive	Competitive	Very competitive	Extremely competitive
14. How do you perceive the competition in the core business sector that your firm works?	☐	☐	☐	☐	☐

	Yes	No
15. Is the firm an active member of an association (AGI, sectorial association, etc.)?	☐	☐

PART 2: Innovation Activities

A. Product (Goods or Services) Innovation

A product innovation is the introduction to market of a <u>new</u> or <u>significantly improved</u> <u>good or service</u> with respect to its capabilities, such as improved user-friendliness, components, software or sub-systems.

	Yes	Is it new to the world (1) or to Ghana (2) or to your firm (3)?	No
16. During the three years from 2010 to 2012, did your enterprise introduce new or significantly improved goods or services?	☐ ➡		☐

17. Using the definitions above, please estimate the percentage of your total turnover in 2012:	2012 turnover distribution (tot must be 100%)
A. Goods and service innovations introduced during 2010 to 2012 that were **new to your market**	%
B. Goods and service innovations introduced during 2010 to 2012 that were only **new to your firm**	%
C. Goods and services that were unchanged or only marginally modified during 2010 to 2012	%

B. Process Innovation

Process innovation is the use or implementation of <u>new</u> or <u>significantly improved</u> process or method for the production or distribution of goods or services or supporting activity.

18. During the three years 2010 to 2012, did your enterprise introduce any:	Yes	Is it new to the world (1) or to Ghana (2) or to your firm (3)?	No
A. New or significantly improved methods of manufacturing or producing goods or services?	☐ ➡		☐
B. New or significantly improved logistics, delivery or distribution methods for your inputs, goods or service?	☐ ➡		☐
C. New or significantly improved supporting activities for your processes, such as maintenance and operating systems for purchasing, accounting or computing?	☐ ➡		☐

C. Management and Marketing Innovation

A management innovation refers to the *implementation of a new management method in the firm's business practices, workplace organisation or external relations* in firm structure or management methods that are intended to improve your firm's use of knowledge, the quality of your goods and services or the efficiency of work flows.

A marketing innovation is the *'Implementation of a new marketing method involving significant changes in product design or packaging, product placement, product promotion or pricing'* or sales methods to increase the appeal of your goods and services or to enter new markets.

19. During the three years 2010 to 2012, did your enterprise introduce some of the following management and marketing innovations:	Yes	Is it new to the world (1), or to Ghana (2)?	No
A. Business management practices New management practices (i.e. supply chain management, business re-engineering, knowledge management, lean production, quality management, first use of alliances, partnerships, outsourcing or subcontracting, etc.). Exclude routine upgrades.	☐ ⟶		☐
B. Human resource management practices New methods of human resource management (i.e. team work, decentralisation, empowerment, performance related pay, training systems)	☐ ⟶		☐
C. New marketing practices E.g., Significant changes to the aesthetic design or packaging of a good or service, new methods of product promotion, use of e-business, new methods of pricing	☐ ⟶		☐

PART 3: *Internal and Domestic Sources of Innovation*

20. **Did these innovations originate during the three years 2010 to 2012 mainly in Ghana?**	Yes	No
A. Ghana	☐	☐
B. ECOWAS sub-Regions	☐	☐
C. Rest of Africa	☐	☐
D. Europe	☐	☐
E. United States	☐	☐
F. China and India	☐	☐
G. Other countries	☐	☐
I. Do not know	☐	☐

21. **How does this innovation become real? Please tick all that apply.**	
A. The product or process was mainly developed within the enterprise.	☐
B. Your company has a research and development department. Scientists and engineers working in this R&D department created it.	☐
C. Technicians in your companies created this as a solution to a problem that constrains the production or competitiveness of the company.	☐
D. Skilled workers in the company find out a better way for the production process after some experiments.	☐
E. You modified the product in response to customers' requirement.	☐
F. Your enterprise adapted or modified goods or services originally developed by other enterprises or institutions	☐
G. Your enterprise created it together with other enterprises or institutions:	
With supplier	☐
With customer	☐
With other firm in the industry	☐
With universities and research institution	☐
With other firm in the same company group	☐
H. Your firm acquired technology originally developed by others by licensing and adapted or modified it.	☐
I. Your firm acquired technology originally developed by others by licensing without any adaptation and modification.	☐

346   The Diffusion of Innovation in Ghana Survey

(cont.)

J. Your firm observed or heard new products or production process or new ways or new ways of organising production and marketing by other companies and imitate it directly.	☐
K. Your firm observed or heard new products or production process or new ways of organising production and marketing by other companies and imitate it with some modification.	☐
L. Other_____	

22. During the three years 2010 to 2012, how important to your enterprise's innovation activities were each of the following information sources?		Degree of importance (Insignificant=1, Crucial = 5)				
		1	2	3	4	5
Internal sources	A. Sources within your enterprise (colleagues)	☐	☐	☐	☐	☐
	B. Sources within your group (if you have subsidiary or associated companies)	☐	☐	☐	☐	☐
Network	C. Member of cluster	☐	☐	☐	☐	☐
	D. Member of associations	☐	☐	☐	☐	☐
Market resources	E. Suppliers of equipment, materials, components or software	☐	☐	☐	☐	☐
	F. Clients or customers	☐	☐	☐	☐	☐
	G. Competitors or other enterprises in your sector	☐	☐	☐	☐	☐
	H. Consultants, commercial labs or private R&D institutes	☐	☐	☐	☐	☐
Institutional sources	I. National universities or other higher education institutions	☐	☐	☐	☐	☐
	J. Government or public research institutes	☐	☐	☐	☐	☐
Other sources	K. Radio	☐	☐	☐	☐	☐
	L. Internet	☐	☐	☐	☐	☐
	M. Conferences, trade fairs, exhibitions	☐	☐	☐	☐	☐
	N. Scientific journals and trade/ technical publications	☐	☐	☐	☐	☐
	O. Professional and industry associations	☐	☐	☐	☐	☐

Collaboration and Innovation

	Yes	No
23. During the three years 2008 to 2010, did your enterprise co-operate on any of your innovation activities with other enterprises or institutions? It is active participation. Exclude pure contracting out of work with no active co-operation.	☐	☐
		Go to Q. 27

24. Please indicate the type/s of co-operation partner and location. Please tick all that apply.	Ghana	ECOWAS	Rest of Africa	Europe	USA	China and India	Other countries	Not collaborated
A. Other enterprises within your enterprise group	☐	☐	☐	☐	☐	☐	☐	☐
B. Suppliers of equipment, materials, components or software	☐	☐	☐	☐	☐	☐	☐	☐
C. Clients or customers	☐	☐	☐	☐	☐	☐	☐	☐
D. Competitors or other enterprises in your sector	☐	☐	☐	☐	☐	☐	☐	☐
E. Consultants, commercial labs or private R&D institutes	☐	☐	☐	☐	☐	☐	☐	☐
F. Universities or other higher education institutions	☐	☐	☐	☐	☐	☐	☐	☐
G. Government or public research institutes (e.g. Research councils)	☐	☐	☐	☐	☐	☐	☐	☐

25. Which type of co-operation partner was the most valuable for your enterprise's innovation activities?
Give corresponding letter from above. For example, clients or customers = 'C'

26. If you have engaged in direct collaboration with foreign partners for innovation, what were the reasons for choosing a foreign partner? Please tick all that apply.	
A. The technology you need is not available in Ghana.	☐
B. We are part of an international marketing/business alliance.	☐
C. We are in the same industry and share same ambition, so we approached each other.	☐
D. Our foreign customer/supplier recommended it to us.	☐
E. The collaborator is a relative or a former friend of one of the key staff of your company.	☐
F. It is forged by an international aid or international collaboration project.	☐
G. Foreignness does not make any difference.	☐
H. Other reason. Please specify _____	

Universities and Innovation

27. If you have NOT collaborated with universities, why? Please tick all that apply.	
A. We do not have such need.	☐
B. They are not interested.	☐
C. We are not connected.	☐

	Yes	No
28. Do you have the intention to collaborate with universities?	☐	☐

	Yes	No
29. Has/Would government funding been/be useful to bring you together?	☐	☐
30. Has/Would government information provision of compatible university departments/staff been/be useful?	☐	☐

31. If you have collaborated with a university outside Africa, why do you choose it? Please give corresponding letter from Q. 25. For example, 'technology you need is not available in Ghana' = 'A'	

SMEs Network / Clusters and Relationship to Innovation

	Yes	No
32. Is your firm located in a cluster consisting of small firms producing similar products?	☐	☐

Go to Q. 34

33. What are the benefits from being a member of a cluster? Please tick all that apply.	
A. Easier to exchange or get relevant production and technology information	☐
B. We can divide the labour. Each firm specialises in producing one or a few parts/components and then another firm in the cluster assemble all the parts/components into final product	☐
C. It provides a pool for resources	☐
D. Easier to collaborate in innovation	☐
E. Easier to collaborate in pricing	☐
F. Availability of specialist service and equipment providers	☐
G. Joint programs to raise skills and enhance efficiency	☐
H. Work sharing	☐

	Yes	No
34. Is your firm a part of a vertical production chain consisting of SMEs?	☐	☐

Go to Q. 38

	Your region	Ghana	ECOWAS	Africa	Globally
35. Where is the network mainly located?	☐	☐	☐	☐	☐

	Yes	No
36. Is such a network formed to produce something that firms in the country would otherwise not be able to produce?	☐	☐
37. Is such a network formed to make existing products cheaper or better quality?	☐	☐

Part 4. Foreign Sources of Knowledge and Innovation

38. During the three years 2010 to 2012, how important to your enterprise's innovation activities were each of the following foreign knowledge sources?		Degree of importance (Insignificant=1, Crucial = 5)				
		1	2	3	4	5
Technology transaction	A. Foreign technology acquired through licensing	☐	☐	☐	☐	☐
Trade and value chain	B. Imported goods in the same industry	☐	☐	☐	☐	☐
	C. Imported goods that input as intermediary goods into your production	☐	☐	☐	☐	☐
	D. Imported machinery and equipment	☐	☐	☐	☐	☐
	E. Observing and imitating competitors in export market	☐	☐	☐	☐	☐
	F. New product or quality requirement raised by customers in export market	☐	☐	☐	☐	☐
	G. Knowledge transferred from foreign suppliers	☐	☐	☐	☐	☐
	H. Knowledge transferred from foreign customers in export market	☐	☐	☐	☐	☐
Foreign invested firms in Ghana	I. Foreign firms in the same industry	☐	☐	☐	☐	☐
	J. In upstream industry	☐	☐	☐	☐	☐
	K. In downstream industry	☐	☐	☐	☐	☐
Innovation Collaboration	L. Foreign research institutions & universities	☐	☐	☐	☐	☐
	M. Foreign competitors	☐	☐	☐	☐	☐
	N. Foreign suppliers	☐	☐	☐	☐	☐
	O. Foreign customers	☐	☐	☐	☐	☐
Labour mobility	P. Returnees employed in your firm	☐	☐	☐	☐	☐
	Q. Foreign workers/managers employed in your firm	☐	☐	☐	☐	☐
	R. Local workers who have worked in MNEs before	☐	☐	☐	☐	☐
Social networks	S. Relatives or friends working/living abroad	☐	☐	☐	☐	☐
Standards and internet	T. Information found via internet	☐	☐	☐	☐	☐
	U. International standards that your firm has to meet	☐	☐	☐	☐	☐
Short term foreign visit & Internet	V. Visits to foreign production sites	☐	☐	☐	☐	☐
	W. Attending international trade fairs	☐	☐	☐	☐	☐

39. How important are the following factors in ensuring success in adopting a foreign innovation?	Degree of importance (Insignificant=1, Crucial = 5)				
	1	2	3	4	5
A. Adaptation of the technology to be used in your firm	☐	☐	☐	☐	☐
B. Capacity to carry out the adaptation needed	☐	☐	☐	☐	☐
C. Assistance from the supplier for the adaptation	☐	☐	☐	☐	☐
D. Assistance from the Ghanaian universities and public research institutions for the adaptation	☐	☐	☐	☐	☐

PART 5: Impact of Innovation

Objectives of innovation

40. How important were each of the following objectives for your products (goods or services) and process innovations introduced during the three years 2010 to 2012?	Importance of objectives Tick "Not relevant" if there were no innovation objectives.			
	Low	Medium	High	Not relevant
A. Increase range of goods or services	☐	☐	☐	☐
B. Replace outdated products or processes	☐	☐	☐	☐
C. Enter new markets	☐	☐	☐	☐
D. Increase market share	☐	☐	☐	☐
E. Improve quality of goods or services	☐	☐	☐	☐
F. Improve flexibility for producing goods or services	☐	☐	☐	☐
G. Increase capacity for producing goods and services	☐	☐	☐	☐
H. Reduce production (labour, materials, energy) costs per unit output	☐	☐	☐	☐
I. Improve working conditions on health and safety	☐	☐	☐	☐
J. Improve supervision and accountability	☐	☐	☐	☐

Impact of Innovations

41. How important or successful were each of the following types of outcomes for your products (goods or services) and process innovations introduced during the three years 2010 to 2012?		Level of success of outcomes Tick "Not relevant" if there were no innovation outcomes.			
		Low	Medium	High	Not relevant
Product oriented effects	A. Increased range of goods or services	☐	☐	☐	☐
	B. Entered new markets	☐	☐	☐	☐
	C. Increased market share	☐	☐	☐	☐
	D. Improved quality of goods or services	☐	☐	☐	☐
	E. Started to export	☐	☐	☐	☐
	F. Expanded export volumes or to new market	☐	☐	☐	☐
Process oriented effects	G. Improved flexibility of production or service provision	☐	☐	☐	☐
	H. Increased capacity of production or service provision	☐	☐	☐	☐
	I. Reduced production costs per unit of labour, materials, energy	☐	☐	☐	☐
Organisational oriented effects	J. Reduced organisational costs	☐	☐	☐	☐
	K. Increased management efficiency	☐	☐	☐	☐
	L. Improved supervision and accountability	☐	☐	☐	☐
Marketing oriented effects	M. Targeted new customers	☐	☐	☐	☐
	N. Entered new geographical markets	☐	☐	☐	☐
Other effects	O. Reduced environmental impacts	☐	☐	☐	☐
	P. Improved working conditions on health and safety	☐	☐	☐	☐
	Q. Met governmental regulatory requirements	☐	☐	☐	☐
	R. Used less energy or generated less pollution.	☐	☐	☐	☐

PART 6: Constraints to Innovation

42. During the three years 2010 to 2012, were any of your innovation activities or projects:	Yes	No	If yes, the main reason is
A. Abandoned in the concept stage	☐	☐	

| B. Abandoned after the activity or project was begun | ☐ | ☐ | |

| C. Seriously delayed | ☐ | ☐ | |

43. During the three years 2010 to 2012, how important were the following factors in hampering your innovation activities or projects or influencing a decision not to innovate?		Degree of importance (Insignificant=1, Crucial = 5 . 00=Irrelevant)					
		1	2	3	4	5	00
Cost factors	A. Lack of funds within your enterprise or group	☐	☐	☐	☐	☐	☐
	B. Lack of finance from sources outside your enterprise	☐	☐	☐	☐	☐	☐
	C. Innovation costs too high	☐	☐	☐	☐	☐	☐
	D. Excessive perceived economic risks	☐	☐	☐	☐	☐	☐
Knowledge factors	E. Lack of qualified personnel	☐	☐	☐	☐	☐	☐
	F. Lack of information on technology	☐	☐	☐	☐	☐	☐
	G. Lack of information on markets	☐	☐	☐	☐	☐	☐
	H. Difficulty in finding co-operation partners for innovation	☐	☐	☐	☐	☐	☐
Market factors	I. Market dominated by established enterprises	☐	☐	☐	☐	☐	☐
		☐	☐	☐	☐	☐	☐

(cont.)

Other factors	J. Uncertain demand for innovative goods or services						
	K. Innovation is easy to imitate	☐	☐	☐	☐	☐	☐
	L. Little competition in the market and hence no need to innovate	☐	☐	☐	☐	☐	☐
	M. Too much competition in the market and too low perceived return of innovation investment	☐	☐	☐	☐	☐	☐
	N. Organisational rigidities within the enterprise	☐	☐	☐	☐	☐	☐
	O. Little reward for innovation in the firm. Workers do not have the incentive to innovate.	☐	☐	☐	☐	☐	☐
	P. Insufficient flexibility of regulations or standards	☐	☐	☐	☐	☐	☐
	Q. Limitations of science and technology public policies	☐	☐	☐	☐	☐	☐
	R. Weak intellectual property rights protection	☐	☐	☐	☐	☐	☐
No need to innovate	S. No need due to prior innovations	☐	☐	☐	☐	☐	☐
	T. No need because of no demand for innovations	☐	☐	☐	☐	☐	☐
Other	U. Other_____						

PART 7: Policies

	Yes	No
44. Did you take advantage of training opportunities from the Governments during the three years 2010 to 2012?	☐	☐

A. If yes, how beneficial was for you? (Not beneficial = 1, Highly beneficial = 5)	

	Did not know it	Applied but did not get it	Too much paperwork
B. If no, why?	☐	☐	☐

	Yes	No
45. Did you take advantage of Subsidized rate loans from the Governments during the three years 2010 to 2012?	☐	☐

A. If yes, how beneficial was for you? (Not beneficial = 1, Highly beneficial = 5)	

	Did not know it	Applied but did not get it	Too much paperwork
B. If no, why?	☐	☐	☐

46. Please rate the perceived importance of the following policy measures for enhancement of innovation capabilities of Ghanaian firms, and the relative implementation in Ghana	Importance (1–5, 5= excellent)	Implementation in Ghana (1–5, 5=excellent. 0=not relevant)
Provide fiscal subsidies		
Allow free tax in export and duties		
Impose higher duties for imported products		
Develop high tech industrial development zone		
Lower corporate taxes		
Provide cheaper interest loans		
Government procurement		
Open the economy to foreign competition and increase competition		
Gov. funding schemes, e.g. the Micro, Small and Medium Enterprise (MSME) Project of the Ministry of Trade and Industry		
Government funding scheme, e.g., The Venture Capital Trust Fund.		

Part 8. Information About Your Firm's Management

47. Please tell us some information about your Managing Director	
A. Level of education	
B. Gender	
C. Age group *(19–25, 26–35, 36–50, over 50)*	
D. Tenure in post *(number of years)*	
E. Tenure in company *(number of years)*	
F. Does the firm's owner own and run other businesses?	
G. Is the firm owned by a single person or does it have multiple owners?	
H. What is the nationality of the largest shareholder?	
I. If multiple ownership, percentage of the largest owner/shareholder?	
J. Is the managing director the owner or largest shareholder of your firm?	

48 Has your firm adopted the following management practices?	Yes	No
A. A written plan	☐	☐
B. A written plan for innovation	☐	☐
C. Performance related pay	☐	☐
D. Clear reward arrangement for adopting/creating any innovation	☐	☐
E. Strategic decision made by a committee or the board of directors	☐	☐
F. Strategic decision made by the managing director alone	☐	☐
G. Total quality management	☐	☐
H. Job rotation	☐	☐

49 Please rate how much you agree/ disagree with each statement below	Degree of importance (Disagree strongly =1, Agree strongly = 5,)					Do not know (00)
	1	2	3	4	5	
A. I plan tasks carefully	☐	☐	☐	☐	☐	
B. I make up my mind quickly	☐	☐	☐	☐	☐	
C. I will pursue my goal despite many failures and oppositions	☐	☐	☐	☐	☐	
D. I am well organised and good at multi-tasking	☐	☐	☐	☐	☐	
E. I browse internet a lot and like to meet new people	☐	☐	☐	☐	☐	
F. I am fully prepared to take risk	☐	☐	☐	☐	☐	
G. I am always optimistic about my future	☐	☐	☐	☐	☐	
H. A person can get rich by taking risks	☐	☐	☐	☐	☐	

Appendix 2 Technical Appendix[*]

Preparatory work and data collection spanned a period of eleven months (February 2013–January 2014). It involved eight stages:
- In-depth case study
- Questionnaire design and survey instruments
- Sampling frame
- Recruitment and training of enumerators
- Pilot survey
- Survey and monitoring
- Firm replacement protocol

In-depth Interview

A preliminary study was conducted between February and March 2013 to collect in-depth case studies about firms' responses to the constraints on innovation, and how and when innovation policies can overcome these barriers. This guided the research team in the sample frame and the designing of the questionnaire. In the preliminary study, a total of ten firms were surveyed and thirty-two in-depth interviews were carried out among managers from different divisions and workers. The firms were selected across sectors and categories. These sectors were garment and textiles, food processing and construction. Under each sector, firms were selected from both the formal and informal sectors, four from the textile and food sectors, and two from the construction business. To capture the different nature of innovation, for the textile and food sector, two firms were selected under a formal setting, and two from the informal sector. The firms were selected using a purposive sampling technique to identify and approach innovative firms. We selected textile, food processing and construction firms from the Association of Ghana Industries database, which, in a previous Innovation Survey in Ghana, had identified themselves as innovators. Amongst the subsample, we then randomly selected the firms to visit. This allowed us to approach only innovative firms.

[*] Part of this technical appendix that relates to DILIC project stage 1 was drafted by Giacomo Zanello, as part of DILIC survey report.

The data was collected through in-depth interviews. The interviews covered four main dimensions: innovation activities, process of innovation, barriers to innovation transmission and space for innovation policies. The interviews were recorded and later transcribed. On occasion, some relevant findings came out during informal discussion with the respondents – before or after the interview. In order to have a comprehensive understanding of the nature and constraints to innovation, interviewees included a range of actors: senior managers, departmental managers (production, marketing and human resources), R&D staff, technicians and workers. For the firms in the informal sectors, the managers and workers were the main source of information since those firms did not have complex functional departments.

Questionnaire Design and Survey Instruments

The design of the survey was based on previous innovation surveys and tailored to the Ghanaian environment, based on the findings from the in-depth interviews and discussion with key local policymakers.

The data were collected with the aid of a personal digital assistant (PDA). PDAs are increasingly used for data collection in developing countries and bring several benefits. The use of PDAs supports the work of enumerators, allowing them to code consistency checks during the interview and systematic skips. Since the data is already entered in a digital format, no other data entry is needed, which saves time and, as a system, is less prone to mistakes. However, PDAs bring some disadvantages compared to paper-based surveys, mainly in terms of the reliability of the devices and the computer skills needed to use them. We took extensive precautions to mitigate these potential drawbacks. The devices we used had already been used in previous data collections and their reliability in terms of battery life and failures had already been tested. Besides the extensive training of the enumerators, we also put in place a protocol to make sure data were constantly backed up and devices constantly charged. In the whole survey, we did not experience any PDA failure at all and no data were lost.

Sampling Frame

We use a different sampling framework for formal and informal firms. The rationale for this hinges on the fact that informal firms may not be recorded on databases for official firms, and therefore we could have under-represented the whole informal sector. We therefore sampled half of the sample from sources that were likely to mainly capture informal firms, and the other half from sources containing mainly formal firms.

Table A.1 *Cluster details (region and sector)*

Region	Sector
Greater Accra	Handicraft producers
Greater Accra	Sawmill
Greater Accra	Metal working
Greater Accra	Mushroom production
Greater Accra	Garment and textiles
Ashanti	Wood workers
Ashanti	Automotive industry and metal working
Central	Garment and textile
Eastern	Palm oil processors
Northern	Shea butter production

For informal firms, we randomly sampled twenty-five firms in ten clusters spread in five regions. Cluster activities ranged from the food and textile sectors to metal and wood working (Table A.1). The choice of clusters and regions was determined by the need to have a sectoral and geographical representation of the Ghanaian informal economy.

We compiled a comprehensive population of firms from which we drew the sample of the formal firms. Three main sources were used:
- The latest available National Industrial Census (2003) by the Ghana Statistical Service
- The Micro, Small and Medium Enterprises database from the Ministry of Trade and Industry
- The D&B database of Ghanaian firms
- The list of members of the Association of Ghana Industries (AGI)

The lists of firms from the different sources were merged and the duplicated firms removed. A total of 4,658 firms were included. The sample was then randomly selected with three levels of stratification: industry sector, size and regional location (see Table A.2, Table A.3 and Table A.4).

The 2nd Round of Survey in Ghana and Tanzania The 2nd round of survey carried out in 2015 used the same sampling framework in Ghana. We have included 498 firms in the survey carried out in Ghana in 2015.

In Tanzania, it was possible to collect information for 278 formal and informal firms in 2015. For the sampling method for the formal sector, the following industries were selected for the survey: food processing & beverages, textile and apparel, plastic and rubber, metal application wood

Table A.2 *Geographical distribution of the firms in the sample*

	Full Sample	Informal	Formal
Greater Accra	249	159	90
Ashanti Region	104	69	35
Brong-Ahafo Region	8	0	8
Central Region	42	27	15
Eastern Region	41	34	7
Northern Region	34	26	8
Upper East Region	4	0	4
Upper West Region	2	0	2
Volta Region	8	6	2
Western Region	10	0	10

Table A.3 *Sectorial distribution of the firms in the sample*

	Full Sample	Informal	Formal
Manufacture of food products	124	90	34
Manufacture of beverages	2	0	2
Manufacture of textiles	23	15	8
Manufacture of wearing apparel	102	52	50
Manufacture of leather and related products	1	1	0
Manufacture of wood and of products of wood and cork	51	36	15
Manufacture of paper and paper products	10	0	10
Printing and reproduction of recorded materials	9	4	5
Manufacture of chemicals and chemical products	1	1	0
Manufacture of basic pharmaceutical products	1	0	1
Manufacture of rubber and plastics products	8	0	8
Manufacture of fabricated metal products	65	45	20
Manufacture of electrical equipment	2	2	0
Manufacture of machinery and equipment	1	0	1
Manufacture of furniture	74	51	23
Other manufacturing	5	4	1
Repair and installation of machinery	21	20	1
Construction of buildings	2	0	2

industry, construction, pharmaceutical, chemicals and ICT. The population of the study includes all manufacturing firms within the selected sectors that are located in Tanga and Dar es Salaam. The information on the population was drawn from various sources, such as the National Bureau of Statistics (NBS), Business Registration and Licensing Agency (BRELA) and the Confederation Tanzanian Industries (CTI).

Table A.4 *Size distribution of the firms in the sample*

	Total sample	Informal	Formal
Micro (< 9 empl.)	367	269	99
Small (10–29 empl.)	86	48	38
Medium (30–99 empl.)	21	4	17
Large (> 99 empl.)	27	0	27

Sampling selection process for the formal sectors was done by stratification by region and by industry, so as to get a representative sample. However, there was one exception. The pharmaceutical sector is very small in Tanzania; we therefore included all industries that we had in the population.

For the sampling method for the informal sector, we randomly selected clusters in the identified sectors that will be surveyed, and will interview a total of 100 firms in the identified clusters.

Recruitment and Training of Enumerators

Ten enumerators were recruited and trained specifically for data collection. The enumerators were selected from Science and Technology Policy Research Institute (STEPRI) staff or were derived from those who had previous experience of data collection in other projects coordinated by STEPRI. In designing the enumerator team, we made sure enumerators were able to speak local languages.

The purpose of the training was to impart skills to the enumerators, particularly to explain the concepts and terms of the survey and the use of the PDA. It was also to train the enumerators in the process of data collection. The training was facilitated by a team of Research Officers from Oxford University and STEPRI. During the three-day training, the facilitators reviewed the questionnaire with the enumerators, offering a platform for the enumerators to interact with facilitators to allow for a possible review of the questionnaire. The enumerators were also taken through the use of the PDAs and were allowed to conduct mock interviews with PDAs to familiarize themselves with the PDA and build their confidence in using PDAs. A discussion of the results from the mock interview was held to help review the questionnaire.

The enumerators were evaluated through a short written test to find out their level of understanding of the survey terms and concepts. The results of the test were critically examined. The enumerators who needed further assistance were given the needed support.

Pilot Survey

In September 2013, a pilot survey was conducted to ensure that the survey design and materials would capture the data necessary to meet the survey objectives. A sample of fifty firms was chosen from the sampled firms located in the Greater Accra Region, and each enumerator surveyed five firms, with a mix of formal and informal firms. The data from the pilot were then analysed and feedback from the enumerators collected. We did not find any major issues, and only minor changes to the coded questionnaire in the PDA were made.

Survey and Monitoring

The data collection of DILIC Stage 1 spanned a period of seven weeks, from Nov. 2013 to Jan. 2014. During this period, survey managers visited several locations (Greater Accra, Eastern region, Ashanti region and Central region) to monitor the progress of the data collection and support the work of the enumerators. The data were downloaded from the PDAs every week and analysed for consistency checks. In a few cases, the enumerators re-visited the firms to double-check the reliability of the data. Most of those instances involved unreliable data or data entry mistakes on the number of employees, turnover or fixed asset variables.

The data collection of DILIC Stage 2 was carried out in Ghana at the end of 2015 and in Tanzania in early 2016.

Firm Replacement Protocol

A third of the firms originally sampled needed to be replaced (Table A.5). Most of those could not be located by the enumerators (24 per cent), others had closed down (8 per cent), and a few firms were not willing to participate in the survey (1 percent). Firms, often, are located in part of cities that do not have street names, and tracking down their exact location can be a challenge. This is the case for most small and informal businesses. During the development, firms may also change location and name, or sometimes move to a different business.

Table A.5 *Total number of firms replaced*

Reasons for replacement	Number of firms	Percentage (%)
Cannot be located	122	24.4
Closed down	38	7.6
Uncooperative	5	1.0
Total	165	33.0

The replacement firms were randomly selected from among the firms working in the same sector and region, and with the same size as the missing firms.

References

Abereijo, I. O., Ilori, M. O., Taiwo, K. A. and Adegbite, S. A. (2007). Assessment of the capabilities for innovation by small and medium industry in Nigeria. *African Journal of Business Management*, 1, 209–217.

Abor, J., Adjasi, C. K. D. and Hayford, M.-C. (2008). How does foreign direct investment affect the export decisions of firms in Ghana? *African Development Review*, 20, 446–465.

Abu-Ghaida, D. and Klasen, S. (2004). The costs of missing the Millennium Development Goals on gender equity. *World Development*, 32(7), 1075–1107.

Acemoglu, D. (2002). Directed technical change. *Review of Economic Studies*, 69 (4), 781–810.

Acs, Z. J., Anselin, L. and Varga, A. (2002). Patents and innovation counts as measures of regional production of new knowledge. *Research Policy*, 31(7), 1069–1086.

Adamides, E. D. and Karacapilidis, N. (2006). Information technology support for the knowledge and social processes of innovation management. *Technovation*, 26(1), 50–59.

ADB. (2013). *Financial Inclusion and Integration through Mobile Payments and Transfer* (Proceedings of Workshop on 'Enhancing Financial Integration through Sound Regulation of Cross-Border Mobile Payments: Opportunities and Challenges'). Tunisia: African Development Bank.

Adeyeye, A. D., Jegede, O. O., Oluwadare, A. J. and Aremu, F. S. (2016). Micro-level determinants of innovation: analysis of the Nigerian manufacturing sector. *Innovation and Development*, 6, 1–14.

AfDB, OECD and UNDP (2014). Global Value Chains and Africa's Industrialisation. African Economic Outlook. Available at www.africaneconomicoutlook.org/fileadmin/uploads/aeo/2014/PDF/E-Book_African_Economic_Outlook_2014.pdf.

African Observatory of Science Technology and Innovation. (2013). Assessing best practices of science, technology and innovation observatories. In AOSTI Working Paper Series. https://knowledge.cta.int/en/content/download/41011/590572/file/Assessing-Best-Practices-of-Science-Technology-and-Innovation-Observatories.pdf

Aggarwal, A. (2000). Deregulation, technology imports and in-house R&D efforts: an analysis of the Indian experience. *Research Policy*, 29, 1081–1093.

Aghion, P. and Jaravel, X. (2015). Knowledge spillovers, innovation and growth. *The Economic Journal*, 125(583), 533–573.

Aghion, P. and Howitt, P. (2009). *The Economics of Growth*, MIT Press.

Aghion, P., Bloom, N., Blundell, R., Griffith, R. and Howitt, P. (2005). Competition and innovation: an inverted-U relationship. *Quarterly Journal of Economics*, 120, 701–728.

Agyapong, F. O., Agyapong, A., Poku, K. and Davis, J. L. (2017). Nexus between social capital and performance of micro and small firms in an emerging economy: the mediating role of innovation. *Cogent Business & Management*, 4, 1309784.

Aikaeli, J. and Mkenda, B. K. (2014). Determinants of informal employment: a case of Tanzania's construction industry. *Botswana Journal of Economics*, 12 (2). DOI:10.2139/ssrn.2706021

Aitken, B. J. and Harrison, A. E. (1999). Do domestic firms benefit from direct foreign investment? Evidence from Venezuela. *American Economic Review*, 89 (3), 605–618.

Aker, J. C. and Mbiti, I. M. (2010). Mobile phones and economic development in Africa. *Journal of Economic Perspectives*, 24(3), 207–232.

Akyuz, Y. and Gore, C. (1996). The investment-profits nexus in East Asian industrialization, *World Development*, 24(3), 461–470.

Allard, G., Martinez, C. A. and Williams, C. (2012). Political instability, pro-business market reforms and their impacts on national systems of innovation. *Research Policy*, 41, 638–651.

Almeida, R. and Fernandes, A. M. (2008). Openness and technological innovations in developing countries: evidence from firm-level surveys. *Journal of Development Studies*, 44, 701–727.

Altenburg, T. (2009). Building inclusive innovation systems in developing countries: challenges for IS research. In *Handbook of Innovation Systems and Developing Countries: Building Domestic Capabilities in a Global Setting* (Lundvall, B.-Å., Joseph, K. J., Chaminade, C. and Vang, J. eds.), pp. 33–56. Cheltenham, UK: Edward Elgar.

Altenburg, T. and Meyer-Stamer, J. (1999). How to promote clusters: policy experiences from Latin America. *World Development*, 27, 1693–1713.

Amankwah-Amoah, J. (2016). The evolution of science, technology and innovation policies: a review of the Ghanaian experience. *Technological Forecasting and Social Change*, 110, 134–142.

Amendolagine, V., Boly, A., Coniglio, N. D., Prota, F. and Seric, A. (2013). FDI and local linkages in developing countries: evidence from sub-Saharan Africa. *World Development*, 50, 41–56.

Amsden, A. (1989). *Asia's Next Giant. South Korea and Late Industrialization*, Oxford: Oxford University Press.

Amsden, A. (2001). *The Rise of 'The Rest'. Challenge to the West from Late-industrializing Economies*, Oxford: Oxford University Press, chapters 1 and 6–10.

Andersson, U., Forsgren, M. and Holm, U. (2002). The strategic impact of external networks: subsidiary performance and competence development in the multinational corporation. *Strategic Management Journal*, 23(11), 979–996.

Anselin, L., Varga, A. and Acs, Z. (1997). Local geographic spillovers between university research and high technology innovations. *Journal of Urban Economics*, 42, 422–448.

Antwi, S. and Zhao, X. (2013). Impact of foreign direct investment and economic growth in Ghana: a cointegration analysis. *International Journal of Business and Social Research*, 3(1), 64–74.

Apple (2017, June 1). Swift Playgrounds. Accessed on 25 September 2017, www .apple.com/uk/swift/playgrounds/

Aralica, Z., Račić, D. and Radić, D. (2008). Innovation propensity in Croatian enterprises: results of a community innovation survey. *South East European Journal of Economics and Business*, 3(1), 77–88.

Archibugi, D. (2001). Pavitt's taxonomy sixteen years on: a review article. *Economics of Innovation and New Technology*, 10(5), 415–425.

Arnold, E. (2004). Evaluating research and innovation policy: a systems world needs systems evaluations. *Research Evaluation*, 13(1), 3–17.

Arup, M., Hawkes, D. and Ugur, M. (2011). *What Is the Impact of Higher Rates of Innovation on Employment in LICs? How Does This Vary by Gender?* p. 53, London: University of Greenwich Business School.

Asiedu, E., Kalonda-Kanyama, I., Ndikumana, L. and Nti-Addae, A. (2013). Access to credit by firms in sub-Saharan Africa: how relevant is gender? *American Economic Review*, 103(3), 293–297.

Asongu, S. A. and Nwachukwu, J. C. (2016). The mobile phone in the diffusion of knowledge for institutional quality in sub-Saharan Africa, *World Development*, 86, 133–147.

Atkinson A. B. and Stiglitz J. E. (1969). A new view of technological change. *Economic Journal*, 79(315), 573–578.

Auffray, C. and Fu, X. (2013). MNEs and managerial knowledge transfer: the case of the construction sector in Ghana. *Journal of Chinese Economic and Business Studies*, 13(4), 285–310.

Auffray, C. and Fu, X. (2015). Chinese MNEs and managerial knowledge transfer in Africa: the case of the construction sector in Ghana. *Journal of Chinese Economic and Business Studies*, 13(4), 285–310.

Aulakh, P. S. (2007). Emerging multinationals from developing economies: motivations, paths and performance. *Journal of International Management*, 13 (3), 235–402.

Autor, D. H. and Dorn, D. (2013, August 24). How Technology Wrecks the Middle Class – *The New York Times*. Accessed on 15 September 2017, https:// opinionator.blogs.nytimes.com/2013/08/24/how-technology-wrecks-the-middle -class/?mcubz=1

Aviram, A. and Eshet-Alkalai, Y. (2006). Towards a theory of digital literacy: three scenarios for the next steps. *European Journal of Open, Distance and E-Learning*, 9(1).

Aw, B. Y. and Hwang, A. R. (1995). Productivity and the export market – a firm-level analysis. *Journal of Development Economics*, 47, 313–332.

Ayyagari, M., Demirguc-Kunt, A. and Maksimovic, V. (2011). Firm innovation in emerging markets: the role of finance, governance, and competition. *Journal of Financial and Quantitative Analysis*, 46, 1545–1580.

Baffes, J. (2002). *Tanzania's Cotton Sector: Constraints and Challenges in a Global Environment*, World Bank.

Bafoutsou, G. and Mentzas, G. (2002). Review and functional classification of collaborative systems. *International Journal of Information Management*, 22(4), 281–305.

Bagachwa, M. S. D. (1992). Choice of technology in small and large firms: grain milling in Tanzania. *World Development*, 20, 97–107.

Bakhshi, H. and Larsen, J. (2005). ICT-specific technological progress in the United Kingdom. *Journal of Macroeconomics*, 27, 648–669.

Balasubramanian, N and Lee, J. (2008). Firm age and innovation. *Industrial and Corporate Change*, 17(5), 1019–1047.

Balasubramanyam, V. N., Salisu, M. and Sapsford, D. (1996). Foreign direct investment and growth in EP and is countries, *The Economic Journal*, 106(434), 92–105.

Baldwin, C., Hienerth, C. and von Hippel, E. (2006). How user innovations become commercial products: a theoretical investigation and case study. *Research Policy*, 35, 1291–1313.

Banerjee, A., Chandrasekhar, A. G., Duflo, E. and Jackson, M. O. (2013). The diffusion of microfinance. *Science*, 341, 1236498. DOI:10.1126/science .1236498

Bardasi, E., Sabarwal, S. and Terrell, K. (2011). How do female entrepreneurs perform? Evidence from three developing regions. *Small Business Economics*, 37, 417–441.

Barro, R. and Sala-i Martin, X. (1997). Technological diffusion, convergence, and growth. *Journal of Economic Growth*, 2(1), 1–26.

Barslund, M., Chiconela, J., Rand, J. and Tarp, F. (2007). Understanding victimization: the case of mozambique. *World Development*, 35(7), 1237–1258.

Bartelsman, E. J. and Doms, M. (2000). Understanding productivity: lessons from longitudinal micro data. *Journal of Economic Literature*, 38(3), 569–594.

Bartz, W., Mohnen, P. and Schweiger, H. (2016). The role of innovation and management practices in determining firm productivity in developing economies. In Working Paper 187. European Bank for Reconstruction and Development, London (UK).

Bashir, T., Khan, K. and Malik, K. (2010). The innovation landscape of Pakistan's North West Frontier Province. *Science and Public Policy*, 37, 181–191.

Basu, S. and Weil, D. N. (1998). Appropriate technology and growth. *Quarterly Journal of Economics*, 113(4), 1025–1054.

Battisti, G. and Stoneman, P. (2010). How innovative are UK firms? Evidence from the Fourth UK Community Innovation Survey on synergies between technological and organizational innovations. *British Journal of Management*, 21(1), 187–206.

Baum, K. (2008). Stata tip 63: modeling proportions. *The Stata Journal*, 8(2), 299–303.

Beason, R. and Weinstein, D. (1996). Growth, economies of scale, and targeting in Japan (1955–1990). *The Review of Economics and Statistics*, 78(2), 286–295.

Bell M. (1984). 'Learning' and the accumulation of industrial technological capacity in developing countries. In *Technological Capability in the Third World*

(Fransman M. and King K. eds.), pp. 178–209. London: Palgrave Macmillan.

Bell, M. and Albu, M. (1999). Knowledge systems and technological dynamism in industrial clusters in developing countries. *World Development*, 27, 1715–1734.

Bell, M. and Pavitt, K. (1992). Accumulating technological capability in developing-countries. *World Bank Economic Review*, 6(1), 257–281.

Bell, M. and Pavitt, K. (1993). Technological accumulation and industrial growth: Contrasts between developed and developing countries. *Industrial and Corporate Change*, 2, 157–210.

Benjamin, N. C. and Mbaye, A. A. (2012). The informal sector, productivity, and enforcement in West Africa: a firm-level analysis. *Review of Development Economics*, 16, 664–680.

Benjamin, N. C. and Mbaye, A. A. (2014). Informality, growth, and development in Africa. UNU-WIDER, Helsinki (Finland). www.wider.unu.edu/publica tion/informality-growth-and-development-africa.

Bergek, A. and Jacobsson, S. (2003). The emergence of a growth industry: a comparative analysis of the German, Dutch and Swedish wind turbine industries. In *Change, Transformation and Development* (Metcalfe, S. and Cantner, U. eds.), pp. 197–227. Heidelberg: Physica-Verlag.

Bergek, A., Jacobsson, S., Carlsson, B., Lindmark, S. and Rickne, A. (2008). Analysing the functional dynamics of technological innovation systems. *A Scheme of Analysis Research Policy*, 37(3), 407–429.

Bhagwat, R. and Sharma, M. K. (2007) Performance measurement of supply chain management: a balanced scorecard approach. *Computers & Industrial Engineering*, 53(1), 43–62.

Bhatti, Y. and Ventresca, M. (2012). The Emerging Market for Frugal Innovation: Fad, Fashion, or Fit? Available at SSRN: http://ssrn.com/abstract=2005983.

Biggart, N. W. and Guillen, M. F. (1999). Developing difference: social organization and the rise of the auto industries of South Korea, Taiwan, Spain, and Argentina. *American Sociological Review*, 64, 722–747.

Black, S. E. and Lynch, L. M. (2001). How to compete: the impact of workplace practices and information technology on productivity. *Review of Economics and Statistics*, 83(3), 434–445.

Blalock, G. and Gertler, P. J. (2008). Welfare gains from foreign direct investment through technology transfer to local suppliers. *Journal of International Economics*, 74, 402–421.

Blalock, G. and Veloso, F. M. (2007). Imports, productivity growth, and supply chain learning. *World Development*, 35, 1134–1151.

Blomström, M. and Kokko, A. (1998). Multinational corporations and spillovers. *Journal of Economic Surveys*, 12, 247–277.

Blomström, M. and Kokko, A. (2001). Foreign direct investment and spillovers of technology. *International Journal of Technology Management*, 22, 435–454.

Bloom, N., Eifert, B., Mahajan, A., McKenzie, D. and Roberts, J. (2013). Does management matter? Evidence from India. *Quarterly Journal of Economics*, 128, 1–51.

Bloom, N., Genakos, C., Sadun, R. and Van Reenen, J. (2012). Management Practices across Firms and Countries. National Bureau of Economic Research, Working Paper 17850, www.nber.org/papers/w17850

Bloom, N., Schankerman, M. and Van Reenen, J. (2013). Identifying technology spillovers and product market rivalry. *Econometrica*, 81(4), 1347–1393.

Blumenthal, T. (1976). Japan's technological strategy. *Journal of Development Economics*, 3, 245–255.

Blundell, R., Dearden, L., Meghir, C. and Sianesi, B. (1999). Human capital investment: the returns from education and training to the individual, the firm and the economy. *Fisc. Stud.*, 20, 1–23.

Boden, R. J., Jr. (1999). Gender inequality in wage earnings and female self-employment selection. *Journal of Socio-Economics*, 28, 351–364.

Bolton, P. and Mathias D. (1994). The firm as a communication network. *The Quarterly Journal of Economics*, 109(4), 809–839.

Bordoff, J. (2016, September 23). How Big Data Changes the Economics of Renewable Energy. Accessed on 14 September 2017, https://blogs.wsj.com/experts/2016/09/23/how-big-data-changes-the-economics-of-renewable-energy/

Borghans, L., Golsteyn, B. H. H., Heckman, J. J. and Meijers, H. (2009). Gender differences in risk aversion and ambiguity aversion. *Journal of the European Economic Association*, 7(2–3), 649–658.

Borrás, S. and Edquist, C. (2013). The choice of innovation policy instruments. *Technological Forecasting and Social Change*, 80, 1513–1522.

Bosire, J. B. (2012). *M-PESA:* Why Kenya? M.A. Thesis (Financial Economics), State University of New York at Buffalo.

Braczyk, H. J., Cooke, P. and Heidenreich, M. (eds.), (1998). *Regional Innovation Systems: The Role of Governance in a Globalized World*, London: UCL Press.

Bradley, S. W., McMullen, J. S., Artz, K. and Simiyu, E. M. (2012). Capital is not enough: innovation in developing economies. *Journal of Management Studies*, 49, 684–717.

Branisa, B., Klasen, S. and Ziegler, M. (2013). Gender inequality in social institutions and gendered development outcomes. *World Development*, 45, 252–268.

Bresnahan, T. F., Brynjolfsson, E. and Hitt, L. M. (2002). Information technology, workplace organization, and the demand for skilled labor: firm-level evidence. *Quarterly Journal of Economics*, 117(1), 339–376.

Bruhn, M., Karlan, D. and Schoar, A. (2010). What capital is missing in developing countries? *American Economic Review: Papers & Proceedings*, 100, 629–633.

Brush, C. G. (1990). Women and enterprise creation: barriers and opportunities, In *Enterprising Women: Local Initiatives for Job Creation* (Gould, S. and Parzen, J. eds.), Paris: OECD.

Brush, C. G. (1992). Research on women business owners: past trends, a new perspective and future directions. *Entrepreneurship Theory and Practice*, 16, 5–30.

Brynjolfsson, E. and Yang, S. (1996). Information technology and productivity: a review of the literature. *Advances in Computers*, 43, 179–214.

Brynjolfsson, E. and McAfee, A. (2011). *Race Against the Machine: How the Digital Revolution is Accelerating Innovation, Driving Productivity, and Irreversibly Transforming Employment and the Economy*, Digital Frontier Press.

Brynjolfsson, E. and McAfee, A. (2014). *The Second Machine Age: Work, Progress, and Prosperity in a Time of Brilliant Technologies*, New York: W. W. Norton.
Brynjolfsson, E. and Hitt, L. M. (2000). Beyond computation: information technology, organizational transformation and business performance. *Journal of Economic Perspectives*, 14(4), 23–48.
Brynjolfsson, E. and Yang, S. (1998). The intangible benefits and costs of computer investments: evidence from the financial markets. *Proceedings of the International Conference on Information Systems*, December 1997, in Atlanta, Georgia.
Brynjolfsson, E. and Hitt, L. M. (1995). Information technology as a factor of production: the role of differences among firms. *Economics of Innovation and New Technology*, 3(3/4), 183–200.
Brynjolfsson, E., Hitt L. M. and Yang, S. (2002). Intangible assets: computers and organizational capital. *Brookings Papers on Economic Activity*, 1, 137–199.
Burke, A. E., FitzRoy, F. R. and Nolan, M. A. (2002). Self- employment wealth and job creation: the roles of gender, non-pecuniary motivation and entrepreneurial ability. *Small Business Economics*, 19, 255–270.
Bwalya, S. M. (2006). Foreign direct investment and technology spillovers: evidence from panel data analysis of manufacturing firms in Zambia. *Journal of Development Economics*, 81, 514–526.
Ca, T. N. (2007). Turning science into business in developing countries: the case of vaccine production in Vietnam. *Journal of Technology Transfer*, 32, 425–434.
Camner, G., Pulver, C. and Sjöblom E. (2009). What Makes a Successful Mobile Money Implementation? Learnings from M-PESA in Kenya and Tanzania. [online]. Sweden: GSMA, p. 3. Accessed 23 October 2017, www.gsma.com/mobilefordevelopment/wpcontent/uploads/2012/03/What-makes-a-success ful-mobile-money-implementation.pdf/
Caniëls, M. C. and Romijn, H. A. (2003a). Firm-level knowledge accumulation and regional dynamics. *Industrial and Corporate Change*, 12(6), 1253–1278.
Caniëls, M. C. and Romijn, H. A. (2003b). Dynamic clusters in developing countries: collective efficiency and beyond. *Oxford Development Studies*, 31(3), 275–292.
Capaldo, A. (2007). Network structure and innovation: the leveraging of a dual network as a distinctive relational capability. *Strategic Management Journal*, 28 (6), 585–608.
Carlsson, B., Jacobsson, S., Holmén, M. and Rickne, A. (2002). Innovation systems: analytical and methodological issues. *Research Policy*, 31, 233–245.
Castiglione, C. (2009). ICT investment and firm technical efficiency. Paper Presented at EWEPA 2010, June, in Pisa, www.semanticscholar.org/paper/IC T-Investments-and-Technical-Efficiency-in-Italian-Castiglione/1126e0aeff6 d647602909ff59a062ce7d339bfba.
CCTV. (2017, May 22). 'Internet+' helps precise poverty alleviation programme in poor village. Accessed on 14 September 2017, http://news.cctv.com/2017/05/22/ARTI8iDKdnyMlN3uu3Rd7R3S170522.shtml
Cerquera, D. and Klein, G. J. (2008). Endogenous firm heterogeneity, ICT and R&D incentives. ZEW Discussion Paper No. 08–126, Mannheim, Germany, https://econpapers.repec.org/paper/zbwzewdip/7516.htm.

Chang, H.-J. and Lin, J. (2009). Should industrial policy in developing countries conform to comparative advantages or defy it? A debate between Justin Lin and Ha-Joon Chang. *Development Policy Review*, 27(5), 483–502.

Change and Economic Theory (Dosi, G. ed.). Francis Pinter, London (UK).

Charles, K. K., Hurst, E. and Notowidigdo, M. J. (2013). Manufacturing decline, housing booms, and non-employment, NBER Working Paper No. 18949, National Bureau of Economic Research, 10.2139/ssrn.2273684.

Chataway, J., Tait, J. and Wield, D. (2006). The governance of agro- and pharmaceutical biotechnology innovation: public policy and industrial strategy. *Technology Analysis & Strategic Management*, 18(2), 169–185.

Chataway, J., Hanlin, R. and Kaplinsky, R. (2013). Inclusive innovation: an architecture for policy development. IKD Working Paper No. 65, http://oro.open.ac.uk/39712/.

Chataway, J., Hanlin, R. and Kaplinsky, R. (2014). Inclusive innovation: an architecture for policy development. *Innovation and Development*, 4(1), 33–54.

Chen K. and Kenney M. (2007). Universities/research institutes and regional innovation systems: the cases of Beijing and Shenzhen. *World Development*, 35(6), 1056–1074.

Chen, C., Watanabe, C. and Griffy-Brown, C. (2007). The co-evolution process of technological innovation–An empirical study of mobile phone vendors and telecommunication service operators in Japan. *Technology in Society*, 29, 1–22.

Chen, J., Guo, Y., Huang, S. and Zhu, H. (2011). The determinants of the choice of innovation source for Chinese firms. *International Journal of Technology Management*, 53, 44–67.

Chen, M., Sebstad, J. and O'Connell, L. (1999). Counting the invisible workforce: the case of homebased workers. *World Development*, 27, 603–610.

Chen, T. and Tang, D. P. (1987). Comparing technical efficiency between import-substitution-oriented and export-oriented foreign firms in a developing-economy. *Journal of Development Economics*, 26, 277–289.

Chesbrough H. (2003). *Open Innovation: The New Imperative for Creating and Profiting from Technology*, Boston, MA: Harvard Business School Press.

Chesbrough, H. and Crowther, A. K. (2006), Beyond high tech: early adopters of open innovation in other industries. *R&D Management*, 36, 229–236.

Chesbrough, H. and Bogers, M. (2014). Explicating open innovation: clarifying an emerging paradigm for understanding innovation. In *New Frontiers in Open Innovation: 3–28* (Chesbrough, H., Vanhaverbeke, W. and West, J. eds.), pp. 3–28. Oxford: Oxford University Press.

Cheung, K. and Ping L. (2004). Spillover effects of FDI on innovation in China: evidence from the provincial data. *China Economic Review*, 15(1), 25–44.

Child, J. (1994). *Management in China during the Age of Reform*, Cambridge, England: Cambridge University Press.

Child, J., Pitkethly, R. and Faulkner, D. (1999). Changes in management practice and the post-acquisition performance achieved by direct investors in the UK. *British Journal of Management*, 10(3), 185–198.

China Science and Technology Information Research Institute (CSTII), (2010). *Statistical data of Chinese Science and Technology Papers*. CSTII, Beijing, China.

Clark, N., Chataway, J., Hanlin, R., Kale, D., Kaplinsky, R., Muraguri, L., Papaioannou, T., Robbins, P. and Wamae, W. (2009). Below the Radar: What Does Innovation in the Asian Driver Economies Have to Offer Other Low-Income Economies. Economic and Social Research Council. Accessed on January 2018, http://oro.open.ac.uk/15241/1/.

Clerides, S. K., Lach, S. and Tybout, J. R. (1998). Is learning by exporting important? Micro-dynamic evidence from Colombia, Mexico, and Morocco. *Quarterly Journal of Economics*, 113, 903–947.

Code Club. (2017, September 25). Countries. Accessed on 25 September 2017, www.codeclubworld.org/about/countries/

Coe, D. T., Helpman, E. and Hoffmaister, A. W. (1997). North-South R&D spillovers. *Economic Journal*, 107, 134–149.

Cohen, W. (2005). Empirical studies of innovative activity. In *Handbook of the Economics of Innovation and Technological Change* (Stoneman, P. ed.), pp. 182–264. Oxford: Blackwell Publishers.

Cohen, W. (2010). Fifty years of empirical studies of innovative activity and performance. In *Handbook of the Economics of Innovation* (Hall, H. B. and Rosenberg, N. eds.), vol. 1. pp. 129–213, Amsterdam: North-Holland, Elsevier.

Cohen, W. M. and Levinthal, D. A. (1990). Absorptive capacity: a new perspective on learning and innovation. *Administrative Science Quarterly*, 35, 128–152.

Cohen, W. M. and Levinthal, D. A. (1989). Innovation and learning: the two faces of R&D. *The Economic Journal*, 99, 569–596.

Cohen, W. M., Nelson, R. R. and Walsh, J. P. (2002). Links and impacts: the influence of public research on industrial R&D. *Management Science*, 48, 1–23.

Cooke, P. (2001). Regional innovation systems, clusters, and the knowledge economy. *Industrial and Corporate Change*, 10(4), 945–974.

Cooper, C. (1989). *Technology and Innovation in International Economy*, The Netherlands: United Nation University Press.

Corrocher, N., Malerba, F. and Montobbio, F. (2007). Schumpeterian patterns of innovative activity in the ICT field. *Research Policy*, 36, 418–432.

Cosh and Hughes (2007). *British Enterprise: Thriving or Surviving? : SME Growth, Innovation and Public Policy 2001–2004*, Cambridge, UK: ESRC Centre for Business Research, University of Cambridge.

Coughlan, S. (2014, December 3). Tablet computers in '70% of schools'. Accessed on 19 September 2017, www.bbc.co.uk/news/education-30216408

Cozzens, S. and Sutz, J. (2014). Innovation in informal settings: reflections and proposals for a research agenda. *Innovation and Development*, 4(1), 5–31.

Crepon, B., Duguet, E. and Mairesse, J. (1998). Research, innovation and productivity: an econometric analysis at the firm level. *Economics of Innovation and New Technology*, 7, 115–158.

Crespo, N. and Fontoura, M. (2007). Determinant factors of FDI spillovers – what do we really know?. *World Development*, 35(3), 410–425.

Criscuolo, C., Haskel, J. and Slaughter, M. (2005). Why Are Some Firms More Innovative? Knowledge Inputs, Knowledge Stocks and the Role of Global

Engagement, NBER Working Paper No. 11479 (June), http://www2.nber.org/conferences/2005/prs05/slaughter.pdf.

Croson, R. and Gneezy, U. (2009). Gender differences in preferences. *Journal of Economic Literature*, 47(2), 448–474.

Cuervo-Cazurra, A. (2012). Extending theory by analyzing developing country multinational companies: solving the Goldilocks debate. *Global Strategy Journal*, 2(3), DOI:10.1111/j.2042-5805.2012.01039.x

Darby, M. R., Zucker, L. G. and Wang, A. (2003). Universities, Joint Ventures, and Success in the Advanced Technology Program. NBER Working Paper No. 9463.

Darby, M. R., Zucker, L. G. and Wang, A. (2004). Joint ventures, universities, and success in the advanced technology program. *Contemporary Economic Policy*, 22(2), 145–161.

Das, J., Do, Q.-T., Shaines, K. and Srikant, S. (2013). U.S. and them: the geography of academic research. *Journal of Development Economics*, 105, 112–130.

Dasgupta, P. and David, P.A. (1994). Toward a new economics of science. *Research Policy*, 23, 487–521.

Davis, P. J. and Abdiyeva, F. (2012). En route to a typology of the female entrepreneur? Similarities and differences among self-employed women. *Journal of Management Policy and Practice*, 13(4), 121–137.

De Mel, S., McKenzie, D. and Woodruff C. (2008). Returns to capital: results from a randomized experiment. *Quarterly Journal of Economics*, 123(4), 1329–1372.

de Mel, S., McKenzie, D. and Woodruff, C. (2009). *Innovative Firms or Innovative Owners? Determinants of Innovation in Micro, Small, and Medium Enterprises*, Washington DC (US): The World Bank.

de Mel, S., McKenzie, D. and Woodruff, C. (2013). The demand for, and consequences of formalization among informal firms in Sri Lanka. *American Economic Journal: Applied Economics*, 5(2), 122–150.

De Waldemar, F. S. (2012). New products and corruption: evidence from Indian firms. *Developing Economies*, 50, 268–284.

Deb, A. and Kubzansky, M. (2012). *Bridging the Gap: The Business Case for Financial Capability. A Report Commissioned and Funded by the Citi Foundation*, Cambridge, MA: Monitor, March.

Dedrick, J., Gurbaxani, V. and Kraemer, K. L. (2003). Information technology and economic performance: a critical review of the empirical evidence. *ACM Computing Surveys*, 35(1), 1–28.

den Hertog, P., Bergman, E. M. and Charles, D. (eds.), (2001). *Innovative Clusters: Drivers of National Innovation Systems*, Paris: OECD Proceedings, 419.

Department for Digital, Culture, Media & Sport. (2017, March 1). Digital skills and inclusion – giving everyone access to the digital skills they need. Accessed 20 September 2017, www.gov.uk/government/publications/uk-digital-strategy/2-digital-skills-and-inclusion-giving-everyone-access-to-the-digital-skills-they-need

Desai, A. (1989). *Indian Technology Imports from SMEs*, New Delhi: National Council for Applied Economic Research.

Dewett, T. and Jones, G. R. (2001). The role of information technology in the organization: a review, model, and assessment. *Journal of Management*, 27(3), 313–346.

DFID. (2012). *Systematic Reviews in International Development: An Initiative to Strengthen Evidence-Informed Policy Making Vol. 2012*, London, www.gov.uk/g overnment/publications/systematic-reviews-in-international-development/sys tematic-reviews-in-international-development.

DiMaggio, P., Hargittai, E., Celeste, C. and Shafer, S. (2004). From unequal access to differentiated use: a literature review and agenda for research on digital inequality. *Social Inequality*. Russell Sage Foundation, www .scholars.northwestern.edu/en/publications/digital-inequality-from-unequal-access-to-differentiated-use

Diyamett, B. and Wangwe, S. (2006). Innovation indicators within sub-Saharan Africa: a specific case for Tanzania. Measuring innovation in OECD and non-OECD countries: selected seminar papers. W. Blankley and et al. Cape Town, South Africa, HSRC Press, www.scholars.northwestern.edu/en/publications/ digital-inequality-from-unequal-access-to-differentiated-use.

Diyamett, B. and Mutambla, M. (2014). Foreign direct investment and local technological capabilities in least developed countries: some evidence from the Tanzanian manufacturing sector. *African Journal of Science, Technology, Innovation and Development*, 6(5), 401–414.

Djankov, S., Miguel, E., Qian, Y., Roland, G. and Zhuravskaya, E. (2005). Who are Russia's entrepreneurs? *Journal of the European Economic Association*, 3 (2–3), 587–597

Djankov, S., Qian, Y., Roland, G. and Zhuravskaya, E. (2007) What makes a successful entrepreneur? Evidence from Brazil, CEFIR/NES Working Paper 104, Moscow, https://econpapers.repec.org/paper/cfrcefirw/w0104.htm.

Dollar, D., Hallward-Driemeier, M. and Mengistae, T. (2005). Investment climate and firm performance in developing economies. *Economic Development and Cultural Change*, 54, 1–31.

Doms, M. and Jensen, J. B. (1998). Comparing wages, skills and productivity between domestically and foreign-owned manufacturing establishments in the United States. In *Geography and Ownerships as Basis for Economic Accounting* (Baldwin, R. E., Lipsey, R. E. and Richardson, J. D. eds.), pp. 235–258. Chicago: University of Chicago Press.

Donckels, R. and Fröhlich, E. (1991). Are family businesses really different? European experiences from STRATOS. *Family Business Review*, 4, 149–160.

Doney, Patricia M., Cannon Joseph P. and Mullen Michael R. (1998). Understanding the influence of national culture on the development of trust. *The Academy of Management Review*, 23(3), 601–620.

Donner, J. (2015). *After Access*. Cambridge, US: MIT Press.

Doron, A. and Jeffrey, R. (2013). *The Great Indian Phone Book*, Cambridge, MA and London, England: Harvard University Press. http://doi.org/10.4159/har vard.9780674074248

Dosi, G. (1988).The nature of the innovative process. In *Technical Change and Economic Theory* (Dosi, G., Freeman, C., Nelson, R., Silverberg, G. and Soete, L. eds.), pp. 221–238. London: Pinter.

Drexler, A., Fischer, G. and Schoar, A. (2014). Keeping it simple: financial literacy and rules of thumb. *American Economic Journal: Applied Economics*, 6, 1–31.

Driffield, N., Love, J. H. and Menghinello, S. (2010). The multinational enterprise as a source of international knowledge flows: direct evidence from Italy. *Journal of International Business Studies*, 41(2), 350–359.

Dunning, J. H. (1998). *American Investment in British Manufacturing Industry*, Taylor & Francis US.

Dunning, J. H. (1993). *Multinational Enterprises and the Global Economy*, Reading, MA: Addison-Wesley.

Durham, J. B. (2004). Absorptive capacity and the effects of foreign direct investment and equity foreign portfolio investment on economic growth. *European Economic Review*, 48(2), 285–306.

Dutta, S., Geiger, T. and Lanvin, B. (2015). *The Global Information Technology Report 2015: ICTs for Inclusive Growth*, Geneva: World Economic Forum, Insight Report.

Dzobo, Noah Komla. (1992). Values in a changing society: man, ancestors and god. In *Person And Community: Ghanaian Philosophical Studies, I. Cultural Heritage and Contemporary Change* (Wiredu, K. and Gyekye, K. eds.), pp. 223–240. Washington, DC: Council for Research in Values and Philosophy.

Eady, M. J. (2015). Eleven design-based principles to facilitate the adoption of internet technologies in Indigenous communities. *International Journal of Social Media and Interactive Learning Environments*, 3(4), 267. http://doi.org/10.1504/IJSMILE.2015.074010

Eaton, J. and Kortum, S. (2002). Technology, geography, and trade. *Econometrica*, 70, 1741–1779.

Economist. (2014). Mobile money in developing Countries. Accessed on 29 October 2017, www.economist.com/news/economic-and-financial-indicators/21618842-mobile-money-developing-countries

Economist. (2017, July 22). Technology is transforming what happens when a child goes to school. Accessed on 19 September 2017, www.economist.com/news/briefing/21725285-reformers-are-using-new-software-personalise-learning-technology-transforming-what-happens

Edelman, L. F., Brush, G. C. and Alkhurafi, N. (2018). The labyrinth of women's entrepreneurship. In *Time for Solutions! Overcoming Gender-related Career Barriers* (Adams, S. M. ed.), Chapter 5, pp. 115–134. Oxford and New York: Routledge.

Edler, J. (2016). The impact of policy measures to stimulate private demand for innovation. In *Handbook of Innovation Policy Impact*. Edward Elgar Publishing.

Edler, J. and Fagerberg, J. (2017). Innovation policy: what, why, and how. *Oxford Review of Economic Policy*, 33(1), 2–23.

Edler, J. and Georghiou, L. (2007). Public procurement and innovation – resurrecting the demand side. *Research Policy*, 36(7), 949–963.

Edler, J., Gök, A., Cunningham, P. and Shapira, P. (2016). Introduction: making sense of innovation policy. In *Handbook of Innovation Policy Impact*. Edward Elgar Publishing.

Edquist, C. and Johnson, B. (1997). Institutions and organizations in systems of innovation. In *Systems of Innovation –Technologies, Institutions and Organizations* (Edquist, C. ed.), pp. 41–63. London: Frances Pinter.

Edwards, S. (1998). Openness, productivity and growth: what do we really know? *Economic Journal*, 108, 383–398.

Egbetokun, A. A., Adeniyi, A. A., Siyanbola, W. O. and Olamade, O. O. (2012). The types and intensity of innovation in developing country SMEs: evidences from a Nigerian subsectoral study. *International Journal of Learning and Intellectual Capital*, 9, 98–112.

Egbetokun, A., Mendi, P. and Mudida, R. (2016). Complementarity in firm-level innovation strategies: a comparative study of Kenya and Nigeria. *Innovation and Development*, 6(1), 87–101.

Eisenhardt, K. M. (1989). Building theories from case-study research. *Academy of Management Review*, 14, 532–550.

Ekesionye E. N. and Okolo A. (2012). Women empowerment and participation in economic activities: indispensable tools for self-reliance and development of Nigerian society. *Educational Research and Review*, 7(1), 10–18.

Ellis, P. (2000). Social ties and foreign market entry. *Journal of International Business Studies*, 31(3), 443–469.

Eom, B-Y. and Lee, K. (2010). Determinants of industry-academy linkages and, their impact on firm performance: the case of Korea as a latecomer in knowledge industrialization. *Research Policy*, 39, 625–639.

EPSRC. (2012, April 18). Largest India-UK ICT research collaboration gets £10 million funding boost that could benefit millions. Accessed on25 September 2017, www.epsrc.ac.uk/newsevents/news/indiaukict/

Ericsson. (2013). ICT in education study (pp. 1–25). www.ericsson.com/en/news/2013/11/ict-in-education

Eshet-Alkalai, Y. (2004). Digital literacy: a conceptual framework for survival skills in the digital era. *Journal of Educational Multimedia and Hypermedia*, 13 (1), 93.

Etzkowitz, H. and Leydesdorff, L. (1997). *Universities and the Global Knowledge Economy: A Triple Helix of University-Industry-Government Relations*, London: Continuum.

Etzkowitz, H. and Leydesdorff, L. (2000). The dynamics of innovation: from national systems and 'Mode 2' to a triple helix of university–industry–government relations, *Research Policy*, 29(2), 109–123.

EU Science Hub. (2013, March 29). Job market fails to unleash ICT potential – European Commission. accessed on 15 September 2015, https://ec.europa.eu/jrc/en/news/job-market-fails-unleash-ict-potential-9692

Eun, J.-H., Lee, K. and Wu, G. (2006). Explaining the 'University-run enterprises' in China: a theoretical framework for university-industry relationship in developing countries and its application to China. *Research Policy*, 35, 1329–1346.

European Commission. (2014, October 10). The Digital Skills and Jobs Coalition. accessed on 18 September 2017, https://ec.europa.eu/digital-single-market/en/digital-skills-jobs-coalition

Fagerberg, J. and Srholec, M. (2008). National innovation systems, capabilities and economic development. *Research Policy*, 37, 1417–1435.

Fagerberg, J. and Verspagen, B. (2009). Innovation studies: the emerging structure of a new scientific field. *Research Policy*, 38, 218–233.

Fagerberg, J., Lundvall, B. Å. and Srholec, M. (2018). Global value chains, national innovation systems and economic development. *The European Journal of Development Research*, 30(3), 533–556.

Fagerberg, J., Srholec, M. and Verspagen, B. (2010). Innovation and economic development. In *Handbook of the Economics of Innovation* (Bronwyn, H. H and Rosenberg, N. eds.), Vol. 2, pp. 833–872. Amsterdam: North-Holland.

Falvey, R., Foster, N. and Greenaway, D. (2007). Relative backwardness, absorptive capacity and knowledge spillovers. *Economics Letters*, 97(3), 230–234.

Feely, A. J. and Harzing, A. W. (2003). Language management in multinational companies. *Cross Cultural Management: An International Journal*, 10(2), 37–52.

FinAccess National Survey (2009). Dynamics of Kenya's changing financial landscape. June. FSD Kenya and the Central Bank of Kenya, https://fsdkenya .org/publication/finaccess-national-survey-2009-dynamics-of-kenyas-changing-financial-landscape/.

Findlay, Ronald. (1978). Relative backwardness, direct foreign investment, and the transfer of technology: a simple dynamic model. *The Quarterly Journal of Economics*, 92(1), 1–16.

Fischer, L. (2004). *The Workflow Handbook 2004*, Lighthouse Point, FL: Future Strategies Inc.

Fisman, R. and Svensson, J. (2007). Are corruption and taxation really harmful to growth? Firm-level evidence, *Journal of Development Economics*, 83, 63–75.

Flanagan, R. J. (2005). *Globalization and Labor Conditions: Working Conditions and Worker Rights in a Global Economy*, New York: Oxford University Press.

Flanagin, A. J. (2002). The elusive benefits of the technology support of knowledge management. *Management Communication Quarterly*, 16(2), 242–248.

Fosfuri, A., Motta, M. and Rønde, T. (2001). Foreign direct investment and spillovers through workers mobility. *Journal of International Economics*, 53(1), 205–222.

Foster, C. and Heeks, R. (2013). Innovation and scaling of ICT for the bottom-of-the-pyramid. *Journal of Information Technology*, 28, 296–315.

Fosu, G. O., Bondzie, E. A. and Okyere G. A. (2014). Does foreign direct investment really affect Ghana's economic growth? *International Journal of Academic Research in Economics and Management Sciences*, 3(1), 148.

Franco, E., Ray, S. and Ray, P. K. (2011). Patterns of innovation practices of multinational-affiliates in emerging economies: evidences from Brazil and India. *World Development*, 39, 1249–1260.

Fransman, M. (1985). Conceptualizing technical change in the third-world in the 1980s: an interpretive survey. *Journal of Development Studies*, 21, 572–652.

Gault, F., Ambali, A. and Mangwende, T. (2016). Innovation in Africa: Measurement, Policy and Global Issues, available at www.merit.unu.edu/pub lications/uploads/1491823855.pdf

Freeman, C. (1987). *Technology Policy and Economic Performance: Lessons from Japan*, London: Pinter.

Freeman, C. (1989). *The Economics of Industrial Innovation*, 2nd ed., London: Francis Pinter.

Freeman, C. and Soete, L. (1997). *The Economics of Industrial Innovation*, London: Pinter.

Frey, C. B. and Osborne, M. (2016). Technology at Work: The Future of Innovation and Employment, 1–108. www.oxfordmartin.ox.ac.uk/publica tions/view/1883

Frey, C. B. and Osborne, M. A. (2017). The future of employment: how susceptible are jobs to computerisation? *Technological Forecasting and Social Change*, 114(C), 254–280.

Frey, C. B. and Rahbari, E. (2016). Do labor-saving technologies spell the death of jobs in the developing world? Note prepared for Brookings Roundtable, www .brookings.edu/wp-content/uploads/2016/07/Global_20160720_Blum_FreyR ahbari.pdf.

Frey, C. B. and Osborne, M. (2013). *The Future of Employment: How Susceptible Are Jobs to Computerisation? Working Paper of Oxford Martin Programme on Technology and Employment*, Oxford Martin School: University of Oxford, September.

Fritsch, M. and Kauffeld-Monz, M. (2010). The impact of network structure on knowledge transfer: an application of social network analysis in the context of regional innovation networks. *The Annals of Regional Science*, 44(1), 21–38.

Fu, X. (2004). *Exports, Foreign Direct Investment and Economic Development in China*, London and New York: Palgrave Macmillan.

Fu, X. (2008). Foreign direct investment, absorptive capacity and regional innovation capabilities: evidence from China. *Oxford Development Studies*, 36, 89–110.

Fu, X. (2011). Processing-trade, FDI and exports of indigenous firms: firm-level evidence from high-technology industries in China. *Oxford Bulletin of Economics and Statistics*, 73(6), 792–817.

Fu, X. (2012). Foreign direct investment and managerial knowledge spillovers through the diffusion of management practices. *Journal of Management Studies*, 49(5), 970–999.

Fu, X. (2015). *China's Path to Innovation*, Cambridge, UK: Cambridge University Press.

Fu, X. and Soete, L. (2010). *The Rise of Technological Power in the South*, London: Palgrave MacMillan.

Fu, X. and Xu, H. (2019). Knowledge transfer in MNEs in Africa: a comparison of Chinese and European MNEs in Ghana. In *Multinationals, Local Capacity Building and Development* (Fu, Essegbey and Frempong, eds.), Cheltenham, UK: Edward Egar.

Fu, X. and Akter, S. (2016). The impact of mobile phone technology on agricultural extension services delivery: evidence from India. *The Journal of Development Studies*, 52(11), 1561–1576. http://doi.org/10.1080/00220388 .2016.1146700

Fu, X. and Buckley, P. J. (2015). Multi-dimensional complementarities and the growth impact of direct investment from China on host developing countries. TMCD Working Paper TMD-WP-69, www.oxfordtmcd.org/publication/multi-dimensional-complementarities-and-growth-impact-direct-investment-china-host-0.

Fu, X. and Gong, Y. (2011). Indigenous and foreign innovation efforts and drivers of technological upgrading: evidence from China. *World Development*, 39, 1213–1225.

Fu, X. and Yang, Q. (2009). World innovation frontier: exploring the innovation gap between the EU and the US. *Research Policy*, 38(7), 1203–1213.

Fu, X. and Zhang, J. (2011). Technology transfer, indigenous innovation and leapfrogging in green technology: the solar-PV industry in China and India. *Journal of Chinese Economic and Business Studies*, 9, 329–347.

Fu, X., Essegbey, G. and Promkon, G. (2019). *MNEs, Knowledge Transfer and Capabilities Upgrading*, Cheltenham, UK: Edward Elgar. Forthcoming.

Fu, X., Zanello, G. and Contreras, C. (2018). *Innovation under Constraints: The Role of Open Innovation in Ghana*, Oxford, UK: University of Oxford, TMCD Centre Working Paper.

Fu, X., Helmers, C. and Zhang, J. (2012). The two faces of foreign management capabilities: FDI and productive efficiency in the UK retail sector. *International Business Review*, 21(1), 71–88.

Fu, X., Pietrobelli, C. and Soete, L. (2011). The role of foreign technology and indigenous innovation in the emerging economies: technological change and catching-up. *World development*, 39(7), 1204–1212.

Fu, X., Zanello, G., Essegbey, G. O., Hou, J. and Mohnen, P. (2014). *Innovation in Low Income Countries: A Survey Report*, Oxford: TMCD and DEGRP.

Fu, X. and Li, J. (2016). Collaboration with foreign universities for innovation: evidence from Chinese manufacturing firms. *International Journal of Technology Management*, 70(2/3), 193–217.

García, F., Jin, B. and Salomon, R. (2013). Does inward foreign direct investment improve the innovative performance of local firms? *Research Policy*, 42(1), 231–244.

Gault, F. (2015). Measuring innovation in all sectors of the economy, UNU-MERIT Working Paper 2015–038, p. 23. (Revised May 2016). www.merit.unu.edu/publications/working-papers/abstract/?id=5832

Gebreeyesus, M. (2009). Innovation and microenterprises growth in Ethiopia. In *Entrepreneurship, Innovation, and Economic Development* (Szirmai, A. Naudé, W. A. and Goedhuys, M. eds.), Oxford (UK): Oxford University Press, www.oxfordscholarship.com/view/10.1093/acprof:oso/9780199596515.001.0001/acprof-9780199596515-chapter-6.

Gebreeyesus, M. and Mohnen, P. (2013). Innovation performance and embeddedness in networks: evidence from the Ethiopian footwear cluster. *World Development*, 41, 302–316.

Geels, F. W. (2004). From sectoral systems of innovation to socio-technical systems. *Research Policy*, 33(6–7), 897–920. DOI:10.1016/j.respol.2004.01.015

Gelfand, M. J., Erez, M. and Aycan, Z. (2007). Cross-cultural organizational behavior. *Annual Review of Psychology*, 58(1), 479–514.

General Electric. (2017, March 30). GE Launches Brilliant Skills Curriculum To Train Workers For Digital Industrial Future. Accessed on 25 September 2017, www.genewsroom.com/press-releases/ge-launches-brilliant-skills-curriculum-train-workers-digital-industrial-future

Gennaioli, N., Porta, R. L., Lopez-de-Silanes, F. and Shleifer, A. (2013). Human capital and regional development. *Quarterly Journal of Economics*, 128 (1), 105–164.

Gereffi, G. and Frederick, S. (2011). The global apparel value chain, trade, and the crisis: challenges and opportunities for developing countries. In *Global Value Chains in a Postcrisis World. A Development Perspective* (Cattaneo, O., Gereffi G. and Staritz, C. eds.), pp. 157–208. Washington, DC: World Bank.

Gereffi, G. and Lee, J. (2012). Why the world suddenly cares about global supply chains. *Journal of Supply Chain Management*, 48(3), 24–32.

Gereffi, G. and Sturgeon, T. J. (2013). Global value chains and industrial policy: the role of emerging economies. In *Global Value Chains in a Changing World* (Elms, D. K. and Low, P. eds.), pp. 329–360. Geneva, Switzerland: WTO.

Gereffi, G. (1994). The organisation of buyer-driven global commodity chains: how U.S. retailers shape overseas production networks. In *Commodity Chains and Global Capitalism* (Gereffi, G. and Korzeniewicz, M. eds.), pp. 95–122. Westport, CT: Praeger.

Gereffi, G. (1999). International trade and industrial upgrading in the apparel commodity chain. *Journal of International Economics*, 48(1), 37–70.

Gereffi, G. (2014). Global value chains in a post-Washington consensus world. *Review of International Political Economy*, 21(1), 9–37.

Gereffi, G. (2005). The global economy: organization, governance, and development. In *The Handbook of Economic Sociology* (Smelser, N. J. and Swedberg, R. eds.), pp. 160–182. Princeton, NJ: Princeton University Press.

Gereffi, G., Humphrey, J. and Sturgeon, T. (2005). The governance of global value chains. *Review of International Political Economy*, 12(1), 78–104.

Geroski, P. A. (1989). Entry, innovation and productivity growth. *The Review of Economics and Statistics*, 74(4), 572–578.

Ghana Statistical Service, (2012). *Labour Force Report*. Available at http://www2 .statsghana.gov.gh/docfiles/publications/Labour_Force/LFS%20REPORT_ fianl_21-3-17.pdf

Ghauri, P. Fu, X. and Vaatanen, J. (2017). *Multinational Enterprises and Sustainable Development*, Bingley, UK: Emerald.

Ghoshal, S. and Bartlett, C. A. (1990). The multinational corporation as an interorganizational network. *Academy of Management Review*, 15(4), 603–626.

Girma, S. and Görg, H., (2003). Foreign Direct Investment, Spillovers and Absorptive Capacity: Evidence from Quantile Regressions. GEP Working Paper No. 2002/14. SSRN Scholarly Paper ID 410742. Rochester, NY: Social Science Research Network.

Girma, S. (2005). Absorptive capacity and productivity spillovers from FDI: a threshold regression analysis. *Oxford Bulletin of Economics and Statistics*, 67 (3), 281–306.

Glass, A. J. and Saggi, K. (2002). Multinational firms and technology transfer. *The Scandinavian Journal of Economics*, 104(4), 495–513.

Glass, A. J. and Saggi, K. (1998). International technology transfer and the technology gap. *Journal of Development Economics*, 55, 369–398.

Global Entrepreneurship Monitor, Smith College, Women's Entrepreneurship 2016/2017 Report (2017). Report, Smith College, Northampton, MA. https:// scholarworks.smith.edu/conway_research/1

Globerman, S., Ries, J. and Vertinsky, I. (1994). The economic performance of foreign affiliates in Canada. *Canadian Journal of Economics*, 27, 143–156.

Godin, B. and Lane, J. P. (2013). Pushes and pulls: hi(S)tory of the demand pull model of innovation. science. *Technology and Human Values*, 38(5), 621–654.

Goedhuys, M. (2007). Learning, product innovation, and firm heterogeneity in developing countries: evidence from Tanzania. *Industrial and Corporate Change*, 16, 269–292.

Goedhuys, M., Janz, N. and Mohnen, P. (2008). What drives productivity in Tanzanian manufacturing firms: technology or business environment? *European Journal of Development Research*, 20, 199–218.

Goedhuys, M., Janz, N. and Mohnen, P. (2014). Knowledge-based productivity in 'low-tech' industries: evidence from firms in developing countries. *Industrial and Corporate Change*, 23, 1–23.

Goes, J. B. and Park, S. H. (1997). Interorganizational links and innovation: the case of hospital services. *Academy of Management Journal*, 40(3), 673–696.

Gök, A., Li, Y., Cunningham, P., Edler, J. and Laredo, P. (2016). Towards a Taxonomy of Science and Innovation Policy Instruments, paper presented to the EU SPRI Conference Lund, June.

Google. (2017, September 15). Google Diversity. Accessed on 15 September 2017, www.google.com/diversity/

Goos, M., Manning, A. and Salomons, A. (2014). Explaining job polarization: routine-biased technological change and offshoring. *American Economic Review*, 104(8), 2509–2526. ISSN 0002-8282

Görg, H. and Greenaway, D. (2004). Much ado about nothing? Do domestic firms really benefit from foreign direct investment? *World Bank Research Observer*, 19(2), 171–197.

Görg, H. and Strobl, E. (2005). Spillovers from foreign firms through worker mobility: an empirical investigation. *The Scandinavian Journal of Economics*, 107 (4), 693–709.

Görg, H. and Strobl, E. (2001). Multinational companies and productivity spillovers: a meta-analysis. *Economic Journal*, 111, 723–739.

Government of Ghana (2010). *Ghana's Revised Science, Technology and Innovation Policy Document*, Ghana: Accra.

Govindarajan, V. and Ramamurti, R. (2011). Reverse innovation, emerging markets, and global strategy. *Global Strategy Journal*, 1, 191–205.

Graetz, G. and Michaels, G. (2015). Robots at Work, CEPR Discussion Paper No. DP10477, March, http://papers.ssrn.com/sol3/papers.cfm?abstract_id=2575781.

Grandstrand O., Bohlin, E., Oskarsson C. and Sjoberg, N. (1992). External technology acquisition in large multi-technology corporations, *R&D Management*, 22, 111–133.

Greenan N., Topiol-Bensaid, A. and Mairesse, J. (2001). Information technology and research and development impacts on productivity and skills: looking for correlations on French firm level data. In *Information Technology, Productivity and Economic Growth* (Pohjola, M. ed.), pp. 119–48. Oxford: Oxford University Press.

Greenan, N. and Mairesse, J. (2000). Computers and productivity in France: some evidence. *Economics of Innovation and New Technology*, 9(3), 275–315.

Greene, P. (2000). Self-employment as an economic behavior: an analysis of self-employed women's human and social capital. *National Journal of Sociology*, 12 (1), 1–55.

Griliches, Z. and Schmookler, J. (September 1963). Inventing and maximizing. *American Economic Review*, LIII(4), 725–729.

Grossman, G. M. and Helpman, E. (1991). *Innovation and Growth in the Global Economy*, Cambridge, MA (US): The MIT Press.

Groves, T., Hong, Y., McMillan, J. and Naughton, B. (1994). Autonomy and incentives in Chinese state enterprises. *Quarterly Journal of Economics*, 109, 183–209.

GSMA. (2014). Digital Entrepreneurship in Kenya 2014. www.gsmaentrepreneurshipkenya.com/gsma_kenya-ar2014-060214-web-single-pgs.pdf

GSMA. (2015). State of the Industry Report on Mobile Money. London, United Kingdom: Groupe Speciale Mobile (GSM) Association report. Accessed on 4 January 2018, www.gsma.com/mobilefordevelopment/wpcontent/uploads/2016/04/SOTIR_2015.pdf

GSMA. (2015, March 23). Bridging the gender gap: mobile access and usage in low- and middle-income countries. Accessed on 15 September 2017, www.gsma.com/mobilefordevelopment/programmes/connected-women/bridging-gender-gap

GSS. (2008). *Ghana Living Standards Survey: Report of the 5th Round*, Ghana: Ghana Statistical Service, Accra.

Guan, J. and Ma, N., (2007). China's emerging presence in nanoscience and nanotechnology: a comparative bibliometric study of several nanoscience 'giants', *Research Policy*, 36(6), 880–886.

Guerzoni, M. and Raiteri, E. (2015). Demand-side vs. supply-side technology policies: hidden treatment and new empirical evidence on the policy mix. *Research Policy*, 44(3), 726–747.

Gulati, R. (2010). Management lessons from the edge. *Academy of Management Perspectives*, 24, 25–27.

Gulbrandsen, M., Mowery, D. and Feldman, M. (2011). Heterogeneity and university–industry relations, *Research Policy*, 40(1), 1–5.

Gurria, A. (2013). *Together We Stand: Inclusive Growth, Speech at OECD Workshop on Inclusive Growth*, Paris: OECD, 3 April.

Guthrie, D. (1997). Between markets and politics: organizational responses to reform in China. *American Journal of Sociology*, 102, 1258–1304.

Haas, M. and Hansen, M. (2005). When using knowledge can hurt performance: the value of organizational capabilities in a management consulting company. *Strategic Management Journal*, 26(1), 1–24.

Haas, M. R. and Cummings, J. N. (2015). Barriers to knowledge seeking within MNC teams: which differences matter most? *Journal of International Business Studies*, 46(1), 36–62.

Haglund, Dan. (2009). In it for the long term? Governance and learning among Chinese investors in Zambia's copper sector. *The China Quarterly*, 199, 627–646.

Hall, B. H. (2004). Innovation and Diffusion. NBER Working Paper Series 10212.

Hall, B. H. (2011). Innovation and Productivity. NBER Working Paper Series 17178.

Hall, J., Matos, S., Sheehan, L. and Silvestre, B. (2012). Entrepreneurship and innovation at the Base of the Pyramid: a recipe for inclusive growth or social exclusion? *Journal of Management Studies*, 49, 785–812.

Hallward-Driemeier, M., Iarossi, G. and Sokoloff, K. L. (2002). Exports and Manufacturing Productivity in East Asia: A Comparative Analysis with Firm-Level Data. NBER Working Paper Series.

Hamilton, G. G. and Biggart, N. W. (1988). Market, culture, and authority – a comparative-analysis of management and organization in the far-east. *American Journal of Sociology*, 94, S52–S94.

Hansen, E. G., Lüdeke-Freund, F., Quan, X. I. and West, J. (2015). Beyond Technology Push vs. Demand Pull: The Evolution of Solar Policy in the U.S., Germany and China. Centre for Sustainability Management (CSM) Leuphana University of Lueneburg Working Paper. [Accessed via Research Gate on 16 December 2018].

Hargittai, E. (2003). How wide a Web?: inequalities in accessing information online. Princeton University, Department of Sociology. https://catalog.princeton.edu/catalog/3930107

Hargittai, E. and Hinnant, A. (2008). Digital inequality differences in young adults' use of the internet. *Communication Research*. http://doi.org/10.1177/0093650208321782

Harzing, A. W. and Feely, A. J. (2008). The language barrier and its implications for HQ-subsidiary relationships. *Cross Cultural Management: An International Journal*, 15(1), 49–61.

Hausman, A. (2005). Innovativeness among small businesses: theory and propositions for future research. *Industrial Marketing Management*, 34, 773–782.

Hayhoe, R. (1996). *China's Universities, 1895–1995: A Century of Cultural Conflict*, New York: Garland Publishing, Inc.

Heeks, R. B., Amalia, M., Kintu, R. and Shah, N. (2013). Inclusive Innovation: Definition, Conceptualization and Future Research Priorities. Development Informatics Working Paper 53, Centre for Development Informatics, University of Manchester, UK. http://themimu

.info/sites/themimu.info/files/documents/Ref_Doc_Definition_Conceptualisat ion_Future_Research_Priorities_2013.pdf

Hekkert, M. P. and Negro, S. O. (2009). Functions of innovation systems as a framework to understand sustainable technological change: empirical evidence for earlier claims. *Technological Forecasting and Social Change*, 76(4), 584–594.

Hekkert, M., Negro, S., Heimeriks, G. and Harmsen, R. (2011). Technological Innovation System Analysis: A Manual for Analysts. www.innovation-system.net/wp-ontent/uploads/2013/03/UU_02rapport_Technological_Innovation_

Hekkert, M., Suurs, R., Negro, S., Smits, R. and Kuhlmann, S. (2007). Functions of innovation systems: a new approach for analyzing technological change. *Technological Forecasting & Social Change*, 74, 413–432.

Henderson, J. C. and Venkatraman, N. (1999). Strategic alignment: leveraging information systems for transforming organizations. *IBM Systems Journal*, 38, 472–484.

Henderson, J. (2005). Language diversity in international management teams. *International Studies of Management & Organization*, 35(1), 66–82.

Hershberg, E., Nabeshima, K. and Yusuf, S. (2007). Opening the ivory tower to business: university-industry linkages and the development of knowledge-intensive clusters in Asian cities, *World Development*, 35(6), 931–940.

Hicks, D. and Katz, J. S. (1996). Science policy for a highly collaborative science system. *Science and Public Policy*, 23, 39–44.

Hinz, M. (2014). Financial inclusion: M-PESA the Best of Both Worlds: Financial Inclusion Flash. Accessed on 23 October 2017, www.bbvaresearch.com/wp-content/uploads/pdf/16844_34099.pdf

Hoecklin, L. A. (1995). *Managing Cultural Differences: Strategies for Competitive Advantage*, Addison-Wesley New York: Economist Intelligence Unit.

Hoffman, K., Parejo, M., Bessant, J. and Perren, L. (1998). Small firms, R&D, technology and innovation in the UK: a literature review. *Technovation*, 18(1), 39–73.

Hong W. (2008). Decline of the center: the decentralizing process of knowledge transfer of Chinese universities from 1985 to 2004. *Research Policy*, 37, 580–595.

Hong, W. (2006). Technology transfer in Chinese universities: is 'mode 2' sufficient for a developing country? In *New Technologies in Global Societies* (Pui-Lam Law, Leopoldina Fortunati and Shanhua Yang eds.), New Jersey: World Scientific Publishers, 21–50.

Huang, J., Makoju, E., Newell, S. and Galliers, R. D. (2003). Opportunities to learn from 'failure' with electronic commerce: a case study of electronic banking. *Journal of Information Technology*, 18, 17–26.

Huang, Y., Jin, L. and Qian, Y. (2013). Does ethnicity pay? Evidence from overseas chinese FDI in China. *Review of Economics and Statistics*, 95(3), 868–883.

Huang, Z. and Palvia, P. (2001). ERP implementation issues in advanced and developing countries. *Business Process Management Journal*, 7(3), 276–284.

Huff, W. (1994). *The Economic Growth of Singapore. Trade and Development in the Twentieth Century*, Cambridge, UK: Cambridge University Press.

Hughes, A. (2010). The multifaceted role of universities, *ESRC Society Now IN FOCUS*, no. 8.

Hughes, N. and Lonie, S. (2007). M-PESA: mobile money for the 'unbanked' turning cellphones into 24-hour tellers in Kenya. *Innovations*, 2(1–2), 63–81.

Hughes, T. P. (1983). *Networks of Power – Electrification in Western Society 1880–1930*, Baltimore: The Johns Hopkins University Press.

Humphrey, J. and Oetero, A. (2000). *Strategies for Diversification and Adding Value to Food Exports: A Value Chain Perspective. United Nations Conference on Trade and Development*, Geneva: UNCTAD, https://digitallibrary.un.org/record/427518?ln=en

Humphrey, J. and Schmitz, H. (1998). Trust and inter-firm relations in developing and transition economies. *Journal of Development Studies*, 34 (4), 32–61.

Humphrey, J. and Schmitz, H. (2000). Governance and Upgrading: Linking Industrial Cluster and Global Value Chain Research. *Institute of Development Studies* (IDS Working Paper 120), www.ids.ac.uk/download.php?file=files/Wp120.pdf.

Humphrey, J. and Schmitz, H. (2002). How does insertion in global value chains affect upgrading in industrial clusters? *Regional Studies*, 36(9), 1017–1027.

Humphrey, J. and Schmitz, H. (2004a). Chain governance and upgrading: taking stock. In *Local Enterprises in the Global Economy*. (Schmitz, H. ed.), pp. 349–382. Cheltenham: Edward Elgar.

Humphrey, J. and Schmitz, H. (2004b). Globalized localities: introduction. In *Local Enterprises in the Global Economy* (Schmitz, H. ed.), pp. 1–21. Cheltenham: Edward Elgar.

Humphrey, J. (2004). Upgrading in Global Value Chains. *ILO*, (Policy Integration Department. World Commission on the Social Dimension of Globalization 28, www.researchgate.net/profile/John_Humphrey8/publication/228131264_Upgrading_in_Global_Value_Chains/links/5b8bf65b92851c1e12432032/Upgrading-in-Global-Value-Chains.pdf.

Humphrey, J. (2003a). Commodities, diversification and poverty reduction. In *FAO Symposium on the State of Agricultural Commodity Market Research*, Rome: FAO, pp. 1–17.

Humphrey, J. (2003b). Opportunities for SMEs in Developing Countries to Upgrade in a Global Economy. *ILO SEED* (Working Paper 43), www.ilo.org/empent/Publications/WCMS_117688/lang–en/index.htm.

Humphrey, J. (2005). Shaping Value Chains for Development: Global Value Chains in Agribusiness. *Deutsche Gesellschaft für Technische Zusammenarbeit (GTZ)*, (Trade Programme), www.ids.ac.uk/publications/shaping-value-chains-for-development-global-value-chains-in-agribusiness/.

Humphrey, J., McCulloch, N. and Ota, M. (2004). The impact of European market changes on employment in the Kenyan horticulture sector. *Journal of International Development*, 16(1), 63–80.

Huzingh, E. (2000). The content and design of web sites: an empirical study. *Information & Management*, 37(3), 123–134.

Hwang, Y., Kim, S., Byun, B., Lee, G. and Lee, H. (2003). *Strategies of Promoting Industry-Academia-Research Institute R&D Partnerships to Cooperation with New Technologies*, Korea: Science & Technology Policy Institute.

ICFGEO. (2016). The Learning Generation: Investing in education for a changing world. Report by the International Commission on Financing Global Education Opportunity. Available at http://report.educationcommission.org/wp-content/uploads/2016/09/Learning_Generation_Full_Report.pdf.

ILO, ITU. (2017, September 18). ILO-ITU Digital Skills for Decent Jobs for Youth Campaign to train 5 million youth with job-ready digital skills. Accessed on 18 September 2017, www.itu.int/en/ITU-D/Digital-Inclusion/Youth-and-Children/Pages/Digital-Skills.aspx

ILO. (2018). *Women and Men in the Informal Economy: A Statistical Picture*. Third edition. Available at www.ilo.org/global/publications/books/WCMS_626831/lang--en/index.htm

Ilori, M. O., Oke, J. S. and Sanni, S. A. (2000). Management of new product development in selected food companies in Nigeria. *Technovation*, 20, 333–342.

Inkpen, A. C. and Tsang, E. W. (2005). Social capital, networks, and knowledge transfer. *The Academy of Management Review*, 30(1), 146–165.

Insah, B. (2013). Foreign direct investment inflows and economic growth in Ghana. *International Journal of Economic Practices and Theories*, 3(2), 115–121.

Institute of Statistical Social and Economic Research (ISSER) (2013). *The State of Ghanaian Economy in 2012*, Accra, Ghana: Legon University Press.

Institute of Statistical Social and Economic Research (ISSER) (2015). *The State of Ghanaian Economy in 2014*, Accra, Ghana: Legon University Press.

Institute of Statistical, Social and Economic Research (ISSER) (2014). *The State of Ghanaian Economy in 2013*, Accra, Ghana: Legon University Press.

Intarakumnerd, P., Chairatana, P. A. and Tangchitpiboon, T. (2002). National innovation system in less successful developing countries: the case of Thailand. *Research Policy*, 31, 1445–1457.

Intel. (2017, September 25). Intel® Learn Program: Technology and Entrepreneurship Course. Accessed on 25 September 2017, www.intel.com/content/www/us/en/education/k12/intel-learn/intel-learn-technology-and-entrepreneurship-syllabus.html

IREK policy brief, (1) (2017). Building capabilities in the wind and solar sub-sectors in Kenya. June.

ITU. (2017). ICT Facts and Figures, 2017. International Telecommunication Union. Available at www.itu.int/en/itu-d/statistics/documents/facts/ictfactsfigures2017.pdf

ITU. (2012). A Bright Future in ICTs Opportunities for a new generation of women. Accessed on 25 September 2017, www.itu.int/en/ITU-D/Digital-Inclusion/Women-and-Girls/Girls-in-ICT-Portal/Pages/Publications.aspx

ITU. (2014). Final WSIS Targets Review: Achievements, Challenges and the Way Forward (pp. 1–434). www.itu.int/en/ITU-D/Statistics/Pages/publications/wsistargets2014.aspx

ITU and UN Women announce 'EQUALS': The Global Partnership for Gender Equality in the Digital Age. Available at www.unwomen.org/en/news/stories/2016/9/press-release-itu-and-un-women-announce-global-partnership-for-gender-equality-in-the-digital-age

Ivanova Yordanova, D. and Alexandrova-Boshnakova, I. (2011). Gender effects on risk-taking of entrepreneurs: evidence from Bulgaria. *International Journal of Entrepreneurial Behaviour and Research*, 17(3), 272–295.

Jack, W. and Suri, T. (2011). Mobile money: the economics of M-PESA. NBER Working Paper No. 16721. National Bureau of Economic Research, Cambridge, MA. www.nber.org/papers/w1672

Jackson, M. (2008). *Social and Economic Networks*, Princeton, US: Princeton University Press.

Jacobsson, S. and Bergek, A. (2004). Transforming the energy sector: the evolution of technological systems in renewable energy technology. *Industrial and Corporate Change*, 13(5), 815–849.

Jacobsson, S. and Johnson, A. (2000). The diffusion of renewable energy technology: an analytical framework and key issues for research. *Energy Policy*, 28(9), 625–640.

Jaffe, A. (1989). Real effects of academic research. *American Economic Review*, 79, 957–70.

Jaffe, A. B. (1986). Technological opportunity and spillovers of R & D: evidence from firms' patents, profits, and market value. *The American Economic Review*, 76(5), 984–1001.

Jaimovich, N. and Siu, H. E. (2012). *The Trend is the Cycle: Job Polarization and Jobless Recoveries. No. w18334*, Cambridge, US: National Bureau of Economic Research.

Jaramillo H., Lugones G. and Salazar, M. (2006). The Bogotá Manual: Standardising innovation indicators for Latin America and the Caribbean, Iberoamerican Network of Science and Technology Indicators (RICYT), Organisation of American States (OAS), www.ovtt.org/sites/default/files/bogota_manual%20english.pdf.

Javorcik, B. S. (2004). Does foreign direct investment increase the productivity of domestic firms? In search of spillovers through backward linkages. *The American Economic Review*, 94, 605–627.

Javorcik, B. S. (2008). Can survey evidence shed light on spillovers from foreign direct investment? *World Bank Research Observer*, 23(2), 139–159.

Javorcik, B. S. and Saggi, K. (2003). Technological asymmetry among foreign investors and mode of entry. World Bank Policy Research Working Paper (3196), https://openknowledge.worldbank.org/handle/10986/14789.

Jennings E. J. and Brush, C, G. (2013). Research on women entrepreneurs: challenges to (and from) the broader entrepreneurship literature? *Academy of Management Annals*, 7(1), 661–713.

Jianakoplos, N. A. and A. Bernasek, (1998). Are women more risk averse?. *Economic Inquiry*, 36(4), 620–630.

Johansson, B., Karlsson, C. and Backman, M. (2007). Innovation policy instruments, Working Paper Series in Economics and Institutions of Innovation 105, Royal Institute of Technology, CESIS - Centre of Excellence for Science and Innovation Studies. https://static.sys.kth.se/itm/wp/cesis/cesiswp105.pdf.

Jones, R. W., Kierzkowski, H. and Chen, L. (2005). What does evidence tell us about fragmentation and outsourcing? *International Review of Economics & Finance*, 14(3), 305–316. DOI:10.1016/j.iref.2004.12.010

Jonker, M., Romijn, H. and Szirmai, A. (2006). Technological effort, technological capabilities and economic performance: a case study of the paper manufacturing sector in West Java. *Technovation*, 26(1), 121–134.

Joshi, A., Labianca, G. and Caligiuri, P. M. (2003). Getting along long distance: understanding conflict in a multinational team through network analysis. *Journal of World Business*, 37(4), 277–284.

Jovanovic, B. (1982). Selection and the evolution of industry. *Econometrica*, 50, 649–670.

Joynt, P. and Warner, M. (2002). *Managing Across Cultures: Issues and Perspectives*, London: Thomson Learning.

Juma, C. (2015). *The New Harvest: Agricultural Innovation in Africa*, Oxford, UK: Oxford University Press.

Kaiser, R. and Kripp, M. (2010, June). Demand-orientation in national systems of innovation: a critical review of current European innovation policy concepts. In DRUID Summer Conference.

Kalakota, R. and Robinson, M. (2000). *Roadmap for Success*, Reading: Addison Wesley Longman.

Kaplinsky, R. and Farooki, M. (2010). What Are the Implications for Global Value Chains When the Market Shifts from the North to the South? *World Bank* (Policy Research Working Paper 5205), https://documents.worldbank.org/en/p ublication/documents-reports/documentdetail/807451468267002335/what-are -the-implications-for-global-value-chains-when-the-market-shifts-from-the -north-to-the-south.

Kaplinsky, R. and Morris, M. (2002). A Handbook for Value Chain Research. *IDRC-International Development Research Center*, http://asiandrivers.open.ac.uk /documents/Value_chain_Handbook_RKMM_Nov_2001.pdf.

Kaplinsky, R. (2011). Schumacher meets Schumpeter: appropriate technology below the radar. *Research Policy*, 40(2), 193–203.

Kaplinsky, R. (2018). Technology and innovation for sustainable development. In *Handbook of Development Economics: Critical Reflections and Emerging Policy Perspectives*, (Nissanke, M. and Campo, J. O. eds.), London: Palgrave Macmillan.

Kaplinsky, R. and Morris, M. (2009). Chinese FDI in Sub-Saharan Africa: engaging with large dragons. *European Journal of Development Research*, 21(4), 551–569.

Kaplinsky, R., Chataway, J., Hanlin, R., Clark, N., Kale, D., Muraguri, L., Papaioannou, T., Robbins, P. and Wamae, W. (2009). Below the radar: what does innovation in emerging economies have to offer other low-income economies? *International Journal of Technology Management and Sustainable Development*, 8(3), 177–197.

Kaplinsky, R., Morris, M. and Readman, J. (2002). Understanding Upgrading Using Value Chain Analysis. University of Sussex, (BAM 1), https://research .brighton.ac.uk/en/publications/understanding-upgrading-using-value-chain -analysis.

Karlan, D. and Valdivia, M. (2011). Teaching entrepreneurship: impact of business training on microfinance clients and institutions. *Review of Economics and Statistics*, 93, 510–527.

Karo, E. and Kattel, R. (2011). Should 'open innovation' change innovation policy thinking in catching-up economies? Considerations for policy analyses. *Innovation The European Journal of Social Science Research*, 24(1–2), 173–198.

Kaše, R., Paauwe, J. and Zupan, N. (2009). HR practices, interpersonal relations, and intrafirm knowledge transfer in knowledge-intensive firms: a social network perspective. *Human Resource Management*, 48(4), 615–639.

Katila, R. (2002). New product search over time: past ideas in their prime? *Academy of Management Journal*, 45(5), 995–1010.

Katrak, H. (1997a). Developing countries' imports of technology, in-house technologies capabilities and efforts: an analysis of the Indian experience. *Journal of Development Economics*, 53, 67–83.

Katrak, H. (1997b). The private use of publicly funded industrial technologies in developing countries: empirical tests for an industrial research institute in India. *World Development*, 25, 1541–1550.

Katz, J. S. and Martin, B. R. (1997). What is research collaboration? *Research Policy*, 26, 1–18.

Kaufmann, A. and Todtling, F. (2001). Science-industry interaction in the process of innovation: the importance of boundary-crossing between systems. *Research Policy*, 30, 791–804.

Keizer, J., Dijkstra, L. and Halman, J. (2002). Explaining innovative efforts of SMEs. An exploratory survey among SMEs in the mechanical and electrical engineering sector in the Netherlands. *Technovation*, 22(1), 1–13.

Keller, W. (1996). Absorptive capacity: on the creation and acquisition of technology in development. *Journal of Development Economics*, 49, 199–227.

Keller, W. (2004). International technology diffusion. *Journal of Economic Literature*, 42, 752–782.

Keller, W. (2001). *Knowledge Spillovers at the World's Technology Frontier*. SSRN Scholarly Paper ID 271703. Rochester, NY: Social Science Research Network.

Kemp, R. and Never, B. (2017). Green transition, industrial policy, and economic development. *Oxford Review of Economic Policy*, 33(1), 66–84.

Kernen, A. and Lam, K. N. (2014). Workforce localization among Chinese state-owned enter- prises SOEs in Ghana. *Journal of Contemporary China*, 23 (90), 1053–1072.

Keupp, M. and Gassmann, O. (2009). The past and the future of international entrepreneurship: a review and suggestions for developing the field. *Journal of Management*, 35(3), 600–633.

Keynes, J. M. (1933). Economic possibilities for our grandchildren (1930). *Essays in Persuasion*, pp. 358–73, www.cambridge.org/core/books/collected-writings-of-john-maynard-keynes/economic-possibilities-for-our-grandchildren-1930/230A7959F87C44AC6E83E406DF126B97.

Khan, F. and Ghadially, R. (2010). Empowerment through ICT education, access and use: a gender analysis of Muslim youth in India. *Journal of International Development*, 22(5), 659–673. http://doi.org/10.1002/jid.1718

Kimenyi, S. M. and Ndung'u, S. N. (2009). Expanding the Financial Services Frontier: Lessons from Mobile Phone Banking in Kenya. Brookings: 1–60. Accessed on file:///f:/mpesa%20case%20study/1016_mobile_phone_kenya_ki menyi.pdf/_on_23/_10/2017.

Kimura, F. and Kiyota, K. (2007). Foreign-owned versus domestically-owned firms: economic performance in Japan. *Review of Development Economics*, 11, 31–48.

Kimura, Y. (2011). Knowledge diffusion and modernization of rural industrial clusters: a paper-manufacturing village in Northern Vietnam. *World Development*, 39, 2105–2118.

Kinda, T. (2010). Investment climate and FDI in developing countries: firm-level evidence. *World Development*, 38, 498–513.

Kitson M., Howells J., Braham R. and Westlake S. (2009). *The Connected University: Driving Recovery and Growth in the UK Economy*, London: NESTA.

Klasen, S. (2002). Low schooling for girls, slower growth for all? Cross-country evidence on the effect of gender inequality in education on economic development. *The World Bank Economic Review*, 16(3), 345–373.

Kleinknecht, A. and Mohnen, P. A. (2002). *Innovation and Firm Performance: Econometric Explorations of Survey Data*, Basingstoke (UK): Palgrave.

Klepper, S. (1996). Entry, exit, growth, and innovation over the product life cycle. *American Economic Review*, 86, 562–583.

Klimenko, M. M. (2004). Industrial targeting, experimentation, and long run specialisation. *Journal of Development Economics*, 73(1), 75–105.

Klobodu, E. K. M. and Adams, S. (2016). Capital flows and economic growth in Ghana. *Journal of African Business*, 17(3), 291–307, DOI:10.1080/15228916 .2016.1169784

Klonner, S. and Nolen, P. J. (2010). Cell phones and rural labor markets: evidence from South Africa. http://doi.org/10.2307/41498426?ref=search-gateway:ab7e002caa4d7a0cb0121c1c840c8ab7

Kohli, R. and Devraj, S. (2003). Measuring information technology payoff: a meta-analysis of structural variables in firm-level empirical research. *Information System Research*, 14(2), 127–145.

Kokko, A., Tansini, R. and Zejan, M. C. (1996). Local technological capability and productivity spillovers from FDI in the Uruguayan manufacturing sector. *The Journal of Development Studies*, 32(4), 602–611.

Kokko, A. (1994). Technology, market characteristics, and spillovers. *Journal of Development Economics*, 43(2), 279–293.

Konté, A. and Ndong, M. (2012). The informal ICT sector and innovation processes in Senegal. In: UNU-MERIT Working Paper. UNU-MERIT, Maastricht (The Netherlands), www.merit.unu.edu/publications/working-papers/abstract/?id=4653.

Korinek A. and Stiglitz, J. (2017). Artificial Intelligence and Its Implications for Income Distribution and Unemployment, NBER Working Paper No. 24174. Available at www.nber.org/papers/w24174.

Kostoff, R. N., Boylan, R. and Simons, G. R. (2004). Disruptive technology roadmaps. *Technological Forecasting & Social Change*, 71, 141–159.

Kraemer-Mbula, E. and Wunsch-Vincent, S. (2016). *The Informal Economy in Developing Nations: Hidden Engine of Innovation?* Cambridge, UK: Cambridge University Press.

Kroll H. and Liefner I. (2008). Spin-off enterprises as a means of technology commercialization in a transforming economy: evidence from three universities in China, *Technovation*, 28, 298–313.

Kruss, G., Adeoti, J. and Nabudere, D. (2012). Universities and knowledge-based development in sub-Saharan Africa: comparing university-firm interaction in Nigeria, Uganda and South Africa. *Journal of Development Studies*, 48, 516–530.

Kshetri, N. (2007). Barriers to E-Commerce and Competitive Business Models in Developing Countries: A Case Study Electronic Commerce Research and Applications, Vol. 6. Available at SSRN: https://ssrn.com/abstract=1269024

Kugler, M. (2006). Spillovers from foreign direct investment: within or between industries? *Journal of Development Economics*, 80, 444–477.

Kuhlmann, S. (2017). Addressing Grand Challenges: Towards Transformative Science and Innovation Policy

Kumar, N. and Saqib, M. (1996). Firm size, opportunities for adaptation and in-house R&D activity in developing countries: the case of Indian manufacturing. *Research Policy*, 25, 713–722.

La Porta, R. and Shleifer, R. (2014). Informality and development. *Journal of Economic Perspectives*, 28(3), 109–126.

La Porta, R. and Shleifer, A. (2008). *The Unofficial Economy and Economic Development*, Washington DC, USA: The Brookings Institution.

La Porta, R. and Shleifer, A. (2014). Informality and development. *Journal of Economic Perspectives*, 28, 109–126.

Lall, S. (1989). *Learning to Industrialise: The Acquisition of Technological Capability by India*, London: Macmillan.

Lall, S. (1992). Technological capabilities and industrialization. *World Development*, 20, 165–186.

Lall, S. (1996). *Learning From the Asian Tigers – Studies in Technology and Industrial Policy*, London: Macmillan.

Lall, S. (1997). Investment, technology and international competitiveness. In *The New Globalism and Developing Countries* (Dunning J. H. and Hamdani K. A. eds.), pp. 232–259. Tokyo: United Nations University Press.

Lall, S. (2000). The technological structure and performance of developing country manufactured exports, 1985–1998. *Oxford Development Studies*, 28 (3), 337–369.

Lall, S. and Streeten, P. (1977). *Foreign Investment, Transnationals, and Developing Countries*, London: Macmillan.

Lall, S. (1980). Vertical inter-firm linkages in LDCs: an empirical study. *Oxford Bulletin of Economics and Statistics*, 42(3), 203–226.

Lankshear, C. and Knobel, M. (2008). *Digital Literacies: Concepts, Policies and Practices*, New York: Peter Lang.

Laranja, M., Uyarra, E. and Flanagan, K. (2008). Policies for science, technology and innovation: translating rationales into regional policies in a multi-level setting. *Research Policy*, 37(5), 823–835.

Lashitew, A. A., Bals, L. and van Tulder, R. (2018). Inclusive business at the base of the pyramid: the role of embeddedness for enabling social innovations. *Journal of Business Ethics*, 162(2), 421–448. https://doi.org/10.1007/s10551-0 18-3995-y

Latour, B. (1996). On actor-network theory: a few clarifications Soziale Welt, 47. Jahrg., H., 369–381, www.jstor.org/stable/40878163?origin=JSTOR-pdf&seq=1.

Laursen, K. and Salter, A. (2006). Open for innovation: the role of openness in explaining innovation performance among UK manufacturing firms. *Strategic Management Journal*, 27(2), 131–150.

Lederman, D. (2009). *The Business of Product Innovation: International Empirical Evidence*, Washington, DC (USA): The World Bank.

Lee, H. and Choi, B. (2003). Knowledge management enablers, processes, and organizational performance: an integrative view and empirical examination. *Journal of Management Information Systems*, 20(1), 179–228.

Lee, S., Gholami, R. and Tong, T. (2005). Time series analysis in the assessment of ICT impact at the aggregate level–Lessons and implications for the new economy. *Information & Management*, 42, 1009–1022.

Lefkowitz, J. (1994). Sex related differences in job attitudes and dispositional variables: now you see them. *Academy of Management Journal*, 37(2), 323–349.

Legros, D. and Galia, F. (2012). Are innovation and R&D the only sources of firms' knowledge that increase productivity? An empirical investigation of French manufacturing firms. *Journal of Productivity Analysis*, 38, 167–181. https://doi.org/10.1007/s11123-011-0254-y

Leiponen, A. and Helfat, C. E. (2010). Innovation objectives, knowledge sources, and the benefits of breadth. *Strategic Management Journal*, 31(2), 224–236.

Li, J. T. (2010). Global R&D alliances in China: collaborations with universities and research institutes. *IEEE Transactions on Engineering Management*, 57(1), 78–87.

Li, X. B. (2009). China's regional innovation capacity in transition: an empirical approach. *Research Policy*, 38, 338–357.

Lindmark, S. and Rickne, A. (2005). Dynamics and Functionality of the Swedish Mobile Internet Innovation System. Paper presented at the 16th European Regional Conference of the International Telecommunications Society (ITS), Porto, www.semanticscholar.org/paper/Dynamics-and-Functionality-of-the-Swe dish-Mobile-Lindmark-Rickne/4c30e72ff67f7855d565df121c027dcb70c4560a.

Kim, L. and Nelson, R. R. (2000). *Technology, Learning, and Innovation: Experiences of Newly Industrializing*, Cambridge, UK: Cambridge University Press.

Liu, X. and White, S. (2001). Comparing innovation systems: a framework and application to China's transitional context. *Research Policy*, 30, 1091–1114.

Liu, Z. (2008). Foreign direct investment and technology spillovers: theory and evidence. *Journal of Development Economics*, 85(1–2), 176–193

Lombard, K. (2001). Female self-employment and demand for flexible, non-standard work schedules. *Economic Inquiry*, 39(2), 214–237.

Lorentzen, J. (2010). Low-income countries and innovation studies: a review of recent literature. *African Journal of Science, Technology, Innovation and Development*, 2, 46–81.

Lucke, M. (1993). The diffusion of process innovations in industrialized and developing countries: a case study of the world textile and steel industries. *World Development*, 21, 1225–1238.

Lundvall, B.- Å., Joseph, K. J., Chaminade, C. and Vang, J. (2009). *Handbook of Innovation Systems and Developing Countries: Building Domestic Capabilities in a Global Setting*, Cheltenham, UK: Edward Elgar.

Lundvall, B., Joseph, K. J., Chamináde, C. and Vang, J. (2011). *Handbook of Innovation Systems and Developing Countries: Building Domestic Capabilities in a Global Setting*, Edward Elgar.

Lundvall, B.-Å. (2016). *The Learning Economy and the Economics of Hope*. London; New York: Anthem Press. www.jstor.org/stable/j.ctt1hj9zjd

Lundvall, B. Å. (1998). The learning economy–challenges to economic theory and policy. In *Institutions and Economic Change* (Nielsen, K. and Johnson, B. eds.), Bath: Edward Elgar, https://vbn.aau.dk/en/publications/the-learning-economy-challenges-to-a-economic-theory-and-policy.

Lundvall, B.-Å., Johnson, B., Andersen, E. S. and Dalum, B. (2002). National systems of production, innovation and competence building. *Research Policy*, 31, 213–231.

Lundvall, B-Å. (1992). *National Systems of Innovation: Towards a Theory of Innovation and Interactive Learning*, London: Pinter.

Luther Osabutey, E. and Debrah, Y. A. (2012). Foreign direct investment and technology transfer policies in Africa: a review of the Ghanaian experience. *Thunderbird International Business Review*, 54(4), 441–456.

Ma, W. (2004). *From Berkeley to Beida and Tsinghua: The Development and Governance of Public Research Universities in the US and China*, Beijing: Educational Science Press.

MacGarvie, M. (2005). The determinants of international knowledge diffusion as measured by patent citations. *Economics Letters*, 87, 121–126.

Magro, E., Navarro, M. and Zabala-Iturriagagoitia, J. M. (2014). Coordination-mix: the hidden face of STI policy. *Review of Policy Research*, 31(5), 367–389.

Mahemba, C. M. and Bruijn, E. J. (2003). Innovation activities by small and medium-sized manufacturing enterprises in Tanzania. *Creativity and Innovation Management*, 12, 162–173.

Mairesse, J. and Mohnen, P. (2002). Accounting for innovation and measuring innovativeness: an illustrative framework and an application. *American Economic Review Papers and Proceedings*, 92(2), 226–230.

Mairesse, J., and Mohnen, P. (2010). Using innovation surveys for econometric analysis. *Handbook of the Economics of Innovation*, 2, 1129–1155.

Malerba, F. (1992). Learning by firms and incremental technical change. *The Economic Journal*, 102(413), 845–859. DOI:10.2307/2234581

Malerba, F. (2005). Sectoral systems of innovation: a framework for linking innovation to the knowledge base, structure and dynamics of sectors. *Economics of Innovation and New Technology*, 14(1–2), 63–82. DOI:10.1080/1043859042000228688

Malerba, F. and Mani, S. (2009). *Sectoral Systems of Innovation and Production in Developing Countries: Actors, Structure and Evolution*, Cheltenham: Edward Elgar.

Mano, Y., Iddrisu, A., Yoshino, Y. and Sonobe, T. (2012). How can micro and small enterprises in Sub-Saharan Africa become more productive? The impacts of experimental basic managerial training. *World Development*, 40, 458–468.

Manolova, T. S., Carter, N. M., Manev, I. M. and Gyoshev, B. S. (2007). The differential effect of men and women entrepreneurs' human capital and networking on growth expectancies in Bulgaria. *Entrepreneurship: Theory and Practice*, 31(3), 407–426.

Mansfield, E. and Lee, J. Y. (1996). The modern university: contributor to industrial innovation and recipient of industrial R&D support. *Research Policy*, 25, 1047–1058.

Mansfield, R. (1968). *Industrial Research and Technological Innovation: An Econometric Analysis*, New York: W. W. Norton, xviii.

Manyika, J., Chui, M., Bughin, J., Dobbs, R., Bisson, P. and Marrs, A. (2013). *Disruptive Technologies: Advances That Will Transform Life, Business, and the Global Economy*, San Francisco: The McKinsey Global Institute (MGI), May.

Markusen, A. (1996). Sticky places in slippery space: a typology of industrial districts. *Economic Geography*, 72(3), 293.

Marr, B. (2017, January 24). A Complete Beginner's Guide To Blockchain. Accessed on 19 September 2017, www.forbes.com/sites/bernardmarr/2017/0 1/24/a-complete-beginners-guide-to-blockchain/

Martin, B. R. (2012). The evolution of science policy and innovation studies. *Research Policy*, 41, 1219–1239.

Mas, I. and Radcliffe, D. (2010). *Mobile Payments go Viral: M-PESA in Kenya (English)*, Washington, DC: World Bank Group. http://documents .worldbank.org/curated/en/638851468048259219/Mobile-payments-go-viral-M-PESA-in-Kenya

Matusik, S. (2000). Absorptive Capacity and Firm Knowledge: Separating the Effects of Public Knowledge, Flexible Firm Boundaries, and Firm Absorptive Abilities. Paper presented at the Organization Science Winter Conference, Keystone.

Maurer, B. (2012). Mobile money: communication, consumption and change in the payments space. *Journal of Development Studies*, 48(5), 589–604. DOI:10 .1080/00220388.2011.621944

Mbaya, C. K. and Estapé-Dubreuil, G. (2016). Gender and opportunity recognition: does social capital rank higher than human capital among poor women?. *International Journal of Entrepreneurship and Small Business*, 27(4), 542–559.

Mbiti, J. S. (1990). *African Religions and Philosophy*, Oxford: Heinemann Educational.

McCormick, D. and Atieno, R. (2002). Linkages between small and large firms in the Kenyan food processing sector. In *Innovation and Small Enterprises in the Third World* (Van Dijk M. P. and Sandee H. eds.), Cheltenham: Edward Elgar.

McDade, B. E. and Malecki, E. J. (1997). Entrepreneurial networking: industrial estates in Ghana. *Tijdschrift Voor Economische En Sociale Geografie*, 88, 262–272.

McIntosh, C. S. and Dorfman, J. H. (1992). Qualitative forecast evaluation: a comparison of two performance measures. *American Journal of Agricultural Economics*, 74, 209–214.

Meagher, K. (2018). Cannibalizing the informal economy: frugal innovation and economic inclusion in Africa. *Special Issue Article. The European Journal of Development Research (2017)*. January, 30(1), 17–33

Meagher, K. (2007). Manufacturing disorder: liberalization, informal enterprise and economic 'ungovernance' in African small firm clusters. *Development and Change*, 38, 473–503.

Meagher, K. (2018). Cannibalizing the informal economy: frugal innovation and economic inclusion in Africa. *The European Journal of Development Research*, 30, 17–33.

Melville, N., Kraemer, K. L. and Gurbaxani, V. (2004). Information technology and organizational performance: an integrative model of IT business value. *MIS Quarterly*, 28(22), 283–322.

Mendi, P. and Mudida, R. (2018). The effect on innovation of beginning informal: empirical evidence from Kenya. *Technological Forecasting and Social Change*, 131, 326–335. https://doi.org/10.1016/j.techfore.2017.06.002

Menon, T. and Pfeffer, J. (2003). Valuing internal vs. external knowledge: explaining the preference for outsiders. *Management Science*, 49(4), 497–513.

MESTI (2017). National Science, Technology and Innovation Policy, Ministry of Environment, Science, Technology and Innovation (MESTI), Accra. https://new-ndpc-static1.s3.amazonaws.com/CACHES/PUBLICATIONS/2016/07/15/DRAFT+MESTI+SMTDP+2014-2017.pdf

Metcalfe, J. R. (1988). The diffusion of innovation: an interpretive survey. In *Technical Change and Economic Theory* (Dosi, G., Freeman, C., Nelson, R., Silverberg, G. and Soete, L. eds.), pp. 560–589. London: Pinter.

Microsoft. (2017, January 26). Microsoft launches digital skills programme for the UK. Accessed on 25 September 2017, https://news.microsoft.com/en-gb/2017/01/26/microsoft-launches-digital-skills-programme-for-the-uk/

Milberg, W. and Winkler, D. (2010). Economic and social upgrading in global production networks: problems of theory and measurement. *Capturing the Gains*, 4 (June). www.capturingthegains.org/pdf/ctg-wp-2010-4.pdf

Milberg, W. and Winkler, D. (2013). *Outsourcing Economics: Global Value Chains in Capitalist Development*, Cambridge: Cambridge University Press.

Milberg, W. (2004). The changing structure of trade linked to global production systems: what are the policy implications? *International Labour Review*, 143 (1–2), 45–90.

Milberg, W., Jiang, X. and Gereffi, G. (2014). Industrial policy in the era of vertically specialized industrialization. In *Transforming Economies: Making Industrial Policy Work for Growth, Jobs and Development* (Salazar-Xirinachs, J. M., Nübler, I. and Kozul-Wright, R. eds.), pp. 151–178. Geneva: UNCTAD-ILO.

Ministry of Commerce (MOC), People's Republic of China. (2015). Statistics of China's outward direct investment. Available at www.mofcom.gov.cn/article/i/dxfw/gzzd/201503/20150300910506.shtml

Ministry of Education (1999). The regulation regarding the protection and management of intellectual properties in higher education institutions. *Act*, 3, No. 8120.

Minniti, M. and Nardone, C. (2007). Being in someone else's shoes: the role of gender in nascent entrepreneurship. *Small Business Economics*, 28(2/3), 223–238.

Minniti, M. and Naudé, W. (2010). What do we know about the patterns and determinants of female entrepreneurship across countries. *European Journal of Development Research*, 22(3), 277–293.

Minniti, M., Arenius, P. and Langowitz, N. (2005). *2004 Global Entrepreneurship Monitor Special Topic Report: Women and Entrepreneurship*, Babson Park, MA: Center for Women's Leadership at Babson College.

Molina-Domene, M. A. and Pietrobelli, C. (2012). Drivers of technological capabilities in developing countries: an econometric analysis of Argentina, Brazil and Chile. *Structural Change and Economic Dynamics*, 23(4), 504–515.

Moran, T., Graham, E. M. and Blomstrom, M. (2005) *Does Foreign Direct Investment Promote Development?* Washington, US: Peterson Institute Press.

Morawczynski, O. and Pickens, M. (2009). *Poor People Using Mobile Financial Services: Observations on Customer Usage and Impact from M-PESA. CGAP Brief. World Bank*, Washington, DC: World Bank. https://openknowledge .worldbank.org/handle/10986/9492

Morawczynski, O. and Krepp, S. (2011). Saving on the mobile: developing innovative financial services to suit poor users. Reports. Pp 51–56. weforum .org. The Mobile Financial Services.

Morris, M. H., Miyasaki, N. N., Watters, C. E. and Coombes, S. M. (2006). The dilemma of growth: understanding venture size choices of women entrepreneurs. *Journal of Small Business Management*, 44(2), 221–244.

Morrison, A., Pietrobelli, C. and Rabellotti, R. (2008). Global value chains and technological capabilities: a framework to study learning and innovation in developing countries. *Oxford Development Studies*, 36(1), 39–58.

Motta, Massimo. (1999). *Foreign Direct Investment and Spillovers Through Workers' Mobility*, London: Centre for Economic Policy Research.

Mowery, D. and Oxley, J. (1995). Inward technology transfer and competitiveness: the role of national innovation system. *Cambridge Journal of Economics*, 19, 67–93.

Mowery, D. C. and Sampat, B. N. (2005). Universities in national innovations systems. In *The Oxford Handbook of Innovation* (Fagerberg, F., Mowery, D. and Nelson, R. eds.), pp. 209–239. New York: Oxford University Press.

Mowery, D. C., Oxley, J. E. and Silverman, B. S. (1996). Strategic alliances and interfirm knowledge transfer. *Strategic Management Journal*, 17, 77–91.

Muhanga M. (2017). Informal sector in urban areas in Tanzania: some socio-demographic, economic and legal aspects. *International Journal of Accounting and Economics Studies*, 5(2), 163–168. DOI:10.14419/ijaes .v5i2.8495

Murphy, J. T. (2002). Networks, trust, and innovation in Tanzania's manufacturing sector. *World Development*, 30, 591–619.

Murphy, J. T. (2007). The challenge of upgrading in African industries: socio-spatial factors and the urban environment in Mwanza, Tanzania. *World Development*, 35, 1754–1778.

Murray, F. (2004). The role of academic inventors in entrepreneurial firms: sharing the laboratory life. *Research Policy*, 33, 643–659.

Muthiora, B. (2015). Enabling mobile money policies in Kenya. Fostering a digital financial revolution. Groupe Speciale Mobile Association (GSMA) report. Accessed on 4 January 2018, www.gsma.com/mobilefordevelopment/wp-content/uploads/2015/02/2015_MMU_Enabling-Mobile-Money-Policies-in-Kenya.pdf

Nakata, C. and Weidner, K. (2012). Enhancing new product adoption at the base of the pyramid: a contextualized model. *Journal of Product Innovation Management*, 29, 21–32.

National Statistics Bureau of China (NBS). Report on the Second National R&D Resources Survey of China. Available at www.stats.gov.cn.

Naudé, W. (2017). Entrepreneurship, Education and the Fourth Industrial Revolution, IZA DP No. 10855. Bonn: IZA Institute of Labor Economics. Available at http://legacy.iza.org/en/webcontent/publications/papers/viewAbstract?dp_id=10855

Ndemo, B. and Maina, W. F. (2007). Women entrepreneurs and strategic decision making. *Management Decision*, 45(1), 118–130.

Ndubisi, O. N. (2007). Evaluating the direct and indirect impact of traits and perceptions on technology adoption by women entrepreneurs in Malaysia. *Academy of Entrepreneurship Journal*, 13(2), 1–20.

Ndung'u, N. (2010). Remarks by Prof. Njuguna Ndung'u, Governor Central Bank of Kenya, Chairman of the Alliance for Financial Inclusion Steering Committee at the Opening Ceremony of the 2010 Alliance for Financial Inclusion (AFI) Global Policy Forum, Bali, Indonesia, September 27, 2010. Accessed on 18 January 2018, www.centralbank.go.ke/images/docs/speeches/2010/AFI%20Global%20Policy%20Forum.pdf

Negro, S. O. (2007). Dynamics of Technological Innovation Systems: The Case of Biomass Energy. PhD Thesis, Utrecht University, Utrecht.

Negro, S. O., Hekkert, M. P. and Smits, R. E. H. M. (2008). Stimulating renewable energy technologies by innovation policy. *Science and Public Policy*, 35(6), 403–416.

Nelson, R. (1986). Institutions supporting technical advance in industry. *American Economic Review*, 76, 186–189.

Nelson, R. (1992). National innovation systems: a retrospective on a study. *Industrial and Corporate Change*, 1, 347–374.

NEPAD Planning and Coordinating Agency (NPCA). (2014). African Innovation Outlook 2014, NPCA, Pretoria, www.nepad.org/file-download/download/public/15191.

Neuman, W. R. (2016). *The Digital Difference*, London, England: Harvard University Press.

Nichter, S. and Goldmark, L. (2009). Small firm growth in developing countries. *World Development*, 37, 1453–1464.

Njiraini, J. and Anyanzwa, J. (2008). Unmasking the storm behind M-PESA, *East African Standard*, 30th December 2008. Accessed on 18 January 2018, www.standardmedia.co.ke/business/article/1144002826/unmasking-the-storm-behind-m-pesa

Nonaka, I. and Nishiguchi, T. (2001). *Knowledge Emergence*, New York: Oxford University Press.

North, D. C. (1994). Institutions Matter. EconWPA, November. http://ideas.repec.org/p/wpa/wuwpeh/9411004.html

Ntara, C. (2015). An analysis of M-PESA use in international transactions, *European Journal of Business and Management*, 7(17), 73–80.

Nyaoma, G. (2010). Director, Banking Department, Central Bank of Kenya, speaking at the first AFI Global Policy Forum in Nairobi, Kenya, www.afi-global.org/sites/default/files/publications/afi_casestudy_mpesa_en.pdf.

OECD. (1992). *Oslo Manual: Guidelines for Collecting and Interpreting Innovation Data*, 1st ed. Paris: OECD Publishing.

OECD. (1994). *Science and Technology Policy: Review and Outlook*, Paris (France): Organisation for Economic Co-operation and Development, www.bookdepository.com/Science-Technology-Policy-Review-Outlook-1994-Oecd/9789264142374.

OECD. (1998). *Science, Technology and Industry Outlook 1998*, Paris: OECD.

OECD. (1999). *Boosting Innovation: The Cluster Approach*, OECD Publishing, www.oecd.org/document/23/0,3343,en_2649_34273_1894871_1_1_1_1,00.html and http://dx.doi.org/10.1787/9789264174399-en

OECD. (2004), Strategic public/private partnerships for innovation in OECD Science, Technology and Innovation Outlook 2004, OECD Publishing, Paris. Accessed on 27 January 2018, http://dx.doi.org/10.1787/sti_in _outlook-2005-5-en

OECD. (2005). *Oslo Manual: Guidelines for Collecting and Interpreting Innovation Data*, 3rd ed. Paris: OECD Publishing.

OECD. (2010). *Are ICT Users More Innovative? An Analysis of ICT-enabled Innovation in OECD Firms*. DSTI/ICCP/IIS(2010)8/REV1, www.oecd.org/economy/growth/are%20ict%20users%20more%20innovative.pdf.

OECD. (2011). *Demand Side Innovation Policies*, Paris, France: OECD Publishing.

OECD. (2015). *System Innovation: Synthesis Report*, Paris: Organization of Economic Cooperation and Development.

OECD. (2016). Strategic public/private partnerships in science, technology and innovation, in OECD Science, Technology and Innovation Outlook 2016, OECD Publishing, Paris. Accessed on 27 January 2018, http://dx.doi.org/10.1787/sti_in_outlook-2016-10-en

OECD. (2012). *Promoting Inclusive Growth: Challenges and Policies*, Paris: OECD.

OECD. (2008). *National Innovation System in China*, Paris: OECD.

OECD. (2016). *Skills for a Digital World. Policy Brief on the Future of Work* (pp. 1–4). Paris: OECD.

OECD. (2017a). *Students, Computers and Learning* (pp. 1–204). OECD Publishing. www.oecd-ilibrary.org/education/students-computers-and-learning_9789264239555-en

OECD. (2017b). Going digital: the future of work for women. www.oecd.org/employment/Going-Digital-the-Future-of-Work-for-Women.pdf

Okon E. E. (2016). Operational Structure of Multinational Enterprises in Africa, IGI Global. DOI:10.4018/978-1-5225-0276-0.ch017

Okoth, J. (2009). Regulator gives M-PESA a clean bill of health. *East African Standard*, 27 January 2009. Accessed on 18 January 2018, www .standardmedia.co.ke/business/article/1144004990/regulator-gives-m-pesa-a-clean-bill-of-health

Onsongo, E. K. (2013). A Multi-level Perspective on Inclusive Innovation: Reflections on Mobile Money in Kenya. https://prezi.com/cwd-vxd5iy-m/a-m ulti-level-perspective-on-inclusive-innovation/.

Onsongo, E. and Schot, J. (2017). Inclusive Innovation and Rapid Sociotechnical Transitions: The Case of Mobile Money in Kenya. SPRU Working Paper Series (SWPS), 2017–07: 1–28.ISSN 2057–6668. Accessed on 4 January 2018, http:// dx.doi.org/10.2139/ssrn.2940184

Overå, R. (2006). Networks, distance, and trust: telecommunications development and changing trading practices in Ghana. *World Development*, 34, 1301–1315.

Oyelaran-Oyeyinka, B. and Lal, K. (2006). Learning new technologies by small and medium enterprises in developing countries. *Technovation*, 26, 220–231.

Oyelaran-Oyeyinka, B. and McCormick, D. (2007). *Industrial Clusters and Innovation Systems in Africa*, Maastricht: United Nations University Press.

Oyelaran-Oyeyinka, B. and Sampath, P. G. Innovation in African Development: Case Studies of Uganda, Tanzania and Kenya, A Report Prepared for World Bank. Available at http://citeseerx.ist.psu.edu/viewdoc/download?doi=10.1.1 .630.5770&rep=rep1&type=pdf

Oyelaran-Oyeyinka, B., Laditan, G. O. A. and Esubiyi, A. O. (1996). Industrial innovation in Sub-Saharan Africa: the manufacturing sector in Nigeria. *Research Policy*, 25, 1081–1096.

Pack, H. (2000). Industrial policy: growth elixir or poison? *The World Bank Research Observer*, 15(1), 47–67.

Pack, H. and Saggi, K. (2006). Is there a case for industrial policy? A critical survey. *The World Bank Research Observer*, 21(2), 267–297.

Palaniappan, C. S. and Ramanigopal, A. M. (2012). A study on problem and prospects of women entrepreneurs with special reference to Erode District. *International Journal of Physical and Social Sciences*, 2(3), 2249–5894.

Papke L. E. and Wooldridge, J. M. (1996). Econometric methods for fractional response variables with an application to 401(k) plan participation rates. *Journal of Applied Econometrics*, 11(6), 619–632.

Park, B. I. and Choi, J. (2014). Foreign direct investment motivations and knowledge acquisition from MNEs in overseas subsidiaries. *Canadian Journal of Administrative Sciences/Revue Canadienne des Sciences de l'Administration*, 31 (2), 104–115.

Park, B. I., Kim, C.-H. and Choi, S. B. (2016). Knowledge spillovers through inward FDI in emerging markets: an empirical examination in the supermarket industry. *European Journal of International Management*, 10(3), 314–342.

Partnership for Gender Equality in the Digital Age. Accessed on 15 September 2017, www.unwomen.org/en/news/stories/2016/9/press-release-itu-an...announce-global-partnership-for-gender-equality-in-the-digital-age

Pavitt, K. (1984). Sectoral patterns of technical change: towards a taxonomy and a theory. *Research Policy*, 13(6), 343–373.

Perkmann, M. and Walsh, K., (2008). Engaging the scholar: three types of academic consulting and their impact on universities and industry. *Research Policy*, 37, 1884–1891.

PLOS. (2017, September 19). Benefits of Open Access Journals. Accessed on 19 September 2017, www.plos.org/open-access/

PNAS. (2017, September 19). Developing Countries Initiatives. Accessed on 19 September 2017, www.pnas.org/site/aboutpnas/developingcountries .xhtml

Polder, M., Van Leeuwen, G., Mohnen, P. and Raymond, W. (2009). Productivity effects of innovation modes. Statistics Netherlands Discussion Paper No. 09033, The Hague, Netherlands. https://econpapers.repec.org/pap er/pramprapa/18893.htm

Poole, J. P. (2013). Knowledge transfers from multinational to domestic firms: evidence from worker mobility. *Review of Economics and Statistics*, 95(2), 393–406.

Porter, M. and Stern, S. (1999) *The New Challenge to America's Prosperity: Findings from the Innovation Index*. Council on Competitiveness, Washington, DC., USA: Council on Competitiveness.

Powell, W. W. and Grodal, S. (2005). Networks of innovators. In *The Oxford Handbook of Innovation* (Fagerberg, F., Mowery, D. and Nelson, R. eds.), pp. 56–85. New York: Oxford University Press.

Powell, W. W., Koput, K. W. and Smith-Doerr, L. (1996). Interorganizational collaboration and the locus of innovation: networks of learning in biotechnology. *Administrative Science Quarterly*, 41, 116–145.

Powell, W. W. and Snellman, K. (2004). The knowledge economy. *Annual Review of Sociology*, 30, 199–220.

Prahalad, C. K. (2012). Bottom of the Pyramid as a source of breakthrough innovations. *Journal of Product Innovation Management*, 29, 6–12.

Prahalad, C. K. and Mashelkar, R. A. (2010). Innovation's holy grail. *Harvard Business Review*, 88, 1–10.

Prahalad, C. K. and Hammond, A. (2002). Serving the world's poor, profitably. *Harvard Business Review*, 80, 48–57.

Prahalad, C. K. and Hart, S. L. (2002). The fortune at the bottom of the pyramid. *Strategy and Business*, 26, 1–14.

P-TECH. (2017, September 25). Public/private partnership is critical to the success of a P-TECH 9–14 school and its students. Accessed on 25 September 2017, www.ptech.org/model/who-creates-a-ptech-school

Pun, K. F., Chin, K. S. and Lau, H. (2000). A review of the Chinese cultural influences on Chinese enterprise management. *International Journal of Management Reviews*, 2(4), 325–338.

PwC. (2016). Financial Services Technology 2020 and Beyond: Embracing disruption (pp. 1–48). www.pwc.com/fstech2020

Radjou, N., Prabhu, J. and Ahuja, S. (2012). *Jugaad Innovation: Think Frugal, Be Flexible, Generate Breakthrough Growth*, New York: Jossey-Bass.

Radosevic, S. (2012). Innovation policy studies between theory and practice: a literature review based analysis. *STI Policy Review*, 3(1), 1–45.

Ramachandran, J., Pant, A. and Pani, S. K. (2012). Building the BoP producer ecosystem: the evolving engagement of Fabindia with Indian handloom artisans. *Journal of Product Innovation Management*, 29, 33–51.

Ramani, S. V., Sadre Ghazi, S. and Duysters, G. (2012). On the diffusion of toilets as bottom of the pyramid innovation: lessons from sanitation entrepreneurs. *Technological Forecasting and Social Change*, 79, 676–687.

Rand, J. and Tarp, F. (2012). Firm level corruption in Vietnam. *Economic Development and Cultural Change*, 60(3), 571–595.

Reagans, R. and McEvily, B. (2003). Network structure and knowledge transfer: the effects of cohesion and range. *Administrative Science Quarterly*, 48(2), 240–267.

Redecker, C. and Johannessen, Ø. (2013). Changing assessment – towards a new assessment paradigm using ICT. *European Journal of Education*, 48(1), 79–96.

Renard, M. F. (2011). China's trade and FDI in Africa. African Development Bank Working Paper Series 126. www.afdb.org/fileadmin/uploads/afdb/Documents/Publications/Working%20126.pdf

Robinson, J. P., Winthrop, R. and McGivney, E. (2016, April 13). Millions Learning: Scaling Up Quality Education in Developing Countries. Accessed on 19 September 2017, www.brookings.edu/research/millions-learning-scaling-up-quality-education-in-developing-countries/

Robson, P. J. A., Haugh, H. M. and Obeng, B. A. (2009). Entrepreneurship and innovation in Ghana: enterprising Africa. *Small Business Economics*, 32, 331–350.

Rodriguez-Clare, A. (1996). Multinationals, linkages, and economic development. *American Economic Review*, 86, 852–873.

Rodrik, D. (2004). Industrial Policy for the Twenty-first Century at www.hks.harvard.edu/fs/drodrik/Research%20papers/UNIDOSep.pdf

Rogers, E. M. (2003). *Diffusion of Innovations*. 5th ed. New York: Free Press.

Romer, P. (1990). Endogenous technological change. *The Journal of Political Economy*, 98(5), S71–S102.

Romer, P. M. (1994). The origins of endogenous growth. *The Journal of Economic Perspectives*, 8(1), 3–22. DOI:10.1257/jep.8.1.3.JSTOR2138148

Ruiz-Mercader, J., Merono-Cerdan, A. L. and Sabater-Sánchez, R. (2006). Information technology and learning: their relationship and impact on organisational performance in small businesses. *International Journal of Information Management*, 26(1), 16–29.

Sadana, M., Mugweru, G., Murithi, J., Cracknell, D. and Wright, G. A. N. (2011). *Analysis of Financial Institutions Riding the M-PESA Rails*, Nairobi, Kenya: MicroSave. www.microsave.net/2011/03/01/analysis-of-financial-institutions-riding-the-m-pesa-rails/

Safaricom. (2018). M-Pesa Timeline. Celebrating Ten Years. www.safaricom.co.ke/mpesa_timeline/timeline.html

Sainsbury, Lord. (2007). *Race to Top: Sainsbury Review of Science and Innovation*, London: HM Treasury.

Sambamurthy, V. and Subramani, M. (2005). Knowledge problems in organizations: foreword to special issue on information technologies and knowledge management. *MIS Quarterly*, 29(1), 1–7.

Sawada, Y., Matsuda, A. and Kimura, H. (2012). On the role of technical cooperation in international technology transfers. *Journal of International Development*, 24, 316–340.

Scherer, F. M. (1982). Interindustry technology flows and productivity growth. *Review of Economics and Statistics*, 64(4) 627–634.

Schmitz, H. (2006). Learning and earning in global garment and footwear chains. *The European Journal of Development Research*, 18(4), 546–571.

Schmookler J. (1966). *Invention and Economic Growth*, Cambridge, US: Harvard University Press.

Schneider, F., Buehn, A. and Montenegro, C. E. (2011). Shadow economies all over the world: new estimates for 162 countries from 1999 to 2007. *International Economic Journal*, 24, 443–461.

Schoepf, B. G. (2018). Health, gender relations and poverty in the AIDS era. In *Courtyards, Markets, City Streets: Urban Women in Africa* (K. Sheldon ed.), (Chapter 7, pp 153–168). Oxford, UK: Routledge.

Schumpeter, J. A. (1934). *The Theory of Economic Development: An Inquiry into Profits, Capital, Credit, Interest, and the Business Cycle*, Cambridge, MA: Harvard University Press.

Schwab, K. (2016). *The Fourth Industrial Revolution*, Geneva, Switzerland: World Economic Forum.

Schwab, K. (2017). The Fourth Industrial Revolution: what it means, how to respond. Accessed on 2017, www.weforum.org/agenda/2016/01/the-fourth-industrial-revolution-what-it-means-and-how-to-respond

Sein, M. K. and Harindranath, G. (2004). Conceptualizing the ICT artifact: toward understanding the role of ICT in national development. *The Information Society*, 20(1), 15–24. http://doi.org/10.1080/01972240490269942

Seker, M. (2011). *Effects of Licensing Reform on Firm Innovation: Evidence from India*, Washington, DC (USA): World Bank.

Seker, M. (2012). Importing, exporting, and innovation in developing countries. *Review of International Economics*, 20, 299–314.

Shi, G. and Pray, C. (2012). Modeling agricultural innovation in a rapidly developing country: the case of Chinese pesticide industry. *Agricultural Economics*, 43, 379–390.

Shin, J. and Park, Y. (2007). Building the national ICT frontier: the case of Korea, *Information Economics & Policy*, 2(2), 249–277.

Shinnar, R. S., Hsu, D. K., Powell, B. C. and Zhou, H. (2018). Entrepreneurial intentions and start-ups: are women or men more likely to enact their intentions? *International Small Business Journal*, 36(1), 60–80.

Sine, W. D., Haveman, H. A. and Tolbert, P. S. (2005). Risky business? Entrepreneurship in the new independent-power sector. *Administrative Science Quarterly*, 50(2), 200–232

Singh, J. (2007). Asymmetry of knowledge spillovers between MNCs and host country firms. *Journal of International Business Studies*, 38, 764–786.

Sirkin, H. L., Zinser, M. and Rose, J. (2015, September 23). How Robots Will Redefine Competitiveness. Accessed on 15 September 2017, www.bcgper spectives.com/content/articles/lean-manufacturing-innovation-robots-redefine -competitiveness/

Soete, L. (1985). International diffusion of technology, industrial-development and technological leapfrogging. *World Development*, 13, 409–422.

Sorenson, O., Rivkin, J. and Fleming, L. (2006). Complexity, networks and knowledge flow. *Research Policy*, 35, 994–1017.

Srholec, M. (2011). A multilevel analysis of innovation in developing countries. *Industrial and Corporate Change*, 20, 1539–1569.

Srholec, M. and Verspagen, B. (2012). The Voyage of the Beagle into innovation: explorations on heterogeneity, selection, and sectors. *Industrial and Corporate Change*, 21(5), 221–1253.

Stewart, F. (1983). Macro-policies for appropriate technology: an introductory classification. *International Labour Review*, 122(3), 279–294.

Strang, D. and Meyer, J. W. (1993). Institutional conditions for diffusion. *Theory and Society*, 22, 487–511.

Strang, D. and Soule, S. A. (1998). Diffusion in organizations and social movements: from hybrid corn to poison pills. *Annual Review of Sociology*, 24, 265–290.

Sultana, R. (2009). Mobile banking: overview of regulatory frame/work in emerging markets. In 4th Communication Policy Research, South Conference. DOI:10 .2139/ssrn.1554160

Suyanto, M., Salim, R. A. and Bloch, H. (2009). Does foreign direct investment lead to productivity spillovers? Firm level evidence from Indonesia. *World Development*, 37, 1861–1876.

Swan, M. (2016), This skills could save your job – and your company, 31 August 2016, in World Economic Forum. Accessed on 20 October 2017, www.weforum.org/agenda/2016/08/this-little-known-skill-will-save-your-job-and-your-company/System_Analysis.pdf.

TechFuture Girls. (2017, September 25). About TechFuture Girls. Accessed on 25 September 2017, www.techfuturegirls.com/about-us/

Thanh, L. and Bodman, P. M. (2011). Remittances or technological diffusion: which drives domestic gains from brain drain? *Applied Economics*, 43, 2277–2285.

The National Academies of Science. (2017). *Information Technology and the U.S. Workforce: Where Are We and Where Do We Go from Here?* Washington, DC: National Academies Press, 1–199.

Thébaud, S. (2015). Business as Plan B: institutional foundations of gender inequality in entrepreneurship across 24 industrialised countries. *Administrative Science Quarterly*, 60(4), 671–711

Thompson, E. R. (2002). Clustering of foreign direct investment and enhanced technology transfer: evidence from Hong Kong garment firms in China. *World Development*, 30, 873–889.

Tigabu, D. A. (2017). Analysing the diffusion and adoption of renewable energy technologies in Africa: the functions of innovation systems perspective. *African Journal of Science, Technology, Innovation and Development*, 10(5), 615–624, DOI:10.1080/20421338.2017.1366130.

Todo, Y. and Miyamoto, K. (2006). Knowledge spillovers from foreign direct investment and the role of local R&D activities: evidence from Indonesia. *Economic Development and Cultural Change*, 55, 173–200.

Trebilcock, A. (2005). Decent work and the informal economy. UNU-WIDER, Helsinki (Finland). www.wider.unu.edu/publication/decent-work-and-informal-economy

Tsai, W. (2001). Knowledge transfer in intraorganizational networks: effects of network position and absorptive capacity on business unit innovation and performance. *Academy of Management Journal*, 44(5), 996–1004.

Tsikata, D., Fenny, A. P. and Aryeetey, E. (2010). Impact of China-Africa investment relations: an in-depth analysis of the case of Ghana. Report at African Economic Research Consortium.

Tushman, M. L. and Anderson, P. (1986). Technological discontinuities and organizational environments. *Administrative Science Quarterly*, 31, 439–465.

Tybout, J. R. (2000). Manufacturing firms in developing countries: how well do they do, and why? *Journal of Economic Literature*, 38, 11–44.

U.K. Department for Education. (2014, January 22). Michael Gove speaks about computing and education technology. Accessed on 21 September 2017, www.gov.uk/government/speeches/michael-gove-speaks-about-computing-and-education-technology

U.S. Department of Education. (2017, January 18). Reimagining the Role of Technology in Education: 2017 National Education Technology Plan Update. Accessed on 19 September 2017, https://tech.ed.gov/netp/

Uddin, A. K. (2006). The role of diffusion of innovations for incremental development in small enterprises. *Technovation*, 26, 274–284.

UNCTAD. (2016). Building Digital Competencies to Benefit from Frontier Technologies. Geneva. Available at https://unctad.org/en/pages/PublicationWebflyer.aspx?publicationid=2449

UN Women. (2017, April 26). International Girls in ICT Day. Accessed on 25 September 2017, www.unwomen.org/en/news/stories/2017/4/feature-international-girls-in-ict-day

UN. (2015). Transforming our world: the 2030 Agenda for Sustainable Development (No. A/RES/70/1) (pp. 1–35). https://sustainabledevelopment.un.org/post2015/transformingourworld/publication

UN. (2016, June 27). No Poverty: Why it matters. Accessed on 14 September 2017, www.un.org/sustainabledevelopment

UNCTAD (2002). WORLD INVESTMENT REPORT 2002 – Transnational Corporations and Export Competitiveness. Geneva.

UNCTAD (2003). WORLD INVESTMENT REPORT 2003 – FDI Policies for Development: National and International Perspectives. Geneva.

UNCTAD. (2016). Robots and industrialization in developing countries, UNCTAD Policy Brief, No. 50, October 2016.

UNCTAD. (2016a, February 29). Foresight for digital development. Accessed on October 2017, http://unctad.org/meetings/en/SessionalDocuments/ecn162016d3_en.pdf

UNCTAD. (2016b, November 8). Robots threaten up to two thirds of developing country jobs, but could be an opportunity too. Accessed on September 2017, http://unctad.org/en/pages/newsdetails.aspx?OriginalVersionID=1369

UNCTAD. (2017). Information economy report: digitalisation, trade and development. Accessed on October 26, http://unctad.org/en/PublicationsLibrary/ie r2017_en.pdf

UNECA. (2015). Economic Report on Africa 2015. Available at www.uneca.org /publications/economic-report-africa-2015

UNESCO. (2005). Towards knowledge societies (pp. 1–220). UNESCO Publishing. www.unesco.org/publications

UNESCO. (2015, January 15). A complex formula: girls and women in science, technology, engineering and mathematics in Asia. Accessed on 18 September 2017, http://unesdoc.unesco.org/images/0023/002315/231519e.pdf

UNESCO. (2017, September 4). Community engagement and online literacy empower girls and women in Pakistan. Accessed on 25 September 2017, http:// en.unesco.org/news/community-engagement-and-online-literacy-empower-girls -and-women-pakistan

UNU-MERIT (2012). Demand-side Innovation Policies at Regional Level. In Technopolis (ed.), Regional Innovation Monitor Thematic Paper 3.

Unwin, T. (2009) *ICT4D: Information and Communication Technology for Development*, Cambridge: Cambridge University Press.

Utterback, J. M. (1974). Innovation in industry and diffusion of technology. *Science*, 183(4125), 620–626.

van der Boor, P., Oliveira, P. and Veloso, F. (2014) Users as innovators in developing countries: the global sources of innovation and diffusion in mobile banking services. *Research Policy*, 43(9), 1594–1607.

van der Panne, G., van Beers, C. and Kleinknecht, A. (2003). Success and failure of innovation: a literature review. *International Journal of Innovation Management*, 7(3), 1–30.

Van Dijk, M. and Szirmai, A. (2006). Industrial policy and technology diffusion: evidence from paper making machinery in Indonesia. *World Development*, 34, 2137–2152.

Van Reenen, J. and Bloom N. (2007). Measuring and explaining management practices across firms and nations, *Quarterly Journal of Economics*, 122(4), 1351–1408. DOI:10.1162/qjec.2007.122.4.1351

Vega-Jurado, J., Gutierrez-Gracia, A. and de Lucio, I. F. (2009). Does external knowledge sourcing matter for innovation? Evidence from the Spanish manufacturing industry. *Industrial and Corporate Change*, 18(4), 634–670.

Vicente, M. and Lopez, A. (2006). Patterns of ICT diffusion across the European Union. *Economics Letters*, 93, 45–51.

Vishwasrao, S. and Bosshardt, W. (2001). Foreign ownership and technology adoption: evidence from Indian firms. *Journal of Development Economics*, 65, 367–387.

Wainaina E. (2016). Safaricom to Roll Out Ready Business Platform Targeting SMEs. Accessed on 14 June, https://techweez.com/2016/06/14/safaricom-to-roll-out-ready-for-business-platform-for-smes/

Wakefield, J. (2016, May 25). Foxconn replaces '60,000 factory workers with robots' – BBC News. Accessed on 15 September 2017, www.bbc.co.uk/news/ technology-36376966

Walder, A. G. (2003). Elite opportunity in transition economies. *American Sociological Review*, 68, 899–916.

Waldkirch, A. and Ofosu, A. (2010). Foreign presence, spillovers, and productivity: evidence from Ghana. *World Development*, 38(8), 1114–1126.

Wang, H. C. (2010). Discovering steam power in China, 1840s-1860s. *Technology and Culture*, 51, 31–54.

Wang, J. Y. and Blomström, M. (1992). Foreign investment and technology transfer: a simple model. *European Economic Review*, 36(1), 137–155.

Wang, M. and Wong, M. C. S. (2012). International R&D transfer and technical efficiency: evidence from panel study using stochastic frontier analysis. *World Development*, 40, 1982–1998.

Wang, P. (1994). Brokers still treat men better than women. *Money*, 23(6), 108–110.

Wangwe, S., Mmari, D., Aikaeli, J., Rutatina, N., Mboghoina, T. and Kinyondo, A. (2014). The performance of the manufacturing sector in Tanzania: challenges and the way forward. UNU-WIDER, WIDER Working Papers, WP/2014/085

Weinhold, D. and Nair-Reichert, U. (2009). Innovation, inequality and intellectual property rights. *World Development*, 37, 889–901.

Wells, B. L., Pfantz, T. J. and Bryne, J. L. (2003). Russian women business owners: evidence of entrepreneurship in a transition economy. *Journal of Developmental Entrepreneurship*, 8(1), 59.

Westwood, R. and Lok, P. (2003). The meaning of work in Chinese contexts a comparative study. *International Journal of Cross Cultural Management*, 3(2) August 1, 139–165.

Westwood, R. and Lok, P. (2003). The meaning of work in Chinese contexts a comparative study. *International Journal of Cross Cultural Management*, 3(2) August 1, 139–165.

White, S. and Liu, X. (1998). Organizational processes to meet new performance criteria: Chinese pharmaceutical firms in transition. *Research Policy*, 27, 369–383.

Williams, M. (2016, July 14). Facebook Diversity Update: Positive Hiring Trends Show Progress. Accessed on 15 September 2017, https://newsroom.fb.com/n ews/2016/07/facebook-diversity-update-positive-hiring-trends-show-progress/

Willoughby, Kelvin W. (1990) *Technology Choice: A Critique of the Appropriate Technology Movement*, London: Intermediate Technology Publications.

Wiseman A. W. and Anderson E. (2012). ICT-integrated education and national innovation systems in the Gulf Cooperation Council (GCC) countries. *Computers & Education*, 59(2012), 607–618.

Wood, A. (ed.), (2003). Symposium on infant industries. *Oxford Development Studies*, 31(1), 3–20.

Wooldridge, J. M. (2011). *Econometric Analysis of Cross Section and Panel Data*. Cambridge, Massachusetts; London, England: The MIT Press.

World Bank. (2012). How We Classify Countries Vol. 2012, https://datahelp desk.worldbank.org/knowledgebase/articles/378834-how-does-the-world-bank-classify-countries.

World Bank. (2016). *World Development Report 2016 : Digital Dividends*, Washington, DC: World Bank. © World Bank. https://openknowledge .worldbank.org/handle/10986/23347 License: CC BY 3.0 IGO

World Bank. (2013a, September 10). ICTs are creating new jobs and making labor markets more innovative, inclusive, and global – World Bank study. Accessed on 14 September 2017, www.worldbank.org/en/news/press-release/2 013/09/10/icts-are...bor-markets-more-innovative-inclusive-and-global-world-bank-study

World Bank. (2013b, December 4). NESAP-ICT | World Bank Blogs. Accessed on 25 September 2017, http://blogs.worldbank.org/category/tags/nesap-ict

World Bank. (2014) *Global Financial Development Report 2014: Financial Inclusion*, Washington, DC: World Bank Publications.

World Bank. (2015). World Bank Data: Patent Applications. Accessed on 26 October, https://data.worldbank.org/indicator/IP.PAT.NRES?locations= XO&view=chart

World Bank. (2016, February 4). Adaption is a key to realizing job gains. Accessed on 26 October 2017, www.worldbank.org/en/topic/ict/brief/will-the-digital-revolution-help-or-hurt-employment

World Bank. (2017, September 18). Literacy rate, adult total % of people ages 15 and above). Accessed on 18 September 2017, https://data.worldbank.org/indi cator/SE.ADT.LITR.ZS

World Economic Forum. (2016). The Future of Jobs: Employment, Skills and Workforce Strategy for the Fourth Industrial Revolution. Global Challenge Insight Report (pp. 1–167). www3.weforum.org/docs/WEF_FOJ_Executive_ Summary_Jobs.pdf

Wu, W. P. (2007). Cultivating research universities and industrial linkages in China: the case of Shanghai, *World Development*, 35(6), 1075–1093.

Wunsch-Vincent, S. and Kraemer-Mbula, E. (2016) *The Informal Economy in Developing Nations: Hidden Engine of Innovation? New Economic Insights and Policies*, Cambridge (UK): Cambridge University Press.

Xiaojing, L. (2017). They made all elderly villagers fall in love with the internet. Accessed on 10 October 10 2017, http://mp.weixin.qq.com/s/3Id3Lc5G5 GDz4rs5XdEKVQ

Xue, L. (1997). A historical perspective of China's innovation system reform: a case study. *Journal of Engineering and Technology Management*, 14, 67–81.

Yang, L. and Maskus, K. E. (2009). Intellectual property rights, technology transfer and exports in developing countries. *Journal of Development Economics*, 90, 231–236.

Yongmin, C. and Puttitanun, T. (2005). Intellectual property rights and innovation in developing countries. *Journal of Development Economics*, 78, 474–493.

Young, S. and Lan, P. (1997). Technology transfer to China through foreign direct investment. *Regional Studies*, 31, 669–679.

Yuan, J. (2002). *The Institutional Logic of University Start-Ups*, Xuzhou, China: The Chinese Mining University Press.

Yuki, Masaki, Maddux, William W., Brewer, Marilynn B. and Takemura, Kosuke. (2005). Cross-cultural differences in relationship- and group-based trust. *Personality and Social Psychology Bulletin*, 31(62) January 1, 48–62.

Yusuf, S. (2008). Intermediating knowledge exchange between universities and businesses, *Research Policy*, 37(8), 1167–1174.

Zack, M. (1999). Developing a knowledge strategy. *California Management Review*, 41(3), 125–145.

Zanello, G., Fu, X., Mohnen, P. and Ventresca, M. (2016). The creation and diffusion of innovation in developing countries: a systematic literature review. *Journal of Economic Surveys*, 30(5), 884–912.

Zhang, J. (2003). *The Development of High-Tech Enterprises in China's Universities*, Wuhan: Huazhong Science and Technology University Press.

Zhang, Y. (2009). Alliance-based network view on Chinese firms' catching-up: case study of Huawei Technologies Co Ltd., UNU-MERIT, Working Paper 2009–039. https://collections.unu.edu/view/UNU:1264

Zhang, Y., Li, H. Y., Li, Y. and Zhou, L. A. (2010). FDI spillovers in an emerging market: the role of foreign firms' country origin diversity and domestic firms' absorptive capacity. *Strategic Management Journal*, 31, 969–989.

Zhao, M. (2006). Conducting R&D in countries with weak intellectual property rights protection. *Management Science*, 52, 1185–1199.

Zheng, W., Yang, B. and McLean, G. N. (2010). Linking organizational culture, structure, strategy, and organizational effectiveness: mediating role of knowledge management. *Journal of Business Research*, 63(7), 763–771.

Zhou, X., Zhao, W., Li, Q. and Cai, H. (2003). Embeddedness and contractual relationships in China's transitional economy. *American Sociological Review*, 68, 75–102.

Index

Printed in the United States
By Bookmasters